T0073326

Programming Languages: Advanced Principles and Systems

Programming Languages: Advanced Principles and Systems

Edited by
Katy Spalding

Willford Press
www.willfordpress.com

Published by Willford Press,
118-35 Queens Blvd., Suite 400,
Forest Hills, NY 11375, USA

Copyright © 2023 Willford Press

This book contains information obtained from authentic and highly regarded sources. Copyright for all individual chapters remain with the respective authors as indicated. All chapters are published with permission under the Creative Commons Attribution License or equivalent. A wide variety of references are listed. Permission and sources are indicated; for detailed attributions, please refer to the permissions page and list of contributors. Reasonable efforts have been made to publish reliable data and information, but the authors, editors and publisher cannot assume any responsibility for the validity of all materials or the consequences of their use.

Trademark Notice: Registered trademark of products or corporate names are used only for explanation and identification without intent to infringe.

ISBN: 978-1-64728-439-8

Cataloging-in-publication Data

Programming languages : advanced principles and systems / edited by Katy Spalding.
p. cm.
Includes bibliographical references and index.
ISBN 978-1-64728-439-8
1. Programming languages (Electronic computers). 2. Languages, Artificial.
3. Electronic data processing. I. Spalding, Katy.
QA76.7 .F86 2023
005.13--dc23

For information on all Willford Press publications
visit our website at www.willfordpress.com

WILLFORD PRESS

Contents

Preface

In my initial years as a student, I used to run to the library at every possible instance to grab a book and learn something new. Books were my primary source of knowledge and I would not have come such a long way without all that I learnt from them. Thus, when I was approached to edit this book; I became understandably nostalgic. It was an absolute honor to be considered worthy of guiding the current generation as well as those to come. I put all my knowledge and hard work into making this book most beneficial for its readers.

A computer programming language refers to any of the different languages used to convey a set of specific instructions to a digital computer. These instructions can be performed directly when represented in machine language. They follow a simple replacement procedure when expressed or translated in a corresponding higher-level language or assembly language. Low-level programming languages include assembly and machine languages. These languages require a programmer to manage all of a computer's features, such as data storage and operations. High-level languages, on the other hand, free a programmer from such concerns and give a notation that is easier for programmers to write and read. Various programming languages include algorithmic languages, business oriented languages, and object oriented languages. This book provides comprehensive insights on advanced principles and systems of programming languages. It is a vital tool for all researching or studying programming languages as it gives incredible insights into emerging trends and concepts.

I wish to thank my publisher for supporting me at every step. I would also like to thank all the authors who have contributed their researches in this book. I hope this book will be a valuable contribution to the progress of the field.

Editor

1

One Step at a Time: A Functional Derivation of Small-Step Evaluators from Big-Step Counterparts

Ferdinand Vesely[1,2(✉)] and Kathleen Fisher[1]

[1] Tufts University, Medford, USA
{fvesely,kfisher}@eecs.tufts.edu
[2] Swansea University, Swansea, UK
f.vesely@swansea.ac.uk

Abstract. Big-step and small-step are two popular flavors of operational semantics. Big-step is often seen as a more natural transcription of informal descriptions, as well as being more convenient for some applications such as interpreter generation or optimization verification. Small-step allows reasoning about non-terminating computations, concurrency and interactions. It is also generally preferred for reasoning about type systems. Instead of having to manually specify equivalent semantics in both styles for different applications, it would be useful to choose one and derive the other in a systematic or, preferably, automatic way.

Transformations of small-step semantics into big-step have been investigated in various forms by Danvy and others. However, it appears that a corresponding transformation from big-step to small-step semantics has not had the same attention. We present a fully automated transformation that maps big-step evaluators written in direct style to their small-step counterparts. Many of the steps in the transformation, which include CPS-conversion, defunctionalisation, and various continuation manipulations, mirror those used by Danvy and his co-authors. For many standard languages, including those with either call-by-value or call-by-need and those with state, the transformation produces small-step semantics that are close in style to handwritten ones. We evaluate the applicability and correctness of the approach on 20 languages with a range of features.

Keywords: Structural operational semantics · Big-step semantics · Small-step semantics · Interpreters · Transformation · Continuation-passing style · Functional programming

1 Introduction

Operational semantics allow language designers to precisely and concisely specify the meaning of programs. Such semantics support formal type soundness proofs [29], give rise (sometimes automatically) to simple interpreters [15,27] and debuggers [14], and document the correct behavior for compilers. There are two popular approaches for defining operational semantics: big-step and small-step. *Big-step semantics* (also referred to as *natural* or *evaluation* semantics) relate initial program configurations directly to final results in one "big" evaluation step. In contrast, *small-step semantics* relate intermediate configurations consisting of the term currently being evaluated and auxiliary information. The initial configuration corresponds to the entire program, and the final result, if there is one, can be obtained by taking the transitive-reflexive closure of the small-step relation. Thus, computation progresses as a series of "small steps."

The two styles have different strengths and weaknesses, making them suitable for different purposes. For example, big-step semantics naturally correspond to definitional interpreters [23], meaning many big-step semantics can essentially be transliterated into a reasonably efficient interpreter in a functional language. Big-step semantics are also more convenient for verifying program optimizations and compilation – using big-step, semantic preservation can be verified (for terminating programs) by induction on the derivation [20, 22].

In contrast, small-step semantics are often better suited for stepping through the evaluation of an example program, and for devising a type system and proving its soundness via the classic syntactic method using progress and preservation proofs [29]. As a result, researchers sometimes develop multiple semantic specifications and then argue for their equivalence [3, 20, 21]. In an ideal situation, the specifier writes down a single specification and then derives the others.

Approaches to deriving big-step semantics from a small-step variant have been investigated on multiple occasions, starting from semantics specified as either interpreters or rules [4, 7, 10, 12, 13]. An obvious question is: what about the reverse direction?

This paper presents a systematic, mechanised transformation from a big-step interpreter into its small-step counterpart. The overall transformation consists of multiple stages performed on an interpreter written in a functional programming language. For the most part, the individual transformations are well known. The key steps in this transformation are to explicitly represent control flow as *continuations*, to defunctionalise these continuations to obtain a datatype of reified continuations, to "tear off" recursive calls to the interpreter, and then to return the reified continuations, which represent the rest of the computation. This process effectively produces a stepping function. The remaining work consists of finding translations from the reified continuations to equivalent terms in the source language. If such a term cannot be found, we introduce a new term constructor. These new constructors correspond to the intermediate auxiliary forms commonly found in handwritten small-step definitions.

We define the transformations on our *evaluator definition language* – an extension of λ-calculus with call-by-value semantics. The language is untyped and, crucially, includes tagged values (variants) and a case analysis construct for building and analysing object language terms. Our algorithm takes as input a big-step interpreter written in this language in the usual style: a main function performing case analysis on a top-level term constructor and recursively calling itself or auxiliary functions. As output, we return the resulting small-step interpreter which we can "pretty-print" as a set of small-step rules in the usual style. Hence our algorithm provides a fully automated path from a restricted class of big-step semantic specifications written as interpreters to corresponding small-step versions.

To evaluate our algorithm, we have applied it to 20 different languages with various features, including languages based on call-by-name and call-by-value λ-calculi, as well as a core imperative language. We extend these base languages with conditionals, loops, and exceptions.

We make the following contributions:

- We present a multi-stage, automated transformation that maps any deterministic big-step evaluator into a small-step counterpart. Section 2 gives an overview of this process. Each stage in the transformation is performed on our *evaluator definition language* – an extended call-by-value λ-calculus. Each stage in the transformation is familiar and principled. Section 4 gives a detailed description.
- We have implemented the transformation process in Haskell and evaluate it on a suite of 20 representative languages in Section 5. We argue that the resulting small-step evaluation rules closely mirror what one would expect from a manually written small-step specification.
- We observe that the same process with minimal modifications can be used to transform a big-step semantics into its *pretty-big-step* [6] counterpart.

2 Overview

In this section, we provide an overview of the transformation steps on a simple example language. The diagram in Fig. 1 shows the transformation pipeline. As the initial step, we first convert the input big-step evaluator into continuation-passing style (CPS). We limit the conversion to the *eval* function itself and leave all other functions in direct style. The resulting continuations take a value as input and advance the computation. In the generalization step, we modify these continuations so that they take an arbitrary term and evaluate it to a value before continuing as before. With this modification, each continuation handles both the general non-value case and the value case itself. The next stage lifts a carefully chosen set of free variables as arguments to continuations, which allows us to define all of them at the same scope level. After generalization and argument lifting, we can invoke continuations directly to switch control, instead of passing them as arguments to the *eval* function. Next we defunctionalize the continuations, converting them into a set of tagged values together with an *apply* function capturing their meaning. This transformation enables the next step, in which we remove recursive tail-calls to *apply*. This allows us to interrupt the interpreter and make it return a continuation or a term: effectively, it yields a stepping function, which is the essence of a small-step semantics. The remainder of the pipeline converts continuations to terms, performs simplifications, and then converts the CPS evaluator back to direct style to obtain the final small-step interpreter. This interpreter can be pretty-printed as a set of small-step rules.

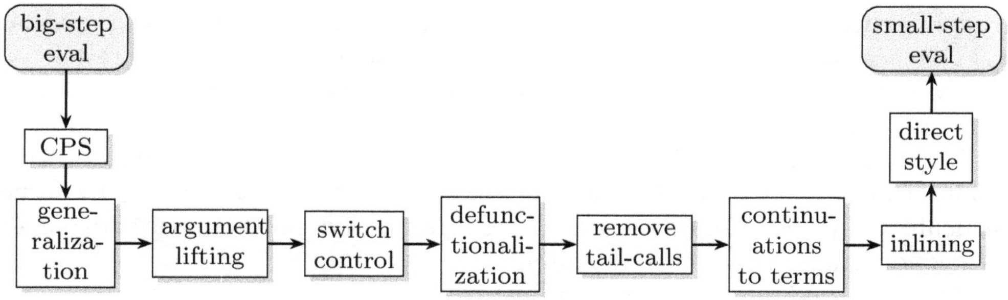

Fig. 1. Transformation overview

Our example language is a λ-calculus with call-by-value semantics. Fig. 2 gives its syntax and big-step rules. We use environments to give meaning to variables. The only values in this language are closures, formed by packaging a λ-abstraction with an environment.

$$x \in \mathit{Var} \qquad \rho \in \mathit{Env} = \mathit{Var} \rightarrow \mathit{Val}$$

$$\begin{aligned} v &::= \mathsf{clo}(x, e, \rho) \\ e &::= \mathsf{var}(x) \\ &\mid \mathsf{val}(v) \\ &\mid \mathsf{lam}(x, e) \\ &\mid \mathsf{app}(e_1, e_2) \end{aligned}$$

$$\frac{}{\rho \vdash \mathsf{val}(v) \Downarrow v} \qquad \frac{\rho(x) = v}{\rho \vdash \mathsf{var}(x) \Downarrow v}$$

$$\frac{}{\rho \vdash \mathsf{lam}(x, e) \Downarrow \mathsf{clo}(x, e, \rho)}$$

$$\frac{\rho \vdash e_1 \Downarrow \mathsf{clo}(x, e, \rho') \qquad \rho \vdash e_2 \Downarrow v_2 \qquad \rho'[x \mapsto v_2] \vdash e \Downarrow v}{\rho \vdash \mathsf{app}(e_1, e_2) \Downarrow v}$$

Fig. 2. Example: Call-by-value λ-calculus, abstract syntax and big-step semantics

We will now give a series of interpreters to illustrate the transformation process. We formally define the syntax of the meta-language in which we write these interpreters in Section 3, but we believe for readers familiar with functional programming the language is intuitive enough to not require a full explanation at this point. Shaded text highlights (often small) changes to subsequent interpreters.

Big-Step Evaluator. We start with an interpreter corresponding directly to the big-step semantics given in Fig. 2. We represent environments as functions – the empty environment returns an error for any variable. The body of the *eval* function consists of a pattern match on the top-level language term. Function abstractions are evaluated to closures by packaging them with the current environment. The only term that requires recursive calls to *eval* is application: both its arguments are evaluated in the current environment, and then its first argument is pattern-matched against a closure, the body of which is then evaluated to a value in an extended environment using a third recursive call to *eval*.

```
let empty = λx. error() in
let update x v ρ = λx'. let xx' = (== x x') in if xx' then v else (ρ x') in
let rec eval e ρ =
  case e of {
    val(v) → v |
    var(x) → let v = (ρ x) in v |
    lam(x, e') → clo(x, e', ρ) |
    app(e1, e2) →
        let v1 = (eval e1 ρ) in
        let v2 = (eval e2 ρ) in
        case v1 of {
          clo(x, e', ρ') →
              let ρ'' = (update x v2 ρ') in
              let v = (eval e' ρ'') in
              v
        }
  }
```

CPS Conversion. Our first transformation introduces a continuation argument to *eval*, capturing the "rest of the computation" [9, 26, 28]. Instead of returning the resulting value directly, *eval* will pass it to the continuation. For our example we need to introduce three continuations – all of them in the case for **app**. The continuation $kapp_1$ captures what remains to be done after evaluating the first argument of **app**, $kapp_2$ captures the computation remaining after evaluating the second argument, and $kclo_1$ the computation remaining after the closure body is fully evaluated. This final continuation simply applies the top-level continuation to the resulting value and might seem redundant; however, its utility will become apparent in the following step. Note that the CPS conversion is limited to the *eval* function, leaving any other functions in the program intact.

```
let rec eval e ρ k =
  case e of {
    val(v) → (k v) |
    var(x) → let v = (ρ x) in (k v) |
    lam(x, e') → (k clo(x, e', ρ)) |
    app(e1, e2) →
      letcont kapp1 v1 =
          letcont kapp2 v2 =
            case v1 of {
              clo(x, e', ρ') →
                  let ρ'' = (update x v2 ρ') in
                  letcont kclo1 v = (k v) in
                  (eval e' ρ'' (λv. (kclo1 v)))
            } in
            (eval e2 ρ (λv2. (kapp2 v2))) in
        (eval e1 ρ (λv1. (kapp1 v1)))
  }
```

Generalization. Next, we modify the continuation definitions so that they handle both the case when the term is a value (the original case) and the case where it is still a term that needs to be evaluated. To achieve this goal, we introduce a case analysis on the input. If the continuation's argument is a value, the evaluation will proceed as before. Otherwise it will call *eval* with itself as the continuation argument. Intuitively, the latter case will correspond to a congruence rule in the resulting small-step semantics and we refer to these as *congruence cases* in the rest of this paper.

```
let rec eval e ρ k = case e of {
    val(v) → (k val(v)) |
    var(x) → let v = (ρ x) in (k val(v)) |
    lam(x, e') → (k val(clo(x, e', ρ))) |
    app(e1, e2) →
        letcont kapp1 e1 =
          case e1 of {
            val(v1) →
              ...
                              case v1 of {
                                clo(x, e', ρ') →
                                  let ρ'' = (update x v2 ρ') in
                                  letcont kclo1 e =
                                    case e of {
                                      val(v) → (k val(v)) |
                                      ELSE(e) → (eval e ρ'' (λe'. (kclo1 e')))
                                    } in
                                  (eval e' ρ'' (λv. (kclo1 v)))
              ...
            ELSE(e1) → (eval e1 ρ (λe1'. (kapp1 e1')))
          } in
        (eval e1 ρ (λv1. (kapp1 v1)))
}
```

Argument Lifting. The free variables inside each continuation can be divided into those that depend on the top-level term and those that parameterize the evaluation. The former category contains variables dependent on subterms of the top-level term, either by standing for a subterm itself, or by being derived from it. In our example, for $kapp_1$, it is the variable e_2, i.e., the right argument of **app**, for $kapp_2$, the variable v_1 as the value resulting from evaluating the left argument, and for $kclo_1$ it is the environment obtained by extending the closure's environment by binding the closure variable to the operand value (ρ'' derived from v_2). We lift variables that fall into the first category, that is, variables derived from the input term. We leave variables that parametrize the evaluation, such as the input environment or the store, unlifted. The rationale is that, eventually, we want the continuations to act as term constructors and they need to carry information not contained in arguments passed to *eval*.

```
let rec eval e ρ k = case e of {
    ...
    app(e1, e2) →
        letcont kapp1 e2 e1 =
            ...
            letcont kapp2 v1 e2 =
              ...
                  letcont kclo1 ρ' e =
                    case e of {
                      val(v) → (k val(v)) |
                      ELSE(e) → (eval e ρ' (λe'. (kclo1 ρ' e')))
                    } in
                  (eval e' ρ'' (λv. (kclo1 ρ'' v)))
              } |
              ELSE(e2) → (eval e2 ρ (λe2'. (kapp2 v1 e2')))
            } in
            (eval e2 ρ (λv2. (kapp2 v1 v2))) |
          ELSE(e1) → (eval e1 ρ (λe1'. (kapp1 e2 e1')))
        } in
        (eval e1 ρ (λv1. (kapp1 e2 v1)))
}
```

Continuations Switch Control. Since continuations now handle the full evaluation of their argument themselves, they can be used to switch stages in the evaluation of a term. Observe how in the resulting evaluator below, the evaluation of an **app** term progresses through stages initiated by $kapp_1$, $kapp_2$, and finally $kclo_1$.

```
let rec eval e ρ k = case e of {
    ...
    app(e1, e2) →
        letcont kapp1 e2 e1 =
          ...
            letcont kapp2 v1 e2 =
              ...
              letcont kclo1 ρ' e =
                ...
              in (kclo1 ρ'' e')
              ...
            in (kapp2 v1 e2) |
          ...
        in (kapp1 e2 e1)
}
```

Defunctionalization. In the next step, we defunctionalize continuations. For each continuation, we introduce a constructor with the corresponding number of arguments. The *apply* function gives the meaning of each defunctionalized continuation.

```
let rec apply eval e_k ρ k = case e_k of {
    kapp1(e2, e1) →
        case e1 of {
          val(v1) → (apply eval kapp2(v1, e2) ρ k) |
          ELSE(e1) → (eval e1 ρ (λe1'. (apply eval kapp1(e2, e1') ρ k)))
        } |
    kapp2(v1, e2) →
        case e2 of {
          val(v2) →
              case v1 of {
                clo(x, e', ρ') →
                    let ρ'' = (update x v2 ρ')
                    in (apply eval kclo1(ρ'', e') ρ k)
              } |
          ELSE(e2) → (eval e2 ρ (λe2'. (apply eval kapp2(v1, e2') ρ k)))
        } |
    kclo1(ρ', e) →
        case e of {
          val(v) → (k val(v)) |
          ELSE(e) → (eval e ρ' (λe'. (apply eval kclo1(ρ', e') ρ k)))
        }
  } in
let rec eval e ρ k = case e of {
    val(v) → (k val(v)) |
    var(x) → let v = (ρ x) in (k val(v)) |
    lam(x, e') → (k val(clo(x, e', ρ))) |
    app(e1, e2) → (apply eval kapp1(e2, e1) ρ k)
  }
```

Remove Tail-Calls. We can now move from a recursive evaluator to a stepping function by modifying the continuation arguments passed to *eval* in congruence cases. Instead of calling *apply* on the defunctionalized continuation, we return the defunctionalized continuation itself. Note, that we leave intact those calls to *apply* that switch control between different continuations (e.g., in the definition of *eval*).

```
let rec apply eval e_k ρ k = case e_k of {
    kapp1(e2, e1) →
        case e1 of {
          val(v1) → (apply eval kapp2(v1, e2) ρ k) |
          ELSE(e1) → (eval e1 ρ (λe1'. (k kapp1(e2, e1'))))
        } |
    kapp2(v1, e2) →
        case e2 of {
          val(v2) → ... (apply eval kclo1(ρ'', e') ρ k) |
          ELSE(e2) → (eval e2 ρ (λe2'. (k kapp2(v1, e2'))))
        } |
    kclo1(ρ', e) →
```

```
        case e of {
          val(v) → (k val(v)) |
          ELSE(e) → (eval e ρ' (λe'. (k kclo1(ρ', e'))))
        }
    } in ...
```

Convert Continuations into Terms. At this point, we have a stepping function that returns either a term or a continuation, but we want a function returning only terms. The most straightforward approach to achieving this goal would be to introduce a term constructor for each defunctionalized continuation constructor. However, many of these continuation constructors can be trivially expressed using constructors already present in the object language. We want to avoid introducing redundant terms, so we aim to reuse existing constructors as much as possible. In our example we observe that **kapp1**(e_2, e_1) corresponds to **app**(e_1, e_2), while **kapp2**(v_1, e_2) to **app**(**val**$(v_1), e_2)$. We might also observe that **kclo1**(ρ', e) would correspond to **app**(**clo**$(x, e, \rho), val(v_2))$ if $\rho' = \text{update } x\ v_2\ \rho$. Our current implementation doesn't handle such cases, however, and so we introduce **kclo1** as a new term constructor.

```
let rec apply eval e_k ρ k = case e_k of {
  kapp1(e2, e1) →
      case e1 of {
        val(v1) → (apply eval kapp2(v1, e2) ρ k) |
        ELSE(e1) → (eval e1 ρ (λe1'. (k app(e1', e2))))
      } |
  kapp2(v1, e2) →
      case e2 of {
        val(v2) →
            case v1 of {
              clo(x, e', ρ') → let ρ'' = (update x v2 ρ') in kclo1(ρ'', e')
            } |
        ELSE(e2) → (eval e2 ρ (λe2'. (k app(val(v1), e2'))))
      } |
  kclo1(ρ', e) →
      case e of {
        val(v) → (k val(v)) |
        ELSE(e) → (eval e ρ' (λe'. (k kclo1(ρ', e'))))
      }
} in
let rec eval e ρ k = case e of {
  ...
  kclo1(ρ', e') → (apply eval kclo1(ρ', e') ρ k)
}
```

Inlining and Simplification. Next, we eliminate the *apply* function by inlining its applications and simplifying the result. At this point we have obtained a small-step interpreter in continuation-passing style.

$$
\begin{array}{l}
\textbf{let rec } \mathit{eval}\ e\ \rho\ k = \textbf{case } e \textbf{ of } \{ \\
\quad \ldots \\
\quad \textsf{app}(e_1, e_2) \rightarrow \\
\qquad \textbf{case } e_1 \textbf{ of } \{ \\
\qquad\quad \textsf{val}(v_1) \rightarrow \\
\qquad\qquad \textbf{case } e_2 \textbf{ of } \{ \\
\qquad\qquad\quad \textsf{val}(v_2) \rightarrow \\
\qquad\qquad\qquad \textbf{case } v_1 \textbf{ of } \{ \\
\qquad\qquad\qquad\quad \textsf{clo}(x, e', \rho') \rightarrow \textbf{let } \rho'' = (\text{update } x\ v_2\ \rho') \textbf{ in } \textsf{kclo1}(\rho'', e') \\
\qquad\qquad\qquad \} \mid \\
\qquad\qquad\quad \textsf{ELSE}(e_2) \rightarrow (\text{eval } e_2\ \rho\ (\boldsymbol{\lambda} e_2'.\ (k\ \textsf{app}(\textsf{val}(v_1), e_2')))) \\
\qquad\qquad \} \mid \\
\qquad\quad \textsf{ELSE}(e_1) \rightarrow (\text{eval } e_1\ \rho\ (\boldsymbol{\lambda} e_1'.\ (k\ \textsf{app}(e_1', e_2)))) \\
\qquad \} \mid \\
\quad \textsf{kclo1}(\rho', e') \rightarrow \\
\qquad \textbf{case } e' \textbf{ of } \{ \\
\qquad\quad \textsf{val}(v) \rightarrow (k\ \textsf{val}(v)) \mid \\
\qquad\quad \textsf{ELSE}(e) \rightarrow (\text{eval } e\ \rho'\ (\boldsymbol{\lambda} e'.\ (k\ \textsf{kclo1}(\rho', e')))) \\
\qquad \} \\
\}
\end{array}
$$

Convert to Direct Style and Remove the Value Case. The final transformation is to convert our small-step interpreter back to direct style. Moreover, we also remove the value case $\textsf{val}(v) \rightarrow \textsf{val}(v)$ as we, usually, do not want values to step.

$$
\begin{array}{l}
\textbf{let rec } \mathit{eval}\ e\ \rho = \textbf{case } e \textbf{ of } \{ \\
\quad \textsf{var}(x) \rightarrow \textbf{let } v = (\rho\ x) \textbf{ in } \textsf{val}(v) \mid \\
\quad \textsf{lam}(x, e') \rightarrow \textsf{val}(\textsf{clo}(x, e', \rho)) \mid \\
\quad \textsf{app}(e_1, e_2) \rightarrow \\
\qquad \textbf{case } e_1 \textbf{ of } \{ \\
\qquad\quad \textsf{val}(v_1) \rightarrow \\
\qquad\qquad \textbf{case } e_2 \textbf{ of } \{ \\
\qquad\qquad\quad \textsf{val}(v_2) \rightarrow \\
\qquad\qquad\qquad \textbf{case } v_1 \textbf{ of } \{ \\
\qquad\qquad\qquad\quad \textsf{clo}(x, e', \rho') \rightarrow \textbf{let } \rho'' = (\text{update } x\ v_2\ \rho') \textbf{ in } \textsf{kclo1}(\rho'', e') \\
\qquad\qquad\qquad \} \mid \\
\qquad\qquad\quad \textsf{ELSE}(e_2) \rightarrow \textbf{let } e_2' = (\text{eval } e_2\ \rho) \textbf{ in } \textsf{app}(\textsf{val}(v_1), e_2') \\
\qquad\qquad \} \mid \\
\qquad\quad \textsf{ELSE}(e_1) \rightarrow \textbf{let } e_1' = (\text{eval } e_1\ \rho) \textbf{ in } \textsf{app}(e_1', e_2) \\
\qquad \} \mid \\
\quad \textsf{kclo1}(\rho', e') \rightarrow \\
\qquad \textbf{case } e' \textbf{ of } \{ \\
\qquad\quad \textsf{val}(v) \rightarrow \textsf{val}(v) \mid \\
\qquad\quad \textsf{ELSE}(e) \rightarrow \textbf{let } e' = (\text{eval } e\ \rho') \textbf{ in } \textsf{kclo1}(\rho', e') \\
\qquad \} \\
\}
\end{array}
$$

Small-Step Evaluator. Fig. 3 shows the small-step rules corresponding to our last interpreter. Barring the introduction of the **kclo1** constructor, the resulting semantics is essentially identical to one we would write manually.

$$1\ \frac{v = \rho\ x}{\rho \vdash \mathsf{var}(x) \rightarrow \mathsf{val}(v)} \qquad 2\ \frac{}{\rho \vdash \mathsf{lam}(x, e') \rightarrow \mathsf{val}(\mathsf{clo}(x, e', \rho))}$$

$$3\ \frac{\rho'' = \mathsf{update}\ x\ v_2\ \rho'}{\rho \vdash \mathsf{app}(\mathsf{val}(\mathsf{clo}(x, e', \rho')), \mathsf{val}(v_2)) \rightarrow \mathbf{kclo1}(\rho'', e')}$$

$$4\ \frac{\rho \vdash e_2 \rightarrow e_2'}{\rho \vdash \mathsf{app}(\mathsf{val}(v_1), e_2) \rightarrow \mathsf{app}(\mathsf{val}(v_1), e_2')} \qquad 5\ \frac{\rho \vdash e_1 \rightarrow e_1'}{\rho \vdash \mathsf{app}(e_1, e_2) \rightarrow \mathsf{app}(e_1', e_2)}$$

$$6\ \frac{}{\rho \vdash \mathbf{kclo1}(\rho', \mathsf{val}(v)) \rightarrow \mathsf{val}(v)} \qquad 7\ \frac{\rho' \vdash e \rightarrow e'}{\rho \vdash \mathbf{kclo1}(\rho', e) \rightarrow \mathbf{kclo1}(\rho', e')}$$

Fig. 3. Resulting small-step semantics

3 Big-Step Specifications

We define our transformations on an untyped extended λ-calculus with call-by-value semantics that allows the straightforward definition of big- and small-step interpreters. We call this language an *evaluator definition language* (EDL).

3.1 Evaluator Definition Language

Table 1 gives the syntax of EDL. We choose to restrict ourselves to A-normal form, which greatly simplifies our partial CPS conversion without compromising readability. Our language has the usual call-by-value semantics, with arguments being evaluated left-to-right. All of the examples of the previous section were written in this language.

Our language has 3 forms of let-binding constructs: the usual (optionally recursive) **let**, a let-construct for evaluator definition, and a let-construct for defining continuations. The behavior of all three constructs is the same, however, we treat them differently during the transformations. The **leteval** construct also comes with the additional static restriction that it may appear only once (i.e., there can be only one evaluator). The **leteval** and **letcont** forms are recursive by default, while **let** has an optional **rec** specifier to create a recursive binding. For simplicity, our language does not offer implicit mutual recursion, so mutual recursion has to be made explicit by inserting additional arguments. We do this when we generate the *apply* function during defunctionalization.

Notation and Presentation. We use vector notation to denote syntactic lists belonging to a particular sort. For example, $\vec{e}$ and $\vec{ae}$ are lists of elements of, respectively, *Expr* and *AExpr*, while $\vec{x}$ is a list of variables. Separators can be spaces (e.g., function arguments) or commas (e.g., constructor arguments or configuration components). We expect the actual separator to be clear from the context. Similarly for lists of expressions: $\vec{e}$, $\vec{ae}$, etc. In let bindings, $f\ x_1\ \ldots\ x_n = e$ and $f = \lambda x_1\ \ldots\ x_n.\ e$ are both syntactic sugar for $f = \lambda x_1.\ \ldots\ \lambda x_n.\ e$.

Table 1. Syntax of the evaluator definition language.

$\mathit{Expr} \ni e ::=$	$\mathbf{let}\ bn = ce\ \mathbf{in}\ e$	(let-binding)
	$\mid \mathbf{let\ rec}\ bn = ce\ \mathbf{in}\ e$	(recursive let-binding)
	$\mid \mathbf{leteval}\ x = ce\ \mathbf{in}\ e$	(evaluator definition)
	$\mid \mathbf{letcont}\ k = ce\ \mathbf{in}\ e$	(continuation definition)
	$\mid ce$	
$\mathit{CExpr} \ni ce ::=$	$(ae\ ae\ \ldots)$	(application)
	$\mid \mathbf{case}\ ae\ \mathbf{of}\ \{\ cas \mid \ldots \mid cas\ \}$	(pattern matching)
	$\mid \mathbf{if}\ ae\ \mathbf{then}\ e\ \mathbf{else}\ e$	(conditional)
	$\mid ae$	
$\mathit{AExpr} \ni ae ::=$	$v \mid op$	(value, operator)
	$\mid x \mid k$	(variable, continuation variable)
	$\mid \boldsymbol{\lambda} bn.\ e$	(λ-abstraction)
	$\mid c(ae, \ldots, ae)$	(constructor application)
	$\mid \langle\ ae, \ldots, ae\ \rangle$	(configuration expression)
$\mathit{Binder} \ni bn ::=$	$x \mid \langle\ x, \ldots, x\ \rangle$	(variable, configuration)
$\mathit{Case} \ni cas ::=$	$c(x, \ldots, x) \rightarrow e$	(constructor pattern)
	$\mid \mathbf{ELSE}(x) \rightarrow e$	(default pattern)
$\mathit{Value} \ni v ::=$	$n \mid b \mid c(v,\ldots,v) \mid \langle\ v,\ldots,v\ \rangle \mid \mathsf{\mathbf{abs}}(\boldsymbol{\lambda} x.e, \rho)$	

4 Transformation Steps

In this section, we formally define each of the transformation steps informally described in Section 2. For each transformation function, we list only the most relevant cases; the remaining cases trivially recurse on the A-normal form (ANF) abstract syntax. We annotate functions with E, CE, and AE to indicate the corresponding ANF syntactic classes. We omit annotations when a function only operates on a single syntactic class. For readability, we annotate meta-variables to hint at their intended use – ρ stands for read-only entities (such as environments), whereas σ stands for read-write or "state-like" entities of a configuration (e.g., stores or exception states). These can be mixed with our notation for syntactic lists, so, for example, $\vec{x}^{\sigma}$ is a sequence of variables referring to state-like entities, while $\vec{ae}^{\rho}$ is a sequence of a-expressions corresponding to read-only entities.

4.1 CPS Conversion

The first stage of the process is a *partial* CPS conversion [8, 25] to make control flow in the evaluator explicit. We limit this transformation to the main evaluator function, i.e., only the function *eval* will take an additional continuation argument and will pass results to it. Because our input language is already in ANF, the conversion is relatively easy to express. In particular, applications of the evaluator are always **let**-bound to a variable (or appear in a tail position), which makes constructing the current continuation straightforward. Below are the relevant clauses of the conversion. For this transformation we assume the following easily checkable properties:

- The evaluator name is globally unique.
- The evaluator is *never* applied partially.
- All bound variables are distinct.

The conversion is defined as three mutually recursive functions with the following signatures:

$$\begin{aligned}\mathsf{cps}_E &: \mathit{Expr} \to (\mathit{CExpr} \to \mathit{Expr}) \to \mathit{Expr}\\ \mathsf{cps}_{CE} &: \mathit{CExpr} \to (\mathit{CExpr} \to \mathit{Expr}) \to \mathit{Expr}\\ \mathsf{cps}_{AE} &: \mathit{AExpr} \to \mathit{AExpr}\end{aligned}$$

In the equations, $\mathcal{K}$, $\mathcal{I}$, $\mathcal{A}_k : \mathit{CExpr} \to \mathit{Expr}$ are meta-continuations; $\mathcal{I}$ injects a *CExpr* into *Expr*.

$$\begin{aligned}&\mathsf{cps}_E\big[\textbf{leteval}\ \mathit{eval}\ \vec{bn} = e_1\ \textbf{in}\ e_2\big]\ \mathcal{K} =\\ &\qquad \textbf{leteval}\ \mathit{eval}\ \vec{bn}\ k = \big(\mathsf{cps}_E\big[e_1\big]\ \mathcal{A}_k\big)\ \textbf{in}\ \big(\mathsf{cps}_E\big[e_2\big]\ \mathcal{K}\big)\\ &\qquad \text{where } k \text{ is a fresh continuation variable}\end{aligned}$$

$$\begin{aligned}&\mathsf{cps}_E\big[\textbf{let}\ bn = (\mathit{eval}\ ae_1\ \vec{ae})\ \textbf{in}\ e\big]\ \mathcal{K} =\\ &\qquad \textbf{letcont}\ k\ bn = \big(\mathsf{cps}_E\ \big[e\big]\ \mathcal{K}\big)\ \textbf{in}\ \mathsf{cps}_{CE}\big[(\mathit{eval}\ ae_1\ \vec{ae})\big]\ \mathcal{A}_k\\ &\qquad \text{where } k \text{ is a fresh continuation variable}\end{aligned}$$

$$\begin{aligned}&\mathsf{cps}_E\ \big[\textbf{let}\ bn = ce\ \textbf{in}\ e\ \big]\ \mathcal{K} =\\ &\qquad \mathsf{renorm}\big[\textbf{let'}\ bn = \big(\mathsf{cps}_{CE}\ \big[ce\big]\ \mathcal{I}\big)\ \textbf{in}\ \big(\mathsf{cps}_E\ \big[e\big]\ \mathcal{K}\big)\big]\end{aligned}$$

$$\begin{aligned}&\mathsf{cps}_{CE}\ \big[(\mathit{eval}\ ae_1\ \vec{ae})\big]\ \mathcal{K} = \ (\mathit{eval}\ \big(\mathsf{cps}_{AE}\ \big[ae_1\big]\big)\ \big(\mathsf{cps}_{AE}\ \big[\vec{ae}\big]\big)\ (\boldsymbol{\lambda} x.\ \mathcal{K}\big[x\big]))\\ &\qquad \text{where } x \text{ is a fresh variable}\end{aligned}$$

$$\mathsf{cps}_{CE}\ \big[ae\big]\ \mathcal{K} = \mathcal{K}\big(\mathsf{cps}_{AE}\ \big[ae\big]\big)$$

$$\mathsf{cps}_{AE}\ \big[\boldsymbol{\lambda} x.e\big] = \boldsymbol{\lambda} x.\ \big(\mathsf{cps}_E\ \big[e\big]\ \mathcal{I}\big)$$

$$\mathsf{cps}_{AE}\ \big[ae\big] = ae$$

where for any k, $\mathcal{A}_k$ is defined as

$$\begin{aligned}\mathcal{A}_k\big[ae\big] &= k\ ae\\ \mathcal{A}_k\big[ce\big] &= \textbf{let}\ x = ce\ \textbf{in}\ k\ x \quad \text{where } x \text{ is fresh}\end{aligned}$$

and

$$\begin{aligned}&\mathsf{renorm}\big[\textbf{let'}\ x = ce\ \textbf{in}\ e\big] = \textbf{let}\ x = ce\ \textbf{in}\ e\\ &\mathsf{renorm}\big[\textbf{let'}\ x = (\textbf{let}\ x' = ce\ \textbf{in}\ e')\ \textbf{in}\ e\big] =\\ &\qquad\qquad \textbf{let}\ x' = ce\ \textbf{in}\ \mathsf{renorm}\big[\textbf{let'}\ x = e'\ \textbf{in}\ e\big]\end{aligned}$$

In the above equations, **let**' is a pseudo-construct used to make renormalization more readable. In essence, it is a non-ANF version of **let** where the bound expression is generalized to *Expr*. Note that renorm only works correctly if $x' \notin \mathsf{fv}(e)$, which is implied by our assumption that all bound variables are distinct.

4.2 Generalization of Continuations

The continuations resulting from the above CPS conversion expect to be applied to value terms. The next step is to generalize (or "lift") the continuations so that they recursively call the evaluator to evaluate non-value arguments. In other words, assuming the term type can be factored into values and computations $V+C$, we convert each continuation k with the type $V \rightarrow V$ into a continuation $k' : V + C \rightarrow V$ using the following schema:

$$\textbf{let rec } k'\ t = \textbf{case } t \textbf{ of } inl\ v \rightarrow k\ v \mid inr\ c \rightarrow eval\ c\ k'$$

The recursive clauses will correspond to congruence rules in the resulting small-step semantics.

The transformation works by finding the unique application site of the continuation and then inserting the corresponding call to *eval* in the non-value case.

$$
\begin{aligned}
\mathsf{gencont}_E\big[\textbf{letcont } k\ \langle\ x,\ \vec{x}^{\sigma}\ \rangle = e_k \textbf{ in } e\big] = \\
\textbf{letcont } k\ \langle\ \hat{x}, \vec{x}^{\sigma}\ \rangle = \\
\textbf{case } \hat{x} \textbf{ of } \{ \\
\mathsf{\textbf{val}}(x) \rightarrow e_k\ ; \\
\textbf{ELSE}(\hat{x}) \rightarrow eval\ \langle\ \hat{x}, \vec{ae}^{\sigma}\ \rangle\ \vec{ae}^{\rho}\ ae_k \\
\} \\
\text{if } \mathsf{findApp}\ k\ e = eval\ \langle\ \_\,, \vec{ae}^{\sigma}\ \rangle\ \vec{ae}^{\rho}\ ae_k
\end{aligned}
$$

where

- findApp $k\ e$ is the unique use site of the continuation k in expression e, that is, the *CExpr* where *eval* is applied with k as its continuation; and
- $\hat{x}$ is a fresh variable associated with x – it stands for "a term corresponding to (the value) x".

Following the CPS conversion, each named continuation is applied exactly once in e, so findApp $k\ e$ is total and returns the continuation's unique use site. Moreover, because the continuation was originally defined and let-bound at that use site, all free variables in findApp $k\ e$ are also free in the definition of k.

When performing this generalization transformation, we also modify tail positions in *eval* that return a value so that they wrap their result in the **val** constructor. That is, if the continuation parameter of *eval* is k, then we rewrite all sites applying k to a configuration as follows:

$$k\ \langle\ ae,\ \vec{ae}^{\sigma}\ \rangle \Rightarrow k\ \langle\ \mathsf{\textbf{val}}(ae),\ \vec{ae}^{\sigma}\ \rangle$$

4.3 Argument Lifting in Continuations

In the next phase, we partially lift free variables in continuations to make them explicit arguments. We perform a *selective* lifting in that we avoid lifting non-term arguments to the evaluation function. These arguments represent entities that parameterize the evaluation of a term. If an entity is modified during evaluation, the modified entity variable gets lifted. In the running example of Section 2, such a lifting occurred for $kclo_1$.

Function lift specifies the transformation at the continuation definition site:

$$\begin{aligned}\mathsf{lift}\ \Xi\ \Delta\ [\mathbf{letcont}\ k\ &= \boldsymbol{\lambda} x.\, e_k\ \mathbf{in}\ e] = \\ \mathbf{letcont}\ k\ &= \boldsymbol{\lambda}\ x_1\ \ldots\ x_n\ x.\,(\mathsf{lift}\ \Xi'\ \Delta'\ [e_k])\ \mathbf{in}\ (\mathsf{lift}\ \Xi'\ \Delta'\ [e])\end{aligned}$$

where

- $\Xi' = \Xi \cup \{k\}$
- $\{x_1, \ldots, x_n\} = \mathsf{fv}\ e_k \cup (\bigcup_{g \in (\mathsf{dom}\ \Delta\ \cap\ \mathsf{fv}\ e_k)} \Delta(g)) - \Xi'$
- $\Delta' = \Delta[k \mapsto (x_1, \ldots, x_n)]$

and at the continuation application site – recall that continuations are always applied fully, but at this point they are only applied to one argument:

$$\mathsf{lift}\ \Xi\ \Delta\ \left[k\ ae\right] = k\ x_1\ \ldots\ x_n\ (\mathsf{lift}\ \Xi\ \Delta\ \left[ae'\right])$$

if $k \in \mathsf{dom}\ \Delta$ and $\Delta(k) = (x_1, \ldots, x_n)$.

Our lifting function is a restricted version of a standard argument-lifting algorithm [19]. The first restriction is that we do not lift all free variables, since we do not aim to float and lift the continuations to the top-level of the program, only to the top-level of the evaluation function. The other difference is that we can use a simpler way to compute the set of lifted parameters due to the absence of mutual recursion between continuations. The correctness of this can be proved using the approach of Fischbach [16].

4.4 Continuations Switch Control Directly

At this point, continuations handle the full evaluation of a term themselves. Instead of calling *eval* with the continuation as an argument, we can call the continuation directly to switch control between evaluation stages of a term. We will replace original *eval* call sites with direct applications of the corresponding continuations. The recursive call to *eval* in congruence cases of continuations will be left untouched, as this is where the continuation's argument will be evaluated to a value. Following from the continuation generalization transformation, this call to *eval* is with the same arguments as in the original site (which we are now replacing). In particular, the *eval* is invoked with the same $\vec{ae}^{\rho}$ arguments in the continuation body as in the original call site.

$$\begin{aligned}&\mathsf{directcont}_E\ \left[\mathbf{letcont}\ k = ce\ \mathbf{in}\ e\right] K = \\ &\qquad \mathbf{letcont}\ k = \mathsf{directcont}_{CE}\ \left[ce\right] K\ \mathbf{in}\ \mathsf{directcont}_E\ \left[e\right](K \uplus \{k\})\end{aligned}$$

$$\mathsf{directcont}_{CE}\left[eval\ \langle\ ae,\ \vec{ae}^{\sigma}\ \rangle\ \vec{ae}^{\rho}\ (\boldsymbol{\lambda} y.\ k\ \vec{x}\ y)\right]\ K = k\ \vec{x}\ \langle\ ae,\ \vec{ae}^{\sigma}\ \rangle \qquad \text{if } k \in K$$

4.5 Defunctionalization

Now we can move towards a first-order representation of continuations which can be further converted into term constructions. We defunctionalize continuations by first collecting all continuations in *eval*, then introducing corresponding constructors (the syntax), and finally generating an *apply* function (the semantics). The collection function accumulates continuation names and their definitions. At the same time it removes the definitions.

$$\mathsf{collect}_E\big[\textbf{letcont}\ k = ce\ \textbf{in}\ e\big] = (\{(k, ce')\} \cup K_{ce} \cup K_e, e')$$

$$\begin{aligned} \text{where } (K_{ce}, ce') &= \mathsf{collect}_{CE}\big[ce\big] \\ (K_e, e') &= \mathsf{collect}_E\big[e\big] \end{aligned}$$

We reuse continuation names for constructors. The *apply* function is generated by simply generating a case analysis on the constructors and reusing the argument names from the continuation function arguments. In addition to the defunctionalized continuations, the generated *apply* function will take the same arguments as *eval*. Because of the absence of mutual recursion in our meta-language, *apply* takes *eval* as an argument.

$$\begin{aligned} &\mathsf{genApply}\ \vec{x}^{\rho}\ \vec{x}^{\sigma}\ k_{top}\ \big\{(k_1, \lambda p_{1,1}\ \ldots p_{1,i}.\ e_1), \ldots, (k_n, \lambda p_{n,1}\ \ldots\ p_{n,j}.\ e_n)\big\} = \\ &\quad \boldsymbol{\lambda} eval\ \langle\ x_k, \vec{x}^{\sigma}\ \rangle\ \vec{x}^{\rho}\ k_{top}. \\ &\qquad \textbf{case}\ x_k\ \textbf{of}\ \{ \\ &\qquad\quad k_1(p_{1,1}, \ldots, p_{1,i}) \ \longrightarrow\ e_1\ ; \\ &\qquad\quad \ldots\ ; \\ &\qquad\quad k_n(p_{n,1}, \ldots, p_{n,j}) \ \longrightarrow\ e_n \\ &\qquad \} \end{aligned}$$

Now we need a way to replace calls to continuations with corresponding calls to *apply*. For $\vec{ae}^{\rho}$ and k_{top} we use the arguments passed to *eval* or *apply* (depending on where we are replacing).

$$\mathsf{replace}_{CE}\big[k\ \vec{ae}_k\ \langle ae, \vec{ae}^{\sigma}\rangle\big](\vec{x}^{\rho}, k_{top}) = \textit{apply eval}\ \langle\ k(\vec{ae}_k, ae),\ \vec{ae}^{\sigma}\ \rangle\ \vec{x}^{\rho}\ k_{top}$$

Finally, the complete defunctionalization is defined in terms of the above three functions.

4.6 Remove Self-recursive Tail-Calls

This is the transformation which converts a recursive evaluator into a stepping function. The transformation itself is very simple: we simply replace the self-recursive calls to *apply* in congruence cases.

$$\begin{aligned} &\mathsf{derec}_{CE}\big[\textit{eval}\ \langle\ ae,\ \vec{ae}^{\sigma}\ \rangle\ \vec{ae}^{\rho}\ (\boldsymbol{\lambda}\langle\ x',\ \vec{x}^{\sigma\prime}\ \rangle.\ \textit{apply eval}\ \langle\ c^{\mathrm{K}}(\vec{ae},\ x'),\ \vec{x}^{\sigma\prime}\ \rangle\ \vec{ae}^{\rho\prime}\ k)\big] = \\ &\quad \textit{eval}\ \langle\ ae,\ \vec{ae}^{\sigma}\ \rangle\ \vec{ae}^{\rho}\ (\boldsymbol{\lambda}\langle\ x',\ \vec{x}^{\sigma\prime}\ \rangle.\ k\ \langle\ c^{\mathrm{K}}(\vec{ae},\ x'),\ \vec{x}^{\sigma\prime}\ \rangle) \end{aligned}$$

Note, that we still leave those invocations of *apply* that serve to switch control through the stages of evaluation. Unless a continuation constructor will become a part of the output language, its application will be inlined in the final phase of our transformation.

4.7 Convert Continuations to Terms

After defunctionalization, we effectively have two sorts of terms: those constructed using the original constructors and those constructed using continuation constructors. Terms in these two sorts are given their semantics by the *eval* and *apply* functions, respectively. To get only one evaluator function at the end of our transformation process, we will join these two sorts, adding extra continuation constructors as new term constructors. We could simply merge *apply* to *eval*, however, this would give us many overlapping constructors. For example, in Section 2, we established that $\mathbf{kapp1}(e_2, e_1) \approx \mathbf{app}(e_1, e_2)$ and $\mathbf{kapp2}(v_1, e_2) \approx \mathbf{app}(\mathbf{val}(v_1), e_2)$. The inference of equivalent term constructors is guided by the following simple principle. For each continuation term $c^{\mathrm{K}}(ae_1, \ldots, ae_n)$ we are looking for a term $c'(ae'_1, \ldots, ae'_m)$, such that, for all $\vec{ae}^{\sigma}$, $\vec{ae}^{\rho}$ and ae_k

$$\begin{aligned} &\mathit{apply}\ \mathit{eval}\ \langle\ c^{\mathrm{K}}(ae_1, \ldots, ae_n), \vec{ae}^{\sigma}\ \rangle\ \vec{ae}^{\rho}\ ae_k \\ &\qquad = \mathit{eval}\ \langle\ c'(ae'_1, \ldots, ae'_m), \vec{ae}^{\sigma}\ \rangle\ \vec{ae}^{\rho}\ ae_k \end{aligned}$$

In our current implementation, we use a conservative approach where, starting from the cases in *eval*, we search for continuations reachable along a control flow path. Variables appearing in the original term are instantiated along the way. Moreover, we collect variables dependent on configuration entities (state). If control flow is split based on information derived from the state, we automatically include any continuation constructors reachable from that point as new constructors in the resulting language and interpreter. This, together with how information flows from the top-level term to subterms in congruence cases, preserves the coupling between state and corresponding subterms between steps.

If, starting from an input term $c(\vec{x})$, an invocation of *apply* on a continuation term $c^{\mathrm{K}}(\vec{ae}_k)$ is reached, and if, after instantiating the variables in the input term $c(\vec{ae})$, the sets of their free variables are equal, then we can introduce a translation from $c^{\mathrm{K}}(\vec{ae}_k)$ into $c(\vec{ae})$. If such a direct path is not found, the c^{K} will become a new term constructor in the language and a case in *eval* is introduced such that the above equation is satisfied.

4.8 Inlining, Simplification and Conversion to Direct Style

To finalize the generation of a small-step interpreter, we inline all invocations of *apply* and simplify the final program. After this, the interpreter will consists of only the *eval* function, still in continuation-passing style. To convert the interpreter to direct style, we simply substitute *eval*'s continuation variable for

$(\boldsymbol{\lambda} x.x)$ and reduce the new redexes. Then we remove the continuation argument performing rewrites following the scheme:

$$\mathit{eval}\ \vec{ae}\ (\boldsymbol{\lambda} bn.\ e) \ \Rightarrow\ \textbf{let}\ bn\ =\ \mathit{eval}\ \vec{ae}\ \textbf{in}\ e$$

Finally, we remove the reflexive case on values (i.e., $\textsf{val}(v) \longrightarrow \textsf{val}(v)$). At this point we have a small-step interpreter in direct form.

4.9 Removing Vacuous Continuations

After performing the above transformation steps, we may end up with some redundant term constructors, which we call "empty" or vacuous. These are constructors which only have one argument and their semantics is equivalent to the argument itself, save for an extra step which returns the computed value. In other words, they are unary constructs which only have two rules in the resulting small-step semantics matching the following pattern.

$$\frac{}{\vec{\rho} \vdash \langle c(\textsf{val}(v)), \vec{\sigma}\rangle \rightarrow \langle \textsf{val}(v), \vec{\sigma}\rangle} \qquad \frac{\vec{\rho} \vdash \langle e, \vec{\sigma}\rangle \rightarrow \langle e', \vec{\sigma}'\rangle}{\vec{\rho} \vdash \langle c(e), \vec{\sigma}\rangle \rightarrow \langle c(e'), \vec{\sigma}'\rangle}$$

Such a construct will result from a continuation, which, even after generalization and argument lifting, merely evaluates its sole argument and returns the corresponding value:

$\textbf{letcont rec}\ k_i\ e = \textbf{case}\ e\ \textbf{of}\ \{$
$\quad \textsf{val}(v) \longrightarrow k\ v\ |$
$\quad \textsf{ELSE}(e) \longrightarrow \mathit{eval}\ e\ (\boldsymbol{\lambda} e'.\ k_i\ e')$
$\}$

These continuations can be easily identified and removed once argument lifting is performed, or at any point in the transformation pipeline, up until *apply* is absorbed into *eval*.

4.10 Detour: Generating Pretty-Big-Step Semantics

It is interesting to see what kind of semantics we get by rearranging or removing some steps of the above process. If, after CPS conversion, we do not generalize the continuations, but instead just lift their arguments and defunctionalize them,[1] we obtain a *pretty-big-step* [6] interpreter. The distinguishing feature of pretty-big-step semantics is that constructs which would normally have rules with multiple premises are factorized into intermediate constructs. As observed by Charguéraud, each intermediate construct corresponds to an intermediate state of the interpreter, which is why, in turn, they naturally correspond to continuations. Here are the pretty-big-step rules generated from the big-step semantics in Fig. 2 (Section 2).

[1] The complete transformation to pretty-big-step style involves these steps: 1. CPS conversion, 2. argument lifting, 3. removal of vacuous continuations, 4. defunctionalization, 5. merging of apply and eval, and 6. conversion to direct style.

$$\frac{}{\rho \vdash \textsf{val}(v) \Downarrow_B^P v} \qquad \frac{\rho \vdash e_1 \Downarrow_B^P v_1 \quad \rho \vdash \textbf{kappl}(e_2, v_1) \Downarrow_B^P v}{\rho \vdash \textsf{app}(e_1, e_2) \Downarrow_B^P v}$$

$$\frac{v = \rho\ x}{\rho \vdash \textsf{var}(x) \Downarrow_B^P v} \qquad \frac{\rho \vdash e_2 \Downarrow_B^P v_2 \quad \rho \vdash \textsf{kapp2}(v_1, v_2) \Downarrow_B^P v}{\rho \vdash \textbf{kappl}(e_2, v_1) \Downarrow_B^P v}$$

$$\frac{}{\rho \vdash \textsf{lam}(x, e') \Downarrow_B^P \textsf{clo}(x, e', \rho)} \qquad \frac{\rho'' = \textsf{update}\ x\ v_2\ \rho' \quad \rho'' \vdash e' \Downarrow_B^P v}{\rho \vdash \textsf{kapp2}(\textsf{clo}(x, e', \rho'), v_2) \Downarrow_B^P v}$$

As we can see, the evaluation of **app** now proceeds through two intermediate constructs, **kappl** and **kapp2**, which correspond to continuations introduced in the CPS conversion. The evaluation of **app**(e_1, e_2) starts by evaluating e_1 to v_1. Then **kappl** is responsible for evaluating e_2 to v_2. Finally, **kapp2** evaluates the closure body just as the third premise of the original rule for **app**. Save for different order of arguments, the resulting intermediate constructs and their rules are identical to Charguéraud's examples.

4.11 Pretty-Printing

For the purpose of presenting and studying the original and transformed semantics, we add a final pretty-printing phase. This amounts to generating inference rules corresponding to the control flow in the interpreter. This pretty-printing stage can be applied to both the big-step and small-step interpreters and was used to generate many of the rules in this paper, as well as for generating the appendix of the full version of this paper [1].

4.12 Correctness

A correctness proof for the full pipeline is not part of our current work. However, several of these steps (partial CPS conversion, partial argument lifting, defunctionalization, conversion to direct style) are instances of well-established techniques. In other cases, such as generalization of continuations (Section 4.2) and removal of self-recursive tail-calls (Section 4.6), we have informal proofs using equational reasoning [1]. The proof for tail-call removal is currently restricted to compositional interpreters.

5 Evaluation

We have evaluated our approach to deriving small-step interpreters on a range of example languages. Table 2 presents an overview of example big-step specifications and their properties, together with their derived small-step counterparts. A full listing of the input and output specifications for these case studies appears in the appendix to the full version of the paper, which is available online [1].

Table 2. Overview of transformed example languages. Input is a given big-step interpreter and our transformations produce a small-step counterpart as output automatically. "Prems" columns only list structural premises: those that check for a big or small step. Unless otherwise stated, environments are used to give meaning to variables and they are represented as functions.

	Big-step		Small-step			
Example	Rules	Prems	Rules	Prems	New	Features
Call-by-value	4	3	7	3	1	
Call-by-value, substitution	4	5	7	4	0	addition
Call-by-value, booleans	13	20	24	11	1	add., conditional, equality
Call-by-value, pairs	7	7	14	7	1	pairs, left/right projection
Call-by-value, dynamic scopes	5	5	10	5	1	add., defunctionalized environments (DEs)
Call-by-value, recursion & iteration	26	44	57	26	6	fixpoint operator, add., sub., let-expressions, applicative for and while loops, cond., strict and "lazy" conjunction, eq., pairs
Call-by-name	5	5	11	5	2	add., DEs
Call-by-name, substitution	4	4	6	3	0	add., DEs
Call-by-name, booleans	13	20	25	11	2	add., cond., eq., DEs
Call-by-name, pairs	7	7	15	7	2	pairs, left/right proj., DEs
Minimal imperative	4	4	6	3	0	add., store without indirection, combined assignment *with* sequencing
While	7	9	14	6	2	add., store w/o indir., assign., seq., while
While, environments	8	10	17	7	3	add., store w/ indir., scoped var. declaration, assign., seq., while
Extended While	17	26	33	15	2	add., subt., mult., seq., store w/o indir., while, cond., "ints as bools", equality, "lazy conj."
Exceptions as state	8	7	11	3	1	add.
Exceptions as values	8	7	10	3	0	add.
Call-by-value, exceptions	21	29	34	12	2	add., div., try block
CBV, exceptions as state	20	26	39	11	8	add., div., handle & try blocks
CBV, non-determinism	7	7	13	5	2	add., choice operator
Store rewinding	8	10	19	8	4	assign., rewinding of the store

For our case studies, we have used call-by-value and call-by-name λ-calculi, and a simple imperative language as base languages and extended them with some common features. Overall, the small-step specifications (as well as the corresponding interpreters) resulting from our transformation are very similar to ones we could find in the literature. The differences are either well justified—for example, by different handling of value terms—or they are due to new term constructors which could be potentially eliminated by a more powerful translation.

We evaluated the correctness of our transformation experimentally, by comparing runs of the original big-step and the transformed small-step interpreters, as well as by inspecting the interpreters themselves. In a few cases, we proved the transformation correct by transcribing the input and output interpreters in Coq (as an evaluation relation coupled with a proof of determinism) and proving them equivalent. From the examples in Table 2, we have done so for "Call-by-value", "Exceptions as state", and a simplified version of "CBV, exceptions as state".

We make a few observations about the resulting semantics here.

New Auxiliary Constructs. In languages that use an environment to look up values bound to variables, new constructs are introduced to keep the updated environment as context. These constructs are simple: they have two arguments – one for the environment (context) and one for the term to be evaluated in that environment. A congruence rule will ensure steps of the term argument in the given context and another rule will return the result. The construct **kclo1** from the λ-calculus based examples is a typical example.

$$\frac{}{\rho \vdash \mathbf{kclo1}(\rho', \mathsf{val}(v)) \rightarrow \mathsf{val}(v)} \qquad \frac{\rho' \vdash t \rightarrow t'}{\rho \vdash \mathbf{kclo1}(\rho', t) \rightarrow \mathbf{kclo1}(\rho', t')}$$

As observed in Section 2, if the environment ρ'' is a result of updating an environment ρ' with a binding of x to v, then the **app** rule

$$\frac{\rho'' = \mathsf{update}\ x\ v\ \rho'}{\rho \vdash \mathbf{app}(\mathbf{clo}(\rho', x, e), v) \rightarrow \mathbf{kclo1}(\rho'', e)}$$

and the above two rules can be replaced with the following rules for **app**:

$$\frac{}{\rho \vdash \mathbf{app}(\mathbf{clo}(x, v, \rho'), v_2) \rightarrow v} \qquad \frac{\rho'' = \mathsf{update}\ x\ v_2\ \rho' \qquad \rho'' \vdash e \rightarrow e'}{\rho \vdash \mathbf{app}(\mathbf{clo}(x, e, \rho'), v_2) \rightarrow \mathbf{app}(\mathbf{clo}(x, e', \rho'), v_2)}$$

Another common type of constructs resulting in a recurring pattern of extra auxiliary constructs are loops. For example, the "While" language listed in Table 2 contains a while-loop with the following big-step rules:

$$\frac{\langle e_b, \sigma\rangle \Downarrow \langle \mathbf{false}, \sigma'\rangle}{\langle \mathbf{while}(e_b, c), \sigma\rangle \Downarrow \langle \mathbf{skip}, \sigma'\rangle}$$

$$\frac{\langle e_b, \sigma\rangle \Downarrow \langle \mathbf{true}, \sigma'\rangle \qquad \langle c, \sigma'\rangle \Downarrow \langle \mathbf{skip}, \sigma''\rangle \qquad \langle \mathbf{while}(e_b, c), \sigma''\rangle \Downarrow \langle v, \sigma'''\rangle}{\langle \mathbf{while}(e_b, c), \sigma\rangle \Downarrow \langle v, \sigma'''\rangle}$$

The automatic transformation of these rules introduces two extra constructs, **kwhile1** and **ktrue1**. The former ensures the full evaluation of the condition expression, keeping a copy of it together with the while's body. The latter construct ensures the full evaluation of while's body, keeping a copy of the body together with the condition expression.

$$\frac{}{\langle \mathbf{while}(e_b, c),\ \sigma\rangle \rightarrow \langle \mathbf{kwhile1}(c, e_b, e_b),\ \sigma\rangle}$$

$$\frac{}{\langle \mathbf{kwhile1}(c, e_b, \mathbf{true}),\ \sigma\rangle \rightarrow \langle \mathbf{ktrue1}(e_b, c, c),\ \sigma\rangle}$$

$$\frac{}{\langle \mathbf{kwhile1}(c, e_b, \mathbf{false}),\ \sigma\rangle \rightarrow \langle \mathbf{skip},\ \sigma\rangle}$$

$$\frac{\langle t,\ \sigma\rangle \rightarrow \langle t',\ \sigma'\rangle}{\langle \mathbf{kwhile1}(c, e_b, t),\ \sigma\rangle \rightarrow \langle \mathbf{kwhile1}(c, e_b, t'),\ \sigma'\rangle}$$

$$\frac{}{\langle \mathbf{ktrue1}(e_b, c, \mathbf{skip}),\ \sigma\rangle \rightarrow \langle \mathbf{while}(e_b, c),\ \sigma\rangle}$$

$$\frac{\langle t,\ \sigma\rangle \rightarrow \langle t',\ \sigma'\rangle}{\langle \mathbf{ktrue1}(e_b, c, t),\ \sigma\rangle \rightarrow \langle \mathbf{ktrue1}(e_b, c, t'),\ \sigma'\rangle}$$

We observe that in a language with a conditional and a sequencing construct we can find terms corresponding to **kwhile1** and **ktrue1:**

$$\begin{aligned}\mathbf{kwhile1}(c, e_b, e_b') &\approx \mathbf{if}(e_b', \mathbf{seq}(c, \mathbf{while}(e_b, c)), \mathbf{skip})\\ \mathbf{ktrue1}(e_b, c, c') &\approx \mathbf{seq}(c', \mathbf{while}(e_b, c))\end{aligned}$$

The small-step semantics of **while** could then be simplified to a single rule.

$$\frac{}{\langle \mathbf{while}(e_b, c), \sigma\rangle \rightarrow \langle \mathbf{if}(e_b, \mathbf{seq}(c, \mathbf{while}(e_b, c)), \mathbf{skip}), \sigma\rangle}$$

Our current, straightforward way of deriving term–continuation equivalents is not capable of finding these equivalences. In future work, we want to explore external tools, such as SMT solvers, to facilitate searching for translations from continuations to terms. This search could be possibly limited to a specific term depth.

Exceptions as Values. We tested our transformations with two ways of representing exceptions in big-step semantics currently supported by our input language: as values and as state. Representing exceptions as values appears to be more common and is used, for example, in the big-step specification of Standard ML [24], or in [6] in connection with *pretty big-step semantics.* Given a big-step specification (or interpreter) in this style, the generated small-step semantics handles exceptions correctly (based on our experiments). However, since exceptions are just values, propagation to top-level is spread out across multiple steps – depending on the depth of the term which raised the exception. The following example illustrates this behavior.

$$\begin{aligned}&\mathbf{add}(1, \mathbf{add}(2, \mathbf{add}(\mathbf{raise}(3), \mathbf{raise}(4)))) \rightarrow \mathbf{add}(1, \mathbf{add}(2, \mathbf{add}(\mathbf{exc}(3), \mathbf{raise}(4))))\\ &\quad \rightarrow \mathbf{add}(1, \mathbf{add}(2, \mathbf{exc}(3))) \rightarrow \mathbf{add}(1, \mathbf{exc}(3)) \rightarrow \mathbf{exc}(3)\end{aligned}$$

Since we expect the input semantics to be deterministic and the propagation of exceptions in the resulting small-step follows the original big-step semantics, this "slow" propagation is not a problem, even if it does not take advantage of "fast" propagation via labels or state. A possible solution we are considering for future work is to let the user flag values in the big-step semantics and translate such values as labels on arrows or a state change to allow propagating them in a single step.

Exceptions as State. Another approach to specifying exceptions is to use a flag in the configuration. Rules may be specified so that they only apply if the incoming state has no exception indicated. As with the exceptions-as-values approach, propagation rules have to be written to terminate a computation early if a computation of a subterm indicates an exception. Observe the exception propagation rule for **add** and the exception handling rule for **try**.

$$\frac{\langle e_1, \sigma, \textbf{ok}\rangle \Downarrow \langle v_1, \sigma', \textbf{ex}\rangle}{\langle \textbf{app}(e_1, e_2), \sigma, \textbf{ok}\rangle \Downarrow \langle \textbf{skip}, \sigma', \textbf{ex}\rangle}$$

$$\frac{\langle e_1, \sigma, \textbf{ok}\rangle \Downarrow \langle v_1, \sigma', \textbf{ex}\rangle \qquad \langle e_2, \sigma', \textbf{ok}\rangle \Downarrow \langle v_2, \sigma'', \textbf{ok}\rangle}{\langle \textbf{try}(e_1, e_2), \sigma, \textbf{ok}\rangle \Downarrow \langle v_2, \sigma'', \textbf{ok}\rangle}$$

Using state to propagate exceptions is mentioned in connection with small-step SOS in [4]. While this approach has the potential advantage of manifesting the currently raised exception immediately at the top-level, it also poses a problem of locality. If an exception is reinserted into the configuration, it might become decoupled from the original site. This can result, for example, in the wrong handler catching the exception in a following step. Our transformation deals with this style of exceptions naturally by preserving more continuations in the final interpreter. After being raised, an exception is inserted into the state and propagated to top-level by congruence rules. However, it will only be caught after the corresponding subterm has been evaluated, or rather, a value has been propagated upwards to signal a completed computation. This behavior corresponds to exception handling in big-step rules, only it is spread out over multiple steps. Continuations are kept in the final language to correspond to stages of computation and thus, to preserve the locality of a raised exception. A handler will only handle an exception once the raising subterm has become a value. Hence, the exception will be intercepted by the innermost handler – even if the exception is visible at the top-level of a step.

Based on our experiments, the exception-as-state handling in the generated small-step interpreters is a truthful unfolding of the big-step evaluation process. This is further supported by our ad-hoc proofs of equivalence between input and output interpreters. However, the generated semantics suffers from a blowup in the number of rules and moves away from the usual small-step propagation and exception handling in congruence rules. We see this as a shortcoming of the transformation. To overcome this, we briefly experimented with a case-floating stage, which would result in catching exceptions in the congruence cases of continuations. Using such transformation, the resulting interpreter would more closely mirror the standard small-step treatment of exceptions as signals. However, the conditions when this transformations should be triggered need to be considered carefully and we leave this for future work.

Limited Non-determinism. In the present work, our aim was to only consider deterministic semantics implemented as an interpreter in a functional programming language. However, since cases of the interpreter are considered independently in the transformation, some forms of non-determinism in the input semantics get translated correctly. For example, the following internal choice construct (cf. CSP's $\sqcap$ operator [5, 17]) gets transformed correctly. The straightforward big-step rules are transformed into small-step rules as expected. Of course, one has to keep in mind that these rules are interpreted as ordered, that is, the first rule in both styles will always apply.

$$\frac{e_1 \Downarrow v_1}{\textsf{choose}(e_1, e_2) \Downarrow v_1} \qquad \frac{}{\textsf{choose}(e_1, e_2) \longrightarrow e_1}$$

$$\frac{e_2 \Downarrow v_2}{\textsf{choose}(e_1, e_2) \Downarrow v_2} \qquad \frac{}{\textsf{choose}(e_1, e_2) \longrightarrow e_2}$$

6 Related Work

In their short paper [18], the authors propose a direct syntactic way of deriving small-step rules from big-step ones. Unlike our approach, based on manipulating control flow in an interpreter, their transformation applies to a set of inference rules. While axioms are copied over directly, for conditional rules a stack is added to the configuration to keep track of evaluation. For each conditional big-step rule, an auxiliary construct and 4 small-step rules are generated. Results of "premise computations" are accumulated and side-conditions are only discharged at the end of such a computation sequence. For this reason, we can view the resulting semantics more as a "leap" semantics, which makes it less suitable for a semantics-based interpreter or debugger. A further disadvantage is that the resulting semantics is far removed from a typical small-step specification with a higher potential for blow-up as 4 rules are introduced for each conditional rule. On the other hand, the delayed unification of meta-variables and discharging of side-conditions potentially makes the transformation applicable to a wider array of languages, including those where control flow is not as explicit.

In [2], the author explores an approach to constructing abstract machines from big-step (natural) specifications. It applies to a class of big-step specifications called *L-attributed big-step semantics*, which allows for sufficiently interesting languages. The extracted abstract machines use a stack of evaluation contexts to keep track of the stages of computations. In contrast, our transformed interpreters rebuild the context via congruence rules in each step. While this is less efficient as a computation strategy, the intermediate results of the computation are visible in the context of the original program, in line with usual SOS specifications.

A significant body of work has been developed on transformations that take a form of small-step semantics (usually an interpreter) and produce a big-step-style interpreter. The relation between semantic specifications, interpreters and abstract machines has been thoroughly investigated, mainly in the context of reduction semantics [10–13, 26]. In particular, our work was inspired by and is based on Danvy's work on refocusing in reduction semantics [13] and on use of CPS conversion and defunctionalization to convert between representations of control in interpreters [11].

A more direct approach to deriving big-step semantics from small-step is taken by authors of [4], where a small-step Modular SOS specification is transformed into a pretty-big-step one. This is done by introducing reflexivity and transitivity rules into a specification, along with a "refocus" rule which effectively compresses a transition sequence into a single step. The original small-step rules are then specialized with respect to these new rules, yielding refocused rules in the style of pretty-big-step semantics [6]. A related approach is by Ciobâcă [7], where big-step rules are generated for a small-step semantics. The big-step rules are, again, close to a pretty-big-step style.

7 Conclusion and Future Work

We have presented a stepwise functional derivation of a small-step interpreter from a big-step one. This derivation proceeds through a sequence of, mostly basic, transformation steps. First, the big-step evaluation function is converted into continuation-passing style to make control-flow explicit. Then, the continuations are generalized (or lifted) to handle non-value inputs. The non-value cases correspond to congruence rules in small-step semantics. After defunctionalization, we remove self-recursive calls, effectively converting the recursive interpreter into a stepping function. The final major step of the transformation is to decide which continuations will have to be introduced as new auxiliary terms into the language. We have evaluated our approach on several languages covering different features. For most of these, the transformation yields small-step semantics which are close to ones we would normally write by hand.

We see this work as an initial exploration of automatic transformations of big-step semantics into small-step counterparts. We identified a few areas where the current process could be significantly improved. These include applying better equational reasoning to identify terms equivalent to continuations, or transforming exceptions as state in a way that would avoid introducing many intermediate terms and would better correspond to usual signal handling in small-step SOS. Another research avenue is to fully verify the transformations in an interactive theorem prover, with the possibility of extracting a correct transformer from the proofs.

Acknowledgements. We would like to thank Jeanne-Marie Musca, Brian LaChance and the anonymous referees for their useful comments and suggestions. This work was supported in part by DARPA award FA8750-15-2-0033.

References

1. https://www.eecs.tufts.edu/~fvesely/esop2019
2. Ager, M.S.: From natural semantics to abstract machines. In: Etalle, S. (ed.) LOPSTR 2004. LNCS, vol. 3573, pp. 245–261. Springer, Heidelberg (2005). https://doi.org/10.1007/11506676_16
3. Amin, N., Rompf, T.: Collapsing towers of interpreters. Proc. ACM Program. Lang. **2**(POPL), 52:1–52:33 (2017). https://doi.org/10.1145/3158140
4. Bach Poulsen, C., Mosses, P.D.: Deriving pretty-big-step semantics from small-step semantics. In: Shao, Z. (ed.) ESOP 2014. LNCS, vol. 8410, pp. 270–289. Springer, Heidelberg (2014). https://doi.org/10.1007/978-3-642-54833-8_15
5. Brookes, S.D., Roscoe, A.W., Walker, D.J.: An operational semantics for CSP. Technical report, Oxford University (1986)
6. Charguéraud, A.: Pretty-big-step semantics. In: Felleisen, M., Gardner, P. (eds.) ESOP 2013. LNCS, vol. 7792, pp. 41–60. Springer, Heidelberg (2013). https://doi.org/10.1007/978-3-642-37036-6_3
7. Ciobâcă, Ş.: From small-step semantics to big-step semantics, automatically. In: Johnsen, E.B., Petre, L. (eds.) IFM 2013. LNCS, vol. 7940, pp. 347–361. Springer, Heidelberg (2013). https://doi.org/10.1007/978-3-642-38613-8_24
8. Danvy, O., Filinski, A.: Representing control: a study of the CPS transformation. Math. Struct. Comput. Sci. **2**(4), 361–391 (1992). https://doi.org/10.1017/S0960129500001535
9. Danvy, O.: On evaluation contexts, continuations, and the rest of computation. In: Thielecke, H. (ed.) Workshop on Continuations, pp. 13–23, Technical report CSR-04-1, Department of Computer Science, Queen Mary's College, Venice, Italy, January 2004
10. Danvy, O.: From reduction-based to reduction-free normalization. Electr. Notes Theor. Comput. Sci. **124**(2), 79–100 (2005). https://doi.org/10.1016/j.entcs.2005.01.007
11. Danvy, O.: Defunctionalized interpreters for programming languages. In: ICFP 2008, pp. 131–142. ACM, New York (2008). https://doi.org/10.1145/1411204.1411206
12. Danvy, O., Johannsen, J., Zerny, I.: A walk in the semantic park. In: PEPM 2011, pp. 1–12. ACM, New York (2011). https://doi.org/10.1145/1929501.1929503
13. Danvy, O., Nielsen, L.R.: Refocusing in reduction semantics. Technical report, BRICS RS-04-26, DAIMI, Department of Computer Science, University of Aarhus, November 2004
14. Ellison, C., Roşu, G.: An executable formal semantics of C with applications. In: POPL 2012, pp. 533–544. ACM, New York (2012). https://doi.org/10.1145/2103656.2103719
15. Felleisen, M., Findler, R.B., Flatt, M.: Semantics Engineering with PLT Redex, 1st edn. The MIT Press, Cambridge (2009)
16. Fischbach, A., Hannan, J.: Specification and correctness of lambda lifting. J. Funct. Program. **13**(3), 509–543 (2003). https://doi.org/10.1017/S0956796802004604
17. Hoare, C.A.R.: Communicating Sequential Processes. Prentice-Hall Inc., Upper Saddle River (1985)

18. Huizing, C., Koymans, R., Kuiper, R.: A small step for mankind. In: Dams, D., Hannemann, U., Steffen, M. (eds.) Concurrency, Compositionality, and Correctness. LNCS, vol. 5930, pp. 66–73. Springer, Heidelberg (2010). https://doi.org/10.1007/978-3-642-11512-7_5
19. Johnsson, T.: Lambda lifting: transforming programs to recursive equations. In: Jouannaud, J.-P. (ed.) FPCA 1985. LNCS, vol. 201, pp. 190–203. Springer, Heidelberg (1985). https://doi.org/10.1007/3-540-15975-4_37
20. Klein, G., Nipkow, T.: A machine-checked model for a Java-like language, virtual machine, and compiler. ACM Trans. Program. Lang. Syst. **28**(4), 619–695 (2006). https://doi.org/10.1145/1146809.1146811
21. Kumar, R., Myreen, M.O., Norrish, M., Owens, S.: CakeML: a verified implementation of ML. In: POPL 2014, pp. 179–191. ACM, New York (2014). https://doi.org/10.1145/2535838.2535841
22. Leroy, X., Grall, H.: Coinductive big-step operational semantics. Inf. Comput. **207**(2), 284–304 (2009). https://doi.org/10.1016/j.ic.2007.12.004
23. Midtgaard, J., Ramsey, N., Larsen, B.: Engineering definitional interpreters. In: PPDP 2013, pp. 121–132. ACM, New York (2013). https://doi.org/10.1145/2505879.2505894
24. Milner, R., Tofte, M., Macqueen, D.: The Definition of Standard ML. MIT Press, Cambridge (1997)
25. Nielsen, L.R.: A selective CPS transformation. Electr. Notes Theor. Comput. Sci. **45**, 311–331 (2001). https://doi.org/10.1016/S1571-0661(04)80969-1
26. Reynolds, J.C.: Definitional interpreters for higher-order programming languages. High. Order Symbolic Comput. **11**(4), 363–397 (1998). https://doi.org/10.1023/A:1010027404223
27. Roşu, G., Şerbănuţă, T.F.: An overview of the K semantic framework. J. Logic Algebraic Program. **79**(6), 397–434 (2010). https://doi.org/10.1016/j.jlap.2010.03.012
28. Strachey, C., Wadsworth, C.P.: Continuations: a mathematical semantics for handling full jumps. High. Order Symbolic Comput. **13**(1), 135–152 (2000). https://doi.org/10.1023/A:1010026413531
29. Wright, A., Felleisen, M.: A syntactic approach to type soundness. Inf. Comput. **115**(1), 38–94 (1994). https://doi.org/10.1006/inco.1994.1093

2

An Abstract Domain for Trees with Numeric Relations

Matthieu Journault[1(✉)], Antoine Miné[1,2(✉)], and Abdelraouf Ouadjaout[1(✉)]

[1] Sorbonne Université, CNRS, Laboratoire d'Informatique de Paris 6, LIP6, 75005 Paris, France
{matthieu.journault,antoine.mine,abdelraouf.ouadjaout}@lip6.fr
[2] Institut universitaire de France, Paris, France

Abstract. We present an abstract domain able to infer invariants on programs manipulating trees. Trees considered in the article are defined over a finite alphabet and can contain unbounded numeric values at their leaves. Our domain can infer the possible shapes of the tree values of each variable and find numeric relations between: the values at the leaves as well as the size and depth of the tree values of different variables. The abstract domain is described as a product of (1) a symbolic domain based on a tree automata representation and (2) a numerical domain lifted, for the occasion, to describe numerical maps with potentially infinite and heterogeneous definition set. In addition to abstract set operations and widening we define concrete and abstract transformers on these environments. We present possible applications, such as the ability to describe memory zones, or track symbolic equalities between program variables. We implemented our domain in a static analysis platform and present preliminary results analyzing a tree-manipulating toy-language.

1 Introduction

The abstract interpretation framework [5] enables the development of sound static analyzers by inferring and proving invariants on reachable states of programs. Invariants in the scope of abstract interpretation are elements of a lattice called an abstract domain. Most domains focus on numeric or pointer variables. By contrast, we propose an abstract domain for variables whose values are tree data-structures. Tree values appear natively in some languages (such as OCaml) and applications (such as the DOM in web programming) or can be encoded through pointer manipulations (as in C). Trees can abstract terms in logic programming. A tree domain can also be useful to collect symbolic expressions appearing in a program.

This work is supported by the European Research Council under Consolidator Grant Agreement 681393 – MOPSA.

```
typedef struct node
{
  int data;
  struct node* next;
} node;

node* append(node* head, int data)
{
  if (head==NULL) {
    return (create(data, NULL));
  } else {
    node *cursor=head;
    while(cursor->next != NULL)
      cursor=cursor->next;
    node* new_node=create(data,NULL);
    cursor->next=new_node;
    return head;
  }
}
```

Program 1: Append to list in C

```
float golden_ratio(int n) {
  int i = 0;
  float r = 1;
  while (i < n) {
    r = 1 + 1 / r;
    i += 1;
  }
  return r;
}
```

Program 2: Golden ratio in C

```
let rec f x n =
  match n with
  | 0 -> []
  | _ -> (x+1)::(x-1)::(f x (n-1))

let () =
  (*Assume x:int and n:int>=0*)
  let t = f x n in
  match t with
  | [] -> ()
  | p :: q when p > x -> ()
  | _ -> assert false
```

Program 3: List type in OCaml

Used Memory Zones. Program 1 describes an `append` function defined in the C language, this function adds an integer at the end of a linked list. The infinite set of unbounded terms of the form `*(*( ...*(head + 4) ...+ 4) + 4)` represents memory zones that are used by the `append` function. Our analyzer is able to infer and represent such sets of terms. This provides the information that Program 1 does not use any of the `data` field of the linked list. Such a function would be fairly commonly called in a real-life project. In a classical top-down static analysis by abstract interpretation, function calls are inlined at each call site. A way to improve scalability is to design modular analyzers able to reuse previous analysis results (as emphasized in [7]). In order to be able to successfully reuse function body analysis, input states must be unified. Moreover the cost of performing the analysis of the body of functions grows with the number of variables that need to be tracked. A common way to deal with both problems is to use framing on the inputs of the functions (as in separation logic [25]). This improves (1) precision: as we know that they are not modified by the function call, (2) body analysis efficiency: as the input state is reduced and finally (3) modularity: as constraints on the usage of the first analysis are relaxed by the removal of constraints.

Symbolic Relations. Program 2 is a C function computing an approximation of the golden ration (as it is the limit of the sequence $r_0 = 1$, $r_{n+1} = 1 + \frac{1}{r_n}$). As classical numerical domains can not represent such numerical relations, methods were proposed to track symbolic equality between expressions (see [23]). However such methods can not handle the unbounded iteration of Program 2. The set of reachable states at the end of Program 2 can be expressed by $\mathtt{r} = 1 + 1/(1 + 1/\ldots 1\ldots)$ with depth `n`. Please note that to infer such results we need to express numerical relations between the size of trees and the numeric variables from the program.

Numerical Environment. Consider now the OCaml Program 3, we want to prove that the `assert false` expression is never reached. This program builds a list of size $2 * \texttt{n}$ with alternating values $\texttt{x} + 1$ and $\texttt{x} - 1$. The assertion states that the head of the list is $\texttt{x} + 1$. After the definition of `t` there are two types of reachable states. (1) Those that have not gone through the loop ($\texttt{t} \mapsto \texttt{[]}, \texttt{x} \mapsto \mathbb{Z}, \texttt{n} \mapsto 0$), and (2) those that have gone through at least one iteration of the loop: ($\texttt{t} \mapsto \texttt{[}a_1\texttt{;}a_2\texttt{;}a_3\texttt{; ...]}, x \mapsto \alpha, \texttt{n} > 0, a_1 \mapsto \alpha + 1, a_2 \mapsto \alpha - 1, a_3 \mapsto \alpha + 1$), where $\alpha \in \mathbb{Z}$. Therefore we need to be able to keep numerical relations between the parametric and unbounded number of numeric values appearing in `t` and numeric variables from the program. Classical numeric domains do not provide out-of-the-box abstractions for sets of partially defined numerical functions, therefore we define such an abstraction. As an example of analysis result, the memory representation obtained by our analysis for `t` describes the set of trees of the form: $\texttt{Cons(}a\texttt{, Cons(}b\texttt{, Cons(}a\texttt{, ..., Nil) ...))}$ where $a = \texttt{x} + 1$ and $b = \texttt{x} - 1$. Therefore we are able to prove that the `assert false` expression is never reached.

Contributions. The main contributions of the article are threefold: (1) The extension of results on tree automata to the abstract interpretation framework by definition of a widening operator, in order to represent the set of tree shapes that a variable can contain. (2) The definition of a numerical domain built upon classical abstract domains able to represent sets of partial numerical maps with heterogeneous and unbounded definition sets. This is necessary to represent the numeric values at the leaves of a set of trees, as trees are unbounded and can contain a different number of leaves. (3) The definition of a novel abstraction for trees that can contain numerical values at their leaves. This last domain combines the abstractions (1) and (2). Moreover it is relational as it can express relations between numerical values found in trees and in the rest of the program, and relations between trees. Finally all results were implemented in an existing framework and experimented on a toy-language.

Limitations. At this point, analyses can only be performed on the toy language presented thereinafter, not on real life code, therefore we do not present any benchmark results, even though examples of analysis results will be put forth. Indeed Programs 1, 2 and 3 were precisely analyzed once encoded into our toy-language (see Programs 4 and 5).

Outline. We start, in Sect. 2, by presenting the concrete semantic we want to abstract. In Sect. 3 we build a first abstraction which forgets numerical values and focuses on abstracting tree shapes. Section 4 presents a novel numerical abstract domain required for the definition of the abstract domain of Sect. 5, which aims at precisely representing numerical constraints between trees and program variables. In Sect. 6 we provide remarks on the implementation and results of the analyzer. Finally Sect. 7 mentions related works while Sect. 8 concludes.

Notations. Classical Galois connections (see [5]) are denoted $(A, \subseteq_A) \underset{\alpha}{\overset{\gamma}{\leftrightarrows}} (B, \subseteq_B)$. When no best abstraction can be defined, we use the *representation* framework (as defined by Bourdoncle in [3], also known as concretization only framework), representations are denoted by $(A, \subseteq_A) \overset{\gamma}{\leftarrow} (B, \subseteq_B)$. $A \twoheadrightarrow B$ denotes the set of partial maps from A to B, and $\lambda_{|A}x.f(x) \in B$ denotes the map in $A \to B$ that associates $f(x)$ to x. Finally when $f \in A \to C$ and $g \in B \to C$, with $A \cap B = \emptyset$, $f \uplus g$ is the function defined on $A \cup B$, that associates $f(x)$ (resp. $g(x)$) to x whenever $x \in A$ (resp. $x \in B$).

2 Syntax and Concrete Semantics

Definition 1. *An* alphabet $\mathcal{F}$ *is a finite set, a* ranked alphabet *is a pair* $\mathcal{R} = (\mathcal{F}, a)$ *where* $\mathcal{F}$ *is an alphabet and* $a \in \mathcal{F} \to \mathbb{N}$. *For* $f \in \mathcal{F}$, *we call* arity *of* f *the value* $a(f)$. *We assume that* $\mathbb{Z}$ *and* $\mathcal{F}$ *are disjoint and we define the set of* natural terms *over* $\mathcal{R}$ *(denoted* $T_{\mathbb{Z}}(\mathcal{R})$*) to be the smallest set defined by:*

- $\mathbb{Z} \subseteq T_{\mathbb{Z}}(\mathcal{R})$
- $\forall p \geq 0,\ f \in \mathcal{F}, t_1,\ \ldots, t_p \in T_{\mathbb{Z}}(\mathcal{R}),\ a(f) = p \Rightarrow f(t_1, \ldots, t_p) \in T_{\mathbb{Z}}(\mathcal{R})$

Moreover when $\mathcal{R}$ *contains at least one symbol of arity* 0, *we define* terms *over* $\mathcal{R}$ *(denoted* $T(\mathcal{R})$*) to be the smallest set defined by:*

- $\forall p \geq 0,\ f \in \mathcal{F}, t_1,\ \ldots, t_p \in T(\mathcal{R}),\ a(f) = p \Rightarrow f(t_1, \ldots, t_p) \in T(\mathcal{R})$

In the following, $\mathcal{F}_n$ *denotes the subset of* $\mathcal{F}$ *of arity* n. *Moreover given a term* $t \in T(\mathcal{R})$ *we denote* $f = \textbf{head}(t) \in \mathcal{F}$ *and* $\textbf{sons}(t)$ *a possibly empty tuple* $(t_1, \ldots, t_n)$ *of elements of* $T(\mathcal{R})$ *such that* $t = f(t_1, \ldots, t_n)$.

Remark 1. Numerical leaves are defined to contain integers, however this could be modified to rationals, real numbers or floats. We are parametric in the type of numeric values, as they are delegated to an underlying numerical domain.

Example 1. Consider the ranked alphabet $\mathcal{R} = \{$*(1), &(1), +(2), x(0)$\}$, $u(n)$ means that symbol u has arity n. Then &x $\in T(\mathcal{R})$, but *(&x+4) $\in T_{\mathbb{Z}}(\mathcal{R})$, and *(&x+4) $\notin T(\mathcal{R})$. Using this alphabet we can model C pointer arithmetic.

Example 2. $U = \{+(x, y) \mid x \leq y\}$ and $V = \{+(x, +(z, y)) \mid x \leq y \wedge z \leq y\}$ are two sets of natural terms over $\mathcal{R} = \{+(2)\}$ which we use as running examples.

$$
\begin{aligned}
\textit{tree-expr} &\triangleq \mid \mathbf{make\_symbolic}(\mathcal{F}, \textit{tree-expr}, \ldots, \textit{tree-expr}) \\
&\quad \mid \mathbf{make\_integer}(\textit{expr}) \\
&\quad \mid \mathbf{get\_son}(\textit{tree-expr}, \textit{expr}) \\
\textit{stmt} &\triangleq \ldots \\
&\quad \mid \mathcal{T} \texttt{ = } \textit{tree-expr}
\end{aligned}
\qquad
\begin{aligned}
\textit{sym-expr} &\triangleq \mid \mathbf{get\_sym\_head}(\textit{tree-expr}) \\
\textit{expr} &\triangleq \ldots \\
&\quad \mid \mathbf{get\_num\_head}(\textit{tree-expr}) \\
&\quad \mid \mathbf{is\_symbol}(\textit{tree-expr}) \\
&\quad \mid \textit{sym-expr} \texttt{ == } \mathcal{F}
\end{aligned}
$$

Fig. 1. Syntax extension of the language

$$
\begin{aligned}
&\mathbb{E}[\![\mathbf{make\_symbolic}(s \in \mathcal{F}_m, T_1, \ldots, T_m)]\!](E, F) = \{s(t_1, \ldots, t_m) \mid \forall i,\ t_i \in \mathbb{E}[\![T_i]\!](E, F)\} \\
&\mathbb{E}[\![\mathbf{make\_integer}(e \in \textit{expr})]\!](E, F) = \mathbb{E}[\![e]\!](E, F) \\
&\mathbb{E}[\![\mathbf{is\_symbol}(T)]\!](E, F) = \{\mathbf{true} \mid \exists t \in \mathbb{E}[\![T]\!](E, F), \exists f \in \mathcal{R},\ t = f(\ldots)\} \\
&\qquad\qquad\qquad\qquad\quad \cup \{\mathbf{false} \mid \exists t \in \mathbb{E}[\![T]\!](E, F), t \in \mathbb{Z}\} \\
&\mathbb{E}[\![\mathbf{get\_son}(T, e)]\!](E, F) = \{t \mid \exists i \in \mathbb{E}[\![e]\!](E, F),\ t' \in \mathbb{E}[\![T]\!](E, F), f \in \mathcal{F}_{m>i}, \\
&\qquad\qquad\qquad\qquad\quad t' = f(t_0, \ldots, t_{m-1}) \wedge t_i = t\} \\
&\mathbb{E}[\![\mathbf{get\_num\_head}(T)]\!](E, F) = \{i \in \mathbb{Z} \mid \exists t \in \mathbb{E}[\![T]\!](E, F),\ t = i\} \\
&\mathbb{E}[\![\mathbf{get\_sym\_head}(T)]\!](E, F) = \{s \in \mathcal{R} \mid \exists t \in \mathbb{E}[\![T]\!](E, F),\ t = s(\ldots)\}
\end{aligned}
$$

Fig. 2. Concrete operations on natural terms

```
int i;
int n;
tree y;
assume(n >= 0);
i = 0;
y = make_symbolic("p",{});
while (i < n) {
  y = make_symbolic("*",
           {make_symbolic("+",
                  {y,
                   make_integer(4)
                  })
           });
  i = i+1;
}
```

Program 4: `*(p+4)` iterated

```
int n; int i; int x; int rep;
tree t;
assume(n>=0);
i = 0;
t = make_symbolic("Nil",{});
while (i < n) {
  t = make_symbolic("Cons",
        {make_integer(x-1), t});
  t = make_symbolic("Cons",
        {make_integer(x+1), t});
  i = i + 1;
 };
if (get_sym_head(t) != "Nil") {
    rep = get_num_head(get_son(t,0));
    assert(rep > x);
 }
```

Program 5: List manipulation

Syntax of the Language and Concrete Operations. We assume already defined a small imperative language and extend it (in Fig. 1) with statements, tree expressions (*tree-expr*) which are expressions that are evaluated to trees, and simple symbol expressions (*sym-expr*) which enable the manipulation of symbols. We add the ability to build a tree which contains only a numerical leaf: **make_integer**(e), the ability to read the i-th son of a tree t: **get_son**(t, i), ... Figure 2 defines concrete operations over the set $\wp(T_{\mathbb{Z}}(\mathcal{R}))$. Figure 2 assumes given a set of program numerical variables $\mathcal{V}$, a set of numerical expressions (over $\mathcal{V}$) denoted *expr*, a set of statements *stmt*, a notion of numerical environment $E \in \mathfrak{E} = \mathcal{V} \to \mathbb{Z}$, a set of tree program variables $\mathcal{T}$, a notion of tree environment $F \in \mathfrak{F} = \mathcal{T} \to \wp(T_{\mathbb{Z}}(\mathcal{R}))$, $D = E \times F$ is our concrete domain. Finally we assume already partially defined on numerical expressions an evaluation function $\mathbb{E}[\![e \in expr]\!](E \in \mathcal{V} \to \mathbb{Z}, F \in \mathcal{T} \to \wp(T_{\mathbb{Z}}(\mathcal{R}))) \in \wp(\mathbb{Z})$. Using this operator we are able to define Program 4 which computes the memory zones used by `append` from Program 1, and Program 5 that simulates the behavior of Program 3.

3 Natural Term Abstraction by Tree Automata

In this section we start by defining a value abstraction for tree sets (in Sect. 3.1), which is then lifted to an environment abstraction (in Sect. 3.2).

3.1 Value Abstraction

As a first abstraction for natural terms, we put aside numerical values and define an abstraction able to describe sets of tree shapes. Tree automata enable the description of set of terms built upon a finite ranked alphabet. The ranked alphabet of the language we want to analyze is extend with the $\square$ symbol to denote potential positions of numerical values.

Definition 2 (Finite tree automata). *A finite tree automaton (FTA) over a ranked alphabet* $\mathcal{R}$ *is a tuple* $(Q, \mathcal{R}, Q_f, \delta)$, *where* Q *is a (finite) set of states,* $Q_f \subseteq Q$ *is the set of final states, and* $\delta \in \wp(\bigcup_{n\in\mathbb{N}} \mathcal{F}_n \times Q^n \times Q)$ *is the set of transitions. We define* $\overline{\delta} : (\bigcup_{n\in\mathbb{N}} \mathcal{F}_n \times Q^n) \to \wp(Q)$ *by:* $\overline{\delta}(f, \overrightarrow{q}) = \{q' \mid (f, \overrightarrow{q}, q') \in \delta\}$. *When* $\overline{\delta}$ *is such that,* $\forall n \in \mathbb{N},\ f \in \mathcal{F}_n,\ \overrightarrow{q} \in Q^n,\ |\overline{\delta}(f, \overrightarrow{q})| = 1$, *we say that the automaton is complete and deterministic (CDFTA). We then abuse notations and denote by* $\delta(f, \overrightarrow{q})$ *the unique element in the set* $\overline{\delta}(f, \overrightarrow{q})$.

Definition 3 (Reachability). *Given a FTA* $\mathcal{A} = (Q, \mathcal{R}, Q_f, \delta)$ *we define, a reachability function* $\text{REACH}_{\mathcal{A}} : T(\mathcal{R}) \to \wp(Q)$

$$\text{REACH}_{\mathcal{A}}(t) = \textbf{let } t_1, \ldots, t_n = \textbf{sons}(t) \textbf{ in} \bigcup_{(q_1,\ldots,q_n)\in(\text{REACH}_{\mathcal{A}}(t_1),\ldots,\text{REACH}_{\mathcal{A}}(t_n))} \overline{\delta}(\textbf{head}(t), (q_1, \ldots, q_n))$$

If **sons**(t) *is the empty tuple (which is the case when t is a constant a), the union is made over a unique element (which is the empty tuple), which then boils down to:* $\overline{\delta}(a, ())$. *If* **sons**(t) *is not the empty tuple and for some* i, $\text{REACH}_{\mathcal{A}}(t_i)$ *is empty, then* $\text{REACH}_{\mathcal{A}}(t)$ *is also empty.*

Example 3. Consider the ranked alphabet $\mathcal{R} = \{f(2), a(0)\}$, and the automaton $\mathcal{A} = (\{u, v\}, \mathcal{R}, \{v\}, \{a() \to u, f(v, v) \to v, f(u, u) \to u, f(u, u) \to v\})$. Then $\text{REACH}_{\mathcal{A}}(a) = \{u\}$, $\text{REACH}_{\mathcal{A}}(f(a, a)) = \{u, v\}$, $\text{REACH}_{\mathcal{A}}(f(f(a, a), a)) = \{u, v\}$.

Definition 4 (Acceptance). *Given a FTA $\mathcal{A} = (Q, \mathcal{R}, Q_f, \delta)$, a term t, we say that t is* accepted *by the automaton if* $\text{REACH}_{\mathcal{A}}(t) \cap Q_f \neq \emptyset$. $\mathcal{L}(\mathcal{A})$ *denotes the set of terms accepted by automaton $\mathcal{A}$.*

Example 4. With the definition of Example 3, $\mathcal{L}(\mathcal{A})$ is the set of terms over $\mathcal{R}$ that contain at least one f.

Definition 5 (Tree regular languages). *A set of terms $\mathcal{T}$ over a ranked alphabet $\mathcal{R}$ is called* tree regular *if there exists a FTA $\mathcal{A}$ over $\mathcal{R}$ such that $\mathcal{L}(\mathcal{A}) = \mathcal{T}$. The set of such languages is denoted $TReg(\mathcal{R})$.*

Remark 2. As for regular languages, for all $\mathcal{A} \in$ FTA there exists $\mathcal{A}' \in$ CDFTA such that $\mathcal{L}(\mathcal{A}) = \mathcal{L}(\mathcal{A}')$, moreover $\mathcal{A}'$ is computable (see [4]).

Example 5.
- As proved in Example 4 the set of all terms over $\{f(2), a(0)\}$ that contain at least one f is tree regular.
- Consider now the ranked alphabet $\{a(1), b(1), \epsilon(0)\}$ and the set of terms $\mathcal{T} = \{\epsilon, a(b(\epsilon)), a(a(b(b(\epsilon)))), \dots\}$. We can prove (in a similar way as for $a^n b^n$ in regular languages) that $\mathcal{T}$ is not tree regular.
- On every ranked alphabet $\mathcal{R}$: every finite language, the empty language and $T(\mathcal{R})$ are tree regular.

Proposition 1. $(TReg(\mathcal{R}), \subseteq, \cap, \cup, .^c, \emptyset, T(\mathcal{R}))$ *is a complemented lattice with infinite height, moreover it is not complete.* $\subseteq, \cap, \cup$ *and complementation* $(.^c)$ *are computable operations on tree automata [4].*

We denote by $\mathcal{R}^\square$ the ranked alphabet $\mathcal{R}$ after adding the symbol $\square$ of arity 0 (we assume that $\square \notin \mathcal{R}$). Given a natural term t, we define $t^\square$ to be the term obtained by replacing every integer with the $\square$ symbol.

Proposition 2. $(\wp(T_{\mathbb{Z}}(\mathcal{R})), \subseteq) \overset{\gamma}{\longleftarrow} (TReg(\mathcal{R}^\square), \subseteq)$ *where* $\gamma(\mathcal{A}) = \{t \mid t^\square \in \mathcal{L}(\mathcal{A})\}$ *is a representation. Moreover with such a γ definition,* $\cup$, $\cap$ *soundly represent the union and the intersection.*

Remark 3. We only have a representation and not a Galois connection as language $\mathcal{T}$ of Example 5 does not have a best tree regular over approximation.

Example 6. Let $\mathcal{R} = \{+(2)\}$ and $\mathcal{A} = (\{0,1\}, \mathcal{R}^\square, \{0,1\}, \{(\square() \to 0, +(0,0) \to 1, +(0,1) \to 1)\})$. Examples of terms recognized by $\mathcal{A}$ are shown on Fig. 3. Natural terms from our running example U and V (defined in Example 2) are also contained in $\gamma(\mathcal{A})$. Moreover as we do not provide numerical constraints: $1 + (3 + 4)$, 23, $1 + (2 + (3 + 4))$ are also elements in $\gamma(\mathcal{A})$.

Due to the infinite height of the lattice, a widening operator is required. In the following, we assume given a constant $w \in \mathbb{N}$, this constant will be used to stabilize increasing chains, the greater the constant, the more precise our widening operator will be.

Definition 6. *Let* $\mathcal{A} = (Q, \mathcal{R}, Q_f, \delta) \in FTA$, *and* $\sim$ *be an equivalence relation on* Q, *such that* $p \sim q \wedge p \in Q_f \Rightarrow q \in Q_f$. *We define* $\mathcal{A}/\sim = (Q/\sim, \mathcal{R}, Q_f/\sim, \bigcup_{(f,q_1,\ldots,q_n,q)\in\delta}\{(f, q_1^{\sim}, \ldots, q_n^{\sim}, q^{\sim})\})$ *where* $q^{\sim}$ *is the equivalence class of* q *in* $\sim$.

Proposition 3. *For every* $\mathcal{A} \in FTA$ *and every* $\sim$ *equivalence relation on its states,* $\mathcal{L}(\mathcal{A}) \subseteq \mathcal{L}(\mathcal{A}/\sim)$.

Therefore following the idea from [9] and in [11], we define a widening operation by quotienting states of automata by an equivalence relation of finite index. We define by induction a special sequence of equivalence relations on states of tree automata: $\sim_1 = \{Q_f, Q \setminus Q_f\}$ and $\sim_{k+1}$ is $\sim_k$ where we split equivalence classes not satisfying the following condition: $\forall f \in \mathcal{F}_n$, $\forall p_1, \ldots, p_n \in Q$, $\forall q_1, \ldots, q_n \in Q$, $(\bigwedge_{i=1}^{n} p_i \sim_k q_i) \Rightarrow \delta(f, p_1, \ldots, p_n) \sim_k \delta(f, q_1, \ldots, q_n)$ and $\forall q \in Q_f$, $q^{\sim_k} \subseteq Q_f$. This sequence of equivalence relations is the Myhill-Nerode sequence (see [4]). This sequence is of length at most the number of states of the automaton (before stabilization). Let $\phi(w) = \max\{i \leq |Q| \mid \text{index of } \sim_i \leq w\}$ (given an integer w, ϕ yields the index of the most precise of the equivalence relationships in the Myhill-Nerode sequence, that contains at most w equivalence classes) and $[\mathcal{A}]_w = \mathcal{A}/\sim_{\phi(w)}$. $[\mathcal{A}]_w$ is therefore a FTA with at most w states such that $\mathcal{L}(\mathcal{A}) \subseteq \mathcal{L}([\mathcal{A}]_w)$. As for regular languages, for every CDFTA a equivalent minimal CDFTA (in the sense of the number of states, and unique modulo state renaming) can be obtained by quotienting the automaton by $\sim_{|Q|}$. Therefore we define a widening operator on CDFTAs, which is then lifted to tree regular languages.

Definition 7 (Widening operator $\triangledown$). $\mathcal{A} \triangledown \mathcal{A}' = [\mathcal{A} \cup \mathcal{A}']_w$.

Proposition 4. *This widening is sound and stabilizes infinite sequences.*

Remark 4. Consider the two following complete and deterministic tree automata: $\mathcal{A} = (\{a, b, h\}, \{+(2)\}, \{a\}, \{\square() \to b, +(b, b) \to a\})$ and $\mathcal{B} = (\{a, b, c, h\}, \{+(2)\}, \{a\}, \{\square() \to b, +(b, b) \to c, +(b, c) \to a\})$ (unmentioned transitions go to h). $\mathcal{A}$ (resp. $\mathcal{B}$) recognizes the tree $+(\square, \square)$ (resp. $+(\square, +(\square, \square))$), it over-approximates U (resp. V) from our running example. $\mathcal{A} \cup \mathcal{B}$ is recognized by the following complete and deterministic tree automaton: $\mathcal{C} = (\{a, b, c, h\}, \{+(2)\}, \{a, c\}, \{\square() \to b, +(b, b) \to c, +(b, c) \to a\})$. If we want to widen $\mathcal{A}$ and $\mathcal{B}$ with parameter 3, the following equivalence relation is computed: $\{\{h\}, \{b\}, \{a, c\}\}$. Merging equivalent states produces $(\{a, b, h\}, \{+(2)\}, \{a\}, \{\square() \to b, +(b, b) \to a, +(b, a) \to a\})$, which contains a loop and over-approximates the union.

3.2 Environment Abstraction

Now that we are given an abstraction for natural term sets, let us show how this is lifted to a notion of abstract natural term environments mapping variables to natural terms. Given a set of natural term variables $\mathcal{T}$, consider $\mathfrak{F}^\sharp = (\mathcal{T} \to \mathrm{TReg}(\mathcal{R}^\Box)) \cup \{\bot\}$ and the set operators defined by the point-wise lifting of operators on $\mathrm{TReg}(\mathcal{R}^\Box)$. We also lift the concretization function $\wp(T_\mathbb{Z}(\mathcal{R})) \leftarrow \mathrm{TReg}(\mathcal{R}^\Box)$ to $\mathfrak{F} \leftarrow \mathfrak{F}^\sharp$. We assume given an abstract numerical environment $E^\sharp$ and an abstract evaluator $\mathbb{E}[\![e]\!]^\sharp$. Abstract transformers $[\![\texttt{make\_symbolic}]\!]^\sharp$, $[\![\texttt{is\_symbol}]\!]^\sharp$, $[\![\texttt{get\_son}(e)]\!]^\sharp$, $[\![\texttt{get\_sym\_head}]\!]^\sharp$ and $[\![\texttt{get\_num\_head}]\!]^\sharp$ are simple tree automata operations. For concision Fig. 4 only provides definitions of two of these operators. Please note that these definitions require all states of the automata to be reachable. An example of use of the `is_symbol` operator can be found in Example 7. Other abstract operators are similar.

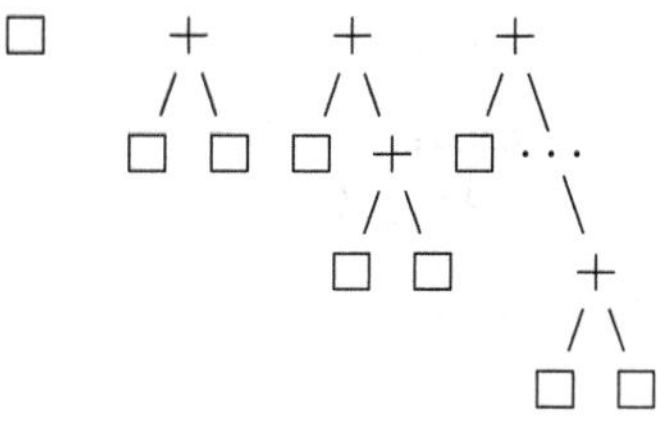

Fig. 3. Example of accepted trees from Example 6

$$\mathbb{E}^\sharp[\![\texttt{make\_integer}(e \in \mathit{expr})]\!](E^\sharp, F^\sharp) = \langle \{a\}, \mathcal{R}, \{a\}, \{\Box() \to a\} \rangle$$

$$\mathbb{E}^\sharp[\![\texttt{get\_son}(T, e \in \mathit{expr})]\!](E^\sharp, F^\sharp) = \bigcup_{\substack{(Q,\mathcal{R},Q_f,\delta) \in \mathbb{E}^\sharp[\![T]\!](E^\sharp, F^\sharp) \\ i \in \mathbb{E}^\sharp[\![e]\!](E^\sharp) \cap \{0,\ldots,m-1\}}} (Q, \mathcal{R}, \{q \in Q \mid \exists p \in Q_f,\ \exists s(p_0, \ldots, p_{m-1}) \to p \in \delta \wedge p_i = q\}, \delta)$$

Fig. 4. Abstract operators

Example 7. Consider the tree automaton $\mathcal{A}$ of Example 6, (Fig. 3), with $F^\sharp = (x \mapsto \mathcal{A})$: $[\![\texttt{get\_sym\_head}(x)]\!]^\sharp(E^\sharp, F^\sharp) = \{+\}$ and $[\![\texttt{get\_num\_head}(x)]\!]^\sharp(E^\sharp, F^\sharp) = \top$.

4 Numerical Abstractions

As emphasized in the introductory example, we rely on numerical domains to introduce constraints on numerical variables found in trees. In a classical numeric abstraction (e.g. intervals [6], octagons [22], polyhedra [8], ...), each abstract element represents a set of maps $\mathcal{V} \to \mathbb{R}$ for a fixed, finite set of variables $\mathcal{V}$. In contrast, our numeric variables are leaves of a possibly infinite set of trees of unbounded size. Hence before starting the presentation of the numerical abstraction for natural terms, we show how to extend in a generic way an abstract element in two steps. Firstly we want to be able to represent a set of maps, where each map is defined over a (possibly different) finite subset of an infinite set of variables (this is done in Sect. 4.1). Secondly, we use summarization variables to relax the finiteness constraint, so as to represent sets of maps over heterogeneous maps over infinitely many variables (done in Sect. 4.2).

4.1 Heterogeneous Support

We define $\mathfrak{M} \triangleq \wp(\mathcal{V} \nrightarrow \mathbb{R})$, the set of partial maps from $\mathcal{V}$, to $\mathbb{R}$. $\mathfrak{M}$ is ordered by the inclusion relation $\subseteq$. In the following $\mathbf{def}(f)$ denotes the definition set of f. We assume defined a representation $(\wp(\mathcal{S} \to \mathbb{R}), \subseteq) \xleftarrow{\gamma_0^{\mathcal{S}}} (N_{\mathcal{S}}, \sqsubseteq_0^{\mathcal{S}})$, for every finite set $\mathcal{S} \subseteq \mathcal{V}$ (such as octagons in $|S|$ dimensions). $N_{\mathcal{S}}$ comes with the usual abstract set operator $\sqcap_0^{\mathcal{S}}$, $\sqcup_0^{\mathcal{S}}$. Moreover if $x \in \mathcal{S}$, $y \notin \mathcal{S}$, $\mathcal{S}'$ is another finite set and $N^\sharp \in N_{\mathcal{S}}$ then $N^\sharp[x \mapsto y] \in N_{\mathcal{S}\cup\{y\}\setminus\{x\}}$ is the abstract element obtained by renaming x into y, $N^\sharp_{|\mathcal{S}'} \in N_{\mathcal{S}'}$ is obtained by existentially quantifying dimensions associated to elements in $\mathcal{S}$ and not in $\mathcal{S}'$ and adding unconstrained dimensions for elements in $\mathcal{S}'$ and not in $\mathcal{S}$. From now on we assume that this last operator is exact (as for intervals, octagons, polyhedra over $\mathbb{R}$). However results from this section can be extended to numerical domains that are able, given $N^\sharp \in N_{\mathcal{S}}$, $N^{\sharp\prime} \in N_{\mathcal{S}'}$, to check if $\gamma_0^{\mathcal{S}}(N^\sharp) \subseteq \gamma_0^{\mathcal{S}'}(N^{\sharp\prime})_{|\mathcal{S}}$. The precision of the extension defined in this subsection would then depend upon the precision of this test in the underlying domain. Finally $[\![.]\!]_0^{\mathcal{S}}$ (resp. $[\![.]\!]_0^{\sharp,\mathcal{S}}$) refers to the classical concrete (resp. abstract) semantic of operators on sets of numerical maps (resp. abstract elements). A classical method for the abstraction of heterogeneous maps is the use of a partitioning of the concrete element according to the definition set of its represented maps. However partitioning induces an increase in numerical operation cost (exponential in the number of variable) which we would like to avoid. Therefore in order to abstract sets of maps with heterogeneous definition sets, we start by abstracting the potential definition set. We choose a simple lower-bound/upper-bound abstraction (l and u in the following definition). Moreover we need to abstract the potential mappings given a definition set: this is done using a classical numerical domain. Contrary to partitioning, we will use only one numerical abstract element, defined on the upper-bound u, to represent all environments (instead of one abstract element by definition set). We also add a $\top$ element, used in the case where the upper bound u is infinite.

Definition 8 (Numerical abstraction). *Let us define the following set:* $\mathfrak{M}^\sharp \triangleq \{\langle N^\sharp, l, u\rangle \mid l, u \in \wp(V) \wedge l$ *and* u *are finite* $\wedge l \subseteq u \wedge N^\sharp \in N_u \wedge N^\sharp \neq \bot_0^u\} \cup \{\top, \bot\}$. *An element of* $\mathfrak{M}^\sharp$ *is therefore: either* $\top$, $\bot$ *or a triple* $\langle N^\sharp, l, u\rangle$ *where* l *and* u *are finite sets of variables such that* $N^\sharp$ *is defined over* u.

Definition 9 (Concretization function). *Abstract elements from* $\mathfrak{M}^\sharp$ *are mapped to* $\mathfrak{M}$ *thanks to the following concretization function:* $\gamma(\bot) = \emptyset$, $\gamma(\top) = \mathfrak{M}$ *and* $\gamma(\langle N^\sharp, l, u\rangle) = \{\rho \in \mathcal{S} \to \mathbb{Z} \mid l \subseteq \mathcal{S} \subseteq u \wedge \rho \in \gamma_0^{\mathcal{S}}(N^\sharp)_{|\mathcal{S}})\}$.

Example 8. As an example consider $\gamma(\langle\{x = y, x \leq 3, z = 0\}, \{x\}, \{x, y, z\}\rangle) = \{(x \mapsto a) \mid a \leq 3\} \cup \{(x \mapsto a, y \mapsto a) \mid a \leq 3\} \cup \{(x \mapsto a, z \mapsto 0) \mid a \leq 3\} \cup \{(x \mapsto a, y \mapsto a, z \mapsto 0) \mid a \leq 3\}$. As intended, the resulting set of maps contains maps with different definition sets.

Definition 10 (Order). *On $\mathfrak{M}^\sharp$ we define the following comparison operator: $\langle N^\sharp, l, u\rangle \sqsubseteq \langle N^{\sharp\prime}, l', u'\rangle \Leftrightarrow l' \subseteq l \subseteq u \subseteq u' \wedge N^\sharp \sqsubseteq_0^u N^{\sharp\prime}_{|u}$, this comparison is trivially extended to $\top$ (resp. $\bot$) as being the biggest (resp. smallest) element in $\mathfrak{M}^\sharp$. In the following $\mathfrak{M}^\sharp_{\mathfrak{p}}$ denotes the subset of $\mathfrak{M}^\sharp$ where $u = \mathfrak{p}$ extended with $\top$ and $\bot$.*

Proposition 5. *γ is monotonic for $\sqsubseteq$.*

Figure 5 provides the definition of the concrete and abstract semantics of the classical numerical statements, `Assume` and `Assign` (denoted $x \leftarrow e$). We denote $\mathbf{vars}(e)$ the set of variables appearing in e. We recall that $[\![\texttt{Assume}(c)]\!]_0^{\mathcal{S}}(E \in \wp(\mathcal{S} \to \mathbb{R})) = \{f \in E \mid \texttt{true} \in \mathbb{E}[\![c]\!](f)\}$ and $[\![x \leftarrow e]\!]_0^{\mathcal{S}}(E \in \wp(\mathcal{S} \to \mathbb{R})) = \{f[x \mapsto e'] \mid f \in E \wedge e' \in \mathbb{E}[\![e]\!](f)\}$. In order to ease the lifting of these classical operators we define $[\![\texttt{stmt}]\!]_0(\mathcal{M} \in \mathfrak{M}) \triangleq \cup_{\mathcal{S}\ \text{finite} \subseteq \mathcal{V}} [\![\texttt{stmt}]\!]_0^{\mathcal{S}}(\mathcal{M} \cap (\mathcal{S} \to \mathbb{R}))$, for every statement `stmt`. Moreover we assume the existence of the following abstract operators: $[\![\texttt{Assume}(c)]\!]_0^{\sharp,u}(N^\sharp)$ and $[\![x \leftarrow e]\!]_0^{\sharp,u} N^\sharp$ abstracting soundly their respective concrete transformers. Note that the concrete semantic of $\texttt{Assume}(c)$ (resp. $x \leftarrow e$) enforces that maps are defined at least on the variables appearing in c (resp. in e and on x). Abstract operators from Fig. 5 are sound with respect to γ and their concrete operators.

$$[\![\texttt{Assume}(c)]\!](\mathcal{M}) = [\![\texttt{Assume}(c)]\!]_0(\{f \mid f \in \mathcal{M} \wedge \mathbf{vars}(c) \subseteq \mathbf{def}(f)\})$$
$$[\![\texttt{Assume}(c)]\!]^\sharp(\langle N^\sharp, l, u\rangle) = \langle [\![\texttt{Assume}(c)]\!]_0^{\sharp,u}(N^\sharp), l \cup \mathbf{vars}(c), u\rangle$$
$$[\![x \leftarrow e]\!](\mathcal{M}) = [\![x \leftarrow e]\!]_0(\{f \mid f \in \mathcal{M} \wedge \mathbf{vars}(e) \cup \{x\} \subseteq \mathbf{def}(f)\})$$
$$[\![x \leftarrow e]\!]^\sharp(\langle N^\sharp, l, u\rangle) = \langle [\![x \leftarrow e]\!]_0^{\sharp,u}(N^\sharp), l \cup \mathbf{vars}(e) \cup \{x\}, u\rangle$$

Fig. 5. Concrete and abstract semantic of usual numerical operators

We now need to define $\sqcup$ that abstracts the classic set operator $\cup$. We can not directly apply the corresponding abstract operator on the numerical component of the abstractions as they might have different definition sets. A first naive solution would be to extend their respective definition set and to perform the abstract operation on the resulting elements: $N^\sharp_{|u \cup u'} \sqcup_0^{u \cup u'} N^{\sharp\prime}_{|u \cup u'}$. However consider $M = \langle\{x = y\}(= U^\sharp), \{x, y\}, \{x, y\}\rangle$ and $N = \langle\{x = z\}(= V^\sharp), \{x, z\}, \{x, z\}\rangle$, where the underlying domain is the octagon domain where elements are represented as a set of linear constraints (e.g. $\{x = y\}$). We have $U^\sharp_{|\{x,y,z\}} = \{x = y\}$ and $V^\sharp_{|\{x,y,z\}} = \{x = z\}$, hence $U^\sharp_{|\{x,y,z\}} \sqcup_0^{\{x,y,z\}} V^\sharp_{|\{x,y,z\}} = \top$. Consider now the abstract element in $\mathfrak{M}^\sharp$: $R = \langle\{x = y, x = z\}(= W^\sharp), \{x\}, \{x, y, z\}\rangle$. The concretization of R over-approximates the union of the concretization of M and N, and its numerical component is more precise than $\top$. We note that the numerical constraints appearing in $W^\sharp$ could be found in $U^\sharp$ or $V^\sharp$, therefore in order to remove the aforementioned imprecision we define a refined abstract union operator, denoted as $\boxed{\star}$, that uses constraints found in the inputs in order to refine its

Algorithm 1. strengthening operator

Input : $X^\sharp$, C: a set of constraints, $U^\sharp \in N_u$: a soundness threshold on environment u, $V^\sharp \in N_v$: a soundness threshold on environment v

Output: $Z^\sharp$ an abstract element over-approximating $U^\sharp$ on u and $V^\sharp$ on v

$Z^\sharp \leftarrow X^\sharp$;
foreach $c \in C$ **do**
  $T^\sharp \leftarrow [\![\mathtt{Assume}(c)]\!]_0^{\sharp, u\cup v}(Z^\sharp)$;
  if $U^\sharp \sqsubseteq_0^u T^\sharp_{|u} \wedge V^\sharp \sqsubseteq_0^v T^\sharp_{|v}$ **then**
    $Z^\sharp \leftarrow T^\sharp$;
  end
return $Z^\sharp$;

result. This is done using the **strenghtening** operator of Algorithm 1 which adds constraints from C that do not make the projection of $X^\sharp$ to u (resp. v) lower than the threshold $U^\sharp$ (resp. $V^\sharp$). We assume that, given an abstract element $U^\sharp$, we can extract a finite set of constraints satisfied by $U^\sharp$, those are denoted **constraints**($U^\sharp$) (the more constraints can be extracted, the more precise the result will be). For example if the numerical domain is the interval domain, constraints have the form $\pm x \geq a$. If the numerical domain is the octagon domain the **constraints** operator yields all the linear relations among variables that define the octagon.

Definition 11 ($\boxast$ operator). *Let $U^\sharp \in N_u$, $V^\sharp \in N_v$ be two numerical environments, let $X^\sharp \in N_{u\cup v}$, let C be a sequence of numerical constraints over $u\cup v$, let $\mathfrak{c} = u \cap v$ we define:*

$$\begin{aligned} U^\sharp \boxast V^\sharp = \ & \textbf{let } X^\sharp = (U^\sharp_{|\mathfrak{c}} \sqcup_0^{\mathfrak{c}} V^\sharp_{|\mathfrak{c}})_{|u\cup v} \textbf{ in} \\ & \textbf{let } C = \textbf{constraints}(U^\sharp) \cup \textbf{constraints}(V^\sharp) \textbf{ in} \\ & \textbf{strengthening}(X^\sharp, C, U^\sharp, V^\sharp) \end{aligned}$$

Remark 5.
- The precision of $\boxast$ depends upon the order of iteration over constraints $c \in C$ in Algorithm 1. Our implementation currently iterates in the order in which constraints are returned from the abstract domains. More clever heuristics will be considered in future work.
- $U^\sharp \boxast V^\sharp$ starts by performing the join over the domain $\mathfrak{c}$, the result is then strengthened. Other **strenghtening**($X^\sharp, U^\sharp \in N_u, V^\sharp \in N_v$) operator could be defined, however in order to ensure soundness of $\boxast$, it must satisfy the following constraints: $U^\sharp \sqsubseteq_0^u$ **strenghtening**($X^\sharp, U^\sharp, V^\sharp$) and $V^\sharp \sqsubseteq_0^v$ **strenghtening**($X^\sharp, U^\sharp, V^\sharp$).

Example 9. Let us now consider the example introduced thereinbefore $U^\sharp \boxast V^\sharp = \{x = y, y = z\} \in N_{\{x,y,z\}}$. Indeed using the notations of Definition 11: $Z^\sharp \triangleq X^\sharp = \top \in N_{\{x,y,z\}}$, $C = \{x = y, y = z\}$, moreover $[\![\mathtt{Assume}(x = y)]\!]_0^{\sharp, u\cup v}(\top) =$

$\{x = y\}(\triangleq T^\sharp)$, $U^\sharp \sqsubseteq_0^{\{x,y\}} \{x = y\} = T^\sharp_{|\{x,y\}}$ and $V^\sharp \sqsubseteq_0^{\{x,z\}} \top = T^\sharp_{|\{x,z\}}$. Therefore constraint $x = y$ is added to $Z^\sharp$. At the next loop iteration: $[\![\texttt{Assume}(x = z)]\!]_0^{\sharp,u\cup v}(\{x = y\}) = \{x = y, x = z\}(\triangleq T^\sharp)$, $U^\sharp \sqsubseteq_0^{\{x,y\}} \{x = y\} = T^\sharp_{|\{x,y\}}$ and $V^\sharp \sqsubseteq_0^{\{x,z\}} \{x = z\} = T^\sharp_{|\{x,z\}}$. Therefore constraint $x = z$ is added to $Z^\sharp$.

Proposition 6 (Soundness of $\sqcup_{\star}$). *let $U^\sharp \in N_u$ and $V^\sharp \in N_v$, then $\gamma_0^u(U^\sharp) \subseteq (\gamma_0^{u\cup v}(U^\sharp \sqcup_{\star} V^\sharp))_{|u}$ and $\gamma_0^v(V^\sharp) \subseteq (\gamma_0^{u\cup v}(U^\sharp \sqcup_{\star} V^\sharp))_{|v}$.*

Definition 12 (Union abstract operators). *We define the following abstract set operator: $\langle N^\sharp, l, u\rangle \sqcup \langle N^{\sharp\prime}, l', u'\rangle \triangleq \langle N^\sharp \sqcup_{\star} N^{\sharp\prime}, l \cap l', u \cup u'\rangle$. This operator soundly abstracts the union. Moreover in order to ensure the stabilization of infinitely increasing chains in $\mathfrak{M}^\sharp$ we define the following widening operator:*

$$\langle N^\sharp, l, u\rangle \triangledown \langle N^{\sharp\prime}, l', u'\rangle = \begin{cases} \langle N^\sharp \triangledown_0^u N^{\sharp\prime}_{|u}, l, u\rangle & \textit{when } l \subseteq l' \wedge u' \subseteq u \\ \langle N^\sharp \sqcup_{\star} N^{\sharp\prime}, l', u\rangle & \textit{when } l' \subset l \wedge u' \subseteq u \\ \top & \textit{otherwise} \end{cases}$$

Remark 6. This widening operator over-approximates to $\top$ whenever the upper-bound on the definition set is growing. This yields a huge loss of information however this numerical domain is designed as a tool domain used by a higher level abstraction in charge of stabilizing the environment before applying the widening, so that this case will not be used in practice.

Subsequent tree abstractions require the definition of the following operators:

- $\langle N^\sharp, l, u\rangle_{|-x} \triangleq \langle N^\sharp_{|u\setminus\{x\}}, l \setminus \{x\}, u \setminus \{x\}\rangle$ and $\langle N^\sharp, l, u\rangle_{|+x} \triangleq \langle N^\sharp_{|u\cup\{x\}}, l \cup \{x\}, u \cup \{x\}\rangle$ which respectively removes (adds) a variable to the numerical environment.
- $\langle N^\sharp, l, u\rangle_{|\mathcal{S}}$ is computed by adding variables in $\mathcal{S}$ and not in u and removing variables in u that are not in $\mathcal{S}$.

4.2 Representation of Maps over Potentially Unbounded Sets

In this subsection we focus on the problem of defining abstract numerical environments on potentially infinite environments. A classical method we use here is variable summarization (see [13]). This is based on the folding of several concrete objects (a potentially infinite number) to an abstract element which summarizes all concrete objects. The folding is encoded in a function f mapping summarized variables to the set of concrete variables they abstract. Given an abstract numerical environment $N^\sharp$ and a mapping from summary variables: $\mathcal{V}'$ to sets of concrete variables $f \in \mathcal{V}' \to \wp(\mathcal{V})$ where $f(v_1) \cap f(v_2) \neq \emptyset \Rightarrow v_1 = v_2$, we define the collapsing of a partial map $\rho \in \mathcal{V} \nrightarrow \mathbb{Z}$ under a summarizing function f:

$$\begin{aligned} \downarrow_f (\rho) = \{\rho' \in \mathcal{V}' \nrightarrow \mathbb{Z} \mid \forall v' \in \mathcal{V}',\ & (f(v') \cap \mathbf{def}(\rho) = \emptyset \wedge \rho'(v') = \mathbf{undefined}) \\ & \vee (\exists v \in \mathcal{V},\ v \in f(v') \cap \mathbf{def}(\rho) \wedge \rho'(v') = \rho(v))\} \end{aligned}$$

Example 10. Consider $\mathcal{V}' = \{x, y, z, t\}$ and $\mathcal{V} = \{a, b, c, d, g, h\}$, the environment $\rho = (a \mapsto 0, b \mapsto 1, c \mapsto 2, d \mapsto 3)$ and finally the summarizing function $f = (x \mapsto \{a\}, y \mapsto \{b, c\}, z \mapsto \{d\}, t \mapsto \{g\})$. Collapsing environment ρ under f yields the set of environments: $(x \mapsto 0, y \mapsto 1, z \mapsto 3)$ and $(x \mapsto 0, y \mapsto 2, z \mapsto 3)$.

Given a summarizing function f we can now define an extension of the concretization function γ of the previous subsection in the following manner:

$$\gamma[f](N^\sharp) = \{\rho \in \mathcal{V} \nrightarrow \mathbb{Z} \mid \downarrow_f (\rho) \subseteq \gamma(N^\sharp)\}$$

Example 11. Going back to Example 10 and considering the numerical abstract element: $N^\sharp = \langle\{x \leq y\}, \{x\}, \{x, y\}\rangle$, we have: $\gamma(N^\sharp) = \{(x \mapsto \alpha) \mid \alpha \in \mathbb{Z}\} \cup \{(x \mapsto \alpha, y \mapsto \beta) \mid \alpha \leq \beta\}$. We have: $m \in \gamma[f](N^\sharp) \Leftrightarrow \downarrow_f (m) \subseteq \gamma(N^\sharp) \Rightarrow \{x\} \subseteq \mathbf{def}(\downarrow_f (m)) \subseteq \{x, y\}$. Therefore if we assume m defined on d then $f(z) \cap \mathbf{def}(m) \neq \emptyset$ hence there would be an element in $\downarrow_f (m)$ defined on z. Hence m is not defined on d, similarly for g. Moreover $\{x\} \subseteq \mathbf{def}(\downarrow_f (m))$ implies that m is defined on a. Finally: defining $S = \{(a \mapsto \alpha) \mid \alpha \in \mathbb{Z}\} \cup \{(a \mapsto \alpha, b \mapsto \beta) \mid \alpha \leq \beta\} \cup \{(a \mapsto \alpha, c \mapsto \beta) \mid \alpha \leq \beta\} \cup \{(a \mapsto \alpha, b \mapsto \beta, c \mapsto \gamma) \mid \alpha \leq \beta \wedge \alpha \leq \gamma\}$. We have: $\gamma[f](N^\sharp) = S \cup (\bigcup_{f \in S}\{f \uplus (h \mapsto \delta) \mid \delta \in \mathbb{Z}\})$.

The abstract domains we will define in the following sections will employ this summarization framework. The manipulation of summarized variables requires the definition of a $\mathbf{fold}(E, x, \mathcal{S})$ (resp. $\mathbf{expand}(E, x, \mathcal{S})$) operator yielding a new environment where x is used as a summary variable for $\mathcal{S}$ (resp. where a summary variable x is desummarized into a set of variables $\mathcal{S}$). Let $\mathcal{S}$ and $\mathcal{S}'$ be two finite sets of elements such that $\mathcal{S}' \cap \mathcal{S} \subseteq \{x\}$, we define: $\mathbf{expand}_0(N^\sharp, x, \mathcal{S}'') = \bigsqcap_{v \in \mathcal{S}''} N^\sharp[x \mapsto v]_{|(\mathcal{S} \setminus \{x\}) \cup \mathcal{S}''}$ and $\mathbf{fold}_0(N^\sharp, x, \mathcal{S}'') = \bigsqcup_{v \in \mathcal{S}''} N^\sharp[v \mapsto x]_{|(\mathcal{S} \setminus \mathcal{S}'') \cup \{x\}}$ (which generalize the one introduced in [13]). These operations are lifted as operators on elements of $\mathfrak{M}^\sharp$:

$$\mathbf{expand}(\langle N^\sharp, l, u\rangle, x, \mathcal{S}) \triangleq \langle \mathbf{expand}_0(N^\sharp, x, \mathcal{S}), l \setminus \{x\}, (u \setminus \{x\}) \cup \mathcal{S}\rangle$$

$$\mathbf{fold}(\langle N^\sharp, l, u\rangle, x, \mathcal{S}) \triangleq \langle \mathbf{fold}_0(N^\sharp, x, \mathcal{S}), \begin{cases} (l \setminus \mathcal{S}) \cup \{x\} & \text{if } \mathcal{S} \subseteq l \\ (l \setminus \mathcal{S}) & \text{otherwise} \end{cases}, (u \setminus \mathcal{S}) \cup \{x\}\rangle$$

5 Natural Term Abstraction by Numerical Constraints

We are now able to represent sets of maps with heterogeneous supports and to lift their concretization (modulo a summarization function) to sets of maps with infinite and heterogeneous supports. Given a tree shape (in the sense of Sect. 3), we can associate a numeric variable to each numeric leaf, and use a numeric abstract element to represent the possible values of these leaves. We will name the variable of each leaf as the path from the root to the leaf, i.e., $\mathcal{V}$ is a set of words in $\{0, ..., n-1\}$ where n is the maximum arity of the considered ranked alphabet. In order to avoid confusion such paths will be denoted $\wr 0, 1, 1 \wr$ for the word $(0, 1, 1)$. A summarized variable then represents a set of such paths. We will abstract such sets as regular expressions. Using the summarization extended to heterogeneous supports presented in the previous section, it will be possible to represent, using a single numeric abstract element, a set of contraints over the numeric leaves of an infinite set of unbounded trees of arbitrary shape.

5.1 Hole Positions and Numerical Constraints

The presentation of our computable abstraction able to represent numerical values in trees is broken down (for presentation purposes) into two consecutive abstractions. The first one is not computable, as natural terms are abstracted as partial environments over tree paths to numerical values. This abstraction looses most of the tree shapes but focuses on their numerical environment. A second abstraction will show how partial environments over paths are abstracted into numerical abstract elements defined over a regular expression environment.

In the following, when $\mathcal{R}$ is a ranked alphabet of maximum arity n, we call *words* sequences of integers, $w = (w_0, \ldots, w_{p-1}) \in \{0, \ldots, (n-1)\}^p$ will be called a word of length p (denoted $|w|$), w_i denotes the i-th integer of the sequence, $\overline{w} = (w_1, \ldots, w_{p-1})$ is the tail of word w, $\mathcal{W}(\mathcal{R}) = \{0, \ldots, (n-1)\}^\star$ is the set of all words over $\{0, \ldots, n-1\}$ of arbitrary size.

Definition 13 (Position in a term). *Given a natural term t and a word w we inductively define the subterm of t at position w (denoted $t_{|w}$) to be:*

$$t_{|w} = \begin{cases} (t_{w_0})_{|\overline{w}} & \textit{when } |w| > 0 \wedge t = f(t_0, \ldots, t_{p-1}) \textit{ with } w_0 < p \\ t & \textit{when } |w| = 0 \\ \textbf{undefined} & \textit{otherwise} \end{cases}$$

Moreover we denote by $\textbf{numeric}(t) = \{w \in \mathbb{N}^\star \mid t_{|w} \in \mathbb{Z}\}$.

Definition 14 (Positioning lattice with exact numerical constraints). *We define $\mathcal{C}(\mathcal{R}) \triangleq \wp(\mathcal{W}(\mathcal{R}) \nrightarrow \mathbb{Z})$, an element of $\mathcal{C}(\mathcal{R})$ is therefore a set of partial maps that are acceptable bindings of positions to integers.*

Proposition 7 (Galois connection with natural terms). *When t is a natural term, $t_{\mathbb{Z}}$ is the partial map: $\lambda_{|\textbf{numeric}(t)} w.t_w$. We have the following Galois connection: $(\wp(T_{\mathbb{Z}}(\mathcal{R})), \subseteq) \underset{\alpha_{\mathcal{C}(\mathcal{R})}}{\overset{\gamma_{\mathcal{C}(\mathcal{R})}}{\leftrightarrows}} (\mathcal{C}(\mathcal{R}), \subseteq)$, with:*

$$\gamma_{\mathcal{C}(\mathcal{R})}(\Gamma) = \{t \in T_{\mathbb{Z}}(\mathcal{R}) \mid t_{\mathbb{Z}} \in \Gamma\} \quad \alpha_{\mathcal{C}(\mathcal{R})}(\mathcal{T}) = \{t_{\mathbb{Z}} \mid t \in \mathcal{T}\}$$

Example 12. Consider our running example (introduced in Example 2), $V = \{+(x, +(z, y)) \mid x \leq y \wedge z \leq y\}$, we have $\alpha_{\mathcal{C}(\mathcal{R})}(V) = \{\wr 0 \int \mapsto \alpha, \wr 1, 0 \int \mapsto \gamma, \wr 1, 1 \int \mapsto \beta \mid \alpha \leq \beta \wedge \gamma \leq \beta\}$. The concretization of which is exactly V.

Example 13. Consider however the ranked alphabet $\{f(2), g(2), a(0)\}$, and the tree a. Its abstraction contains only the empty map, the concretization of which is the set of all terms that do not contain any numerical value. For example: $f(g(a, a), a), g(a, a), \ldots$. This emphasizes that we loose information on:

- the labels in the natural terms: we only have the path from the root of the term to leaves with numerical labels, not the actual symbols along the path.
- the shape of the natural terms: we do not keep any information on subterms that do not contain numerical values.

Now that we have abstracted away the shape of the terms, we are left with numerical environments with potentially infinite dimensions (that are words over the alphabet $\{0, \dots, n-1\}$) and different definition sets. Therefore following the idea of Sect. 4 we want to define a summarization for sets of words over the alphabet $\{0, \dots, n-1\}$. A summarization of such a language can be expressed as a partition into sub-languages. The set of regular languages over the alphabet $\{0, \dots, n-1\}$ is a subset of the set of languages over this alphabet, that is closed under common set operations. Hence given a set $\{r_1, \dots, r_m\}$ of regular expressions (with respective recognized language $\{L_1, \dots, L_m\}$), we summarize all words in L_i inside a common variable r_i and therefore $\uparrow \{r_1, \dots, r_m\}$ denotes the summarization function: $\lambda r_i.L_i$. In the following, Reg_n denotes the set of regular expressions over the alphabet $A_n = \{0, \dots, n-1\}$. As for tree regular expressions, $(\text{Reg}_n, \subset, \cap, \cup, .^c, \emptyset, A_n^\star)$ is a (non complete) complemented lattice of infinite height, upon which we can define a widening operator $\triangledown$ (see [10]) in a similar manner as for tree regular expressions (this widening is also parameterized by an integer constant). We recall moreover that operators $\subset, \cap, \cup$ and complementation $(.^c)$ are computable, and that every finite set of words is regular. Moreover we have the following representation: $(A_n^\star, \sqsubseteq) \xleftarrow{\gamma_{\text{Reg}_n} = Id} (\text{Reg}_n, \sqsubseteq)$. Finally in order to disambiguate regular expressions from integers we will typeset them within $\lfloor . \rfloor$ in a bold font as in: $\lfloor \mathbf{0 + 0.1^\star} \rfloor$.

Example 14. Using notations from Sect. 4.2, $\mathcal{V}' = \text{Reg}_n$ and $\mathcal{V} = \mathcal{W}(\mathcal{R})$. Consider our running example (introduced in Example 2), natural terms from $V = \{+(x, +(z, y)) \mid x \leq y \wedge z \leq y\}$ contain three paths to numerical values: $\wr 0 \int$, $\wr 1, 0 \int$ and $\wr 1, 1 \int$. Numerical constraints on $\wr 0 \int$ and $\wr 1, 0 \int$ are similar, therefore the two paths are summarized into one regular expression: $\lfloor \mathbf{0 + 1.0} \rfloor$, $\wr 1, 1 \int$ is left alone in its regular expression: $\lfloor \mathbf{1.1} \rfloor$. The two constraints $x \leq y \wedge z \leq y$ can now be expressed as one: $\lfloor \mathbf{0 + 1.0} \rfloor \leq \lfloor \mathbf{1.1} \rfloor$.

In Example 14, we saw that tree paths with similar numerical constraints can be summarized in one regular expression. However, for precision purposes, we do not want to summarize all tree paths into one regular expression. Hence, we will keep several disjoint regular expressions, which we call a subpartitioning.

Definition 15 (Subpartitioning). *Given a regular expression s, a subpartitioning of s is a set $\{s_1, \dots, s_n\}$ of regular expressions such that $\forall i \neq j,\ s_i \cap s_j = \emptyset$ and $\bigcup_{i=1}^n s_i \subseteq s$. We note $P(s)$ the set of all subpartitioning of s. Moreover if $S = \{s_1, \dots, s_n\}$ is a set of regular expressions, $[S]_\emptyset = S \setminus \{\emptyset\}$.*

Remark 7. Contrary to a partitioning of s, we do not require that the set of partitions covers s. Indeed when a set of tree paths is unconstrained we can just remove it from the partitioning, therefore no dimension in the numerical abstract environment will be allocated for this path.

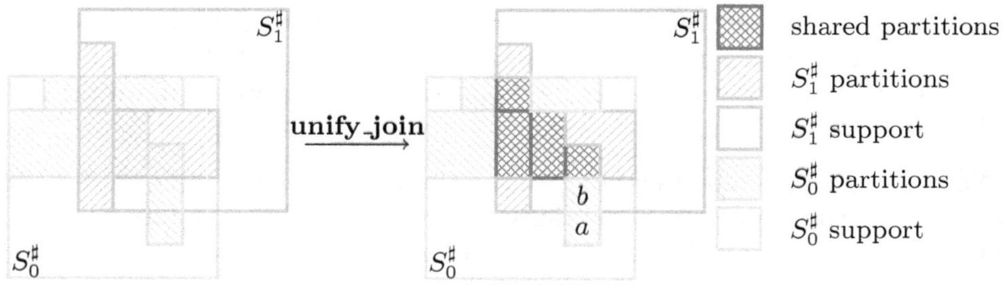

Fig. 6. Unification operator

Definition 16 (Positioning lattice with numerical abstraction). *Given a ranked alphabet* $\mathcal{R}$*, where the maximum arity of symbols is* n*, we define* $\mathcal{C}^\sharp(\mathcal{R}) = \{\langle s, \mathfrak{p}, R^\sharp\rangle \mid s \in Reg_n, \mathfrak{p} \in P(s), R^\sharp \in \mathfrak{M}_\mathfrak{p}^\sharp\}$*. Therefore* $\mathcal{C}^\sharp(\mathcal{R})$ *are triples containing:*

- s*: (called support) a regular expression coding for positions at which numerical values can be located.*
- $\mathfrak{p}$*: a subpartitioning of* s*. Elements of the same partition are subject to the same numerical constraints. Note that these partitions are regular.*
- $R^\sharp$*: an abstract numeric element where a dimension is associated to each partition, this dimension plays the role of a summary dimension.*

Remark 8. In the following, numerical abstract elements described in the form $\{c\}$, where c is a set of constraints, refer to $\langle c, \mathbf{vars}(c), \mathbf{vars}(c)\rangle \in \mathfrak{M}^\sharp$.

Algorithm 2. unify_join operator

Input : $\langle s, \{p_1, \ldots, p_n\}, R^\sharp\rangle, \langle s', \{p'_1, \ldots, p'_m\}, R^{\sharp\prime}\rangle$ two abstract elements
Output: two unified abstract elements

$(\underline{c_{i,j}})_{i\le n, j\le m} \leftarrow p_i \cap p'_j$;
$(\underline{p_i})_{i\le n} \leftarrow p_i \cap s'^c$;
$(\underline{p'_j})_{j\le m} \leftarrow p'_j \cap s^c$;
$(\underline{q_i})_{i\le n} \leftarrow p_i \cap s' \cap (\cup_{j\le m}\underline{c_{i,j}})^c$;
$(\underline{q'_j})_{j\le m} \leftarrow p'_j \cap s \cap (\cup_{i\le n}\underline{c_{i,j}})^c$;
$\underline{R^\sharp} \leftarrow R^\sharp$;
$\underline{R^{\sharp\prime}} \leftarrow R^{\sharp\prime}$;
for $i = 1$ **to** n **do**
  $\underline{R^\sharp} \leftarrow$ **expand**$(\underline{R^\sharp}, p_i, [\{\underline{c_{i,j}}\}_{j\le m} \cup \{\underline{p_i}\} \cup \{\underline{q_i}\}]_\emptyset)$;
for $j = 1$ **to** m **do**
  $\underline{R^{\sharp\prime}} \leftarrow$ **expand**$(\underline{R^{\sharp\prime}}, p'_j, [\{\underline{c_{i,j}}\}_{i\le n} \cup \{\underline{p'_j}\} \cup \{\underline{q'_j}\}]_\emptyset)$;
return $\langle s, \bigcup_{i\le n, j\le m}[\{\underline{q_i}, \underline{p_i}, \underline{c_{i,j}}\}]_\emptyset, \underline{R^\sharp}\rangle, \langle s', \bigcup_{i\le n, j\le m}[\{\underline{q'_i}, \underline{p'_j}, \underline{c_{i,j}}\}]_\emptyset, \underline{R^{\sharp\prime}}\rangle$;

Unification. The previous definition shows that two elements $U^\sharp = \langle s, \mathfrak{p}, R^\sharp \rangle$ and $V^\sharp = \langle s', \mathfrak{p}', R^{\sharp\prime} \rangle$ can have different subpartitionings ($\mathfrak{p}$ and $\mathfrak{p}'$). However the partitions in $\mathfrak{p}$ and in $\mathfrak{p}'$ might overlap, thus giving constraints to similar tree paths. Therefore in order to define the classical operators: $\sqsubseteq, \sqcup$ and ∇, we need to unify the two abstract elements ($U^\sharp$ and $V^\sharp$) so that given a tree path and the partition in which it is contained in $U^\sharp$, it is contained in the same partition in $V^\sharp$. This will enable us to rely on abstract operators on the numerical domain. In order to perform unification, we rely on the **expand** and **fold** operators. Indeed consider our running example, $U^\sharp = \langle \lfloor \mathbf{0} + \mathbf{1} \rfloor, \{\lfloor \mathbf{0} \rfloor, \lfloor \mathbf{1} \rfloor\}, \{\lfloor \mathbf{0} \rfloor \le \lfloor \mathbf{1} \rfloor\} \rangle$ and $V^\sharp = \langle \lfloor \mathbf{0} + \mathbf{1}.(\mathbf{0}+\mathbf{1}) \rfloor, \{\lfloor \mathbf{0} + \mathbf{1.0} \rfloor, \lfloor \mathbf{1.1} \rfloor\}, \{\lfloor \mathbf{0} + \mathbf{1.0} \rfloor \le \lfloor \mathbf{1.1} \rfloor\} \rangle$. We see that constraints on tree path $\wr 0 \int$ is given: in $U^\sharp$ by partition $\lfloor \mathbf{0} \rfloor$ and in $V^\sharp$ by partition $\lfloor \mathbf{0} + \mathbf{1.0} \rfloor$. However we can split the partition $\lfloor \mathbf{0} + \mathbf{1.0} \rfloor$ into two partitions: $\lfloor \mathbf{0} \rfloor$ and $\lfloor \mathbf{1.0} \rfloor$, and expand variable $\lfloor \mathbf{0} + \mathbf{1.0} \rfloor$ into the two variables $\lfloor \mathbf{0} \rfloor$ and $\lfloor \mathbf{1.0} \rfloor$ in the numeric component: $\mathbf{expand}(\{\lfloor \mathbf{0} + \mathbf{1.0} \rfloor \le \lfloor \mathbf{1.1} \rfloor\}, \lfloor \mathbf{0} + \mathbf{1.0} \rfloor, \{\lfloor \mathbf{0} \rfloor, \lfloor \mathbf{1.0} \rfloor\}) = \{\lfloor \mathbf{0} \rfloor \le \lfloor \mathbf{1.1} \rfloor, \lfloor \mathbf{1.0} \rfloor \le \lfloor \mathbf{1.1} \rfloor\}$. Once $U^\sharp$ and $V^\sharp$ are unified we can rely on the numerical join to soundly abstract the union. Note that splitting partitions is more precise than merging them. Indeed, consider the example where: in $U^\sharp$ we have $\lfloor \mathbf{0} \rfloor \ge 0$ and $\lfloor \mathbf{1} \rfloor \le 0$ and in $V^\sharp$ we have $\lfloor \mathbf{0} + \mathbf{1} \rfloor = 0$. Splitting partition in $V^\sharp$ yields: $\lfloor \mathbf{0} \rfloor = 0, \lfloor \mathbf{1} \rfloor = 0$, after joining we get $\lfloor \mathbf{0} \rfloor \ge 0, \lfloor \mathbf{1} \rfloor \le 0$. Whereas merging partitions in $U^\sharp$ yields $\lfloor \mathbf{0} + \mathbf{1} \rfloor$ unconstrained, after joining we also get that $\lfloor \mathbf{0}+\mathbf{1} \rfloor$ is unconstrained. However unifying by splitting or merging partitions in both abstract elements might result in an over-approximation of the initial elements. This does not pose a threat to the soundness of the join operator, but it does for the inclusion test. Unifying by splitting partitions induces an increase in the number of partitions which we want to avoid when trying to stabilize abstract elements in the widening. Hence, we define three unification operators:

- An operator **unify_join** that splits partitions from $U^\sharp$ and $V^\sharp$, this operator might induce an over-approximation for both $U^\sharp$ and $V^\sharp$ and is used in the join operation. This operator is presented in Algorithm 2, and illustrated in Fig. 6.
- An operator **unify_subset** that does not modify $V^\sharp$ (in order to avoid over-approximated it), we only split and merge (using the **fold** operator) partitions from $U^\sharp$ as, if the over-approximated $U^\sharp$ is smaller than $V^\sharp$, then so is the original $U^\sharp$.
- An operator **unify_widen** that unifies $U^\sharp$ and $V^\sharp$ by only merging partitions so that the number of partitions does not increase. This operator is used in the widening definition.

Operators **unify_subset** and **unify_widen** are very similar to **unify_join**.

Definition 17 (Comparison $\sqsubseteq_{\mathcal{C}^\sharp(\mathcal{R})}$). *Using* **unify_subset** *we define a relation on $\mathcal{C}^\sharp(\mathcal{R})$: $\sqsubseteq_{\mathcal{C}^\sharp(\mathcal{R})} = \{(U^\sharp, V^\sharp) \mid (\langle s, \mathfrak{p}, N^\sharp \rangle, \langle s', \mathfrak{p}', N^{\sharp\prime} \rangle) = \mathbf{unify\_subset}(U^\sharp, V^\sharp) \Rightarrow s \subseteq s' \wedge \forall b \in \mathfrak{p}', (b \subseteq s^c \vee \exists! a \in \mathfrak{p}, b \cap s = a) \wedge N^\sharp \sqsubseteq N^{\sharp\prime}[\phi]\}$ where ϕ is the renaming from $\mathfrak{p}'$ into $\mathfrak{p}$ that renames b to a when such an a exists.*

Example 15. Going back to our running example: $U^\sharp = \langle\lfloor\mathbf{0}+\mathbf{1}\rfloor, \{\lfloor\mathbf{0}\rfloor, \lfloor\mathbf{1}\rfloor\}, \{\lfloor\mathbf{0}\rfloor \le \lfloor\mathbf{1}\rfloor\}(=A^\sharp)\rangle$ and $V^\sharp = \langle\lfloor\mathbf{0}+\mathbf{1}.(\mathbf{0}+\mathbf{1})\rfloor, \{\lfloor\mathbf{0}+\mathbf{1}.\mathbf{0}\rfloor, \lfloor\mathbf{1}.\mathbf{1}\rfloor\}, \{\lfloor\mathbf{0}+\mathbf{1}.\mathbf{0}\rfloor \le \lfloor\mathbf{1}.\mathbf{1}\rfloor\}\rangle$. We have $s \not\subseteq s'$ hence $U^\sharp \not\sqsubseteq V^\sharp$. However if we now consider $W^\sharp$: $\langle\lfloor(\epsilon+\mathbf{1}).(\mathbf{0}+\mathbf{1})\rfloor, \{\lfloor(\epsilon+\mathbf{1}).\mathbf{0}\rfloor, \lfloor(\epsilon+\mathbf{1}).\mathbf{1}\rfloor\}, \{\lfloor(\epsilon+\mathbf{1}).\mathbf{0}\rfloor \le \lfloor(\epsilon+\mathbf{1}).\mathbf{1}\rfloor\}(=B^\sharp)\rangle$. $W^\sharp$ is already unified with $U^\sharp$, we have $s \subseteq s'$ and $\phi : (\lfloor(\epsilon+\mathbf{1}).\mathbf{0}\rfloor \mapsto \mathbf{0}, \lfloor(\epsilon+\mathbf{1}).\mathbf{1}\rfloor \mapsto \lfloor\mathbf{1}\rfloor)$. Moreover $A^\sharp \sqsubseteq B^\sharp[\phi] = \{\lfloor\mathbf{0}\rfloor \le \lfloor\mathbf{1}\rfloor\}$. Hence $U^\sharp \sqsubseteq W^\sharp$.

Proposition 8. *We have:* $(\mathcal{C}(\mathcal{R}), \sqsubseteq_{\mathcal{C}(\mathcal{R})}) \xleftarrow{\gamma_1} (\mathcal{C}^\sharp(\mathcal{R}), \sqsubseteq_{\mathcal{C}^\sharp(\mathcal{R})})$, *where:* $\gamma_1(\langle s, \mathfrak{p}, R^\sharp\rangle) = \{f \mid \mathbf{def}(f) \subseteq \gamma_{Reg_n}(s) \wedge f \in \gamma[\uparrow \mathfrak{p}](R^\sharp)\}$. *By composition we get:* $(\wp(T_{\mathbb{Z}}(\mathcal{R})), \subseteq) \xleftarrow{\gamma_2} (\mathcal{C}^\sharp(\mathcal{R}), \sqsubseteq_{\mathcal{C}^\sharp\mathcal{R}})$, *with* $\gamma_2 = \gamma_{\mathcal{C}(\mathcal{R})} \circ \gamma_1$.

Example 16. Going back to our running example: $V^\sharp = \langle\lfloor\mathbf{0}+\mathbf{1}.(\mathbf{0}+\mathbf{1})\rfloor, \{\lfloor\mathbf{0}+\mathbf{1}.\mathbf{0}\rfloor, \lfloor\mathbf{1}.\mathbf{1}\rfloor\}, \{\lfloor\mathbf{0}+\mathbf{1}.\mathbf{0}\rfloor \le \lfloor\mathbf{1}.\mathbf{1}\rfloor\}\rangle$. We have: $\uparrow \mathfrak{p} = (\lfloor\mathbf{0}+\mathbf{1}.\mathbf{0}\rfloor \mapsto \{\wr 0 \int, \wr 1, 0 \int\}, \lfloor\mathbf{1}\rfloor \mapsto \wr 1 \int)$. Hence, $\gamma_1(V^\sharp) = \{(\wr 0 \int \mapsto \alpha, \wr 1 \int \mapsto \beta) \mid \alpha \le \beta\} \cup \{(\wr 1, 0 \int \mapsto \alpha, \wr 1 \int \mapsto \beta) \mid \alpha \le \beta\} \cup \{(\wr 0 \int \mapsto \alpha, \wr 1, 0 \int \mapsto \gamma, \wr 1 \int \mapsto \beta) \mid \alpha \le \beta \wedge \gamma \le \beta\}$. The product with tree automata refines this result so that only the last set is left.

We now define the $\sqcup$ operator that relies on the **unify_join** operator of Algorithm 2. Once elements are unified we can distinguish three kinds of partitions: (1) Partitions found in both abstract elements (e.g. ● in Fig. 6). (2) Partitions found in only one of the two, which do not overlap over the support of the other abstract element (denoted u^o), these are outer-partitions. Information on such partitions can be soundly kept when joining two abstract elements (e.g. partition a in Fig. 6). (3) Partitions found in only one of the two, which overlap over the support of the other abstract element, these are inner-partitions. Information on such partitions can not be soundly kept when joining two abstract elements. (e.g. partition b in Fig. 6). Therefore in the following definition of the join operator, we compute (once elements are unified) the common partitions and both outer-partitions and merge them to form the resulting subpartitioning.

Definition 18 (Union abstract operator). *Given* $U^\sharp, V^\sharp \in \mathcal{C}^\sharp(\mathcal{R})$, *if* $(\langle s, \mathfrak{p}, R^\sharp\rangle, \langle s', \mathfrak{p}', R^{\sharp\prime}\rangle) = \mathbf{unify\_join}(U^\sharp, V^\sharp)$, *let* $\mathfrak{c}$ *be* $\mathfrak{p} \cup \mathfrak{p}'$, *let* u^o *(*$U^\sharp$ *outer-partition) be* $\{e \in \mathfrak{p} \mid e \subseteq s'^c\}$, *let* v^o *(*$V^\sharp$ *outer-partition) be* $\{e \in \mathfrak{p}' \mid e \subseteq s^c\}$, *we then define:*

$$U^\sharp \sqcup_{\mathcal{C}^\sharp(\mathcal{R})} V^\sharp = \langle s \cup s', \mathfrak{c} \cup u^o \cup v^o, R^\sharp_{|\mathfrak{c}\cup u^o} \sqcup R^{\sharp\prime}_{|\mathfrak{c}\cup v^o}\rangle$$

Proposition 9. *We have:* $\gamma_1(U^\sharp) \cup \gamma_1(V^\sharp) \subseteq \gamma_1(U^\sharp \sqcup_{\mathcal{C}^\sharp(\mathcal{R})} V^\sharp)$.

Example 17. Consider the two following abstract elements (this is the particular case of our running example where all numerical values are equal): $V^\sharp = \langle\lfloor\mathbf{0}+\mathbf{1}.(\mathbf{0}+\mathbf{1})\rfloor(=s), \{\lfloor\mathbf{0}+\mathbf{1}.\mathbf{0}\rfloor(=a), \lfloor\mathbf{1}.\mathbf{1}\rfloor(=b), \{a=b\}\}\rangle$, and $U^\sharp = \langle\lfloor\mathbf{0}+\mathbf{1}\rfloor(=s'), \{\lfloor\mathbf{0}\rfloor(=c), \lfloor\mathbf{1}\rfloor(=d)\}, \{c=d\}\rangle$. Intuitively $U^\sharp$ could encode the term $(x+x)$ and $V^\sharp$ the term $(x+(x+x))$. The unification of those two elements is: $V_1^\sharp = \langle s, \{c, b, \lfloor\mathbf{1}.\mathbf{0}\rfloor(=e)\}, R^\sharp\rangle$ where $R^\sharp = \langle\{c=b, e=b\}, \{b\}, \{c, b, e\}\rangle$ and $U_1^\sharp = U^\sharp$, moreover the common environment ($\mathfrak{c}$ in previous definition) is: $\{c\}$,

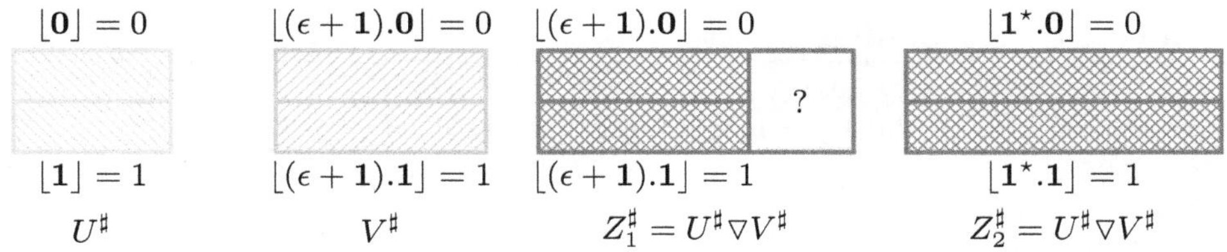

Fig. 7. Widening illustration

$V^\sharp$ outer-partitioning is $\{e, f\}$, $U^\sharp$ outer-partitioning is $\{d\}$. Hence: the numerical component resulting of the join is: $\langle\{c = d\}, \{c, d\}, \{c, d\}\rangle \sqcup \langle\{c = b, e = b\}, \{b\}, \{c, b, e\}\rangle$ which is: $\langle\{c = b, e = b, c = d\}, \emptyset, \{c, d, e, b\}\rangle$. We see here that using a naive numerical join operator, we would not have been able to get such a precise result (the numerical join would have yielded $\top$).

unify_widen $\mathcal{C}^\sharp(\mathcal{R})$ contains infinite increasing chains, therefore, we need to provide a widening operator. As for the other operators, widening is computed on unified abstract elements. A **unify_widen** operator is defined: it produces $U^\sharp$ and $V^\sharp$, over-approximations of its inputs with the same number of partitions. Moreover it ensures that each partition of $U^\sharp$ intersects exactly one partition of $V^\sharp$. This can be obtained by iterative merging partitions that overlap in both arguments until the abstract elements have the exact same partitions. Therefore from the result of **unify_widen** we can extract a list of pairs (a, b) where a is a partition from $U^\sharp$, b is a partition from $V^\sharp$ and $a \cap b \neq \emptyset$. This defines a bijection from partitions of $U^\sharp$ onto partitions of $V^\sharp$.

compose. In order to ensure stabilization we first need to stabilize the supports on which abstract elements are defined. This is easily done using the automaton widening ($s_1 \nabla s_2$ in Algorithm 3). Figure 7 illustrates the following simple example: $U^\sharp$ is an abstract element with support $\lfloor \mathbf{0} + \mathbf{1} \rfloor$, two partitions $u = \lfloor \mathbf{0} \rfloor$ and $u' = \lfloor \mathbf{1} \rfloor$, and numerical constraints $u' = 1$ and $u = 0$. $V^\sharp$ is an abstract element with support $\lfloor (\epsilon + \mathbf{1}).(\mathbf{0} + \mathbf{1}) \rfloor$, two partitions $v = \lfloor (\epsilon + \mathbf{1}).\mathbf{0} \rfloor$ and $v' = \lfloor (\epsilon + \mathbf{1}).\mathbf{1} \rfloor$ with the numerical constraints that $v = 0$ and $v' = 1$. Supports are unstable, therefore we start by widening them, which yields a new support: $\lfloor \mathbf{1}^\star.(\mathbf{0} + \mathbf{1}) \rfloor$. The unification of $U^\sharp$ and $V^\sharp$ leaves subpartitionings unchanged and yields the bijection $(u \mapsto v, u' \mapsto v')$. Given this information we now need to provide a new subpartitioning for the result of the widening. We see in this example that we could soundly use the subpartitioning from $V^\sharp$, this would produce the abstract element $Z_1^\sharp$ depicted in Fig. 7. However due to the widening of the support, paths of the form $\wr 1, 1, 1, 0 \int$ are in the support of the result but are left unconstrained as they are not in any of the partitions. Therefore we need to use the opportunity of the extension of the support to place constraints on the newly added paths. In order to do so we would like to force the extension of the existing partitions from $U^\sharp$ and $V^\sharp$ into the new support. Therefore we need to define a **compose** operator that produces a sound new partition, given: (1) a pair a, b of partitions (such as the one produced by

Algorithm 3. widening operator

Input : $U^\sharp, V^\sharp$ two abstract elements

$(\langle s_1, \mathfrak{p}_1, R_1^\sharp\rangle, \langle s_2, \mathfrak{p}_2, R_2^\sharp\rangle) \leftarrow$ **unify_widen**$(U^\sharp, V^\sharp)$;

$s \leftarrow s_1 \nabla s_2$;

$r \leftarrow s \setminus (s_1 \cup s_2)$;

foreach $a \in \mathfrak{p}_1$ **do**

  $b \leftarrow$ the unique element from $\mathfrak{p}_2$ such that $b \cap a \neq \emptyset$;

  $p \leftarrow$ **compose**(a, b, s_1, s_2, r);

  $\mathfrak{p} \leftarrow \{p\} \cup \mathfrak{p}$;

  $R_1^{\sharp\star} \leftarrow R_1^{\sharp\star}[a \mapsto p]$;

  $R_2^{\sharp\star} \leftarrow R_1^{\sharp\star}[b \mapsto p]$;

  $r \leftarrow r \setminus p$;

if $\mathfrak{p} = \mathfrak{p}_1$ **then**

  return $\langle s, \mathfrak{p}, R_1^{\sharp\star} \nabla R_2^{\sharp\star}\rangle$;

else

  return $\langle s, \mathfrak{p}, R_1^{\sharp\star} \sqcup R_2^{\sharp\star}\rangle$;

unify_widen), (2) the support s_1 (resp s_2) in which a (resp. b) lives and (3) a space to occupy r. The following criteria must be verified by the resulting partition p in order to be sound and to terminate: $p \cap s_1 = a$, $p \cap s_2 = b$ and $p \setminus (s_1 \cup s_2) \subseteq r$. A variety of **compose** operators could be defined, we chose: **compose**$(a, b, s_1, s_2, r) = a \cup (b \cap (s_2 \setminus s_1)) \cup ((a \nabla (a \cup b)) \cap r)$. The idea is the following: we keep a (as it is always sound thanks to the definition of the **unify_widen** operator), we keep the part from b that satisfies the soundness condition, and we extend into the space left to occupy according to the automata widening of a and $a \cup b$. In our example, considering the pair (u, v), this would translate as: $a = \mathbf{0}$, $b \cap (s_2 \setminus s_1) = \lfloor \mathbf{1.0} \rfloor$ and $(a \nabla (a \cup b)) \cap r = \lfloor \mathbf{0} \rfloor \nabla \lfloor (\epsilon + 1).\mathbf{0} \rfloor \cap \lfloor \mathbf{1}^{\geq 2}(\mathbf{0}+\mathbf{1}) \rfloor = \lfloor \mathbf{1}^{\geq 2}.\mathbf{0} \rfloor$. We get the new partition: $\lfloor \mathbf{1}^\star.\mathbf{0} \rfloor$. Doing the same with the pair (v, v') yields $\lfloor \mathbf{1}^\star.\mathbf{1} \rfloor$. Finally we get the abstract element $Z_2^\sharp$ from Fig. 7, which is more precise than $Z_1^\sharp$.

Definition 19 (Widening). *Algorithm 3 provides the definition of a widening operator using the* **unify_widen** *operator and parameterized by a* **compose** *function.*

Widening Stabilization. Our abstraction contains three components: (1) a support that describes the set of paths (2) a subpartitioning of this support and (3) a numerical component giving constraints on partitions in the subpartitioning. We show how the widening operator stabilizes all three components.

- Regular expression widening is used on supports when widening is called. Therefore ensuring support stabilization.
- Once supports are stable (this means $s_2 \subseteq s_1$), we have $p = a$ for every pair (a, b) of partitions. Meaning that once shapes stabilize, the only modifications

allowed on the subpartitionings are those made by the **unify_widen** operator. Each partition resulting from the operator is the union of input partitions, hence the subpartitioning will stabilize.
- Once subpartitionings are stable ($\mathfrak{p}_1 = \mathfrak{p}$ in Algorithm 3) numerical widening is applied on the numerical component in order to ensure stabilization.

Example 18 (Numerical example). Consider the simple example where: $\mathcal{R} = \{f(2)\}$, $U^\sharp = \langle \lfloor \mathbf{0} + \mathbf{1} \rfloor, \{\lfloor \mathbf{0} \rfloor, \lfloor \mathbf{1} \rfloor\}, \{\lfloor \mathbf{1} \rfloor = \lfloor \mathbf{0} \rfloor\}\rangle$ and $V^\sharp = \langle \lfloor \mathbf{0} + \mathbf{1} \rfloor, \{\lfloor \mathbf{0} \rfloor, \lfloor \mathbf{1} \rfloor\}, \{\lfloor \mathbf{1} \rfloor \geq \lfloor \mathbf{0} \rfloor, \lfloor \mathbf{1} \rfloor \leq \lfloor \mathbf{0} \rfloor + 1\}\rangle$. $U^\sharp$ and $V^\sharp$ have the same shape, therefore widening will be performed on the numerical component of the abstraction, therefore: $U^\sharp \triangledown V^\sharp = \langle \lfloor \mathbf{0} + \mathbf{1} \rfloor, \{\lfloor \mathbf{0} \rfloor, \lfloor \mathbf{1} \rfloor\}, \{\lfloor \mathbf{1} \rfloor \geq \lfloor \mathbf{0} \rfloor\}\rangle$.

Reducing Dimensionality and Improving Precision. As emphasized by the previous examples, definitions and illustrations, the numerical component of an abstract state is used as a container for constraints on regular expressions, every node in a regular expression must then satisfy all numerical constraints on the underlying regular expression. Therefore when two nodes of a tree satisfy the same constraints, they should be stored in the same partition so as to reduce the dimension of the numerical domain (thus improving efficiency). Moreover the widening operator provided in Algorithm 3 relies (for precision) on the fact that partitions are built by similarity of constraints, therefore partition merging, when it does not result in an over-approximation, also leads to a precision gain. The unification operator defined in Algorithm 2 tends to split partitions whereas the widening operator defined in Algorithm 3 tends to merge them. In order to reduce dimensionality, we would like to define a **reduce** : $\mathcal{C}^\sharp(\mathcal{R}) \to \mathcal{C}^\sharp(\mathcal{R})$ operator, that folds variables with similar constraints into one. Please note that $\forall S \cap S' \subseteq \{x\}$, $x \in S$ and $R^\sharp \in N_S$, we have that $R^\sharp \sqsubseteq_{N_S} \mathbf{expand}(\mathbf{fold}(R^\sharp, x, S'), x, S')$. This means that when variables are folded into one, expanding them afterwards would yield a bigger abstract element. For example, consider the octagon $R^\sharp = \{x \geq 2, y \geq 2, x = y\}$ then $\mathbf{fold}(R^\sharp, z, \{x, y\}) = \{z \geq 2\} (\triangleq R^{\sharp\prime})$ and $\mathbf{expand}(R^{\sharp\prime}, z, \{x, y\}) = \{x \geq 2, y \geq 2\}$. However if we consider $R^\sharp = \{x \geq 2, y \geq 2\}$ then $\mathbf{fold}(\mathbf{expand}(R^\sharp, z, \{x, y\}), z, \{x, y\}) = R^\sharp$. Therefore if we assume given a score function $\mathbf{score}(R^\sharp, x, S')$ ranging in $[0, 1]$ such that $\mathbf{score}(R^\sharp, x, S') = 1 \Leftrightarrow R^\sharp = \mathbf{expand}(\mathbf{fold}(R^\sharp, x, S'), x, S')$, we are able to define a generic **reduce** operator parameterized by a value α. This **reduce** operator merges partitions until no more set of partitions has a high enough score according to the **score** function. Finding a good **score** function is a work in progress. As a first approximation we used the following trivial one: $\mathbf{score}_0(R^\sharp, S) = 1$ when $\mathbf{expand}(\mathbf{fold}(R^\sharp, x, S), x, S) = R^\sharp$ and 0 otherwise. This $\mathbf{score}_0$ guarantees there is no loss of precision, but can miss opportunities for simplification.

Example 19. Consider the following example: $U^\sharp = \langle \lfloor \mathbf{0} + \mathbf{1} \rfloor, \{\lfloor \mathbf{0} \rfloor, \lfloor \mathbf{1} \rfloor\}, \{\lfloor \mathbf{0} \rfloor = 0, \lfloor \mathbf{1} \rfloor = 0\}\rangle$. Relations on $\lfloor \mathbf{0} \rfloor$ and $\lfloor \mathbf{1} \rfloor$ can be expressed in one relation using the summarizing variable $\lfloor \mathbf{0} + \mathbf{1} \rfloor$. This yields: $\mathbf{reduce}(U^\sharp) = \langle \lfloor \mathbf{0} + \mathbf{1} \rfloor, \{\lfloor \mathbf{0} + \mathbf{1} \rfloor\}, \{\lfloor \mathbf{0} + \mathbf{1} \rfloor = 0\}\rangle$. Note that $\mathbf{expand}(\{\lfloor \mathbf{0} + \mathbf{1} \rfloor = 0\}, \lfloor \mathbf{0} + \mathbf{1} \rfloor, \{\lfloor \mathbf{1} \rfloor, \lfloor \mathbf{0} \rfloor\}) = \{\lfloor \mathbf{0} \rfloor = 0, \lfloor \mathbf{1} \rfloor = 0\}$. Therefore no information is lost.

Abstract Semantic of Operators. As for tree automata, abstract semantic of operators defined in Sect. 2 can be defined as simple transformations on regular automata. Indeed the `make_symbolic(`$s \in \mathcal{R}$`)` (resp. `get_son`) operator, amounts to adding (resp. removing) an integer letter to: (1) the partitions in the subpartitioning and (2) the support. `make_integer(`$e \in expr$`)` amounts to building an abstract element with support $\lfloor\epsilon\rfloor$ and a subpartitioning containing only $\{\lfloor\epsilon\rfloor\}$, on which we put the constraint that it is equal to e. `is_symbol` needs only split the support and each partition, in the two language $L = \{\epsilon\}$ and $A_n^\star \setminus L$. Indeed in order to restrict to terms having only an integer as root, the support must be reduced to ϵ. The `get_sym_head` operator always yields the whole ranked alphabet (as this was abstracted away and will be refined by the automaton abstraction). Finally for `get_num_head`: (1) if the empty path $\wr\int$ is in the support we produce the set of integers satisfying the numerical constraints on the partition containing ϵ, and $\top$ in case no such partition could be found, and (2) otherwise we know that no numerical value is produced.

5.2 Product of Tree Automata and Numerical Constraints

The abstraction by tree automata defined in Sect. 3 and the abstraction by numerical constraints on tree paths defined in Sect. 5.1 provide non comparable information on the set of terms they abstract. Indeed the former describes precisely the shape of the term but can not express numerical constraints whereas the latter abstracts away most of the shape and focuses on numerical constraints. To benefit from both kinds of information, we use a reduced product between the two domains. Both abstractions in the product contain information on potential integer positions. The position of the $\Box$ symbol in the tree automaton abstraction and the support in the numerical constraints abstractions both yield this information. We remove the support component from the product as the information can be retrieved from the tree abstraction. The definitions of the abstract operators in Sect. 5.1 require the support to be a regular language. We show in this subsection how to retrieve the support of a tree automaton with holes and that it is regular.

Given a FTA$(Q, \mathcal{R}, Q_f, \delta)$ over a ranked alphabet $\mathcal{R}$ with maximum arity n. We assume that every node in Q is reachable. Consider the following system over variables v_p for $p \in Q$ with values in the set of languages over the alphabet A_n (. designates the classical concatenation operator lifted to languages):

$$\{v_p = \bigcup_{(s,(q_1,\ldots,q_m),q)\in\delta | q_i = p} v_q.\{i\} \cup \begin{cases} \{\epsilon\} & \text{if } p \in Q_f \\ \emptyset & \text{otherwise} \end{cases} \mid p \in Q\}$$

Every language $\{i\}$ for $i \in \mathbb{N}$ is regular and does not contain ϵ, moreover $\emptyset$ and $\{\epsilon\}$ are regular languages. By application of Arden's rule (see [18]) and Gauss elimination we can compute the unique solution of this system, moreover every v_p is regular. Variable v_p is defined so that: $w \in v_p$ if and only if there exists a tree t recognized by the automaton such that $p \in \text{REACH}(t_{|w})$. If $\Box \in \mathcal{R}$ we have that the regular language: $\cup_{(\Box,(),p)\in\delta} v_p$ represents exactly the potential positions of integers in trees accepted by the tree automaton.

Height and Size. The product is enriched with a simple height and size abstraction: numerical variables (encoding heights and sizes) are added to the numerical component of the abstraction.

5.3 Environment Abstraction

In the previous section, we designed abstractions for sets of trees. However in order to be able to tackle the examples from the introductory section (Sect. 1) we need to design an abstraction able to represent maps from a set of variables to natural terms. In Sect. 3 we have shown how to lift abstractions on natural terms to abstractions of environments over a given finite set of finite term variables $\mathcal{T}$. We apply the same mechanism here to lift the product presented in Sect. 5.2. However lifting the product would result in abstract environments being maps from natural term variables to abstractions containing a numerical environment. In order to be able to express numerical relations between two sets of natural terms or even between numerical program variables and numerical values of natural terms we factor away the numerical environment so that it is shared by all natural term abstractions in the term environment and by the program variables in the numerical environment. Therefore the final abstraction is a pair $(m, R^\sharp)$ where: (1) m is a map from $\mathcal{T}$ to an abstract element that is a product of the automaton abstraction and the hole positioning abstraction. Moreover as all the numerical constraints are stored in a common numerical environment the product abstraction amounts to a pair $(\mathcal{A}, \mathfrak{p})$ where $\mathcal{A}$ is an element of the automaton abstraction and $\mathfrak{p}$ is a partitioning of its support. (2) $R^\sharp$ is an element of $\mathfrak{M}^\sharp$ binding in the same numerical element: numerical program variables and all partitions found in the mapping m.

6 Implementation and Example

6.1 Implementation

The analyzer was implemented in OCaml ($\sim$5000 loc) in the novel and still in development MOPSA framework (see [21]). MOPSA enables a modular development of static analyzers defined by abstract interpretation. An analyzer is built by choosing abstract domains, and combining them according to the user specification. MOPSA comes with pre-existing iterators and domains (e.g. interprocedural analysis, loop iterators, numerical domains, ...), and new ones can be added (e.g. tree abstract domain). A key feature of MOPSA is the ability of an abstract domain to use the abstract knowledge it maintains to transform dynamically expressions into other expressions that can be manipulated more easily by further domains, providing a flexible way to combine relational domains. For instance, assume that a domain abstracts arrays by associating a scalar variable a_0, a_1, ..., to each element $a[0]$, $a[1]$, ..., of an array a, and delegating the abstraction of the array contents to a numeric domain for scalars. It can then evaluate $\mathbb{E}^\sharp[\![2 * a[i] + i]\!](i \mapsto [0,1])$ into the disjunction

$(2 * a_0 + i, i \mapsto [0,0]) \vee (2 * a_1 + i, i \mapsto [1,1])$, indicating that $2 * a[i] + i$ is equivalent to $2 * a_0 + i$ in the sub-environment where $i = 0$ and to $2 * a_1 + i$ in the sub-environment where $i = 1$. Each term of the disjunction contains an array-free expression that can be handled by the scalar domain in the corresponding sub-environment. In the abstract, expressions can be evaluated by induction on the syntax into symbolic expressions to retain the full power of relational domains and disjunctive reasoning (see [21] for more details). We exploit this feature in our implementation to combine our tree abstractions. We implemented (in the MOPSA framework) libraries for regular and tree regular languages that offer the usual lattice interface enriched with a widening operator. These libraries can be reused for the definition of other abstract domains. The overall complexity of the analysis is driven by the complexity of the lattice operations in the regular and tree regular libraries. These are exponential in the number of states of the considered automata, which is bounded by the widening parameter.

6.2 Examples of Analysis

Numerical variables of the form $\mathtt{t}.x$, where $\mathtt{t}$ is a natural term variable, represent a variable allocated for tree $\mathtt{t}$. For example: $\mathtt{t}.r$ where r is a regular expression is the variable allocated for partition r in tree $\mathtt{t}$.

C Introductory Example. Let us consider the introductory example Program 4. The loop invariant inferred with our analysis is the following abstract element: $U^\sharp = (\mathtt{y} \mapsto (\mathcal{A}, \{\lfloor \mathbf{0}.(\mathbf{0}.\mathbf{0})^\star.\mathbf{1} \rfloor (= r)\}), R^\sharp)$, with $\mathcal{A} = \langle \{a,b,c,d\}, \{*(1), +(2), \Box(0), (p,0)\}, \{c\}, \{*(d) \to c, +(c,a) \to d, \Box() \to a, p \to c\} \rangle$, and $R^\sharp$ satisfies the constraints: $\{\mathtt{i} \geq 0, \mathtt{i} \leq \mathtt{n}, \mathtt{y}.r = 4\}$. This describes precisely the set of terms of the form: p, $*(p{+}4)$, $*(*(p{+}4){+}4)$, ... As mentioned in Sect. 6.1 evaluations of tree expressions yield pairs containing an expression and an abstract environment. Tree expressions are pairs $(\mathcal{A}, \mathfrak{p})$, partitions in $\mathfrak{p}$ are bound by the adjoined environment. Let us now present the result of the evaluation of the `make_integer(4)` expression in the abstract environment $U^\sharp$. Here we get the expression $(\mathcal{A}', \{\lfloor \epsilon \rfloor\})$ (where $\mathcal{A}'$ recognizes only $\Box$) in the environment: $(\mathtt{y} \mapsto (\mathcal{A}, \{r\}), R^{\sharp\prime})$ where $R^{\sharp\prime} = R^\sharp \cup \{\lfloor \epsilon \rfloor = 4\}$. This emphasizes how the environment is used to give constraints on the adjoined expression. This transports numerical relations from the leafs of the expression up to the assigned variable $\mathtt{t}$.

OCaml Introductory Example. Let us now consider the introductory example Program 5. The inferred loop invariant is the following ($r = \lfloor (\mathbf{1}.\mathbf{1})^\star.\mathbf{0} \rfloor$ and $r' = \lfloor (\mathbf{1}.\mathbf{1})^\star.\mathbf{1}.\mathbf{0} \rfloor$): $(\mathtt{t} \mapsto (\mathcal{A}, \{r, r'\}), R^\sharp)$ and $R^\sharp$ satisfies the constraints: $\{\mathtt{t}.r' = \mathtt{x} - 1, \mathtt{t}.r = \mathtt{t}.r' + 2, i \geq 0, i \leq \mathtt{n}\}$ and $\mathcal{A} = (\{a,b,c,d\}, \{\mathtt{Cons}(2), \mathtt{Nil}(0), \Box(0)\}, \{a\}, \{\mathtt{Cons}(c,a) \to d, \mathtt{Cons}(c,d) \to a, \mathtt{Nil} \to a, \Box \to c\})$. Please note that at the end of the `while` loops the two numerical environments that need to be joined are not defined over the same set of variables (in the environments that have not gone through the loop, variables $\mathtt{t}.r'$ and $\mathtt{t}.r$ are not present). However thanks to the $\boxtimes$ operator, we do not have to loose the numerical relations between these variables and x. Hence we are able to prove that the assertion holds.

The analyzer was able to successfully analyze and infer the expected invariants for both examples.

7 Related Works

Previous works on sets of trees abstractions [20] were able to recognize larger classes of tree languages than tree automata. However we focused here on the abstraction of trees labeled with numerical values, therefore the work closest to ours would be [12]. Indeed it defines tree automata where leaves can be elements of a lattice (for example an interval). They are therefore able to represent sets of natural terms, but can not express numerical relations between the leaves of trees. Moreover they rely on a partitioning of the leaf lattice for tree automata operations. In [1] (and [2]) tree automata and regular automata are used for the model checking of programs manipulating C pointers and structures. Other uses have been made of tree automata in verification: shape analysis of C programs as in [15], computation of an over-approximation of terms computable by attackers of cryptographic protocols as in [24]. Widening regular languages by the computation of an equivalence relation of bounded index is also done in [9] and in [11]. As mentioned, variable summarization is often used to represent unbounded memory locations as in [17] or [14]. Moreover numerical abstract domains able to handle optional variables have been defined such as [19]. Finally termination analyses have been proposed for the analysis of programs manipulating tree structures (AVL, red-black trees) see [16].

8 Conclusion

In this article we presented a relational abstract environment for sets of trees over a finite algebra, with numerically labeled leaves. We emphasized the potential applications of being able to describe such trees: description of reachable memory zones, tracking symbolic equalities between program variables, description of tree like structures. In order to improve the precision of the analysis while not blowing up its cost we defined a novel abstraction for sets of maps with heterogeneous supports. This numeric abstraction is able to represent optional dimensions in numerical domains without losing relations with optional variables. All domains presented in the article were implemented as a library in the MOPSA framework.

References

1. Bouajjani, A., Habermehl, P., Rogalewicz, A., Vojnar, T.: Abstract regular tree model checking of complex dynamic data structures. In: Yi, K. (ed.) SAS 2006. LNCS, vol. 4134, pp. 52–70. Springer, Heidelberg (2006). https://doi.org/10.1007/11823230_5
2. Bouajjani, A., Habermehl, P., Vojnar, T.: Abstract regular model checking. In: Alur, R., Peled, D.A. (eds.) CAV 2004. LNCS, vol. 3114, pp. 372–386. Springer, Heidelberg (2004). https://doi.org/10.1007/978-3-540-27813-9_29
3. Bourdoncle, F.: Sémantiques des Langages Impératifs d'Ordre Supérieur et Interprétation Abstraite. Ph.D. thesis, Ecole polytechnique (1992)
4. Comon, H., et al.: Tree automata techniques and applications (2007). Release October, 12th 2007
5. Cousot, P., Cousot, R.: Abstract interpretation: a unified lattice model for static analysis of programs by construction or approximation of fixpoints. In: Proceedings of POPL, pp. 238–252. ACM (1977)
6. Cousot, P., Cousot, R.: Static determination of dynamic properties of generalized type unions. In: Language Design for Reliable Software, pp. 77–94 (1977)
7. Cousot, P., Cousot, R.: Modular static program analysis. In: Horspool, R.N. (ed.) CC 2002. LNCS, vol. 2304, pp. 159–179. Springer, Heidelberg (2002). https://doi.org/10.1007/3-540-45937-5_13
8. Cousot, P., Halbwachs, N.: Automatic discovery of linear restraints among variables of a program. In: Proceedings of POPL, pp. 84–96. ACM Press (1978)
9. Feret, J.: Abstract interpretation-based static analysis of mobile ambients. In: Cousot, P. (ed.) SAS 2001. LNCS, vol. 2126, pp. 412–430. Springer, Heidelberg (2001). https://doi.org/10.1007/3-540-47764-0_24
10. Le Gall, T.: Abstract lattices for the verification of systèmes with stacks and queues. Ph.D. thesis, University of Rennes 1, France (2008)
11. Le Gall, T., Jeannet, B., Jéron, T.: Verification of communication protocols using abstract interpretation of FIFO queues. In: Johnson, M., Vene, V. (eds.) AMAST 2006. LNCS, vol. 4019, pp. 204–219. Springer, Heidelberg (2006). https://doi.org/10.1007/11784180_17
12. Genet, T., Le Gall, T., Legay, A., Murat, V.: Tree regular model checking for lattice-based automata. CoRR, abs/1203.1495 (2012)
13. Gopan, D., DiMaio, F., Dor, N., Reps, T., Sagiv, M.: Numeric domains with summarized dimensions. In: Jensen, K., Podelski, A. (eds.) TACAS 2004. LNCS, vol. 2988, pp. 512–529. Springer, Heidelberg (2004). https://doi.org/10.1007/978-3-540-24730-2_38
14. Gopan, D., Reps, T.W., Sagiv, S.: A framework for numeric analysis of array operations. In: Proceedings of POPL, pp. 338–350. ACM (2005)
15. Habermehl, P., Holík, L., Rogalewicz, A., Šimáček, J., Vojnar, T.: Forest automata for verification of heap manipulation. In: Gopalakrishnan, G., Qadeer, S. (eds.) CAV 2011. LNCS, vol. 6806, pp. 424–440. Springer, Heidelberg (2011). https://doi.org/10.1007/978-3-642-22110-1_34
16. Habermehl, P., Iosif, R., Rogalewicz, A., Vojnar, T.: Proving termination of tree manipulating programs. In: Namjoshi, K.S., Yoneda, T., Higashino, T., Okamura, Y. (eds.) ATVA 2007. LNCS, vol. 4762, pp. 145–161. Springer, Heidelberg (2007). https://doi.org/10.1007/978-3-540-75596-8_12
17. Halbwachs, N., Péron, M.: Discovering properties about arrays in simple programs. In: Proceedings of PLDI, pp. 339–348. ACM (2008)

18. Hopcroft, J.E., Motwani, R., Ullman, J.D.: Introduction to Automata Theory, Languages, and Computation, 3rd edn. Addison-Wesley Longman Publishing Co., Inc, Boston (2006)
19. Liu, J., Rival, X.: Abstraction of optional numerical values. In: Feng, X., Park, S. (eds.) APLAS 2015. LNCS, vol. 9458, pp. 146–166. Springer, Cham (2015). https://doi.org/10.1007/978-3-319-26529-2_9
20. Mauborgne, L.: Representation of sets of trees for abstract interpretation. Ph.D. thesis, Ecole polytechnique (1999)
21. Miné, A., Ouadjaout, A., Journault, M.: Design of a modular platform for static analysis. In: The Ninth Workshop on Tools for Automatic Program Analysis (TAPAS 2018), Fribourg-en-Brisgau, Germany, August 2018. https://hal.sorbonne-universite.fr/hal-01870001/file/mine-al-tapas18.pdf
22. Miné, A.: The octagon abstract domain. In: Proceedings of WCRE, p. 310. IEEE Computer Society (2001)
23. Miné, A.: Symbolic methods to enhance the precision of numerical abstract domains. In: Emerson, E.A., Namjoshi, K.S. (eds.) VMCAI 2006. LNCS, vol. 3855, pp. 348–363. Springer, Heidelberg (2005). https://doi.org/10.1007/11609773_23
24. Monniaux, D.: Abstracting cryptographic protocols with tree automata. In: Cortesi, A., Filé, G. (eds.) SAS 1999. LNCS, vol. 1694, pp. 149–163. Springer, Heidelberg (1999). https://doi.org/10.1007/3-540-48294-6_10
25. Reynolds, J.C.: Separation logic: a logic for shared mutable data structures. In: Proceedings of 17th IEEE (LICS 2002), pp. 55–74. IEEE Computer Society (2002)

3

Time Credits and Time Receipts in Iris

Glen Mével[1], Jacques-Henri Jourdan[2(✉)], and François Pottier[1]

[1] Inria, Paris, France
[2] CNRS, LRI, Univ. Paris Sud, Université Paris Saclay, Orsay, France
jacques-henri.jourdan@lri.fr

Abstract. We present a machine-checked extension of the program logic Iris with time credits and time receipts, two dual means of reasoning about time. Whereas time credits are used to establish an upper bound on a program's execution time, time receipts can be used to establish a lower bound. More strikingly, time receipts can be used to prove that certain undesirable events—such as integer overflows—cannot occur until a very long time has elapsed. We present several machine-checked applications of time credits and time receipts, including an application where both concepts are exploited.

"Alice: How long is forever? White Rabbit: Sometimes, just one second."
— Lewis Carroll, *Alice in Wonderland*

1 Introduction

A program logic, such as Hoare logic or Separation Logic, is a set of deduction rules that can be used to reason about the behavior of a program. To this day, considerable effort has been invested in developing ever-more-powerful program logics that control the *extensional* behavior of programs, that is, logics that guarantee that a program safely computes a valid final result. A lesser effort has been devoted to logics that allow reasoning not just about safety and functional correctness, but also about *intensional* aspects of a program's behavior, such as its time consumption and space usage.

In this paper, we are interested in narrowing the gap between these lines of work. We present a formal study of two mechanisms by which a standard program logic can be extended with means of reasoning about time. As a starting point, we take Iris [11–14], a powerful evolution of Concurrent Separation Logic [3]. We extend Iris with two elementary time-related concepts, namely *time credits* [1, 4,9] and *time receipts*.

Time credits and time receipts are independent concepts: it makes sense to extend a program logic with either of them in isolation or with both of them simultaneously. They are dual concepts: every computation step *consumes one time credit* and *produces one time receipt*. They are purely static: they do not exist at runtime. We view them as Iris assertions. Thus, they can appear in the correctness statements that we formulate about programs and in the proofs of these statements.

Time credits can be used to establish an upper bound on the execution time of a program. Dually, time receipts can be used to establish a lower bound, and (as explained shortly) can be used to prove that certain undesirable events cannot occur until a very long time has elapsed.

Until now, time credits have been presented as an ad hoc extension of some fixed flavor of Separation Logic [1,4,9]. In contrast, we propose a construction which in principle allows time credits to be introduced on top of an arbitrary "base logic", provided this base logic is a sufficiently rich variety of Separation Logic. In order to make our definitions and proofs more concrete, we use Iris as the base logic. Our construction involves *composing* the base logic with a program transformation that inserts a *tick*() instruction in front of every computation step. As far as a user of the composite logic is concerned, the *tick*() instruction and the assertion \$1, which represents one time credit, are abstract: the only fact to which the user has access is the Hoare triple $\{\$1\}$ *tick*() $\{\mathsf{True}\}$, which states that "*tick*() consumes one time credit".

There are two reasons why we choose Iris [12] as the base logic. First, in the proof of soundness of the composite logic, we must exhibit concrete definitions of *tick* and \$1 such that $\{\$1\}$ *tick*() $\{\mathsf{True}\}$ holds. Several features of Iris, such as ghost state and shared invariants, play a key role in this construction. Second, at the user level, the power of Iris can also play a crucial role. To illustrate this, we present the first machine-checked reconstruction of Okasaki's debits [19] in terms of time credits. The construction makes crucial use of both time credits and Iris' ghost monotonic state and shared invariants.

Time receipts are a new concept, a contribution of this paper. To extend a base logic with time receipts, we follow the exact same route as above: we compose the base logic with the *same* program transformation as above, which we refer to as "the tick translation". In the eyes of a user of the composite logic, the *tick*() instruction and the assertion ⧗1, which represents one time receipt, are again abstract: this time, the only published fact about *tick* is the triple $\{\mathsf{True}\}$ *tick*() {⧗1}, which states that "*tick*() produces one time receipt".

Thus far, the symmetry between time credits and time receipts seems perfect: whereas time credits allow establishing an upper bound on the cost of a program fragment, time receipts allow establishing a lower bound. This raises a pragmatic question, though: why invest effort, time and money into a formal proof that a piece of code is slow? What might be the point of such an endeavor? Taking inspiration from Clochard *et al.* [5], we answer this question by turning slowness into a quality. If there is a certain point at which a process might fail, then by showing that this process is slow, we can show that failure is far away into the future. More specifically, Clochard *et al.* propose two abstract types of integer counters, dubbed "one-time" integers and "peano" integers, and provide a paper proof that these counters cannot overflow in a feasible time: that is, it would take infeasible time (say, centuries) for an execution to reach a point where overflow actually occurs. To reflect this idea, we abandon the symmetry between time credits and time receipts and publish a fact about time receipts which has no counterpart on the time-credit side. This fact is an implication: ⧗$N \Rrightarrow_{\top} \mathsf{False}$, that is, "$N$ time receipts imply False". The global parameter N can be adjusted so as to represent one's idea of a running time that is infeasible, perhaps due to physical limitations, perhaps due to assumptions about the conditions in which the software is operated. In this paper, we explain what it means for the composite program logic to remain sound in the presence of this axiom, and provide a formal proof that Iris, extended with time receipts, is indeed sound. Furthermore, we verify that Clochard *et al.*'s ad hoc concepts of "one-time" integers and "peano" integers can be reconstructed in terms of time receipts, a more fundamental concept.

Finally, to demonstrate the combined use of time credits and receipts, we present a proof of the Union-Find data structure, where credits are used to express an amortized time complexity bound and receipts are used to prove that a node's integer rank cannot overflow, even if it is stored in very few bits.

In summary, the contributions of this paper are as follows:

1. A way of extending an off-the-shelf program logic with time credits and/or receipts, by composition with a program transformation.
2. Extensions of Iris with time credits and receipts, accompanied with machine-checked proofs of soundness.
3. A machine-checked reconstruction of Okasaki's debits as a library in Iris with time credits.
4. A machine-checked reconstruction of Clochard *et al.*'s "one-time" integers and "peano" integers in Iris with time receipts.
5. A machine-checked verification of Union-Find in Iris with time credits and receipts, offering both an amortized complexity bound and a safety guarantee despite the use of machine integers of very limited width.

All of the results reported in this paper have been checked in Coq [17].

2 A User's Overview of Time Credits and Time Receipts

2.1 Time Credits

A small number of axioms, presented in Fig. 1, govern time credits. The assertion $\$n$ denotes n time credits. The splitting axiom, a logical equivalence, means that *time credits can be split and combined.* Because Iris is an affine logic, it is implicitly understood that *time credits cannot be duplicated, but can be thrown away.*

The axiom $\mathsf{timeless}(\$n)$ means that time credits are independent of Iris' step-indexing. In practice, this allows an Iris invariant that involves time credits to be acquired without causing a "later" modality to appear [12, §5.7]. The reader can safely ignore this detail.

The last axiom, a Hoare triple, means that *every computation step requires and consumes one time credit.* As in Iris, the postconditions of our Hoare triples are λ-abstractions: they take as a parameter the return value of the term. At this point, *tick* () can be thought of as a pseudo-instruction that has no runtime effect and is implicitly inserted in front of every computation step.

$\$: \mathbb{N} \to iProp$	— there is such a thing as "n time credits"
$\mathsf{timeless}(\$n)$	— an Iris technicality
$\mathsf{True} \Rrightarrow_\top \$0$	— zero credits can be created out of thin air
$\$(n_1 + n_2) \equiv \$n_1 \ast \$n_2$	— credits can be split and combined
$tick : Val$	— there is a *tick* pseudo-op
$\{\$1\}\ tick\ (v)\ \{\lambda w.\, w = v\}$	— *tick* consumes one credit

Fig. 1. The axiomatic interface *TCIntf* of time credits

$⧗ : \mathbb{N} \to iProp$	— there is such a thing as "n time receipts"
$\mathsf{timeless}(⧗ n)$	— an Iris technicality
$\mathsf{True} \Rrightarrow_\top ⧗ 0$	— zero receipts can be created out of thin air
$⧗(n_1 + n_2) \equiv ⧗ n_1 \ast ⧗ n_2$	— receipts can be split and combined
$tick : Val$	— there is a *tick* pseudo-op
$\{\mathsf{True}\}\ tick\ (v)\ \{\lambda w.\, w = v \ast ⧗ 1\}$	— *tick* produces one receipt
$⧗ N \Rrightarrow_\top \mathsf{False}$	— no machine runs for N time steps

Fig. 2. The axiomatic interface of exclusive time receipts (further enriched in Fig. 3)

Time credits can be used to express *worst-case time complexity guarantees.* For instance, a sorting algorithm could have the following specification:

$$\begin{array}{c}\{array(a, xs) \ast n = |xs| \ast \$(6n \log n)\} \\ sort(a) \\ \{array(a, xs') \wedge xs' = \ldots\}\end{array}$$

Here, $array(a, xs)$ asserts the existence and unique ownership of an array at address a, holding the sequence of elements xs. This Hoare triple guarantees not only that the function call $sort(a)$ runs safely and has the effect of sorting the array at address a, but also that $sort(a)$ runs in at most $6n \log n$ time steps, where n is the length of the sequence xs, that is, the length of the array. Indeed, only $6n \log n$ time credits are provided in the precondition, so the algorithm does not have permission to run for a greater number of steps.

2.2 Time Receipts

In contrast with time credits, time receipts are a new concept, a contribution of this paper. We distinguish two forms of time receipts. The most basic form, *exclusive time receipts*, is the dual of time credits, in the sense that *every computation step produces one time receipt.* The second form, *persistent time receipts*, exhibits slightly different properties. Inspired by Clochard *et al.* [5], we show that time receipts can be used to *prove that certain undesirable events, such as integer overflows, cannot occur unless a program is allowed to execute for a very, very long time*—typically centuries. In the following, we explain that exclusive time receipts allow reconstructing Clochard *et al.*'s "one-time" integers [5, §3.2], which are so named because they are not duplicable, whereas persistent time receipts allow reconstructing their "peano" integers [5, §3.2], which are so named because they do not support unrestricted addition.

Exclusive time receipts. The assertion ⧗n denotes n time receipts. Like time credits, these time receipts are "exclusive", by which we mean that they are not duplicable. The basic laws that govern exclusive time receipts appear in Fig. 2. They are the same laws that govern time credits, with two differences. The first difference is that time receipts are the dual of time credits: the specification of *tick*, in this case, states that *every computation step produces one time receipt.*[1] The second difference lies in the last axiom of Fig. 2, which has no analogue in Fig. 1, and which we explain below.

In practice, how do we expect time receipts to be exploited? They can be used to prove lower bounds on the execution time of a program: if the Hoare triple $\{\mathsf{True}\}\ p\ \{⧗ n\}$ holds, then the execution of the program p cannot terminate in less than n steps. Inspired by Clochard *et al.* [5], we note that time receipts can also be used to *prove that certain undesirable events cannot occur in a feasible time.* This is done as follows. Let N be a fixed integer, chosen large enough that a modern processor cannot possibly execute N operations in a feasible time.[2] The last axiom of Fig. 2, $⧗ N \Rrightarrow_\top \mathsf{False}$, states that N time receipts imply a contradiction.[3] This axiom informally means that *we won't compute for N time steps*, because we cannot, or because we promise not to do such a thing. A consequence of this axiom is that ⧗n implies $n < N$: that is, *if we have observed n time steps, then n must be small.*

Adopting this axiom weakens the guarantee offered by the program logic. A Hoare triple $\{\mathsf{True}\}\ p\ \{\mathsf{True}\}$ no longer implies that the program p is forever safe. Instead, it means that p is $(N-1)$-safe: the execution of p cannot go wrong until at least $N - 1$ steps have been taken. Because N is very large, for many practical purposes, this is good enough.

How can this axiom be exploited in practice? We hinted above that it can be used to prove the absence of certain integer overflows. Suppose that we wish to use signed w-bit machine integers as a representation of mathematical integers. (For instance, let w be 64.) Whenever we perform an arithmetic operation, such as an addition, we must prove that no overflow can occur. This is reflected in the specification of the addition of two machine integers:

$$\begin{gathered}\{\iota(x_1) = n_1 \ * \ \iota(x_2) = n_2 \ * \ -2^{w-1} \le n_1 + n_2 < 2^{w-1}\} \\ add(x_1, x_2) \\ \{\lambda x.\, \iota(x) = n_1 + n_2\}\end{gathered}$$

Here, the variables x_i denote machine integers, while the auxiliary variables n_i denote mathematical integers, and the function ι is the injection of machine integers into mathematical integers. The conjunct $-2^{w-1} \le n_1 + n_2 < 2^{w-1}$ in the precondition represents an obligation to prove that no overflow can occur.

1 For now, we discuss time credits and time receipts separately, which is why we have different specifications for *tick* in either case. They are combined in Sect. 6.

2 For a specific example, let N be 2^{63}. Clochard *et al.* note that, even at the rate of one billion operations per second, it takes more than 292 years to execute 2^{63} operations. On a 64-bit machine, 2^{63} is also the maximum representable signed integer, plus one.

3 The connective $\Rrightarrow_\top$ is an Iris view shift, that is, a transition that can involve a side effect on ghost state.

Suppose now that the machine integers x_1 and x_2 represent the lengths of two disjoint linked lists that we wish to concatenate. To construct each of these lists, we must have spent a certain amount of time: as proofs of this work, let us assume that the assertions $\mathbf{⧗} n_1$ and $\mathbf{⧗} n_2$ are at hand. Let us further assume that the word size w is sufficiently large that it takes a very long time to count up to the largest machine integer. That is, let us make the following assumption:

$$N \leq 2^{w-1} \qquad \text{(large word size assumption)}$$

(E.g., with $N = 2^{63}$ and $w = 64$, this holds.) Then, we can prove that the addition of x_1 and x_2 is permitted. This goes as follows. From the separating conjunction $\mathbf{⧗} n_1 * \mathbf{⧗} n_2$, we get $\mathbf{⧗}(n_1 + n_2)$. The existence of these time receipts allows us to deduce $0 \leq n_1 + n_2 < N$, which implies $0 \leq n_1 + n_2 < 2^{w-1}$. Thus, the precondition of the addition operation $add(x_1, x_2)$ is met.

In summary, we have just verified that the addition of two machine integers satisfies the following alternative specification:

$$\begin{gathered} \{\iota(x_1) = n_1 * \mathbf{⧗} n_1 * \iota(x_2) = n_2 * \mathbf{⧗} n_2\} \\ add(x_1, x_2) \\ \{\lambda x.\, \iota(x) = n_1 + n_2 * \mathbf{⧗}(n_1 + n_2)\} \end{gathered}$$

This can be made more readable and more abstract by defining a "clock" to be a machine integer x accompanied with $\iota(x)$ time receipts:

$$clock(x) \triangleq \exists n.(\iota(x) = n * \mathbf{⧗} n)$$

Then, the above specification of addition can be reformulated as follows:

$$\begin{gathered} \{clock(x_1) * clock(x_2)\} \\ add(x_1, x_2) \\ \{\lambda x.\, clock(x) * \iota(x) = \iota(x_1) + \iota(x_2)\} \end{gathered}$$

In other words, clocks support unrestricted addition, without any risk of overflow. However, because time receipts cannot be duplicated, neither can clocks: $clock(x)$ does not entail $clock(x) * clock(x)$. In other words, a clock is uniquely owned. One can think of a clock x as a *hard-earned integer*: the owner of this clock has spent x units of time to obtain it.

Clocks are a reconstruction of Clochard *et al.*'s "one-time integers" [5], which support unrestricted addition, but cannot be duplicated. Whereas Clochard *et al.* view one-time integers as a primitive concept, and offer a direct paper proof of their soundness, we have just reconstructed them in terms of a more elementary notion, namely time receipts, and in the setting of a more powerful program logic, whose soundness is machine-checked, namely Iris.

Persistent time receipts. In addition to exclusive time receipts, it is useful to introduce a persistent form of time receipts.[4] The axioms that govern both exclusive and persistent time receipts appear in Fig. 3.

[4] Instead of viewing persistent time receipts as a primitive concept, one could define them as a library on top of exclusive time receipts. Unfortunately, this construction leads to slightly weaker laws, which is why we prefer to view them as primitive.

$⧗ : \mathbb{N} \to iProp$	— there is such a thing as "n exclusive time receipts"
$⧖ : \mathbb{N} \to iProp$	— and "a persistent receipt for n steps"
$\mathsf{timeless}(⧗ n) \wedge \mathsf{timeless}(⧖ n)$	— an Iris technicality
$\mathsf{persistent}(⧖ n)$	— persistent receipts are persistent
$\mathsf{True} \Rrightarrow_{\top} ⧗ 0$	— zero receipts can be created out of thin air
$⧗(n_1 + n_2) \equiv ⧗ n_1 \ast ⧗ n_2$	— exclusive receipts obey addition
$⧖ \max(n_1, n_2) \equiv ⧖ n_1 \ast ⧖ n_2$	— persistent receipts obey maximum
$⧗ n \Rrightarrow_{\top} ⧗ n \ast ⧖ n$	— taking a snapshot of n exclusive receipts yields a persistent receipt for n steps
$⧖ N \Rrightarrow_{\top} \mathsf{False}$	— no machine runs for N time steps
$tick : Val$	— there is a *tick* pseudo-op
$\{⧖ n\}$ $tick\ (v)$ $\{\lambda w.\, w = v \ast ⧗ 1 \ast ⧖(n+1)\}$	— *tick* produces one exclusive receipt, and can increment an existing persistent receipt

Fig. 3. The axiomatic interface *TRIntf* of time receipts

We write $⧖ n$ for a persistent receipt, a witness that at least n units of time have elapsed. (We avoid the terminology "n persistent time receipts", in the plural form, because persistent time receipts are not additive. We view $⧖ n$ as one receipt whose face value is n.) This assertion is persistent, which in Iris terminology means that once it holds, it holds forever. This implies, in particular, that it is duplicable: $⧖ n \equiv ⧖ n \ast ⧖ n$. It is created just by observing the existence of n exclusive time receipts, as stated by the following axiom, also listed in Fig. 3: $⧗ n \Rrightarrow_{\top} ⧗ n \ast ⧖ n$. Intuitively, someone who has access to the assertion $⧖ n$ is someone who knows that n units of work have been performed, even though they have not necessarily "personally" performed that work. Because this knowledge is not exclusive, the conjunction $⧖ n_1 \ast ⧖ n_2$ does not entail $⧖(n_1 + n_2)$. Instead, we have the following axiom, also listed in Fig. 3: $⧖(\max(n_1, n_2)) \equiv ⧖ n_1 \ast ⧖ n_2$.

More subtly, the specification of *tick* in Fig. 3 is stronger than the one in Fig. 2. According to this strengthened specification, *tick* () does not just produce an exclusive receipt $⧗ 1$. In addition to that, if a persistent time receipt $⧖ n$ is at hand, then *tick* () is able to increment it and to produce a new persistent receipt $⧖(n+1)$, thus reflecting the informal idea that a *new* unit of time has just been spent. A user who does not wish to make use of this feature can pick $n = 0$ and recover the specification of *tick* in Fig. 2 as a special case.

Finally, because $⧖ n$ means that n steps have been taken, and because we promise never to reach N steps, we adopt the axiom $⧖ N \Rrightarrow_{\top} \mathsf{False}$, also listed in Fig. 3. It implies the earlier axiom $⧗ N \Rrightarrow_{\top} \mathsf{False}$, which is therefore not explicitly shown in Fig. 3.

In practice, how are persistent time receipts exploited? By analogy with clocks, let us define a predicate for a machine integer x accompanied with $\iota(x)$ persistent time receipts:

$$snapclock(x) \triangleq \exists n.(\iota(x) = n \ast ⧖ n)$$

By construction, this predicate is persistent, therefore duplicable:

$$snapclock(x) \equiv snapclock(x) \ * \ snapclock(x)$$

We refer to this concept as a "snapclock", as it is not a clock, but can be thought of as a snapshot of some clock. Thanks to the axiom $\text{⧗} k \Rrightarrow_{\top} \text{⧗} k \ * \ \text{⧖} k$, we have:

$$clock(x) \Rrightarrow_{\top} clock(x) \ * \ snapclock(x)$$

Furthermore, snapclocks have the valuable property that, by performing just one step of extra work, a snapclock can be incremented, yielding a new snapclock that is greater by one. That is, the following Hoare triple holds:

$$\begin{array}{c}\{snapclock(x)\} \\ tick\ (); add(x, 1) \\ \{\lambda x'.\ snapclock(x') \ * \ \iota(x') = \iota(x) + 1\}\end{array}$$

The proof is not difficult. Unfolding $snapclock(x)$ in the precondition yields $\text{⧖} n$, where $\iota(x) = n$. As per the strengthened specification of *tick*, the execution of *tick* () then yields $\text{⧗} 1 \ * \ \text{⧖}(n+1)$. As in the case of clocks, the assertion $\text{⧖}(n+1)$ implies $0 \leq n+1 < 2^{w-1}$, which means that no overflow can occur. Finally, $\text{⧗} 1$ is thrown away and $\text{⧖}(n+1)$ is used to justify $snapclock(x')$ in the postcondition.

Adding two arbitrary snapclocks x_1 and x_2 is illegal: from the sole assumption $snapclock(x_1) \ * \ snapclock(x_2)$, one cannot prove that the addition of x_1 and x_2 won't cause an overflow, and one cannot prove that its result is a valid snapclock. However, snapclocks do support a restricted form of addition. The addition of two snapclocks x_1 and x_2 is safe, and produces a valid snapclock x, provided it is known ahead of time that its result is less than some preexisting snapclock y:

$$\begin{array}{c}\{snapclock(x_1) \ * \ snapclock(x_2) \ * \ \iota(x_1 + x_2) \leq \iota(y) \ * \ snapclock(y)\} \\ add(x_1, x_2) \\ \{\lambda x.\ snapclock(x) \ * \ \iota(x) = \iota(x_1) + \iota(x_2)\}\end{array}$$

Snapclocks are a reconstruction of Clochard *et al.*'s "peano integers" [5], which are so named because they do not support unrestricted addition. Clocks and snapclocks represent different compromises: whereas clocks support addition but not duplication, snapclocks support duplication but not addition. They are useful in different scenarios: as a rule of thumb, if an integer counter is involved in the implementation of a mutable data structure, then one should attempt to view it as a clock; if it is involved in the implementation of a persistent data structure, then one should attempt to view it as a snapclock.

3 HeapLang and the Tick Translation

In the next section (Sect. 4), we extend Iris with time credits, yielding a new program logic Iris$^{\$}$. We do this *without modifying* Iris. Instead, we *compose* Iris with a program transformation, the "tick translation", which inserts *tick*()

instructions into the code in front of every computation step. In the construction of $\text{Iris}^{⧗}$, our extension of Iris with time receipts, the tick translation is exploited in a similar way (Sect. 5). In this section, we define the tick translation and state some of its properties.

Iris is a generic program logic: it can be instantiated with an arbitrary calculus for which a small-step operational semantics is available [12]. Ideally, our extension of Iris should take place at this generic level, so that it, too, can be instantiated for an arbitrary calculus. Unfortunately, it seems difficult to define the tick translation and to prove it correct in a generic manner. For this reason, we choose to work in the setting of HeapLang [12], an untyped λ-calculus equipped with Booleans, signed machine integers, products, sums, recursive functions, references, and shared-memory concurrency. The three standard operations on mutable references, namely allocation, reading, and writing, are available. A compare-and-set operation **CAS** (e_1, e_2, e_3) and an operation for spawning a new thread are also provided. As the syntax and operational semantics of HeapLang are standard and very much irrelevant in this paper, we omit them. They appear in our online repository [17].

The tick translation transforms a HeapLang expression e to a HeapLang expression $\langle\!\langle e \rangle\!\rangle_{tick}$. It is parameterized by a value *tick*. Its effect is to insert a call to *tick* in front of every operation in the source expression e. The translation of a function application, for instance, is as follows:

$$\langle\!\langle e_1\ (e_2) \rangle\!\rangle_{tick} = tick\ (\langle\!\langle e_1 \rangle\!\rangle_{tick})\ (\langle\!\langle e_2 \rangle\!\rangle_{tick})$$

For convenience, we assume that *tick* can be passed an arbitrary value v as an argument, and returns v. Because evaluation in HeapLang is call-by-value and happens to be right-to-left[5], the above definition means that, after evaluating the argument $\langle\!\langle e_2 \rangle\!\rangle_{tick}$ and the function $\langle\!\langle e_1 \rangle\!\rangle_{tick}$, we invoke *tick*, then carry on with the function call. This translation is syntactically well-behaved: it preserves the property of being a value, and commutes with substitution. This holds for every value *tick*.

$$\begin{aligned} tick_c \triangleq \mathtt{rec}\ & self(x) = \\ & \mathtt{let}\ k = !\, c\ \mathtt{in} \\ & \mathtt{if}\ k = 0\ \mathtt{then}\ oops\ () \\ & \mathtt{else\ if}\ \mathbf{CAS}(c, k, k-1)\ \mathtt{then}\ x\ \mathtt{else}\ self\ (x) \end{aligned}$$

Fig. 4. Implementation of $tick_c$ in HeapLang

As far the end user is concerned, *tick* remains abstract (Sect. 2). Yet, in our constructions of $\text{Iris}^{\$}$ and $\text{Iris}^{⧗}$, we must provide a concrete implementation of it in HeapLang. This implementation, named $tick_c$, appears in Fig. 4. A global

[5] If HeapLang used left-to-right evaluation, the definition of the translation would be slightly different, but the lemmas that we prove would be the same.

integer counter c stores the number of computation steps that the program is still allowed to take. The call $\mathit{tick}_c\,()$ decrements a global counter c, if this counter holds a nonzero value, and otherwise invokes $\mathit{oops}\,()$.

At this point, the memory location c and the value oops are parameters.

We stress that tick_c plays a role only in the proofs of soundness of Iris$^{\$}$ and Iris$^{⧗}$. It is never actually executed, nor is it shown to the end user.

Once tick is instantiated with tick_c, one can prove that the translation is correct in the following sense: the translated code takes the same computation steps as the source code and additionally keeps track of how many steps are taken. More specifically, if the source code can make n computation steps, and if c is initialized with a value m that is sufficiently large (that is, $m \geq n$), then the translated code can make n computation steps as well, and c is decremented from m to $m - n$ in the process.

Lemma 1 (Reduction Preservation). *Assume there is a reduction sequence:*

$$(T_1, \sigma_1) \rightarrow^n_{\mathsf{tp}} (T_2, \sigma_2)$$

Assume c is fresh for this reduction sequence. Let $m \geq n$. Then, there exists a reduction sequence:

$$(\langle\!\langle T_1 \rangle\!\rangle, \langle\!\langle \sigma_1 \rangle\!\rangle\,[c \leftarrow m]) \rightarrow^*_{\mathsf{tp}} (\langle\!\langle T_2 \rangle\!\rangle, \langle\!\langle \sigma_2 \rangle\!\rangle\,[c \leftarrow m - n])$$

In this statement, the metavariable T stands for a thread pool, while σ stands for a heap. The relation $\rightarrow_{\mathsf{tp}}$ is HeapLang's "threadpool reduction". For the sake of brevity, we write just $\langle\!\langle e \rangle\!\rangle$ for $\langle\!\langle e \rangle\!\rangle_{\mathit{tick}_c}$, that is, for the translation of the expression e, where tick is instantiated with tick_c. This notation is implicitly dependent on the parameters c and oops.

The above lemma holds for every choice of oops. Indeed, because the counter c initially holds the value m, and because we have $m \geq n$, the counter is never about to fall below zero, so oops is never invoked.

The next lemma also holds for every choice of oops. It states that if the translated program is safe and if the counter c has not yet reached zero then the source program is not just about to crash.

Lemma 2 (Immediate Safety Preservation). *Assume c is fresh for e. Let $m > 0$. If the configuration $(\langle\!\langle e \rangle\!\rangle, \langle\!\langle \sigma \rangle\!\rangle\,[c \leftarrow m])$ is safe, then either e is a value or the configuration (e, σ) is reducible.*

By combining Lemmas 1 and 2 and by contraposition, we find that safety is preserved backwards, as follows: if, when the counter c is initialized with m, the translated program $\langle\!\langle e \rangle\!\rangle$ is safe, then the source program e is m-safe.

Lemma 3 (Safety Preservation). *If for every location c the configuration $(\langle\!\langle T \rangle\!\rangle, \langle\!\langle \sigma \rangle\!\rangle\,[c \leftarrow m])$ is safe, then the configuration (T, σ) is m-safe.*

4 Iris with Time Credits

The authors of Iris [12] have used Coq both to check that Iris is sound and to offer an implementation of Iris that can be used to carry out proofs of programs. The two are tied: if $\{\mathsf{True}\}\ p\ \{\mathsf{True}\}$ can be established by applying the proof rules of Iris, then one gets a self-contained Coq proof that the program p is safe.

In this section, we temporarily focus on time credits and explain how we extend Iris with time credits, yielding a new program logic Iris$^{\$}$. The new logic is defined in Coq and still offers an end-to-end guarantee: if $\{\$k\}\ p\ \{\mathsf{True}\}$ can be established in Coq by applying the proof rules of Iris$^{\$}$, then one has proved in Coq that p is safe and runs in at most k steps.

To define Iris$^{\$}$, we compose Iris with the tick translation. We are then able to argue that, because this program transformation is operationally correct (that is, it faithfully accounts for the passing of time), and because Iris is sound (that is, it faithfully approximates the behavior of programs), the result of the composition is a sound program logic that is able to reason about time.

In the following, we view the interface *TCIntf* as explicitly parameterized over \$ and *tick*. Thus, we write "*TCIntf* (\$) *tick*" for the separating conjunction of all items in Fig. 1 except the declarations of \$ and *tick*.

We require the end user, who wishes to perform proofs of programs in Iris$^{\$}$, to work with Iris$^{\$}$ triples, which are defined as follows:

Definition 1 (Iris$^{\$}$ triple). *An* Iris$^{\$}$ triple $\{P\}\ e\ \{\Phi\}_{\$}$ *is syntactic sugar for:*

$$\forall(\$: \mathbb{N} \rightarrow iProp) \quad \forall tick \qquad TCIntf\ (\$)\ tick \ \twoheadrightarrow\ \{P\}\ \langle\!\langle e \rangle\!\rangle_{tick}\ \{\Phi\}$$

Thus, an Iris$^{\$}$ triple is in reality an Iris triple about the instrumented expression $\langle\!\langle e \rangle\!\rangle_{tick}$. While proving this Iris triple, the end user is given an abstract view of the predicate \$ and the instruction *tick*. He does not have access to their concrete definitions, but does have access to the laws that govern them.

We prove that Iris$^{\$}$ is sound in the following sense:

Theorem 1 (Soundness of Iris$^{\$}$). *If* $\{\$n\}\ e\ \{\mathsf{True}\}_{\$}$ *holds, then the machine configuration* $(e, \varnothing)$*, where* $\varnothing$ *is the empty heap, is safe and terminates in at most* n *steps.*

In other words, a program that is initially granted n time credits cannot run for more than n steps. To establish this theorem, we proceed roughly as follows:

1. we provide a concrete definition of *tick*;
2. we provide a concrete definition of \$ and prove that *TCIntf* (\$) *tick* holds;
3. this yields $\{\$n\}\ \langle\!\langle e \rangle\!\rangle_{tick}\ \{\mathsf{True}\}$; from this and from the correctness of the tick translation, we deduce that e cannot crash or run for more than n steps.

Step 1. Our first step is to provide an implementation of *tick*. As announced earlier (Sect. 3), we use $tick_c$ (Fig. 4). We instantiate the parameter *oops* with *crash*, an arbitrary function whose application is unsafe. (That is, *crash* is chosen so that *crash* () reduces to a stuck term.) For the moment, c remains a parameter.

With these concrete choices of *tick* and *oops*, the translation transforms an out-of-time-budget condition into a hard crash. Because Iris forbids crashes, Iris$^{\$}$, which is the composition of the translation with Iris, will forbid out-of-time-budget conditions, as desired.

For technical reasons, we need two more lemmas about the translation, whose proofs rely on the fact that *oops* is instantiated with *crash*. They are slightly modified or strengthened variants of Lemmas 2 and 3. First, if the source code can take one step, then the translated code, supplied with zero budget, crashes. Second, if the translated code, supplied with a runtime budget of m, does *not* crash, then the source code terminates in at most m steps.

Lemma 4 (Credit Exhaustion). *Suppose the configuration* (T, σ) *is reducible. Then, for all* c*, the configuration* $(\langle\!\langle T \rangle\!\rangle, \langle\!\langle \sigma \rangle\!\rangle\,[c \leftarrow 0])$ *is unsafe.*

Lemma 5 (Safety Preservation, Strengthened). *If for every location* c *the configuration* $(\langle\!\langle T \rangle\!\rangle, \langle\!\langle \sigma \rangle\!\rangle\,[c \leftarrow m])$ *is safe, then* (T, σ) *is safe and terminates in at most* m *steps.*

Step 2. Our second step, roughly, is to exhibit a definition of $\$: \mathbb{N} \rightarrow \mathit{iProp}$ such that $\mathit{TCIntf}\ (\$)\ \mathit{tick}_c$ is satisfied. That is, we would like to prove something along the lines of: $\exists(\$: \mathbb{N} \rightarrow \mathit{iProp})\quad \mathit{TCIntf}\ (\$)\ \mathit{tick}_c$. However, these informal sentences do not quite make sense. This formula is not an ordinary proposition: it is an Iris assertion, of type *iProp*. Thus, it does not make sense to say that this formula "is true" in an absolute manner. Instead, we prove in Iris that we can *make this assertion true* by performing a view shift, that is, a number of operations that have no runtime effect, such as allocating a ghost location and imposing an invariant that ties this ghost state with the physical state of the counter c. This is stated as follows:

Lemma 6 (Time Credit Initialization). *For every* c *and* n*, the following Iris view shift holds:*

$$(c \mapsto n) \ \Rrightarrow_{\top}\ \exists(\$: \mathbb{N} \rightarrow \mathit{iProp}) \quad (\mathit{TCIntf}\ (\$)\ \mathit{tick}_c \ * \ \$n)$$

In this statement, on the left-hand side of the view shift symbol, we find the "points-to" assertion $c \mapsto n$, which represents the unique ownership of the memory location c and the assumption that its initial value is n. This assertion no longer appears on the right-hand side of the view shift. This reflects the fact that, when the view shift takes place, it becomes impossible to access c directly; the only way of accessing it is via the operation tick_c.

On the right-hand side of the view shift symbol, beyond the existential quantifier, we find a conjunction of the assertion $\mathit{TCIntf}\ (\$)\ \mathit{tick}_c$, which means that the laws of time credits are satisfied, and $\$n$, which means that there are initially n time credits in existence.

In the interest of space, we provide only a brief summary of the proof of Lemma 6; the reader is referred to the extended version of this paper [18, Appendix A] for more details. In short, the assertion $\$1$ is defined in such a way that it represents an exclusive contribution of one unit to the current value of the global counter c. In other words, we install the following invariant: at every time, the current value of c is (at least) the sum of all time credits in existence. Thus, the assertion $\$1$ guarantees that c is nonzero, and can be viewed as a permission to decrement c by one. This allows us to prove that the specification of *tick* in Fig. 1 is satisfied by our concrete implementation $tick_c$. In particular, $tick_c$ cannot cause a crash: indeed, under the precondition $\$1$, c is not in danger of falling below zero, and *crash* () is not executed—it is in fact dead code.

Step 3. In the last reasoning step, we complete the proof of Theorem 1. The proof is roughly as follows. Suppose the end user has established $\{\$n\}\, e\, \{\mathsf{True}\}_{\$}$. By Safety Preservation, Strengthened (Lemma 5), to prove that $(e, \varnothing)$ is safe and runs in at most n steps, it suffices to show (for an arbitrary location c) that the translated expression $\langle\!\langle e \rangle\!\rangle$, executed in the initial heap $\varnothing\,[c \leftarrow n]$, is safe. To do so, beginning with this initial heap, we perform Time Credit Initialization, that is, we execute the view shift whose statement appears in Lemma 6. This yields an abstract predicate $\$$ as well as the assertions *TCIntf* ($\$$) *tick* and $\$n$. At this point, we unfold the Iris$^{\$}$ triple $\{\$n\}\, e\, \{\mathsf{True}\}_{\$}$, yielding an implication (see Definition 1), and apply it to $\$$, to $tick_c$, and to the hypothesis *TCIntf* ($\$$) *tick*. This yields the Iris triple $\{\$n\}\ \langle\!\langle e \rangle\!\rangle\ \{\mathsf{True}\}$. Because we have $\$n$ at hand and because Iris is sound [12], this implies that $\langle\!\langle e \rangle\!\rangle$ is safe. This concludes the proof.

This last step is, we believe, where the modularity of our approach shines. Iris' soundness theorem is re-used as a black box, without change. In fact, any program logic other than Iris could be used as a basis for our construction, as along as it is expressive enough to prove Time Credit Initialization (Lemma 6). The last ingredient, Safety Preservation, Strengthened (Lemma 5), involves only the operational semantics of HeapLang, and is independent of Iris.

This was just an informal account of our proof. For further details, the reader is referred to the online repository [17].

5 Iris with Time Receipts

In this section, we extend Iris with time receipts and prove the soundness of the new logic, dubbed Iris$^{⧗}$. To do so, we follow the scheme established in the previous section (Sect. 4), and compose Iris with the tick translation.

From here on, let us view the interface of time receipts as parameterized over ⧗, ⧖, and *tick*. Thus, we write "*TRIntf* (⧗) (⧖) *tick*" for the separating conjunction of all items in Fig. 3 except the declarations of ⧗, ⧖, and *tick*.

As in the case of credits, the user is given an abstract view of time receipts:

Definition 2 (Iris$^{⧗}$ triple). *An* Iris$^{⧗}$ triple $\{P\}\, e\, \{\Phi\}_{⧗}$ *is syntactic sugar for:*

$$\forall (⧗, ⧖ : \mathbb{N} \to iProp) \quad \forall tick \qquad TRIntf\ (⧗)\ (⧖)\ tick \ \ \text{-}\!\!*\ \ \{P\}\ \langle\!\langle e \rangle\!\rangle_{tick}\ \{\Phi\}$$

Theorem 2 (Soundness of Iris$^{⧗}$). *If* $\{\mathsf{True}\}\, e\, \{\mathsf{True}\}_{⧗}$ *holds, then the machine configuration* $(e, \varnothing)$ *is* $(N-1)$*-safe.*

As indicated earlier, we assume that the end user is interested in proving that crashes cannot occur until a very long time has elapsed, which is why we state the theorem in this way.[6] Whereas an Iris triple $\{\mathsf{True}\}\, e\, \{\mathsf{True}\}$ guarantees that e is safe, the Iris$^{⧗}$ triple $\{\mathsf{True}\}\, e\, \{\mathsf{True}\}_{⧗}$ guarantees that it takes at least $N-1$ steps of computation for e to crash. In this statement, N is the global parameter that appears in the axiom $⧖ N \Rrightarrow_{\top} \mathsf{False}$ (Fig. 3). Compared with Iris, Iris$^{⧗}$ provides a weaker safety guarantee, but offers additional reasoning principles, leading to increased convenience and modularity.

In order to establish Theorem 2, we again proceed in three steps:

1. provide a concrete definition of *tick*;
2. provide concrete definitions of $⧗, ⧖$ and prove that $\mathit{TRIntf}\ (⧗)\ (⧖)\ \mathit{tick}$ holds;
3. from $\{\mathsf{True}\}\ \langle\!\langle e \rangle\!\rangle_{\mathit{tick}}\ \{\mathsf{True}\}$, deduce that e is $(N-1)$-safe.

Step 1. In this step, we keep our concrete implementation of *tick*, namely tick_c (Fig. 4). One difference with the case of time credits, though, is that we plan to initialize c with $N-1$. Another difference is that, this time, we instantiate the parameter *oops* with *loop*, where *loop* () is an arbitrary divergent term.[7]

Step 2. The next step is to prove that we are able to establish the time receipt interface. We prove the following:

Lemma 7 (Time Receipt Initialization). *For every location c, the following Iris view shift holds:*

$$(c \mapsto N-1) \quad \Rrightarrow_{\top} \quad \exists(⧗, ⧖ : \mathbb{N} \to \mathit{iProp}) \quad \mathit{TRIntf}\ (⧗)\ (⧖)\ \mathit{tick}_c$$

We provide only a brief summary of the proof of Lemma 7; for further details, the reader is referred to the extended version of this paper [18, Appendix B]. Roughly speaking, we install the invariant that c holds $N-1-i$, where i is some number that satisfies $0 \le i < N$. We define $⧗ n$ as an exclusive contribution of n units to the current value of i, and define $⧖ n$ as an observation that i is at least n. (i grows with time, so such an observation is stable.) As part of the proof of the above lemma, we check that the specification of *tick* holds:

$$\{⧖ n\}\ \mathit{tick}\ (v)\ \{\lambda w.\, w = v\ *\ ⧗ 1\ *\ ⧖(n+1)\}$$

In contrast with the case of time credits, in this case, the precondition $⧖ n$ does *not* guarantee that c holds a nonzero value. Thus, it *is* possible for *tick*() to be executed when c is zero. This is not a problem, though, because *loop*() is safe to execute in any situation: it satisfies the Hoare triple $\{\mathsf{True}\}\ \mathit{loop}()\ \{\mathsf{False}\}$. In other words, when c is about to fall below zero and therefore the invariant $i < N$ seems about to be broken, *loop* () saves the day by running away and never allowing execution to continue normally.

---

[6] If the user instead wishes to establish a lower bound on a program's execution time, this is possible as well.

[7] In fact, it is not essential that *loop*() diverges. What matters is that *loop* satisfy the Iris triple $\{\mathsf{True}\}\ \mathit{loop}()\ \{\mathsf{False}\}$. A fatal runtime error that Iris does *not* rule out would work just as well, as it satisfies the same specification.

Step 3. In the last reasoning step, we complete the proof of Theorem 2. Suppose the end user has established $\{\mathsf{True}\}\, e\, \{\mathsf{True}\}_{⧗}$. By Safety Preservation (Lemma 3), to prove that $(e, \varnothing)$ is $(N-1)$-safe, it suffices to show (for an arbitrary location c) that $\langle\!\langle e \rangle\!\rangle$, executed in the initial heap $\varnothing\,[c \leftarrow N-1]$, is safe. To do so, beginning with this initial heap, we perform Time Receipt Initialization, that is, we execute the view shift whose statement appears in Lemma 7. This yields two abstract predicates ⧗ and ⧖ as well as the assertion TRIntf (⧗) (⧖) tick. At this point, we unfold $\{\mathsf{True}\}\, e\, \{\mathsf{True}\}_{⧗}$ (see Definition 2), yielding an implication, and apply this implication, yielding the Iris triple $\{\mathsf{True}\}\, \langle\!\langle e \rangle\!\rangle\, \{\mathsf{True}\}$. Because Iris is sound [12], this implies that $\langle\!\langle e \rangle\!\rangle$ is safe. This concludes the proof. For further detail, the reader is again referred to our online repository [17].

6 Marrying Time Credits and Time Receipts

It seems desirable to combine time credits and time receipts in a single program logic, Iris$^{\$⧗}$. We have done so [17]. In short, following the scheme of Sects. 4 and 5, the definition of Iris$^{\$⧗}$ involves composing Iris with the tick translation. This time, *tick* serves two purposes: it consumes one time credit *and* produces one exclusive time receipt (and increments a persistent time receipt). Thus, its specification is as follows:

$$\{\$1 \ast ⧖ n\}\ \mathit{tick}\,(v)\ \{\lambda w.\, w = v \ast ⧗ 1 \ast ⧖(n+1)\}$$

Let us write $\mathit{TCTRIntf}$ (\$) (⧗) (⧖) tick for the combined interface of time credits and time receipts. This interface combines all of the axioms of Figs. 1 and 3, but declares a single *tick* function[8] and proposes a single specification for it, which is the one shown above.

Definition 3 (Iris$^{\$⧗}$ triple). *An* Iris$^{\$⧗}$ triple $\{P\}\, e\, \{\Phi\}_{\$⧗}$ *stands for:*

$$\forall\, (\$)\, (⧗)\, (⧖)\, \mathit{tick} \qquad \mathit{TCTRIntf}\ (\$)\ (⧗)\ (⧖)\ \mathit{tick}\ \twoheadrightarrow\ \{P\}\ \langle\!\langle e \rangle\!\rangle_{\mathit{tick}}\ \{\Phi\}$$

Theorem 3 (Soundness of Iris$^{\$⧗}$). *If* $\{\$n\}\, e\, \{\mathsf{True}\}_{\$⧗}$ *holds then the machine configuration* $(e, \varnothing)$ *is* $(N-1)$*-safe. If furthermore* $n < N$ *holds, then this machine configuration terminates in at most* n *steps.*

Iris$^{\$⧗}$ allows exploiting time credits to prove time complexity bounds and, at the same time, exploiting time receipts to prove the absence of certain integer overflows. Our verification of Union-Find (Sect. 8) illustrates these two aspects.

Guéneau *et al.* [7] use time credits to reason about asymptotic complexity, that is, about the manner in which a program's complexity grows as the size of its input grows towards infinity. Does such asymptotic reasoning make sense in Iris$^{\$⧗}$, where no program is ever executed for N time steps or beyond? It

[8] Even though the interface provides only one *tick* function, it gets instantiated in the soundness theorem with different implementations depending on whether there are more than N time credits or not.

seems to be the case that if a program p satisfies the triple $\{\$n\}\; p\; \{\Phi\}_{\$⧗}$, then it also satisfies the stronger triple $\{\$\min(n, N)\}\; p\; \{\Phi\}_{\$⧗}$, therefore also satisfies $\{\$N\}\; p\; \{\Phi\}_{\$⧗}$. Can one therefore conclude that p has "constant time complexity"? We believe not. Provided N is considered a parameter, as opposed to a constant, one *cannot* claim that "N is $O(1)$", so $\{\$\min(n, N)\}\; p\; \{\Phi\}_{\$⧗}$ does not imply that "p runs in constant time". In other words, a universal quantification on N should come *after* the existential quantifier that is implicit in the O notation. We have not yet attempted to implement this idea; this remains a topic for further investigation.

7 Application: Thunks in Iris$^{\$}$

In this section, we illustrate the power of Iris$^{\$}$ by constructing an implementation of thunks as a library in Iris$^{\$}$. A *thunk*, also known as a *suspension*, is a very simple data structure that represents a suspended computation. There are two operations on thunks, namely *create*, which constructs a new thunk, and *force*, which demands the result of a thunk. A thunk memoizes its result, so that even if it is forced multiple times, the computation only takes place once.

Okasaki [19] proposes a methodology for reasoning about the amortized time complexity of computations that involve shared thunks. For every thunk, he keeps track of a *debit*, which can be thought of as an amount of credit that one must still pay before one is allowed to force this thunk. A ghost operation, *pay*, changes one's view of a thunk, by reducing the debit associated with this thunk. *force* can be applied only to a zero-debit thunk, and has amortized cost $O(1)$. Indeed, if this thunk has been forced already, then *force* really requires constant time; and if this thunk is being forced for the first time, then the cost of performing the suspended computation must have been paid for in advance, possibly in several installments, via *pay*. This discipline is sound even in the presence of sharing, that is, of multiple pointers to a thunk. Indeed, whereas duplicating a credit is unsound, duplicating a debit leads to an over-approximation of the true cost, hence is sound. Danielsson [6] formulates Okasaki's ideas as a type system, which he proves sound in Agda. Pilkiewicz and Pottier [20] reconstruct this type discipline in the setting of a lower-level type system, equipped with basic notions of time credits, hidden state, and monotonic state. Unfortunately, their type system is presented in an informal manner and does not come with a proof of type soundness.

We reproduce Pilkiewicz and Pottier's construction in the formal setting of Iris$^{\$}$. Indeed, Iris$^{\$}$ offers all of the necessary ingredients, namely time credits, hidden state (invariants, in Iris terminology) and monotonic state (a special case of Iris' ghost state). Our reconstruction is carried out inside Coq [17].

7.1 Concurrency and Reentrancy

One new problem that arises here is that Okasaki's analysis, which is valid in a sequential setting, potentially becomes invalid in a concurrent setting. Suppose we wish to allow multiple threads to safely share access to a thunk. A natural, simple-minded approach would be to equip every thunk with a lock and allow competition over this lock. Then, unfortunately, forcing would become a blocking operation: one thread could waste time waiting for another thread to finish forcing. In fact, in the absence of a fairness assumption about the scheduler, an unbounded amount of time could be wasted in this way. This appears to invalidate the property that *force* has amortized cost $O(1)$.

Technically, the manner in which this problem manifests itself in Iris$^{\$}$ is in the specification of locks. Whereas in Iris a spin lock can be implemented and proved correct with respect to a simple and well-understood specification [2], in Iris$^{\$}$, it cannot. The *lock*() method contains a potentially infinite loop: therefore, no finite amount of time credits is sufficient to prove that *lock*() is safe. This issue is discussed in greater depth later on (Sect. 9).

A distinct yet related problem is reentrancy. Arguably, an implementation of thunks should guarantee that a suspended computation is evaluated at most once. This guarantee seems particularly useful when the computation has a side effect: the user can then rely on the fact that this side effect occurs at most once. However, this property does not naturally hold: in the presence of heap-allocated mutable state, it is possible to construct an ill-behaved "reentrant" thunk which, when forced, attempts to recursively force itself. Thus, something must be done to dynamically reject or statically prevent reentrancy. In Pilkiewicz and Pottier's code [20], reentrancy is detected at runtime, thanks to a three-color scheme, and causes a fatal runtime failure. In a concurrent system where each thunk is equipped with a lock, reentrancy is also detected at runtime, and turned into deadlock; but we have explained earlier why we wish to avoid locks.

Fortunately, Iris provides us with a static mechanism for forbidding both concurrency and reentrancy. We introduce a unique token $\lightning$, which can be thought of as "permission to use the thunk API", and set things up so that *pay* and *force* require and return $\lightning$. This forbids concurrency: two operations on thunks cannot take place concurrently. Furthermore, when a user-supplied suspended computation is executed, the token $\lightning$ is *not* transmitted to it. This forbids reentrancy.[9] The implementation of this token relies on Iris' "nonatomic invariants" (Sect. 7.4). With these restrictions, we are able to prove that Okasaki's discipline is sound.

7.2 Implementation of Thunks

A simple implementation of thunks in HeapLang appears in Fig. 5. A thunk can be in one of two states: *White f* and *Black v*. A white thunk is unevaluated:

[9] Therefore, a suspended computation cannot force *any* thunk. This is admittedly a very severe restriction, which rules out many useful applications of thunks. In fact, we have implemented a more flexible discipline, where thunks can be grouped in multiple "regions" and there is one token per region instead of a single global $\lightning$ token. This discipline allows concurrent or reentrant operations on provably distinct thunks, yet can still be proven sound.

$$
\begin{array}{rl}
\mathit{create} \triangleq & \lambda f.\, \mathtt{ref}(\mathit{White}\ f) \\
\mathit{force} \triangleq & \lambda t.\, \mathtt{match}\ !\, t\ \mathtt{with} \\
& \quad \mathit{White}\ f \Rightarrow \mathtt{let}\ v = f\ ()\ \mathtt{in}\ t \leftarrow \mathit{Black}\ v\ ;\ v \\
& \quad \mid \mathit{Black}\ v \Rightarrow v \\
& \quad \mathtt{end}
\end{array}
$$

Fig. 5. An implementation of thunks

$\mathsf{isThunk} : \mathit{Loc} \to \mathbb{N} \to (\mathit{Val} \to \mathit{iProp}) \to \mathit{iProp}$	— there exist "thunks"
$\mathsf{persistent}(\mathsf{isThunk}\ t\ n\ \Phi)$	— thunks can be shared
$n_1 \leq n_2 \mathrel{-\!\!*}$ $\mathsf{isThunk}\ t\ n_1\ \Phi \mathrel{-\!\!*} \mathsf{isThunk}\ t\ n_2\ \Phi$	— it is sound to overestimate a debt
$\lightning : \mathit{iProp}$	— there exist "thunderbolts"
$\lightning$	— the user is handed one
$\{\$3 * \{\$n\}\ \langle\langle f\ ()\rangle\rangle\ \{\Phi\}\}$ $\langle\langle \mathit{create}\ (f)\rangle\rangle$ $\{\lambda t.\, \mathsf{isThunk}\ t\ n\ \Phi\}$	— a computation of cost n gives rise to an n-debit thunk; the cost is $O(1)$
$(\forall v.\, \mathsf{duplicable}(\Phi\ v)) \mathrel{-\!\!*}$ $\{\$11 * \mathsf{isThunk}\ t\ 0\ \Phi * \lightning\}$ $\langle\langle \mathit{force}\ (t)\rangle\rangle$ $\{\lambda v.\, \Phi\ v * \lightning\}$	— a 0-debit thunk can be forced; the thunderbolt is required; the cost is $O(1)$
$\mathsf{isThunk}\ t\ n\ \Phi * \$k * \lightning$ $\Rrightarrow_{\top}\ \mathsf{isThunk}\ t\ (n-k)\ \Phi * \lightning$	— paying reduces one's debt

Fig. 6. A simple specification of thunks in Iris$^{\$}$

the function f represents a suspended computation. A black thunk is evaluated: the value v is the result of the computation that has been performed already. Two colors are sufficient: because our static discipline rules out reentrancy, there is no need for a third color, whose purpose would be to dynamically detect an attempt to force a thunk that is already being forced.

7.3 Specification of Thunks in Iris$^{\$}$

Our specification of thunks appears in Fig. 6. It declares an abstract predicate $\mathsf{isThunk}\ t\ n\ \Phi$, which asserts that t is a valid thunk, that the debt associated with this thunk is n, and that this thunk (once forced) produces a value that satisfies the postcondition Φ. The number n, a *debit*, is the number of credits that remain to be paid before this thunk can be forced. The postcondition Φ is chosen by the user when a thunk is created. It must be duplicable (this is required in the specification of *force*) because *force* can be invoked several times and we must guarantee, every time, that the result v satisfies $\Phi\ v$.

The second axiom states that $\mathsf{isThunk}\ t\ n\ \Phi$ is a persistent assertion. This means that a valid thunk, once created, remains a valid thunk forever. Among other things, it is permitted to create two pointers to a single thunk and to reason independently about each of these pointers.

The third axiom states that isThunk $t\ n\ \Phi$ is covariant in its parameter n. Overestimating a debt still leads to a correct analysis of a program's worst-case time complexity.

Next, the specification declares an abstract assertion $\lightning$, and provides the user with one copy of this assertion. We refer to it as "the thunderbolt".

The next item in Fig. 6 is the specification of *create*. It is higher-order: the precondition of *create* contains a specification of the function f that is passed as an argument to *create*. This axiom states that, if f represents a computation of cost n, then *create* (f) produces an n-debit thunk. The cost of creation itself is 3 credits. This specification is somewhat simplistic, as it does not allow the function f to have a nontrivial precondition. It is possible to offer a richer specification; we eschew it in favor of simplicity.

Next comes the specification of *force*. Only a 0-debit thunk can be forced. The result is a value v that satisfies Φ. The (amortized) cost of forcing is 11 credits. The thunderbolt appears in the pre- and postcondition of *force*, forbidding any concurrent attempts to force a thunk.

The last axiom in Fig. 6 corresponds to *pay*. It is a view shift, a ghost operation. By paying k credits, one turns an n-debit thunk into an $(n-k)$-debit thunk. At runtime, nothing happens: it is the same thunk before and after the payment. Yet, after the view shift, we have a new view of the number of debits associated with this thunk. Here, paying requires the thunderbolt. It should be possible to remove this requirement; we have not yet attempted to do so.

7.4 Proof of Thunks in Iris$^{\$}$

After implementing thunks in HeapLang (Sect. 7.2) and expressing their specification in Iris$^{\$}$ (Sect. 7.3), there remains to prove that this specification can be established. We sketch the key ideas of this proof.

Following Pilkiewicz and Pottier [20], when a new thunk is created, we install a new Iris invariant, which describes this thunk. The invariant is as follows:

$$\mathit{ThunkInv}\ t\ \gamma\ \mathit{nc}\ \Phi \triangleq$$
$$\exists ac.\ \left(\boxed{\bullet\, ac}^{\gamma} \ast \begin{cases} \quad \exists f.\ t \mapsto \mathit{White}\ f \ast \{\$nc\}\, f\, ()\, \{\Phi\} \ast \$ac \\ \vee\ \exists v.\ t \mapsto \mathit{Black}\ v \end{cases} \right)$$

γ is a ghost location, which we allocate at the same time as the thunk t. It holds elements of the authoritative monoid $\textsc{Auth}(\mathbb{N}, \max)$ [12]. The variable nc, for "necessary credits", is the cost of the suspended computation: it appears in the precondition of f. The variable ac, for "available credits", is the number of credits that have been paid so far. The disjunction inside the invariant states that:

- either the thunk is white, in which case we have ac credits at hand;
- or the thunk is black, in which case we have no credits at hand, as they have been spent already.

The predicate $\mathsf{isThunk}\ t\ n\ \Phi$ is then defined as follows:

$$\mathsf{isThunk}\ t\ n\ \Phi \triangleq$$
$$\exists \gamma, nc.\ \left(\boxed{\circ\,(nc - n)}^{\gamma} * \mathsf{NaInv}(\mathit{ThunkInv}\ t\ \gamma\ nc\ \Phi) \right)$$

The non-authoritative assertion $\boxed{\circ\,(nc - n)}^{\gamma}$ inside $\mathsf{isThunk}\ t\ n\ \Phi$, confronted with the authoritative assertion $\boxed{\bullet\, ac}^{\gamma}$ that can be obtained by acquiring the invariant, implies the inequality $nc - n \leq ac$, therefore $nc \leq ac + n$. That is, the credits paid so far (ac) plus the credits that remain to be paid (n) are sufficient to cover for the actual cost of the computation (nc). In particular, in the proof of *force*, we have a 0-debit thunk, so $nc \leq ac$ holds. In the case where the thunk is white, this means that the ac credits that we have at hand are sufficient to justify the call f (), which requires nc credits.

The final aspect that remains to be explained is our use of $\mathsf{NaInv}(\cdots)$, an Iris "nonatomic invariant". Indeed, in this proof, we cannot rely on Iris' primitive invariants. A primitive invariant can be acquired only for the duration of an atomic instruction [12]. In our implementation of thunks (Fig. 5), however, we need a "critical section" that encompasses several instructions. That is, we must acquire the invariant before dereferencing t, and (in the case where this thunk is white) we cannot release it until we have marked this thunk black. Fortunately, Iris provides a library of "nonatomic invariants" for this very purpose. (This library is used in the RustBelt project [10] to implement Rust's type `Cell`.) This library offers separate ghost operations for acquiring and releasing an invariant. Acquiring an invariant consumes a unique token, which is recovered when the invariant is released: this guarantees that an invariant cannot be acquired twice, or in other words, that two threads cannot be in a critical section at the same time. The unique token involved in this protocol is the one that we expose to the end user as "the thunderbolt".

8 Application: Union-Find in Iris$^{\$⧗}$

As an illustration of the use of both time credits and time receipts, we formally verify the functional correctness and time complexity of an implementation of the Union-Find data structure. Our proof [17] is based on Charguéraud and Pottier's work [4]. We port their code from OCaml to HeapLang, and port their proof from Separation Logic with Time Credits to Iris$^{\$⧗}$. At this point, the proof exploits just Iris$^{\$}$, a subset of Iris$^{\$⧗}$. The mathematical analysis of Union-Find, which represents a large part of the proof, is unchanged. Our contribution lies in the fact that we modify the data structure to represent ranks as machine integers instead of unbounded integers, and exploit time receipts in Iris$^{\$⧗}$ to establish the absence of overflow. We equip HeapLang with signed machine integers whose bit width is a parameter w. Under the hypothesis $\log \log N < w - 1$, we are able to prove that, even though the code uses limited-width machine integers, no overflow can occur in a feasible time. If for instance N is 2^{63}, then this condition boils down to $w \geq 7$. Ranks can be stored in just 7 bits without risking overflow.

As in Charguéraud and Pottier's work, the Union-Find library advertises an abstract representation predicate $\mathsf{isUF}\,D\,R\,V$, which describes a well-formed, uniquely-owned Union-Find data structure. The parameter D, a set of nodes, is the domain of the data structure. The parameter R, a function, maps a node to the representative element of its equivalence class. The parameter V, also a function, maps a node to a payload value associated with its equivalence class. We do not show the specification of every operation. Instead, we focus on *union*, which merges two equivalence classes. We establish the following Iris$^{\$\text{⧗}}$ triple:

$$\left.\begin{array}{r}\log\log N < w - 1\\ x \in D\\ y \in D\end{array}\right\} \quad \Rightarrow \quad \begin{array}{c}\{\mathsf{isUF}\,D\,R\,V \;*\; \$(44\alpha(|D|) + 152)\}\\ \mathit{union}\;(x, y)\\ \left\{\lambda z.\; \begin{array}{c}\mathsf{isUF}\,D\,R'\,V' \;*\\ z = R(x) \lor z = R(y)\end{array}\right\}_{\$\text{⧗}}\end{array}$$

where the functions R' and V' are defined as follows:[10]

$$(R'(w), V'(w)) = \begin{cases}(z, \quad V(z)) & \text{if } R(w) = R(x) \text{ or } R(w) = R(y)\\ (R(w), V(w)) & \text{otherwise}\end{cases}$$

The hypotheses $x \in D$ and $y \in D$ and the conjunct $\mathsf{isUF}\,D\,R\,V$ in the precondition require that x and y be two nodes in a valid Union-Find data structure. The postcondition $\lambda z.\;\ldots$ describes the state of the data structure after the operation and the return value z.

The conjunct $\$(44\alpha(|D|) + 152)$ in the precondition indicates that *union* has time complexity $O(\alpha(n))$, where α is an inverse of Ackermann's function and n is the number of nodes in the data structure. This is an amortized bound; the predicate isUF also contains a certain number of time credits, known as the potential of the data structure, which are used to justify *union* operations whose actual cost exceeds the advertised cost. The constants 44 and 152 differ from those found in Charguéraud and Pottier's specification [4] because Iris$^{\$\text{⧗}}$ counts every computation step, whereas they count only function calls. Abstracting these constants by using O notation, as proposed by Guéneau *et al.* [7], would be desirable, but we have not attempted to do so yet.

The main novelty, with respect to Charguéraud and Pottier's specification, is the hypothesis $\log\log N < w - 1$, which is required to prove that no overflow can occur when the rank of a node is incremented. In our proof, N and w are parameters; once their values are chosen, this hypothesis is easily discharged, once and for all. In the absence of time receipts, we would have to publish the hypothesis $\log\log n < w - 1$, where n is the cardinal of D, forcing every (direct and indirect) user of the data structure to keep track of this requirement.

For the proof to go through, we store n time receipts in the data structure: that is, we include the conjunct $\text{⧗}\,n$, where n stands for $|D|$, in the definition of the invariant $\mathsf{isUF}\,D\,R\,V$. The operation of creating a new node takes at least one

[10] This definition of R' and V' has free variables x, y, z, therefore in reality must appear inside the postcondition. Here, it is presented separately, for greater readability.

step, therefore produces one new time receipt, which is used to prove that the invariant is preserved by this operation. At any point, then, from the invariant, and from the basic laws of time receipts, we can deduce that $n < N$ holds. Furthermore, it is easy to show that a rank is at most $\log n$. Therefore, a rank is at most $\log N$. In combination with the hypothesis $\log\log N < w - 1$, this suffices to prove that a rank is at most $2^{w-1} - 1$, the largest signed machine integer, and therefore that no overflow can occur in the computation of a rank.

Clochard *et al.* [5, §2] already present Union-Find as a motivating example among several others. They write that "there is obviously no danger of arithmetic overflow here, since [ranks] are only obtained by successive increments by one". This argument would be formalized in their system by representing ranks as either "one-time" or "peano" integers (in our terminology, clocks or snapclocks). This argument could be expressed in Iris$^{\$⧗}$, but would lead to requiring $\log N < w - 1$. In contrast, we use a more refined argument: we note that ranks are logarithmic in n, the number of nodes, and that n itself can never overflow. This leads us to the much weaker requirement $\log\log N < w - 1$, which means that a rank can be stored in very few bits. We believe that this argument cannot be expressed in Clochard *et al.*'s system.

9 Discussion

One feature of Iris and HeapLang that deserves further discussion is concurrency. Iris is an evolution of Concurrent Separation Logic, and HeapLang has shared-memory concurrency. How does this impact our reasoning about time? At a purely formal level, this does not have any impact: Theorems 1, 2, 3 and their proofs are essentially oblivious to the absence or presence of concurrency in the programming language. At a more informal level, though, this impacts our interpretation of the real-world meaning of these theorems. Whereas in a sequential setting a "number of computation steps" can be equated (up to a constant factor) with "time", in a concurrent setting, a "number of computation steps" is referred to as "work", and is related to "time" only up to a factor of p, the number of processors. In short, our system measures work, not time. The number of available processors should be taken into account when choosing a specific value of N: this value must be so large that N computation steps are infeasible even by p processors. With this in mind, we believe that our system can still be used to prove properties that have physical relevance.

In short, our new program logics, Iris$^{\$}$, Iris$^{⧗}$, and Iris$^{\$⧗}$, tolerate concurrency. Yet, is it fair to say that they have "good support" for reasoning about concurrent programs? We believe not yet, and this is an area for future research. The main open issue is that we do not at this time have good support for reasoning about the time complexity of programs that perform busy-waiting on some resource. The root of the difficulty, already mentioned during the presentation of thunks (Sect. 7.1), is that one thread can fail to make progress, due to interference with another thread. A retry is then necessary, wasting time. In a spin lock, for instance, the "compare-and-set" (CAS) instruction that attempts to acquire the lock can fail. There is no bound on the number of attempts that are required until the lock is eventually acquired. Thus, in Iris$^{\$}$, we are currently unable to assign *any* specification to the *lock* method of a spin lock.

In the future, we wish to take inspiration from Hoffmann, Marmar and Shao [9], who use time credits in Concurrent Separation Logic to establish the lock-freedom of several concurrent data structures. The key idea is to formalize the informal argument that "failure of a thread to make progress is caused by successful progress in another thread". Hoffmann *et al.* set up a "quantitative compensation scheme", that is, a protocol by which successful progress in one thread (say, a successful CAS operation) must transmit a number of time credits to every thread that has encountered a corresponding failure and therefore must retry. Quite interestingly, this protocol is not hardwired into the reasoning rule for CAS. In fact, CAS itself is not primitive; it is encoded in terms of an atomic $\{\ldots\}$ construct. The protocol is set up by the user, by exploiting the basic tools of Concurrent Separation Logic, including shared invariants. Thus, it should be possible in Iris$^{\$}$ to reproduce Hoffmann *et al.*'s reasoning and to assign useful specifications to certain lock-free data structures. Furthermore, we believe that, under a fairness assumption, it should be possible to assign Iris$^{\$}$ specifications also to coarse-grained data structures, which involve locks. Roughly speaking, under a fair scheduler, the maximum time spent waiting for a lock is the maximum number of threads that may compete for this lock, multiplied by the maximum cost of a critical section protected by this lock. Whether and how this can be formalized is a topic of future research.

The axiom $⧖ N \Rrightarrow_{\top} \mathsf{False}$ comes with a few caveats that should be mentioned. The same caveats apply to Clochard *et al.*'s system [5], and are known to them.

One caveat is that it is possible in theory to use this axiom to write and justify surprising programs. For instance, in Iris$^{⧗}$, the loop "*for* $i = 1$ *to* N *do* () *done*" satisfies the specification $\{\mathsf{True}\} — \{\mathsf{False}\}$: that is, it is possible to prove that this loop "never ends". As a consequence, this loop also satisfies every specification of the form $\{\mathsf{True}\} — \{\Phi\}$. On the face of it, this loop would appear to be a valid solution to every programming assignment! In practice, it is up to the user to exhibit taste and to refrain from exploiting such a paradox. In reality, the situation is no worse than that in plain Iris, a logic of partial correctness, where the infinite loop "*while true do* () *done*" also satisfies $\{\mathsf{True}\} — \{\mathsf{False}\}$.

Another important caveat is that the compiler must in principle be instructed to never optimize ticks away. If, for instance, the compiler was allowed to recognize that the loop "*for* $i = 1$ *to* N *do* () *done*" does nothing, and to replace this loop with a no-op, then this loop, which according to Iris$^{⧗}$ "never ends", would in reality end immediately. We would thereby be in danger of proving that a source program cannot crash unless it is allowed to run for centuries, whereas in reality the corresponding compiled program does crash in a short time. In practice, this danger can be avoided by actually instrumenting the source code with *tick*() instructions and by presenting *tick* to the compiler as an unknown external function, which cannot be optimized away. However, this seems a pity, as it disables many compiler optimizations.

We believe that, despite these pitfalls, time receipts can be a useful tool. We hope that, in the future, better ways of avoiding these pitfalls will be discovered.

10 Related Work

Time credits in an affine Separation Logic are not a new concept. Atkey [1] introduces them in the setting of Separation Logic. Pilkiewicz and Pottier [20] exploit them in an informal reconstruction of Danielsson's type discipline for lazy thunks [6], which itself is inspired by Okasaki's work [19]. Several authors subsequently exploit time credits in machine-checked proofs of correctness and time complexity of algorithms and data structures [4, 7, 22]. Hoffmann, Marmar and Shao [9], whose work was discussed earlier in this paper (Sect. 9), use time credits in Concurrent Separation Logic to prove that several concurrent data structure implementations are lock-free.

At a metatheoretic level, Charguéraud and Pottier [4] provide a machine-checked proof of soundness of a Separation Logic with time credits. Haslbeck and Nipkow [8] compare three program logics that can provide worst-case time complexity guarantees, including Separation Logic with time credits.

To the best of our knowledge, affine (exclusive and persistent) time receipts are new, and the axiom $⧖ N \Rrightarrow_{\top} \mathsf{False}$ is new as well. It is inspired by Clochard *et al.*'s idea that "programs cannot run for centuries" [5], but distills this idea into a simpler form.

Our implementation of thunks and our reconstruction of Okasaki's debits [19] in terms of credits are inspired by earlier work [6, 20]. Although Okasaki's analysis assumes a sequential setting, we adapt it to a concurrent setting by explicitly forbidding concurrent operations on thunks; to do so, we rely on Iris nonatomic invariants. In contrast, Danielsson [6] views thunks as a primitive construct in an otherwise pure language. He equips the language with a type discipline, where the type *Thunk*, which is indexed with a debit, forms a monad, and he provides a direct proof of type soundness. The manner in which Danielsson inserts *tick* instructions into programs is a precursor of our tick translation; this idea can in fact be traced at least as far back as Moran and Sands [16]. Pilkiewicz and Pottier [20] sketch an encoding of debits in terms of credits. Because they work in a sequential setting, they are able to install a shared invariant by exploiting the anti-frame rule [21], whereas we use Iris' nonatomic invariants for this purpose. The anti-frame rule does not rule out reentrancy, so they must detect it at runtime, whereas in our case both concurrency and reentrancy are ruled out by our use of nonatomic invariants.

Madhavan *et al.* [15] present an automated system that infers and verifies resource bounds for higher-order functional programs with thunks (and, more generally, with memoization tables). They transform the source program to an instrumented form where the state is explicit and can be described by monotone assertions. For instance, it is possible to assert that a thunk has been forced already (which guarantees that forcing it again has constant cost). This seems analogous in Okasaki's terminology to asserting that a thunk has zero debits, also a monotone assertion. We presently do not know whether Madhavan *et al.*'s system could be encoded into a lower-level program logic such as Iris$^{\$}$; it would be interesting to find out.

11 Conclusion

We have presented two mechanisms, namely time credits and time receipts, by which Iris, a state-of-the-art concurrent program logic, can be extended with means of reasoning about time. We have established soundness theorems that state precisely what guarantees are offered by the extended program logics Iris$^{\$}$, Iris$^{⧗}$, and Iris$^{\$⧗}$. We have defined these new logics modularly, by composing Iris with a program transformation. The three proofs follow a similar pattern: the soundness theorem of Iris is composed with a simulation lemma about the tick translation. We have illustrated the power of the new logics by reconstructing Okasaki's debit-based analysis of thunks, by reconstructing Clochard *et al.*'s technique for proving the absence of certain integer overflows, and by presenting an analysis of Union-Find that exploits both time credits and time receipts.

One limitation of our work is that all of our metatheoretic results are specific to HeapLang, and would have to be reproduced, following the same pattern, if one wished to instantiate Iris$^{\$⧗}$ for another programming language. It would be desirable to make our statements and proofs generic. In future work, we would also like to better understand what can be proved about the time complexity of concurrent programs that involve waiting. Can the time spent waiting be bounded? What specification can one give to a lock, or a thunk that is protected by a lock? A fairness hypothesis about the scheduler seems to be required, but it is not clear yet how to state and exploit such a hypothesis. Hoffmann, Marmar and Shao [9] have carried out pioneering work in this area, but have dealt only with lock-free data structures and only with situations where the number of competing threads is fixed. It would be interesting to transpose their work into Iris$^{\$}$ and to develop it further.

References

1. Atkey, R.: Amortised resource analysis with separation logic. Log. Methods Comput. Sci. **7**(2:17) (2011). http://bentnib.org/amortised-sep-logic-journal.pdf
2. Birkedal, L.: Lecture11: CAS and spin locks, November 2017. https://iris-project.org/tutorial-pdfs/lecture11-cas-spin-lock.pdf
3. Brookes, S., O'Hearn, P.W.: Concurrent separation logic. SIGLOG News **3**(3), 47–65 (2016). http://siglog.hosting.acm.org/wp-content/uploads/2016/07/siglognews9.pdf#page=49
4. Charguéraud, A., Pottier, F.: Verifying the correctness and amortized complexity of a union-find implementation in separation logic with time credits. J. Autom. Reason. (2017). http://gallium.inria.fr/~fpottier/publis/chargueraud-pottier-uf-sltc.pdf

5. Clochard, M., Filliâtre, J.-C., Paskevich, A.: How to avoid proving the absence of integer overflows. In: Gurfinkel, A., Seshia, S.A. (eds.) VSTTE 2015. LNCS, vol. 9593, pp. 94–109. Springer, Cham (2016). https://doi.org/10.1007/978-3-319-29613-5_6. https://hal.inria.fr/al-01162661
6. Danielsson, N.A.: Lightweight semiformal time complexity analysis for purely functional data structures. In: Principles of Programming Languages (POPL) (2008). http://www.cse.chalmers.se/~nad/publications/danielsson-popl2008.pdf
7. Guéneau, A., Charguéraud, A., Pottier, F.: A fistful of dollars: formalizing asymptotic complexity claims via deductive program verification. In: Ahmed, A. (ed.) ESOP 2018. LNCS, vol. 10801, pp. 533–560. Springer, Cham (2018). https://doi.org/10.1007/978-3-319-89884-1_19. http://gallium.inria.fr/~fpottier/publis/gueneau-chargeraud-pottier-esop2018.pdf
8. Haslbeck, M.P.L., Nipkow, T.: Hoare logics for time bounds: a study in meta theory. In: Beyer, D., Huisman, M. (eds.) TACAS 2018. LNCS, vol. 10805, pp. 155–171. Springer, Cham (2018). https://doi.org/10.1007/978-3-319-89960-2_9. https://www21.in.tum.de/~nipkow/pubs/tacas18.pdf
9. Hoffmann, J., Marmar, M., Shao, Z.: Quantitative reasoning for proving lock-freedom. In: Logic in Computer Science (LICS), pp. 124–133 (2013). http://www.cs.cmu.edu/~janh/papers/lockfree2013.pdf
10. Jung, R., Jourdan, J.H., Krebbers, R., Dreyer, D.: RustBelt: securing the foundations of the rust programming language. PACMPL **2**(POPL), 66:1–66:34 (2018). https://people.mpi-sws.org/~dreyer/papers/rustbelt/paper.pdf
11. Jung, R., Krebbers, R., Birkedal, L., Dreyer, D.: Higher-order ghost state. In: International Conference on Functional Programming (ICFP), pp. 256–269 (2016). http://iris-project.org/pdfs/2016-icfp-iris2-final.pdf
12. Jung, R., Krebbers, R., Jourdan, J.H., Bizjak, A., Birkedal, L., Dreyer, D.: Iris from the ground up: a modular foundation for higher-order concurrent separation logic. J. Funct. Program. **28**, e20 (2018). https://people.mpi-sws.org/~dreyer/papers/iris-ground-up/paper.pdf
13. Jung, R., et al.: Iris: monoids and invariants as an orthogonal basis for concurrent reasoning. In: Principles of Programming Languages (POPL), pp. 637–650 (2015). http://plv.mpi-sws.org/iris/paper.pdf
14. Krebbers, R., Jung, R., Bizjak, A., Jourdan, J.-H., Dreyer, D., Birkedal, L.: The essence of higher-order concurrent separation logic. In: Yang, H. (ed.) ESOP 2017. LNCS, vol. 10201, pp. 696–723. Springer, Heidelberg (2017). https://doi.org/10.1007/978-3-662-54434-1_26. http://iris-project.org/pdfs/2017-esop-iris3-final.pdf
15. Madhavan, R., Kulal, S., Kuncak, V.: Contract-based resource verification for higher-order functions with memoization. In: Principles of Programming Languages (POPL), pp. 330–343 (2017). http://lara.epfl.ch/~kandhada/orb-popl17.pdf
16. Moran, A., Sands, D.: Improvement in a lazy context: an operational theory for call-by-need. In: Principles of Programming Languages (POPL), pp. 43–56 (1999). http://www.cse.chalmers.se/~dave/papers/cbneed-theory.pdf
17. Mével, G., Jourdan, J.H., Pottier, F.: Time credits and time receipts in Iris – Coq proofs, October 2018. https://gitlab.inria.fr/gmevel/iris-time-proofs
18. Mével, G., Jourdan, J.H., Pottier, F.: Time credits and time receipts in Iris – extended version (2019). https://jhjourdan.mketjh.fr/pdf/mevel2019time.pdf
19. Okasaki, C.: Purely Functional Data Structures. Cambridge University Press, Cambridge (1999). http://www.cambridge.org/us/catalogue/catalogue.asp?isbn=0521663504

20. Pilkiewicz, A., Pottier, F.: The essence of monotonic state. In: Types in Language Design and Implementation (TLDI) (2011). http://gallium.inria.fr/~fpottier/publis/pilkiewicz-pottier-monotonicity.pdf
21. Pottier, F.: Hiding local state in direct style: a higher-order anti-frame rule. In: Logic in Computer Science (LICS), pp. 331–340 (2008). http://gallium.inria.fr/~fpottier/publis/fpottier-antiframe-2008.pdf
22. Zhan, B., Haslbeck, M.P.L.: Verifying asymptotic time complexity of imperative programs in Isabelle. In: Galmiche, D., Schulz, S., Sebastiani, R. (eds.) IJCAR 2018. LNCS (LNAI), vol. 10900, pp. 532–548. Springer, Cham (2018). https://doi.org/10.1007/978-3-319-94205-6_35. arxiv:1802.01336

4

A Categorical Model of an i/o-typed π-calculus

Ken Sakayori(✉) and Takeshi Tsukada

The University of Tokyo, Tokyo, Japan
sakayori@kb.is.s.u-tokyo.ac.jp

Abstract. This paper introduces a new categorical structure that is a model of a variant of the **i**/**o**-typed π-calculus, in the same way that a cartesian closed category is a model of the λ-calculus. To the best of our knowledge, no categorical model has been given for the **i**/**o**-typed π-calculus, in contrast to session-typed calculi, to which corresponding logic and categorical structure were given. The categorical structure introduced in this paper has a simple definition, combining two well-known structures, namely, closed Freyd category and compact closed category. The former is a model of effectful computation in a general setting, and the latter describes connections via channels, which cause the effect we focus on in this paper. To demonstrate the relevance of the categorical model, we show by a semantic consideration that the π-calculus is equivalent to a core calculus of Concurrent ML.

Keywords: π-calculus · Categorical type theory · Compact closed category · Closed Freyd category

1 Introduction

The Curry-Howard-Lambek correspondence reveals the trinity of the simply-typed λ-calculus, propositional intuitionistic logic and cartesian closed category. Via the correspondence, a type of the calculus can be seen as a formula of the logic, and as an object of a category; a term can be seen as a proof and as a morphism (see, e.g., [23]). Since its discovery, a number of variations have been proposed and studied.

In concurrency theory, a correspondence between a process calculus and logic was established by Caires, Pfenning and Toninho [8,9] and later by Wadler [48]. What they found is that session types [18,20] can be seen as formulas of linear logic [14], and processes as proofs. This remarkable result has inspired lots of work (e.g. [3,4,10,25,45,46]).

This correspondence is, however, not completely satisfactory as pointed out in [3,26], as well as by Wadler himself [48]. The session-typed calculi in [9,48] corresponding to linear logic have only well-behaved processes, because the session type systems guarantee deadlock-freedom and race-freedom of well-typed processes. This strong guarantee is often useful for programmers writing processes in the typed calculus, but can be seen as a significant limitation of expressive power. For example, it prevents us from modelling wild concurrent systems or programs that might fall into deadlocks or race conditions.

This paper describes an approach to a Curry-Howard-Lambek correspondence for concurrency in the presence of deadlocks and race conditions, from the viewpoint of categorical type theory.

What Is the Categorical Model of the π-calculus? We focus on the π-calculus [30, 31] in this paper. This is not only because the π-calculus is widely used and powerful, but also because of a classical result by Sangiorgi [39, 42], which is the starting point of our development.

Sangiorgi, in the early 90s, gave translations between the conventional, first-order π-calculus and its higher-order variant [39, 42]. This translation allows us to regard the π-calculus as a higher-order programming language.

Let us review the observation by Sangiorgi, using a core of the asynchronous π-calculus: $P ::= \mathbf{0} \mid (P|Q) \mid \bar{a}\langle x\rangle \mid a(x).P$.[1] The idea is to decompose the input-prefixing $a(x).P$ into a and $(x).P$. Let us write $a[(x).P]$ for $a(x).P$ to emphasise the decomposition. Then a reduction can also be decomposed as

$$\bar{a}\langle x\rangle \mid a[(y).P] \mid Q \;\longrightarrow\; [(y).P]\langle x\rangle \mid Q \;\longrightarrow\; P\{x/y\} \mid Q,$$

where the first step is the communication and the second step is the β-reduction (i.e. $(\lambda y.P)\,x \longrightarrow P\{x/y\}$ in the λ-calculus notation). Hence we regard

- an output $\bar{a}\langle x\rangle$ as an application of a function $\bar{a}$ to x, and
- an input $a(x).P$ as an abstraction $(x).P$ (or $\lambda x.P$) "located" at $a[-]$.

Now, ignoring the mysterious operator $a[-]$, what we had are the core operations of functional programming languages (i.e. abstraction and application). This functional programming language is effectful; in fact, communication via channels is a side effect.

This observation leads us to base our categorical model for the π-calculus on a model for effectful functional programs. Among several models, we choose *closed Freyd category* [37] for modelling the functional part.

Then what is the categorical counterpart of $a[-]$? As this operation seems responsible for communication, this question can be rephrased as: what is the categorical structure for communication? An observation by Abramsky et al. [2] answered this question. They pointed out the importance of *compact closed category* [21] in concurrency theory, which nicely describes CCS-like processes interconnected via ports.

By combining the two structures described above, this paper introduces a categorical structure, which we call *compact closed Freyd category*, as a categorical model of the π-calculus.[2] Despite its simplicity, compact closed Freyd

[1] This calculus slightly differs from the calculus we shall introduce in Sect. 2, but the differences are not important here.

[2] Here is the reason why we do not use a monad for modelling the effect: it is unclear for us how to integrate a monad with the compact closed structure. On the contrary, a Freyd category has a (pre)monoidal category as its component; we can simply require that it is compact closed.

category captures the strong expressive power of the π-calculus. The compact closed structure allows us to connect ports in an arbitrary way, in return for the possibility of deadlocks; the Freyd structure allows us to duplicate objects, and duplication of input channels introduces the possibility of race conditions.

Reconstructing Calculi. This paper introduces two calculi that are sound and complete with respect to the compact closed Freyd category model. One is a variant of the π-calculus, named π_F; the design of π_F is based on the observations described above. The other is a higher-order programming language λ_{ch} defined as an instance of the computational λ-calculus [33]. Designing λ_{ch} is not so difficult because we can make use of the correspondence between computational λ-calculus and closed Freyd category (see Sect. 4). The λ_{ch}-calculus have operations for creating a channel and for sending a value via the channel and, therefore, can be seen as a core calculus of *Concurrent ML* (or *CML*) [38].

Since the higher-order calculus λ_{ch} and π_F correspond to the same categorical model, we can obtain translations between these calculi by simple semantic computations. These translations are "correct by definition" and, interestingly, coincide with those between higher-order and first-order π-calculus [39,42].

On β- vs. $\beta\eta$-theories. The categorical analysis of this paper reveals that many conventional behavioural equivalences for the π-calculus are problematic from a viewpoint of categorical type theory. The problem is that they induce only *semicategories*, which may not have identities for some objects. This is a reminiscent of the β-theory of the λ-calculus, of which categorical model is given by semi-categorical notions [16].

Adding a single rule (which we call the *η-rule*) resolves the problem. Our categorical type theory deals with only equivalences that admits the η-rule, and the simplicity of the theory of this paper essentially relies on the η-rule.

Interestingly the η-rule seems to explain some phenomenon in the literature. For example, Sangiorgi observed that a syntactic constraint called *locality* [28,49] is essential for his translation [39,42]. The correctness of the translation can be proved without using the η-rule, when one restricts the calculus local; we expect that Sangiorgi's observation can be related to this phenomenon.

Contributions. This paper introduces a new variant of the **i**/**o**-typed π-calculus, which we call π_F. A remarkable feature of π_F is that it has a categorical counterpart, called compact closed Freyd category. The correspondence is fairly firm; the categorical semantics is sound and complete, and the term model is the classifying category. The relevance of the model is demonstrated by a semantic reconstruction of Sangiorgi's translation [39,42]. These results open a new frontier in the Curry-Howard-Lambek correspondence for concurrency; session-type is not the only base for a Curry-Howard-Lambek correspondence for π-calculi.

Organisation of this Paper. Section 2 introduces the calculus π_F and discuss equivalences on processes. Section 3 gives the categorical semantics of π_F and shows soundness and completeness. A connection to a higher-order programming language with channels is studied in Sect. 4. In Sect. 5, we (1) discuss how our work relates to linear logic and (2) present some ideas for how to extend the application range of our model. We discuss related work in Sect. 6 and conclude in Sect. 7. Omitted proofs, as well as detailed definitions, are available in the full version.

2 A Polyadic, Asynchronous π-calculus with i/o-types

This section introduces a variant of π-calculus, named π_F. It is based on a fairly standard calculus, namely polyadic and asynchronous π-calculus with **i**/**o**-types, but the details are carefully designed so that π_F has a categorical model.

2.1 The π_F-calculus

This subsection defines the calculus π_F, which is based on an asynchronous variant of the polyadic π-calculus with **i**/**o**-types in [35]. The aim of this subsection is to explain what are the differences from the conventional π-calculus. Although π_F has some uncommon features, each of them was studied in the literature; see Related Work (Sect. 6) for related ideas and calculi.

Types. The set of *types*, ranged over by S and T, is given by

$$S, T ::= \mathbf{ch}^o[T_1, \ldots, T_n] \mid \mathbf{ch}^i[T_1, \ldots, T_n] \qquad (n \geq 0).$$

The type $\mathbf{ch}^o[T_1, \ldots, T_n]$ is for output channels sending n arguments of types $T_1, \ldots, T_n$. The type $\mathbf{ch}^i[T_1, \ldots, T_n]$ is for input channels. The *dual* $T^\perp$ of type T is defined by $\mathbf{ch}^o[\vec{T}]^\perp \stackrel{\text{def}}{=} \mathbf{ch}^i[\vec{T}]$ and $\mathbf{ch}^i[\vec{T}]^\perp \stackrel{\text{def}}{=} \mathbf{ch}^o[\vec{T}]$. For a sequence $\vec{T} \stackrel{\text{def}}{=} T_1, \ldots, T_n$ of types, we write $\vec{T}^\perp$ for $T_1^\perp, \ldots, T_n^\perp$.

An important difference from [35] is that no channel allows both input and output operations. We will refer this feature of π_F as **i**/**o**-*separation.*

Processes. Let $\mathcal{N}$ be a denumerable set of *names*, ranged over by x, y and z. Each name is either input-only or output-only, because of **i**/**o**-separation.

The set of *processes*, ranged over by P, Q and R, is defined by

$$P, Q, R ::= \mathbf{0} \mid (P|Q) \mid (\boldsymbol{\nu}_{\mathbf{ch}^o[\vec{T}]}\, xy)P \mid x\langle \vec{y} \rangle \mid !x(\vec{y}).P.$$

The notion of *free names*, as well as *bound names*, is defined as usual. The set of free names (resp. bound names) of P is written as $\mathbf{fn}(P)$ (resp. $\mathbf{bn}(P)$). We allow tacit renaming of bound names, and identify α-equivalent processes.

The meaning of the constructs should be clear, except for $(\boldsymbol{\nu}_T\, xy)P$ which is less common. The process $\mathbf{0}$ is the inaction; $P \mid Q$ is a parallel composition; $x\langle \vec{y} \rangle$ is an output; and $!x(\vec{x}).P$ is a replicated input. The restriction $(\boldsymbol{\nu}_T\, xy)P$ hides the names x and y of type T and $T^\perp$ and, at the same time, establishes a connection between x and y. Communication takes place only over bound names explicitly connected by $\boldsymbol{\nu}$. This is in contrast to the conventional π-calculus, in which input-output correspondence is *a priori* (i.e. $\bar{a}$ is the output to a).

$$\frac{}{\Gamma \vdash \mathbf{0} : \diamond} \qquad \frac{\Gamma \vdash P : \diamond \qquad \Gamma \vdash Q : \diamond}{\Gamma \vdash P \mid Q : \diamond} \qquad \frac{\Gamma, x : \mathbf{ch}^o[\vec{T}], y : \mathbf{ch}^i[\vec{T}] \vdash P : \diamond}{\Gamma \vdash (\boldsymbol{\nu}_{\mathbf{ch}^o[\vec{T}]}\, xy)P : \diamond}$$

$$\frac{(x : \mathbf{ch}^i[\vec{T}]) \in \Gamma \qquad \Gamma, \vec{y} : \vec{T} \vdash P : \diamond}{\Gamma \vdash\, !x(\vec{y}).P : \diamond} \qquad \frac{(x : \mathbf{ch}^o[\vec{T}]) \in \Gamma \qquad \vec{y} : \vec{T} \subseteq \Gamma}{\Gamma \vdash x\langle\vec{y}\rangle : \diamond}$$

Fig. 1. Typing rules for processes

The π_F-calculus does not have non-replicated input $x(\vec{y}).P$.

Typing Rules. A *type environment* Γ is a finite sequence of type bindings of the form $x\colon T$. We assume the names in Γ are pairwise distinct. If $\vec{x} = x_1, \ldots, x_n$ and $\vec{T} = T_1, \ldots, T_n$, we write $\vec{x}\colon \vec{T}$ for $x_1\colon T_1, \ldots, x_n\colon T_n$. We write $(\vec{x}\colon \vec{T}) \subseteq \Gamma$ to mean $x_i\colon T_i \in \Gamma$ for every i.

A *type judgement* is of the form $\Gamma \vdash P : \diamond$, meaning that P is a well-typed process under Γ. The typing rules are listed in Fig. 1.

Notation 1. We define $(\boldsymbol{\nu}_{\mathbf{ch}^i[\vec{T}]}\, xy)P$ as $(\boldsymbol{\nu}_{\mathbf{ch}^o[\vec{T}]}\, yx)P$; then $(\boldsymbol{\nu}_T\, xy)P$ is defined for every T. We abbreviate $(\boldsymbol{\nu}_{T_1}\, x_1y_1)\ldots(\boldsymbol{\nu}_{T_n}\, x_ny_n)P$ as $(\boldsymbol{\nu}_{\vec{T}}\, \vec{x}\vec{y})P$. We often omit type annotations and write $(\boldsymbol{\nu}xy)$ for $(\boldsymbol{\nu}_T\, xy)$ and $(\boldsymbol{\nu}\vec{x}\vec{y})$ for $(\boldsymbol{\nu}_{\vec{T}}\, \vec{x}\vec{y})$. We use a and b for names of input channel types and $\bar{a}$ and $\bar{b}$ for output. Note that a and $\bar{a}$ are connected only if they are bound by the same occurrence of $\boldsymbol{\nu}$. □

Operational Semantics. *Structural congruence*, written $\equiv$, is the smallest congruence relation on processes that satisfies the following rules:

$$P \mid \mathbf{0} \equiv P \qquad P \mid Q \equiv Q \mid P \qquad (P \mid Q) \mid R \equiv P \mid (Q \mid R)$$
$$(\boldsymbol{\nu}xy)(P \mid Q) \equiv ((\boldsymbol{\nu}xy)P) \mid Q \qquad (\boldsymbol{\nu}wx)(\boldsymbol{\nu}yz)P \equiv (\boldsymbol{\nu}yz)(\boldsymbol{\nu}wx)P$$

where $x, y \notin \mathbf{fn}(Q)$ in the fourth rule and w, x, y, z are distinct in the fifth rule.

The *reduction relation* on processes, written $\longrightarrow$, is defined by the base rule

$$(\boldsymbol{\nu}\vec{w}\vec{z})(\boldsymbol{\nu}\bar{a}a)(!a(\vec{x}).P \mid \bar{a}\langle\vec{y}\rangle \mid Q) \longrightarrow (\boldsymbol{\nu}\vec{w}\vec{z})(\boldsymbol{\nu}\bar{a}a)(!a(\vec{x}).P \mid P\{\vec{y}/\vec{x}\} \mid Q)$$

(where $P\{\vec{x}/\vec{y}\}$ is the capture-avoiding substitution) and the structural rule which concludes $P \longrightarrow Q$ from $\exists P'\, Q'.\ P \equiv P' \longrightarrow Q' \equiv Q$. Note that, unlike conventional π-calculi, communication only occurs over bound names connected by ν. We write $\longrightarrow^*$ for the reflexive and transitive closure of $\longrightarrow$.

It should be clear that deadlocks and racy communications can be expressed in π_F. An example of race is $(\boldsymbol{\nu}\bar{a}a)(\bar{a}\langle\vec{y}\rangle \mid !a(\vec{x}).P \mid !a(\vec{x}).Q)$, where two input actions are trying to consume the output regarded as a resource. A similar process $(\boldsymbol{\nu}\bar{a}a)(!a(\vec{x}).P \mid \bar{a}\langle\vec{y}\rangle \mid \bar{a}\langle\vec{z}\rangle)$ does not have a race since the receiver $!a(\vec{x}).P$ is replicated. In general, race conditions on output actions do not occur in π_F.

2.2 Equivalences on Processes

To establish a Curry-Howard-Lambek correspondence is to find a nice algebraic or categorical structure of terms. For example, the original Curry-Howard-Lambek correspondence reveals the cartesian closed structure of λ-terms.

Such a nice structure would become visible only when appropriate notions of composition and of equivalence could be identified, such as substitution and $\beta\eta$-equivalence for the λ-calculus.

As for process calculi, so-called "parallel composition + hiding" paradigm [17] has been used to compose processes. Given typed processes

$$\vec{x} : \vec{T},\ \vec{y} : \vec{S} \vdash P : \diamond \quad \text{and} \quad \vec{w} : \vec{S}^{\perp},\ \vec{u} : \vec{U} \vdash Q : \diamond,$$

their composite via $(\vec{y}, \vec{w})$ is defined as

$$\vec{x} : \vec{T},\ \vec{u} : \vec{U} \vdash (\boldsymbol{\nu}_{\vec{S}}\, \vec{y}\vec{w})(P \mid Q) : \diamond.$$

This kind of composition appears quite often in logical studies of π-calculi [1, 5, 19]. It also plays a central role in *interaction category paradigm* proposed by Abramsky, Gay and Nagarajan [2].

So it remains to determine an equivalence on π-calculus processes, appropriate for our purpose. This subsection approaches the problem from two directions:

- Examining behavioural equivalences proposed and studied in the literature
- Developing a new equivalence based on categorical considerations

Let us clarify the notion of equivalence discussed below. An *equation-in-context* is a judgement of the form $\Gamma \vdash P = Q$, where $\Gamma \vdash P : \diamond$ and $\Gamma \vdash Q : \diamond$. An *equivalence* $\mathcal{E}$ is a set of equations-in-context that is reflexive, transitive and symmetric (e.g. $(\Gamma \vdash P = P) \in \mathcal{E}$ for every $\Gamma \vdash P : \diamond$).

Behavioural Equivalences. As mentioned above, we are interested in the structure of π_F-processes modulo existing behavioural equivalences. Among the various behavioural equivalence, we start with studying *barbed congruence* [32], which is one of the most widely used equivalences.

We define (asynchronous and weak) barbed congruence for π_F. For each name $\bar{a}$, we write $P{\downarrow_{\bar{a}}}$ if $P \equiv (\boldsymbol{\nu}\vec{x}\vec{y})(\bar{a}\langle\vec{z}\rangle \mid Q)$ and $\bar{a}$ is free, and $P{\Downarrow_{\bar{a}}}$ if $\exists Q.\, P \longrightarrow^{*} Q{\downarrow_{\bar{a}}}$. A (Γ/Δ)-*context* is a context C such that $\Gamma \vdash C[P] : \diamond$ for every $\Delta \vdash P : \diamond$.

Definition 1. *A* barbed bisimulation *is a symmetric relation $\mathcal{R}$ on processes such that, whenever $P \mathrel{\mathcal{R}} Q$, (1) $P{\downarrow_{\bar{a}}}$ implies $Q{\Downarrow_{\bar{a}}}$ and (2) $P \longrightarrow P'$ implies $\exists Q'.\, (Q \longrightarrow^{*} Q') \wedge (P' \mathrel{\mathcal{R}} Q')$.* Barbed bisimilarity $\overset{\bullet}{\approx}$ *is the largest barbed bisimulation. Typed processes $\Delta \vdash P : \diamond$ and $\Delta \vdash Q : \diamond$ are* barbed congruent at Δ, *written $\Delta \vdash P \cong^{c} Q$, if $C[P] \overset{\bullet}{\approx} C[Q]$ for every (Γ/Δ)-context C.* □

Let us consider a category-like structure $\mathcal{C}$ in which an object is a type and a morphism is an equivalence class of π_F-processes modulo barbed congruence. More precisely, a morphism from T to S is a process $x\colon T,\ y\colon S^{\perp} \vdash P\colon \diamond$ modulo barbed congruence (and renaming of free names x and y). Then the composition (i.e. "parallel composition + hiding") is well-defined on equivalence classes, because barbed congruence is a congruence. This is a fairly natural setting.

We have a strikingly negative result.

Theorem 1. *$\mathcal{C}$ is not a category.*

Proof. In every category, if $f : A \longrightarrow A$ is a left-identity on A (i.e. $f \circ g = g$ for every $g : A \longrightarrow A$), then f is the identity on A. The process $a : \mathbf{ch}^o[], \bar{b} : \mathbf{ch}^i[] \vdash\ !a().\bar{b}\langle\rangle : \diamond$ seen as a morphism $(\mathbf{ch}^o[]) \longrightarrow (\mathbf{ch}^o[])$ is a left-identity but not the identity. The former means that c: $\mathbf{ch}^o[]$, $\bar{b}$: $\mathbf{ch}^i[] \vdash \big((\boldsymbol{\nu}\bar{a}a)(!a().\bar{b}\langle\rangle \mid P)\big) \approx^c P\{\bar{b}/\bar{a}\}$ for every c: $\mathbf{ch}^o[]$, $\bar{a}$: $\mathbf{ch}^i[] \vdash P$: $\diamond$, which is a consequence of the *replicator theorems* [35]. To prove the latter, observe that $(\boldsymbol{\nu}\bar{b}b)(!a().\bar{b}\langle\rangle \mid \mathbf{0})$ and $\mathbf{0}$ are not barbed congruent. Indeed the context $C \stackrel{\text{def}}{=} (\boldsymbol{\nu}\bar{a}a)(\bar{a}\langle\rangle \mid !a().\bar{o}\langle\rangle \mid [])$ distinguishes the processes, where $\bar{o}$ is the observable. □

Note that race condition is essential for the proof, specifically, for the part proving that the process $!a().\bar{b}\langle\rangle$ is not the identity. A race condition occurs in $C[(\boldsymbol{\nu}\bar{b}b)(!a().\bar{b}\langle\rangle \mid \mathbf{0})]$, where $\bar{a}$ in C has two receivers.

The process $!a().\bar{b}\langle\rangle$ is called *forwarder*, and forwarders will play a central role in this paper. Its general form is $a \hookrightarrow \bar{b} \stackrel{\text{def}}{=}\ !a(\vec{x}).\bar{b}\langle\vec{x}\rangle$. When $x : T$ and $y : T^\perp$, we write $x \leftrightharpoons y$ to mean $x \hookrightarrow y$ if $T = \mathbf{ch}^i[\vec{S}]$ and otherwise $y \hookrightarrow x$.

Remark 1. The argument in the proof of Theorem 1 is widely applicable to **i**/**o**-typed calculi, not specific to π_F. In particular, **i**/**o**-separation (i.e. absence of $\mathbf{ch}^{i/o}[\vec{T}]$) is not the cause, but the existence of $\mathbf{ch}^o[\vec{T}]$ or $\mathbf{ch}^i[\vec{T}]$ is. □

Remark 2. Session-typed calculi in Caires, Pfenning and Toninho [8,9], which correspond to linear logic, do not seem to suffer from this problem. In our understanding, this is because of race-freedom of their calculi. □

To obtain a category, we should think of a coarser equivalence that identifies $(\boldsymbol{\nu}\bar{b}b)(!a().\bar{b}\langle\rangle \mid \mathbf{0})$ with $\mathbf{0}$. Such an equivalence should be very coarse; even *must-testing equivalence* [11] fails to equate them. As long as we have checked, only *may-testing equivalence* [11] defined below satisfies the requirement.

Definition 2. *Typed processes $\Delta \vdash P : \diamond$ and $\Delta \vdash Q : \diamond$ are* may-testing equivalent at Δ, *written $\Delta \vdash P =_{may} Q$, if $C[P]\Downarrow_{\bar{a}} \Leftrightarrow C[Q]\Downarrow_{\bar{a}}$ for every (Γ/Δ)-context C and name $\bar{a}$.* □

As we shall see, π_F-processes modulo may-testing equivalence behaves well. May-testing equivalence is, however, often too coarse.

Category-Driven Approach. In this approach, we first guess an appropriate categorical structure sufficient for interpreting π_F, based on intuitions discussed in Introduction (see also Sect. 3.1), and then design an equivalence so that it is sound and complete with respect to the categorical semantics.

Figure 2 defines the equivalence, described as a set of rules. A π_F*-theory* is an equivalence that behaves well from the categorical perspective.

$$\frac{a \notin \mathbf{fn}(P, C) \qquad \bar{a} \notin \mathbf{bn}(C)}{\Gamma \vdash (\boldsymbol{\nu}\bar{a}a)(!a(\vec{x}).P \mid C[\bar{a}\langle\vec{y}\rangle]) = (\boldsymbol{\nu}\bar{a}a)(!a(\vec{x}).P \mid C[P\{\vec{y}/\vec{x}\}])}\ \text{(E-Beta)}$$

$$\frac{a, \bar{a} \notin \mathbf{fn}(P)}{\Gamma \vdash (\boldsymbol{\nu}\bar{a}a)!a(\vec{y}).P = \mathbf{0}}\ \text{(E-GC)} \qquad \frac{\bar{a}, a \notin \mathbf{fn}(\bar{c}\langle\vec{x}\rangle)}{\Gamma \vdash \bar{c}\langle\vec{x}\rangle = (\boldsymbol{\nu}\bar{a}a)(a \hookrightarrow \bar{b} \mid \bar{c}\langle\vec{x}\{\bar{a}/\bar{b}\}\rangle)}\ \text{(E-FOut)}$$

$$\frac{b, \bar{a} \notin \mathbf{fn}(P)}{\Gamma \vdash (\boldsymbol{\nu}\bar{a}a)(b \hookrightarrow \bar{a} \mid P) = P\{b/a\}}\ \text{(E-Eta)}$$

$$\frac{P \equiv Q}{\Gamma \vdash P = Q}\ \text{(E-SCong)} \qquad \frac{\Delta \vdash P = Q \qquad C\colon \Gamma/\Delta\text{-context}}{\Gamma \vdash C[P] = C[Q]}\ \text{(E-Ctx)}$$

Fig. 2. Inference rules of equations-in-context. Each rule has implicit assumptions that the both sides of the equation are well-typed processes.

Definition 3. *An equivalence* $\mathcal{E}$ *is a* π_F-theory *if it is closed under the rules in Fig. 2. Any set* Ax *of equations-in-context has the minimum theory* $Th(Ax)$ *that contains* Ax*. We write* $Ax \rhd \Gamma \vdash P = Q$ *if* $(\Gamma \vdash P = Q) \in Th(Ax)$*.* □

Let us examine each rule in Fig. 2.

The rule (E-Beta) should be compared with the reduction relation. When $C = ([\,] \mid Q)$, then (E-Beta) claims

$$(\boldsymbol{\nu}\bar{a}a)(!a(\vec{x}).P \mid \bar{a}\langle\vec{y}\rangle \mid Q) = (\boldsymbol{\nu}\bar{a}a)(!a(\vec{x}).P \mid P\{\vec{y}/\vec{x}\} \mid Q)$$

provided that $a \notin \mathbf{fn}(P, Q)$, which is indeed an instance of the reduction.

A significant difference from reduction is the side condition. It is essential in the presence of race conditions. Without the side condition, every π_F-theory would be forced to contain the symmetric and transitive closure of the reduction relation; thus it would identify $P \mid (\boldsymbol{\nu}\bar{a}a)(!a().P \mid !a().Q)$ with $Q \mid (\boldsymbol{\nu}\bar{a}a)(!a().P \mid !a().Q)$ for every processes P and Q (where $\bar{a}, a$ are fresh), because

$$\begin{array}{rcl} (\boldsymbol{\nu}\bar{a}a)(\bar{a}\langle\rangle \mid !a().P \mid !a().Q) & \longrightarrow & P \mid (\boldsymbol{\nu}\bar{a}a)(!a().P \mid !a().Q) \\ (\boldsymbol{\nu}\bar{a}a)(\bar{a}\langle\rangle \mid !a().P \mid !a().Q) & \longrightarrow & Q \mid (\boldsymbol{\nu}\bar{a}a)(!a().P \mid !a().Q). \end{array}$$

The side condition prevents π_F-theories from collapsing.

Another, relatively minor, difference is that application of (E-Beta) is not limited to the contexts of the form $[\,] \mid Q$. This kind of extension can be found in, for example, work by Honda and Laurent [19] studying π-calculus from a logical perspective.

The rule (E-GC) runs "garbage-collection". Because no one can send a message to the hidden name a, the process $!a(\vec{x}).P$ will never be invoked and thus is safely discarded. This rule is sound with respect to many behavioural equivalences, including barbed congruence. Rules of this kind often appear in the literature studying logical aspects of concurrent calculi (as in Honda and Laurent [19] and Wadler [48]). There is, however, a subtle difference in the side condition: (E-GC) requires that a and $\bar{a}$ do not appear at all in P.

The rule (E-FOut) can be seen as the η-rule of abstractions, as in the λ-calculus and in the higher-order π-calculus [39]. In the latter, an output name $\bar{b}$ can be identified with an abstraction $(\vec{y}).\bar{b}\langle\vec{y}\rangle$. Then we have, for example,

$$(\boldsymbol{\nu}\bar{a}a)(a \hookrightarrow \bar{b} \mid \bar{c}\langle\bar{a}\rangle) \;=\; (\boldsymbol{\nu}\bar{a}a)(a \hookrightarrow \bar{b} \mid \bar{c}\langle\, (\vec{y}).\bar{a}\langle\vec{y}\rangle\,\rangle) \;=\; \bar{c}\langle\, (\vec{y}).\bar{b}\langle\vec{y}\rangle\,\rangle \;=\; \bar{c}\langle\bar{b}\rangle$$

where we use (E-Beta) and (E-GC) in the second step. An important usage of (E-FOut) is to replace an output of free names with that of bound names. This kind of operation has been studied in [7,28] as a part of translations from the π-calculus to its local/internal fragments.[3]

The rule (E-Eta) requires the forwarders are left-identities, directly describing the requirement discussed above.[4]

The rules (E-SCong) and (E-Ctx) are easy to understand. The former requires that structurally congruent processes should be identified; the latter says that a π_F-theory is a congruence.

These rules can be justified from the operational viewpoint, as well. A well-known result on the **i/o**-typed π-calculus (see, e.g., [35,43]) shows the following propositions.

Proposition 1. *Barbed congruence is closed under all rules but* (E-Eta). □

Proposition 2. *May-testing equivalence is a* π_F*-theory.* □

In particular, the latter means that may-testing equivalence is in the scope of the categorical framework of this paper; see Theorem 5.

3 Categorical Semantics

This section introduces the class of *compact closed Freyd categories* and discusses the interpretation of the π_F-calculus in the categories. We show that the categorical semantics is sound and complete with respect to the equational theory given in Sect. 2.2, and that the syntax of the π_F-calculus induces a model.

This section, by its nature, is slightly theoretical compared with other sections. Section 3.1 explains the ideas of this section without heavily using categorical notions; the subsequent subsections require familiarity with categorical type theory.

3.1 Overview

As mentioned in Sect. 1, the categorical model of π_F is *compact closed Freyd category*, which has both closed Freyd and compact closed structures. Here we

---

[3] Free outputs can be eliminated from π_F-processes by using the rules (E-FOut) and (E-Eta), i.e. external mobility can be encoded by internal mobility [7,40]. If the calculus is local [28,49], then we do not need (E-Eta) to eliminate free outputs.

[4] A forwarder behaves as a right-identity with respect to every π_F-theory. This is a consequence of rules (E-Beta), (E-GC) and (E-FOut).

informally discuss what is a compact closed Freyd category and how to interpret π_F by using syntactic representation.

A *closed Freyd category* is a model of higher-order programs with side effects. It has, among others, the structures to interpret the function type $A \Rightarrow B$ and its constructor and destructor, namely, abstraction $\lambda x.t$ and application $t\,u$. It also has a mechanism for unrestricted duplication of variables; in terms of logic, contraction is admissible.

A *compact closed category* can be seen as MLL [14] with the left rule:

$$\frac{\Gamma, A^*, A \vdash I}{\Gamma \vdash I} \qquad \left[\frac{\Gamma \vdash A^* \qquad \Delta \vdash A}{\Gamma, \Delta \vdash I}\right].$$

(The right rule is the companion, which itself is derivable in MLL.)

A *compact closed Freyd category* has all the constructs. It has the structures corresponding to the following type constructors:

$$\text{(closed Freyd)} \quad I, A \otimes B, A \Rightarrow B \qquad \text{(compact closed)} \quad I, A \otimes B, A^*.$$

Note that the pair type $A \otimes B$ (as well as the unit I) coming from the closed Freyd structure is identified with that from the compact closed structure. Inference rules for a compact closed Freyd category is those for functional languages and the above rules of the compact closed structure.

Interpreting π_F in a compact closed Freyd category is to interpret it by using these constructs. As mentioned in Sect. 1, following Sangiorgi [39], we regard

- an output $\bar{a}\langle \vec{x} \rangle$ as an application of a function $\bar{a}$ to a tuple $\langle \vec{x} \rangle$, and
- an input $!a(\vec{x}).P$ as an abstraction $(\vec{x}).P$ (or $\lambda\vec{x}.P$) located at a.

We interpret the output action by using the function application. Hence the type $\mathbf{ch}^o[T]$ is regarded as a function type $T \Rightarrow I$ (where the unit type I is the type for processes i.e. $\diamond$); then the typing rule for output actions becomes

$$\frac{\Gamma, \bar{a}\colon (T \Rightarrow I), x\colon T \vdash \bar{a} : T \Rightarrow I \qquad \Gamma, \bar{a}\colon (T \Rightarrow I), x\colon T \vdash x : T}{\Gamma, \bar{a}\colon (T \Rightarrow I), x\colon T \vdash \bar{a}\langle x \rangle : I}$$

The type $\mathbf{ch}^i[T]$ is understood as $(T \Rightarrow I)^*$; the input-prefixing rule becomes

$$\frac{\dfrac{}{\Gamma, a\colon (T \Rightarrow I)^* \vdash a : (T \Rightarrow I)^*} \qquad \dfrac{\Gamma, a\colon (T \Rightarrow I)^*, x\colon T \vdash P : I}{\Gamma, a\colon (T \Rightarrow I)^* \vdash (x).P : T \Rightarrow I}}{\Gamma, a\colon (T \Rightarrow I)^* \vdash !a(x).P : I}$$

This derivation directly expresses the intuition that an input-prefixing is abstraction followed by allocation; here allocation is interpreted by using the compact closed structure, i.e. connection of ports. The name restriction also has a natural derivation:

$$\frac{\Gamma, a\colon (T \Rightarrow I)^*, \bar{a}\colon (T \Rightarrow I) \vdash P : I}{\Gamma \vdash (\boldsymbol{\nu}\bar{a}a)P : I}$$

3.2 Compact Closed Freyd Category

Let us formalise the ideas given in Sect. 3.1. Hereafter in this section, we assume basic knowledge of category theory and of categorical type theory.

We recall the definitions of compact closed category and closed Freyd category. For simplicity, the structures below are strict and chosen; a functor is required to preserve the chosen structures on the nose.

Definition 4 (Compact closed category [21]**).** *Let $(\mathcal{C}, \otimes, I)$ be a symmetric strict monoidal category. The* dual *of an object A in $\mathcal{C}$ is an object A^* equipped with* unit *$\eta_A : I \longrightarrow A \otimes A^*$ and* counit *$\epsilon_A : A^* \otimes A \longrightarrow I$ that satisfy the "triangle identities" $(\eta_A \otimes \mathrm{id}_A); (\mathrm{id}_A \otimes \epsilon_A) = \mathrm{id}_A$ and $(\mathrm{id}_{A^*} \otimes \eta_A); (\epsilon_A \otimes \mathrm{id}_{A^*}) = \mathrm{id}_{A^*}$. The category $\mathcal{C}$ is* compact closed *if each object is equipped with a chosen dual.* □

Definition 5 (Closed Freyd category [37]**).** *A* Freyd category *is given by (1) a category with chosen finite products $(\mathcal{C}, \otimes, I)$, called* value category*, (2) a symmetric strict monoidal category $(\mathcal{K}, \otimes, I, \mathbf{symm})$, called* producer category*, and (3) an identity-on-object strict symmetric monoidal functor $J : \mathcal{C} \to \mathcal{K}$. A Freyd category is a* closed Freyd category *if the functor $J(-) \otimes A : \mathcal{C} \to \mathcal{K}$ has the (chosen) right adjoint $A \Rightarrow - : \mathcal{K} \to \mathcal{C}$ for every object A. We write $\Lambda_{A,B,C}$ for the natural bijection $\mathcal{K}(J(A) \otimes B, C) \longrightarrow \mathcal{C}(A, B \Rightarrow C)$ and $\mathbf{eval}_{A,B}$ for $\Lambda^{-1}(\mathrm{id}_{A \Rightarrow B}) : (A \Rightarrow B) \otimes A \longrightarrow B$ in $\mathcal{K}$.* □

Remark 3. The above definition is a restriction of the original one [37], in which $\mathcal{K}$ is a *premonoidal* [36] category. This change reflects concurrency of the calculus. In fact, it validates the following law, expressed by the syntax of the computational λ-calculus [33],

$$\mathbf{let}\, x = M \,\mathbf{in}\, \mathbf{let}\, y = N \,\mathbf{in}\, L \quad = \quad \mathbf{let}\, y = N \,\mathbf{in}\, \mathbf{let}\, x = M \,\mathbf{in}\, L.$$

Then one can evaluate M by using the left form and N by using the right form. This law allows us to evaluate M and N in arbitrary order, or concurrently. □

We now introduce the categorical structure corresponding to the π_F-calculus.

Definition 6 (Compact closed Freyd category). *A* compact closed Freyd category *is a Freyd category $J : \mathcal{C} \longrightarrow \mathcal{K}$ such that (1) $\mathcal{K}$ is compact closed, and (2) J has the (chosen) right adjoint $I \Rightarrow - : \mathcal{K} \to \mathcal{C}$.* □

We shall often write J for a compact closed Freyd category $J : \mathcal{C} \rightleftarrows \mathcal{K}$ (with $J \dashv$).

A compact closed Freyd category is a closed Freyd category:

$$\mathcal{K}(J(A) \otimes B, C) \;\cong\; \mathcal{K}(J(A), B^* \otimes C) \;\cong\; \mathcal{C}(A, I \Rightarrow (B^* \otimes C)).$$

Example 1. The most basic example of a compact closed Freyd category is (the strict monoidal version of) $J : \mathbf{Sets} \rightleftarrows \mathbf{Rel} : \mathcal{P}$ (with $J \dashv \mathcal{P}$). Here J is the identity-on-object functor that maps a function to its graph and $\mathcal{P}$ is the "power set functor"

$$[\![\mathbf{ch}^i[T_1,\ldots,T_n]]\!] \stackrel{\text{def}}{=} (([\![T_1]\!] \otimes \cdots \otimes [\![T_n]\!]) \Rightarrow I)^*$$
$$[\![\mathbf{ch}^o[T_1,\ldots,T_n]]\!] \stackrel{\text{def}}{=} ([\![T_1]\!] \otimes \cdots \otimes [\![T_n]\!]) \Rightarrow I$$

$$[\![\Gamma \vdash \mathbf{0} : \diamond]\!] \stackrel{\text{def}}{=} J(!_\Gamma)$$
$$[\![\Gamma \vdash !a(\vec{x}).P : \diamond]\!] \stackrel{\text{def}}{=} J(\langle \pi_a^\Gamma, \Lambda_{\Gamma,\vec{T},I}([\![\Gamma, \vec{x} : \vec{T} \vdash P : \diamond]\!])\rangle); \epsilon_{\mathbf{ch}[\vec{T}]}$$
$$[\![\Gamma \vdash \bar{a}\langle\vec{x}\rangle : \diamond]\!] \stackrel{\text{def}}{=} J(\langle \pi_{\bar{a}}^\Gamma, \pi_{x_1}^\Gamma, \ldots, \pi_{x_n}^\Gamma\rangle); \mathbf{eval}_{\vec{T},I}$$
$$[\![\Gamma \vdash P \mid Q : \diamond]\!] \stackrel{\text{def}}{=} J(\Delta_\Gamma); ([\![\Gamma \vdash P : \diamond]\!] \otimes [\![\Gamma \vdash Q : \diamond]\!])$$
$$[\![\Gamma \vdash (\nu xy)P : \diamond]\!] \stackrel{\text{def}}{=} (\mathrm{id}_\Gamma \otimes \eta_T); [\![\Gamma, x : T, y : T^\perp \vdash P : \diamond]\!]$$

Fig. 3. Interpretation of types and processes. Here $!_\Gamma$, Δ_Γ and π_y^Γ are maps in $\mathcal{C}$ induced by the cartesian structure, namely, $!_\Gamma \colon [\![\Gamma]\!] \longrightarrow I$ is the terminal map, $\Delta_\Gamma \colon [\![\Gamma]\!] \longrightarrow [\![\Gamma]\!] \otimes [\![\Gamma]\!]$ is the diagonal map and, when $\Gamma = (y_1 \colon T_1, \ldots, y_n \colon T_n)$ and $x = y_j$, the morphism $\pi_x^\Gamma : [\![\Gamma]\!] \longrightarrow [\![T_j]\!]$ is the j-th projection. The interpretation of a type environment $x_1 \colon T_1, \ldots, x_n \colon T_n$ is $[\![T_1]\!] \otimes \cdots \otimes [\![T_n]\!]$.

that maps a relation $\mathcal{R} \subseteq A \times B$ to a function $\mathcal{P}(\mathcal{R}) \stackrel{\text{def}}{=} \{(S_A, S_B) \mid S_B = \{b \mid a \in S_A, a \;\mathcal{R}\; b\}\}$. Another example is obtained by replacing sets with posets, functions with monotone functions and relations with downward closed relations. □

Example 2. A more sophisticated example is taken from Laird's game-semantic model of π-calculus [22]. Precisely speaking, the model in [22] itself is not compact closed Freyd, but its variant (with non-negative arenas) is. This model is important since it is fully abstract w.r.t. may-testing equivalence [22, Theorem 1]; hence our framework has a model that captures the may-testing equivalence. □

3.3 Interpretation

Given a compact closed Freyd category $J \colon \mathcal{C} \rightleftarrows \mathcal{K}$ (with $\perp$), this section defines the interpretation $[\![-]\!]_J$. It maps types and type environments to objects as usual, and a well-typed process $\Gamma \vdash P : \diamond$ to a morphism $[\![P]\!] \colon [\![\Gamma]\!] \to I$ in $\mathcal{K}$ (recall that the tensor unit I is the interpretation of the type for processes).

Figure 3 defines the interpretation of types and processes. It simply formalises the ideas presented in Sect. 3.1: for example, the interpretation of $!a(\vec{x}).P$ is the abstraction Λ (from the closed Freyd structure) followed by location ϵ (from the compact closed structure). There are some points worth noting.

- $(A \Rightarrow I)^*$ is *not* isomorphic to $A^* \Rightarrow I$, $A \Rightarrow I$ nor $I \Rightarrow A$. Indeed $(A \Rightarrow I)^*$ cannot be simplified. Do not confuse it with a valid law $I \Rightarrow (A^*) \cong A \Rightarrow I$.
- A parallel composition is interpreted as a pair. Recall that two components of a pair are evaluated in parallel in this setting (cf. Remark 3).
- All but the last rule use the cartesian structure of $\mathcal{C}$ in order to duplicate or discard the environment.

Example 3. Let us consider $y : T \vdash (\boldsymbol{\nu}\bar{a}a)(\bar{a}\langle y\rangle \mid !a(x).P) : \diamond$, where $\bar{a}, a, y \notin \mathbf{fn}(P)$ and $a \colon \mathbf{ch}^i[T]$. By (E-Beta) and (E-GC), this process is equal to $P\{y/x\}$. It is natural to expect that the interpretations of the two processes coincide; indeed it is. As the following calculation indicates, our semantics factorises the reduction into two steps: (1) the "transmission" of the closure $\lambda\vec{x}.P$ by the triangle identity of the compact closed structure, and (2) the β-reduction modelled by **eval** of the closed Freyd structure:

$$\begin{aligned}
&[\![y : T \vdash (\boldsymbol{\nu}\bar{a}a)(\bar{a}\langle y\rangle \mid !a(x).P) : \diamond]\!] \\
&= (\mathrm{id}_T \otimes \eta_{\mathbf{ch}^o[T]}); [\![y : T, \bar{a} : \mathbf{ch}^o[T], a : \mathbf{ch}^i[T] \vdash \bar{a}\langle y\rangle \mid !a(x).P : \diamond]\!] \\
&= (\mathrm{id} \otimes \eta); ([\![y : T, \bar{a} : \mathbf{ch}^o[T] \vdash \bar{a}\langle y\rangle : \diamond]\!] \otimes [\![a : \mathbf{ch}^i[T] \vdash !a(x).P : \diamond]\!]) \\
&= (\mathrm{id} \otimes \eta); ((\mathbf{symm}_{T,\mathbf{ch}^o[T]}; \mathbf{eval}_{T,I}) \otimes (\mathrm{id}_{\mathbf{ch}[T]^*} \otimes J(\Lambda([\![x : T \vdash P : \diamond]\!])));\epsilon_{T\Rightarrow I} \\
&= (\mathrm{id}_T \otimes J(\Lambda([\![x : T \vdash P : \diamond]\!]))); \mathbf{symm}_{T,\mathbf{ch}^o[T]}; \mathbf{eval}_{T,I} \quad \text{(By triangle identity)} \\
&= (J(\Lambda([\![x : T \vdash P : \diamond]\!])) \otimes \mathrm{id}_T); \mathbf{eval}_{T,I} \\
&= [\![x : T \vdash P]\!] \qquad \text{(By the universality of } \mathbf{eval}\text{)} \\
&= [\![y : T \vdash P\{y/x\} : \diamond]\!].
\end{aligned}$$

(Here we implicitly use derived rules for weakening and exchange.) □

Example 4. The interpretation of a forwarder $a : \mathbf{ch}^i[\vec{T}], \bar{b} : \mathbf{ch}^o[\vec{T}] \vdash a \hookrightarrow \bar{b} : \diamond$ is the counit $\epsilon_{\mathbf{ch}^o[\vec{T}]} \colon [\![\mathbf{ch}^o[\vec{T}]]\!]^* \otimes [\![\mathbf{ch}^o[\vec{T}]]\!] \longrightarrow I$ in $\mathcal{K}$, which is the one-sided form of the identity. Recall that a forwarder is the identity in every π_F-theory. □

The semantics is sound and complete. That means, a judgement $Ax \rhd \Gamma \vdash P = Q$ is provable if and only if $\Gamma \vdash P = Q$ is valid in all models J of Ax.

Here we define the related notions and prove soundness; completeness is the topic of the next subsection.

Definition 7. *An equational judgement $\Gamma \vdash P = Q$ is* valid in J *if $[\![\Gamma \vdash P : \diamond]\!]_J = [\![\Gamma \vdash Q : \diamond]\!]_J$. Given a set Ax of non-logical axioms, J is a* model of Ax, *written $J \models Ax$, if it validates all judgements in Ax. We write $Ax \rhd \Gamma \Vdash P = Q$ if $\Gamma \vdash P = Q$ is valid in every J such that $J \models Ax$.* □

Theorem 2 (Soundness). *If $Ax \rhd \Gamma \vdash P = Q$, then $Ax \rhd \Gamma \Vdash P = Q$.* □

3.4 Term Model

A *term model* is a category whose objects are type environments and whose morphisms are terms (i.e. processes in this setting). This section gives a construction of the term model, by which we show completeness. This subsection basically follows the standard arguments in categorical type theory; we mainly focus on the features unique to our model, giving a sketch to the common part.

Given a set Ax of axioms, we define the term model $J_{Ax} \colon \mathcal{C}_{Ax} \rightleftarrows \mathcal{K}_{Ax}$ (with $\perp$), which we also write as $Cl(Ax)$.

The definition of the producer category $\mathcal{K}_{Ax}$ follows the standard recipe. As usual, its objects are finite lists of types. The monoidal product $\vec{T} \otimes \vec{S}$ is the concatenation of the lists and the dual $\vec{T}^*$ is $\vec{T}^{\perp}$. Given objects $\vec{T}$ and $\vec{S}$, a morphism from $\vec{T}$ to $\vec{S}$ is a process $\vec{x}\colon \vec{T},\ \vec{y}\colon \vec{S}^{\perp} \vdash P : \diamond$ (modulo renaming of variables $\vec{x}$ and $\vec{y}$). If $Ax \rhd \vec{x}\colon \vec{T},\ \vec{y}\colon \vec{S}^{\perp} \vdash P = Q$ is provable, then P and Q are regarded as the same morphism. Composition of morphisms is defined as "parallel composition plus hiding": For morphisms $P : \vec{T} \longrightarrow \vec{S}$ and $Q : \vec{S} \longrightarrow \vec{U}$, i.e. processes such that $\vec{x}\colon \vec{T},\ \vec{y}\colon \vec{S}^{\perp} \vdash P : \diamond$ and $\vec{z}\colon \vec{S},\ \vec{w}\colon \vec{U}^{\perp} \vdash Q : \diamond$, their composite is $\vec{x}\colon \vec{T}, \vec{w}\colon \vec{U}^{\perp} \vdash (\boldsymbol{\nu}\vec{y}\vec{z})(P \mid Q) : \diamond$. The monoidal product $P \otimes Q$ of morphisms is the parallel composition $P \mid Q$. The identity, as well as the symmetry of the monoidal product and the unit and counit of the compact closed structure, is a parallel composition of forwarders: for example, the identity on $\vec{S}$ is $\vec{x} : \vec{S}, \vec{y} : \vec{S}^{\perp} \vdash x_1 \leftrightharpoons y_1 \mid \cdots \mid x_n \leftrightharpoons y_n : \diamond$ where n is the length of $\vec{S}$. The facts that most structural morphisms are forwarders and that forwarders compose are the keys to show that $\mathcal{K}_{Ax}$ is a compact closed category.

We then see the definition of $\mathcal{C}_{Ax}$, of which the definition of morphisms has a subtle point. The objects of $\mathcal{C}_{Ax}$ are by definition the same as $\mathcal{K}_{Ax}$, i.e. lists of types. The definition of morphisms relies on the notion of *values*. The values are defined by the grammar $V ::= x \mid (\vec{x}).P$, where P is a process and $(\vec{x}).P$ is called an *abstraction*. Typing rules for values are as follows:

$$\frac{x : T \in \Gamma}{\Gamma \vdash x : T} \qquad \frac{\Gamma, \vec{x}\colon \vec{T} \vdash P}{\Gamma \vdash (\vec{x}).P : \mathbf{ch}^o[\vec{T}]}.$$

(To understand the right rule, recall that $[\![\mathbf{ch}^o[\vec{T}]]\!] = [\![\vec{T}]\!] \Rightarrow I$.) A morphism from $\vec{T}$ to $\vec{S} = (S_1, \ldots, S_n)$ is an n-tuple $(V_1, \ldots, V_n)$ of values of type $\vec{x}\colon \vec{T} \vdash V_i\colon S_i$ for each i (modulo renaming of $\vec{x}$). Composition is intuitively defined by "substitution followed by β-reduction" whose definition is omitted here.[5]

The functor J_{Ax} places the values to the channels. For example, let $\vec{T} = (\mathbf{ch}^i[U_1], \mathbf{ch}^o[U_2])$ and consider the morphism in $\mathcal{C}_{Ax}$ given by

$$a\colon \mathbf{ch}^i[T_1], \bar{b}\colon \mathbf{ch}^o[T_2] \vdash (a, \bar{b}, (\vec{x}).P) : (\mathbf{ch}^i[T_1], \mathbf{ch}^o[T_2], \mathbf{ch}^o[\vec{S}])$$

where $\vec{S}$ is the type for $\vec{x}$. The image of this morphism by the functor J_{Ax} is

$$a\colon \mathbf{ch}^i[T_1], \bar{b}\colon \mathbf{ch}^o[T_2], \bar{c}\colon \mathbf{ch}^o[T_1], d\colon \mathbf{ch}^i[T_2], e\colon \mathbf{ch}^i[\vec{S}] \vdash a \hookrightarrow \bar{c} \mid d \hookrightarrow \bar{b} \mid !e(\vec{x}).P\colon \diamond.$$

This example contains all the three ways to place a value to a given channel.

Theorem 3. *$Cl(Ax)$ is a compact closed Freyd category for every Ax.* □

In the model $Cl(Ax)$, the interpretation of a process $\Gamma \vdash P : \diamond$ is the equivalence class that P belongs to. This fact leads to completeness.

---

[5] Here is a subtle technical issue that we shall not address in this paper; see the long version for the formal definition. We think, however, that this paragraph conveys a precise intuition.

Theorem 4 (Completeness). *If* $Ax \rhd \Gamma \Vdash P = Q$*, then* $Ax \rhd \Gamma \vdash P = Q$*.* □

Theorem 5. *There exists a compact closed Freyd category* J *that is fully abstract w.r.t. may-testing equivalence, i.e.* $\Gamma \vdash P =_{may} Q$ *iff* $[\![P]\!]_J = [\![Q]\!]_J$*.*

Proof. Let J be the term model $Cl(=_{may})$ and use Proposition 2. □

3.5 Theory/Model Correspondence

It is natural to expect that $Cl(Ax)$ is the *classifying category* as in the standard categorical type theory. This means, to give a model of Ax in J is equivalent to give a structure-preserving functor $Cl(Ax) \longrightarrow J$. This subsection clarifies and studies this claim.

The set $\mathrm{Mod}(Ax, J)$ of models of Ax in J is defined as follows. If $J \models Ax$, then $\mathrm{Mod}(Ax, J)$ is a singleton set[6]; otherwise $\mathrm{Mod}(Ax, J)$ is the empty set.

We then define the notion of structure-preserving functors.

Definition 8. *A* strict compact closed Freyd functor *from* $J\colon \mathcal{C} \underset{\perp}{\rightleftarrows} \mathcal{K}\colon I \Rightarrow (-)$ *to* $J'\colon \mathcal{C}' \underset{\perp}{\rightleftarrows} \mathcal{K}'\colon I \Rightarrow' (-)$ *is a pair of functor* (Φ, Ψ) *such that*

- Φ *is a strict finite product preserving functor from* $\mathcal{C}$ *to* $\mathcal{C}'$*,*
- Ψ *is a strict symmetric monoidal functor from* $\mathcal{K}$ *to* $\mathcal{K}'$ *that preserves the chosen compact closed structures (i.e. units and counits) on the nose, and*
- (Φ, Ψ) *is a map of adjoints between* $J \dashv I \Rightarrow (-)$ *and* $J' \dashv I \Rightarrow' (-)$*.*

□

The collection of (small) compact closed Freyd categories and strict compact closed Freyd functors form a 1-category, which we write as *CCFC*.

Now the question is whether $\mathrm{Mod}(Ax, J) \overset{?}{\cong} \mathit{CCFC}(Cl(Ax), J)$ in **Set**.

Unfortunately this does not hold. More precisely, the left-to-right inclusion does not hold in general. This means that the term model satisfies some additional axioms reflecting some aspects of the π_F-calculus.

The additional axioms reflect the definition of the dual $\vec{T}^*$ in the term model; we have $\vec{T}^* \overset{\text{def}}{=} \vec{T}^{\perp}$ by definition, and thus $\vec{T}^{**} = \vec{T}$ and $(\vec{T} \otimes \vec{S})^* = \vec{T}^* \otimes \vec{S}^*$. It might be surprising that these equations are harmful because isomorphisms $A^{**} \cong A$ and $(A \otimes B)^* \cong A^* \otimes B^*$ exist in every compact closed category. The point is that the equations also require $\mathcal{C}$ to have isomorphisms $A^{**} \cong A$ and $(A \otimes B)^* \cong A^* \otimes B^*$ (witnessed by the respective identities).

We formally define the additional axioms, which we call **(I)** and **(D)**:

(I) The canonical isomorphism $A^{**} \longrightarrow A$ in $\mathcal{K}$ is the identity.
(D) The canonical isomorphism $(A \otimes B)^* \longrightarrow A^* \otimes B^*$ in $\mathcal{K}$ is the identity.

Theorem 6. $\mathrm{Mod}(Ax, J) \cong \mathit{CCFC}(Cl(Ax), J)$ *if* J *satisfies* ***(I)*** *and* ***(D)****.* □

---

6 Because we consider only the empty signature, the set of valuations is singleton.

$$\sigma ::= \tau \to \tau' \qquad \xi ::= \sigma \qquad \tau ::= (\xi_1, \ldots, \xi_n) \qquad\qquad \xi ::= \cdots \mid \sigma^*$$
$$V ::= x \mid \lambda\langle\vec{x}\rangle.M \qquad\qquad V ::= \cdots \mid \mathbf{channel}_\sigma \mid \mathbf{send}_\sigma$$
$$M ::= \langle\vec{V}\rangle \mid V\ \langle\vec{V}\rangle \mid \mathbf{let}\ \langle\vec{x}\rangle = M\ \mathbf{in}\ M'$$

(a) λ_c (b) λ_{ch} (difference from λ_c)

Fig. 4. Syntax of types and terms of the λ_c- and λ_{ch}-calculi. The syntax of λ_c is adapted to the setting of this paper.

4 A Concurrent λ-calculus and (de)compilation

In order to demonstrate the relevance of our semantic framework, this section tries to give a semantic reconstruction of fully-abstract compilation and decompilation from a higher-order calculus to the (first-order) π-calculus, such as [39, 42]. We first design an instance of the computational λ-calculus [33], named λ_{ch}, that is sound and complete with respect to compact closed Freyd categories. It is obtained by a straightforward extension of the coincidence between the computational λ-calculus and closed Freyd categories (Sect. 4.1). There are translations between π_F and λ_{ch} since both are sound and complete with respect to compact closed Freyd categories. Section 4.2 actually calculates the translations, and compare them with those in [39, 42].

4.1 The λ_{ch}-calculus

The λ_{ch}-calculus is a computational λ-calculus with additional constructors dealing with channels. This section introduces and explains the calculus.

The situation is nicely expressed by the following intuitive equation:

$$\frac{\lambda_{ch}}{\lambda_c} \approx \frac{(\text{compact closed Freyd category} + \mathbf{I} + \mathbf{D})}{(\text{closed Freyd category})}.$$

The base calculus λ_c is the *computational λ-calculus*, which corresponds to closed Freyd category [33, 37]. It is a call-by-value higher-order programming language, given in Fig. 4(a). Our calculus λ_{ch} is obtained by adding type and term constructors originating from the compact closed structure, which λ_c does not have.

Syntax. As for types, λ_{ch} has a new constructor coming from the dual object A^*. Normalising occurrences of the dual A^* using the axioms **(I)** $A^{**} = A$ and **(D)** $(A \otimes B)^* = A^* \otimes B^*$, we obtain the following grammar of types:

$$\sigma ::= \tau \to \tau' \qquad \xi ::= \sigma \mid \sigma^* \qquad \tau ::= (\xi_1, \ldots, \xi_n)$$

where $n \geq 0$ and $(\xi_1, \ldots, \xi_n)$ is an alternative notation for $\xi_1 \otimes \cdots \otimes \xi_n$. Compared with λ_c, the only new type is the dual type σ^* of a function type σ.

As for terms, λ_{ch} has constructors corresponding to the unit and counit

$$\eta_A : I \longrightarrow A \otimes A^* \qquad \epsilon_A : A^* \otimes A \longrightarrow I \qquad \text{(for each object } A)$$

of the compact closed structure. We simply add these morphisms as constants:

$$\frac{}{\Gamma \vdash \mathbf{channel}_\sigma : () \to (\sigma, \sigma^*)} \quad \text{and} \quad \frac{}{\Gamma \vdash \mathbf{send}_\sigma : (\sigma^*, \sigma) \to ()}.$$

We shall often omit the subscript σ.

In summary, we obtain the syntax of λ_{ch} shown in Fig. 4. Interestingly, λ_{ch} can be seen as a very core of Concurrent ML [38], a practical higher-order concurrent language, although λ_{ch} is developed from purely semantic considerations.

Semantics. Let us first discuss the intuitive meanings of the new constructors. The type σ^* is for *output channels*; **channel** $\langle\rangle$ creates and returns a pair of an input channel and an output channel that are connected; and **send** $\langle \alpha, V\rangle$ sends the value V via the output channel α. The following points are worth noting.

- λ_{ch} has no type constructor for *input channels*. The type system does not distinguish between input channels for type σ and values of type σ.
- λ_{ch} has no *receive* constructor. Receiving operation is implicit and on demand, delayed as much as possible.
- The send operator broadcasts a value via a channel. Several receivers may receive the same value from the same channel.

The first two points reflect the asynchrony of π_F, and the last point reflects the absence of non-replicated input (cf. Sect. 4.2).

Based on this intuition, we develop the operational, axiomatic and categorical semantics of λ_{ch}. We shall use the following abbreviations:

$$(\nu xy)M \overset{\text{def}}{=} \mathbf{let}\,\langle x, y\rangle = \mathbf{channel}\,\langle\rangle\,\mathbf{in}\,M \qquad M \parallel N \overset{\text{def}}{=} \mathbf{let}\,\langle\rangle = M\,\mathbf{in}\,N.$$

Operational Semantics. Assume an infinite set $\mathcal{X}$ of *channels*, ranged over by α and β. For each channel α, we write α for the input name and $\bar{\alpha}$ for the output name, both of which are values. A *configuration* is a tuple $(M, \vec{\alpha}, \mu)$ of a term M, a sequence $\vec{\alpha}$ of generated channels and a sequence μ of performed send operations, i.e. $\mu = (\mathbf{send}\,\langle\bar{\beta}_1, V_1\rangle, \dots, \mathbf{send}\,\langle\bar{\beta}_k, V_k\rangle)$. The *reduction relation* is defined by the following rules for channels

$$\begin{array}{rcll}
(E[\mathbf{channel}\,\langle\rangle],\ \vec{\alpha},\ \mu) & \longrightarrow & (E[\langle\beta, \bar{\beta}\rangle],\ \vec{\alpha}\cdot\beta,\ \mu) & (\beta \notin \vec{\alpha}) \\
(E[\mathbf{send}\,\langle\bar{\beta}, V\rangle],\ \vec{\alpha},\ \mu) & \longrightarrow & (E[\langle\rangle],\ \vec{\alpha},\ \mu\cdot\mathbf{send}\,\langle\bar{\beta}, V\rangle) & \\
(E[\beta\, V],\ \vec{\alpha},\ \mu) & \longrightarrow & (E[W\, V],\ \vec{\alpha},\ \mu) & (\mathbf{send}\,\langle\bar{\beta}, W\rangle \in \mu).
\end{array}$$

in addition to the standard rules for λ-abstractions and let-expressions, which change only M. Here the set of *evaluation contexts* is given by the grammar:

$$E ::= [] \mid \mathbf{let}\,\langle\vec{x}\rangle = E\,\mathbf{in}\,M \mid \mathbf{let}\,\langle\vec{x}\rangle = M\,\mathbf{in}\,E.$$

Note that M and N in $\mathbf{let}\,\langle\vec{x}\rangle = M\,\mathbf{in}\,N$ are evaluated in parallel (cf. Remark 3). This justifies the notation $M \parallel N$, an abbreviation for $\mathbf{let}\,\langle\rangle = M\,\mathbf{in}\,N$.

Axiomatic Semantics. The inference rules of the equational logic for λ_{ch} are those for λ_c with the rule of concurrent evaluation

$$\mathbf{let}\,\langle\vec{x}\rangle = M\,\mathbf{in}\,\mathbf{let}\,\langle\vec{y}\rangle = N\,\mathbf{in}\,L \quad = \quad \mathbf{let}\,\langle\vec{y}\rangle = N\,\mathbf{in}\,\mathbf{let}\,\langle\vec{x}\rangle = M\,\mathbf{in}\,L;$$

the β- and η-rules for channels

$$\begin{aligned}(\boldsymbol{\nu}x\bar{x})(\mathbf{send}\,\langle\bar{x},V\rangle \parallel M) &= (\boldsymbol{\nu}x\bar{x})(\mathbf{send}\,\langle\bar{x},V\rangle \parallel M\{V/x\})\\ (\boldsymbol{\nu}y\bar{y})(\mathbf{send}\,\langle\bar{z},y\rangle \parallel N) &= N\{\bar{z}/\bar{y}\}\end{aligned}$$

where $\bar{x} \notin \mathbf{Fv}(V) \cup \mathbf{Fv}(M)$, $y \notin \mathbf{Fv}(N)$ and $\bar{z} \neq \bar{y}$; and a GC rule.

Categorical Semantics. One can interpret λ_{ch}-terms in a compact closed Freyd category with **(I)** and **(D)**. The interpretation of the λ_c-calculus part is standard [24,37]; the constant $\mathbf{channel}_\sigma$ (resp. $\mathbf{send}_\sigma$) is interpreted as the "closure" whose body is η_σ (resp. ϵ_σ) as expected.

$$\begin{aligned}[\![\Gamma \vdash \mathbf{channel}_\sigma : () \to (\sigma,\sigma^*)]\!] &\stackrel{\text{def}}{=} J(!_\Gamma; \Lambda_{I,I,\sigma\otimes\sigma^*}(\eta_\sigma))\\ [\![\Gamma \vdash \mathbf{send}_\sigma : (\sigma^*,\sigma) \to ()]\!] &\stackrel{\text{def}}{=} J(!_\Gamma; \Lambda_{I,\sigma\otimes\sigma^*,I}(\epsilon_\sigma)).\end{aligned}$$

The categorical semantics is sound and complete with respect to the equational theory of the λ_{ch}-calculus. The proofs are basically straightforward but there is a subtle issue in the definition of the term model: we have different definitions of the right adjoint $I \Rightarrow (-)$, which are of course equivalent but do not coincide on the nose. Our choice here is $I \Rightarrow \langle\vec{\xi}\rangle \stackrel{\text{def}}{=} (\vec{\xi}^{\perp}) \to ()$.

4.2 Translations Between λ_{ch} and π_F

The higher-order calculus λ_{ch} is equivalent to π_F. This is because both calculi correspond to the same class of categories, namely, the class of compact closed Freyd categories with **(I)** and **(D)**, i.e.,

$$(\lambda_{ch}) \;\approx\; (\text{compact closed Freyd category} + \mathbf{I} + \mathbf{D}) \;\approx\; (\pi_F).$$

This subsection studies translations derived from this semantic correspondence.

The translations are defined by the interpretations in the term models. For example, the translation $(\!|-|\!)$ from λ_{ch} to π_F is induced by the interpretation of λ_{ch}-terms in the term model $\mathit{Cl}(\emptyset)$. The interpretation $[\![M]\!]_{\mathit{Cl}(\emptyset)}$ of a λ_{ch}-term M is an equivalence class of π_F-processes, since a morphism in $\mathit{Cl}(\emptyset)$ is an equivalence class of π_F-processes. The translation $(\!|M|\!)$ is defined by choosing a representative of the equivalence class. The other direction $[\!\{-\}\!]$ is obtained by the interpretation of π_F in the term model of λ_{ch}.

Figures 5 and 6 are concrete definitions of the translations for a natural choice of representatives. Let us discuss the translations in more details.

The translation from π_F to λ_{ch} (Fig. 5) is easy to understand. It directly expresses the higher-order view of the first-order π-calculus. For example, an

$$[\![\mathbf{ch}^o[\vec{T}]]\!] \stackrel{\text{def}}{=} [\![\vec{T}]\!] \to () \qquad [\![\mathbf{ch}^i[\vec{T}]]\!] \stackrel{\text{def}}{=} ([\![\vec{T}]\!] \to ())^* \qquad [\![(T_1, \ldots, T_n)]\!] \stackrel{\text{def}}{=} ([\![T_1]\!], \ldots, [\![T_n]\!])$$

$$[\![\mathbf{0}]\!] \stackrel{\text{def}}{=} \langle\rangle \qquad [\![P \mid Q]\!] \stackrel{\text{def}}{=} [\![P]\!] \parallel [\![Q]\!] \qquad [\![(\boldsymbol{\nu}xy)P]\!] \stackrel{\text{def}}{=} (\boldsymbol{\nu}xy)[\![P]\!]$$

$$[\![\bar{a}\langle\vec{x}\rangle]\!] \stackrel{\text{def}}{=} \bar{a}\,\langle\vec{x}\rangle \qquad [\![!a(\vec{x}).P]\!] \stackrel{\text{def}}{=} \mathbf{send}\,\langle a, \lambda(\vec{x}).[\![P]\!]\rangle$$

Fig. 5. Translation from π_F to λ_{ch}

$$(\!|\tau_1 \to \tau_2|\!) \stackrel{\text{def}}{=} \mathbf{ch}^o[(\!|\tau_1|\!), (\!|\tau_2|\!)^\perp] \qquad (\!|\sigma^*|\!) \stackrel{\text{def}}{=} (\!|\sigma|\!)^\perp \qquad (\!|(\tau_1, \ldots, \tau_n)|\!) \stackrel{\text{def}}{=} ((\!|\tau_1|\!), \ldots, (\!|\tau_n|\!))$$

$$(\!|x|\!)_p \stackrel{\text{def}}{=} (p \leftrightharpoons x) \qquad (\!|\lambda\vec{x}.M|\!)_p \stackrel{\text{def}}{=} !p(\vec{x}, \vec{q}).(\!|M|\!)_{\vec{q}} \qquad (\!|\langle\vec{V}\rangle|\!)_{\vec{p}} \stackrel{\text{def}}{=} (\!|V_1|\!)_{p_1} \mid \cdots \mid (\!|V_n|\!)_{p_n}$$

$$(\!|V\,\langle\vec{W}\rangle|\!)_{\vec{p}} \stackrel{\text{def}}{=} (\boldsymbol{\nu}a\bar{a})(\boldsymbol{\nu}\vec{r}\vec{s})((\!|V|\!)_a \mid (\!|\langle\vec{W}\rangle|\!)_{\vec{s}} \mid \bar{a}\langle\vec{r}, \vec{p}\rangle)$$

$$(\!|\mathbf{let}\,\langle\vec{x}\rangle = M\,\mathbf{in}\,N|\!)_{\vec{p}} \stackrel{\text{def}}{=} (\boldsymbol{\nu}\vec{x}\vec{q})((\!|M|\!)_{\vec{q}} \mid (\!|N|\!)_{\vec{p}})$$

$$(\!|\mathbf{channel}|\!)_p \stackrel{\text{def}}{=} !p(x, y).x \hookrightarrow y \qquad (\!|\mathbf{send}|\!)_p \stackrel{\text{def}}{=} !p(x, y).x \hookrightarrow y$$

Fig. 6. Translation from λ_{ch} to π_F

output action is mapped to an application and an input-prefixing $!a(\vec{x}).P$ to a send operation of the value $\lambda\langle\vec{x}\rangle.P$ via the channel a.

An interesting (and perhaps confusing) phenomenon is that an input channel in π_F is mapped to an output channel in λ_{ch}. This can be explained as follows. In the name-passing viewpoint, the reduction

$$(\boldsymbol{\nu}xy)(!y(\vec{z}).P \mid x\langle\vec{u}\rangle) \quad\longrightarrow\quad (\boldsymbol{\nu}xy)(!y(\vec{z}).P \mid P\{\vec{u}/\vec{z}\})$$

sends $\vec{u}$ to the process $!y(\vec{z}).P$, and thus x is output and y is input. In the process-passing viewpoint, the abstraction $(\vec{z}).P$ is sent to the location of x, and thus y is the output and x is the input.

Next, we explain the translation from λ_{ch} to π_F (Fig. 6).

Let us first examine the translation of types. The most non-trivial part is the translation of a function type $\tau_1 \to \tau_2$. A key to understand the translation is the isomorphism $\tau_1 \to \tau_2 \cong \tau_1 \otimes \tau_2^\perp \to ()$. The latter form of function type corresponds to an output channel type in π_F. Hence a function is understood as a process additionally taking channels to which the return values are passed.

The translation $(\!|M|\!)_{\vec{p}}$ of a λ_{ch}-term $\Gamma \vdash M : (\xi_1, \ldots, \xi_n)$ takes extra parameters $\vec{p} = p_1, \ldots, p_n$ to which the values should be placed. This is a consequence of the definition in the π_F-term model that a morphism $\vec{T} \longrightarrow \vec{S}$ is a process $\vec{x}\colon \vec{T},\ \vec{y}\colon \vec{S}^\perp \vdash P : \diamond$. Here $\vec{p}$ corresponds to $\vec{y}$, Γ to $\vec{x}\colon \vec{T}$ and $\vec{\xi}$ to $\vec{S}$.

Now it is not so difficult to understand the interpretations of constructs in the λ_c-calculus. For example, the abstraction $(\!|\lambda\langle\vec{x}\rangle.M|\!)_p$ is mapped to an abstraction $(\vec{x}, \vec{q}).(\!|M|\!)_{\vec{q}}$ placed at p, which takes additional channels $\vec{q}$ to which the results of the evaluation of M should be sent.

It might be surprising that the interpretations of **channel** and **send** coincide. This is because of the one-sided formulation of π_F. In the two-sided formulation, the unit η and counit ϵ of the compact closed structure, corresponding to **channel** and **send**, can be written as logical inference rules

$$(\!|\mathbf{0}|\!) \stackrel{\text{def}}{=} \mathbf{0} \qquad (\!|P \mid Q|\!) \stackrel{\text{def}}{=} (\!|P|\!) \mid (\!|Q|\!) \qquad (\!|(\boldsymbol{\nu}xy)P|\!) \stackrel{\text{def}}{=} (\boldsymbol{\nu}xy)(\!|P|\!) \qquad (\!|!x\,v|\!) \stackrel{\text{def}}{=} (\!|v|\!)_x$$

$$(\!|v\langle w_1,\dots,w_n\rangle|\!) \stackrel{\text{def}}{=} (\boldsymbol{\nu}\bar{a}a)(\boldsymbol{\nu}\bar{b}_1b_1)\dots(\boldsymbol{\nu}\bar{b}_nb_n)((\!|v|\!)_a \mid (\!|w_1|\!)_{b_1} \mid \cdots \mid (\!|w_n|\!)_{b_n} \mid \bar{a}\langle\bar{b}_1,\dots,\bar{b}_n\rangle)$$

$$(\!|x|\!)_a \stackrel{\text{def}}{=} (a \hookrightarrow x) \qquad (\!|(\vec{x}).P|\!)_a \stackrel{\text{def}}{=} !a(\vec{x}).(\!|P|\!)$$

Fig. 7. Translation from AHOπ to π_F

$$\frac{\Gamma, A, A^{\perp} \vdash \Delta}{\Gamma \vdash \Delta} \quad \text{and} \quad \frac{\Gamma \vdash A^{\perp}, A, \Delta}{\Gamma \vdash \Delta},$$

which are different. In the one-sided formulation, however, they become

$$\frac{\Gamma, A, A^{\perp}, \Delta^{\perp} \vdash}{\Gamma, \Delta^{\perp} \vdash}.$$

Hence η and ϵ (or **channel** and **send**) cannot be distinguished in π_F.

The translation $(\!|-|\!)$ must be the inverse of $[\![-]\!]$ because both the term models are the initial compact closed Freyd category with **(I)** and **(D)**. That means, $\emptyset \rhd \Gamma \vdash P = (\!|[\![P]\!]|\!)$ and $\emptyset \rhd \Gamma \vdash M = [\![(\!|M|\!)]\!]$ are provable for every P and M. This result is independent of the choice of representatives.

4.3 Relation to Other Calculi and Translations

A number of higher-order concurrent calculi, as well as their translations to the first-order π-calculus, have been proposed and studied (e.g. [29,39,40,42,45,47]). The calculus λ_{ch} and the translations have a lot of ideas in common with those calculi and translations; see Sect. 6.

This subsection mainly discusses the relationship to the translations by Sangiorgi [42] (see also [43]) between *asynchronous higher-order* π*-calculus* (*AHO*π for short) and *asynchronous local* π*-calculus* ($L\pi$ for short). Here we focus on this work because it is closest to ours. We shall see that our semantic or categorical development provides us with a semantic reconstruction of Sangiorgi's translations, as well as an extension.

A variant of AHOπ can be seen as a fragment of λ_{ch}. The syntax of processes of AHOπ and representation by λ_{ch}-terms are given as follow:

$$\begin{array}{llllllll} v, w ::= x \mid & (\vec{x}).P & P, Q ::= \mathbf{0} \mid & (P \mid Q) \mid & (\boldsymbol{\nu}xy)P \mid & !x\,v & \mid v\langle\vec{w}\rangle \\ \quad x & \lambda\langle\vec{x}\rangle.P & \langle\rangle & P \parallel Q & (\boldsymbol{\nu}xy)P & \mathbf{send}\,\langle x, v\rangle & v\,\langle\vec{w}\rangle. \end{array}$$

(It slightly differs from the original syntax, as $\boldsymbol{\nu}$ binds a pair of names.)

This fragment is nicely described as the limitation on types:

$$\sigma ::= (\vec{\sigma}) \to () \qquad \xi ::= \sigma \mid \sigma^* \qquad \tau ::= ().$$

Recall that σ is a type for abstractions, ξ is a type for variables, and τ is a type for terms. This limitation means that (1) an abstraction cannot take a channel as an argument, and (2) a term M must be of the unit type, i.e. a process.

Once regarding AHOπ as a fragment of λ_{ch}, the translation from AHOπ to π_F is obtained by restricting $(\!|-|\!)$ to AHOπ. The resulting translation is in Fig. 7. As mentioned, the translation is the same as that of Sangiorgi [42] except for minor differences due to the slight change of the syntax.

Sangiorgi also gave a translation in the opposite direction, from Lπ to AHOπ in the same paper. The calculus Lπ is a fragment of the π-calculus in which only output channels can be passed. The **i**/**o**-separation of π_F allows us to characterise the local version of π_F by a limitation on types. In the local variant, the output channel type is restricted to $T ::= \mathbf{ch}^o[\vec{T}]$, expressing that only output channels can be passed via an output channel. Then the definition of type environment should be changed accordingly: $\Gamma ::= \cdot \mid x : T \mid x : T^{\perp}$ (since the syntactic class represented by T is not closed under the dual $(-)^{\perp}$ in the local setting).

Interestingly the limitation on types in AHOπ coincides with that in Lπ, when one identify $\mathbf{ch}^o[\vec{T}]$ with $(\vec{T}) \to ()$ (as we have done in many places). In other words, the syntactic restrictions of AHOπ and Lπ are the same semantic conditions described in different syntax. As a consequence, the image of Lπ by $[\![-]\!]$ is indeed in AHOπ.

Remark 4. There is, however, a notable difference from Sangiorgi's work [42]. Sangiorgi proved that the translation is fully-abstract with respect to barbed congruence; in contrast, we only show that $\vdash M = N$ iff $\vdash (\!|M|\!) = (\!|N|\!)$. In particular, the η-rule is inevitable for our argument. The presence of the η-rules significantly simplifies the argument, at the cost of operational justification (recall that the η-rule is not sound with respect to barbed congruence).

It is natural to ask how one can reconstruct the full-abstraction result with respect to barbed congruence. An interesting observation is that, if M and N are AHOπ processes, then $\vdash^{\ominus} M = N$ iff $\vdash^{\ominus} (\!|M|\!) = (\!|N|\!)$, where $\vdash^{\ominus}$ means provability without using η-rules. We expect that this semantic observation explains why locality is essential as noted in [42]; we leave the details for future work. □

5 Discussions

Connection to Logics. We have so far studied a connection between compact closed Freyd category and π-calculus. Here we briefly discuss the missing piece of the Curry-Howard-Lambek correspondence, namely logic.

The model of this paper is closely related to linear logic. Actually, every compact closed Freyd category is a model of linear logic (more precisely, MELL), as an instance of linear-non-linear model [6] (see, e.g., [27] for categorical models of linear logic). The interpretation of formulas is shown in Table 1. It differs from the translations by Abramsky [1] and Bellin and Scott [5] and from the Curry-Howard correspondence for session types by Caires and Pfenning [8], but resembles the connection between a variant of local π-calculus and a polarised linear logic by Honda and Laurent [19]; a detailed analysis of the translation is left for future work.

The logic corresponding to compact closed Freyd category should be a proper extension of linear logic, since compact closed Freyd categories form a proper

Table 1. The categorical and π_F-calculus interpretations of MELL formulas

linear logic (formula)	compact closed Freyd category (object)	π_F-calculus (type environment)
$A \otimes B$ $A \parr B$	$A \otimes B$	$x : A, y : B$
$!A$	$I \Rightarrow A$	$x : \mathbf{ch}^o[A^\perp]$
$?A$	$(A \Rightarrow I)^*$	$x : \mathbf{ch}^i[A]$

subclass of linear-non-linear models. For example, the following rules are invalid in linear logic but admissible in compact closed Freyd categories:

$$\frac{\vdash \Gamma \qquad \vdash \Delta}{\vdash \Gamma, \Delta} \qquad \frac{\vdash \Gamma, A, B \qquad \vdash \Delta, A^\perp, B^\perp}{\vdash \Gamma, \Delta} \qquad \frac{\vdash \Gamma, A, A^\perp}{\vdash \Gamma}.$$

These rules, especially the second rule called *multicut*, were often studied in concurrency theory; see Abramsky et al. [2] for their relevance to concurrency.

Do the above rules fill the gap between linear logic and compact closed Freyd category? Recent work by Hasegawa [15] suggests that MELL with above rules is still weaker than compact closed Freyd category. First observe that the above rules can be interpreted in any linear-non-linear model of which the monoidal category is compact closed. Hasegawa showed that a linear-non-linear model whose monoidal category is compact closed induces a closed Freyd category of which the monoidal category is *traced* (and vice versa) but the induced Freyd category is not necessarily compact closed. Hence the logic corresponding to compact closed Freyd category has further axioms or rules in addition to the above ones. A reasonable candidate for the additional axiom is $! \cong ?$; interestingly, Atkey et al. [3] reached a similar rule from a different perspective. Further investigation is left for future work.

Non-empty Signature. The categorical type theory for the λ-calculus considers a family parameterised by *signatures*, consisting of atomic types and constants. It covers, for example, the λ-calculus with natural number type and arithmetic constants (such as addition and multiplication), as well as a calculus with integer reference type and read and update functions.

Although this paper only considers the calculus with the empty signature, which has no additional type nor constant, extending our theory to handle non-empty signatures is, in a sense, not difficult. The easiest way is to apply the established theory of the computational λ-calculus [33,37]. As we have seen in Sect. 4, the π_F-calculus can be seen as a computational λ-calculus λ_{ch} having constants for manipulating channels; hence the π_F-calculus with additional constants is λ_{ch} with the additional constants, which is still in the family of computational λ-calculus.

The π_F-calculus with non-empty signature has several applications. We shall briefly discuss some of them.

An important example of π_F with non-empty signature is the calculus with non-replicated input, which we regard as a calculus with additional "process constants" but without any additional type. A key observation is that every non-replicated input process $a(\vec{x}).P$ can be expressed as

$$a(\vec{x}).P \approx^c (\boldsymbol{\nu}\bar{b}b)(a(\vec{x}).\bar{b}\langle\vec{x}\rangle \mid !b(\vec{x}).P) \qquad (\approx^c \text{ is weak barbed congruence})$$

and thus it suffices to deal with non-replicated input processes in special form, namely $a : \mathbf{ch}^i[\vec{T}],\ \bar{b} : \mathbf{ch}^o[\vec{T}] \vdash a(\vec{x}).\bar{b}\langle\vec{x}\rangle : \diamond$. Adding these processes as constants and the computational rules of $a(\vec{x}).\bar{b}\langle\vec{x}\rangle$ as equational axioms results in a calculus with non-replicated inputs. The categorical model is a compact closed Freyd category with distinguished morphisms $(A \Rightarrow I) \longrightarrow (A \Rightarrow I)$ for each object A which satisfy certain axioms.

This technique is applicable to synchronous output as well. Because

$$\bar{a}\langle\vec{x}\rangle.P \approx^c (\boldsymbol{\nu}\bar{b}b)(\bar{a}\langle\vec{x}\rangle.\bar{b}\langle\rangle \mid !b().P),$$

it suffices to consider constants representing $\bar{a} : \mathbf{ch}^o[\vec{T}], \vec{x} : \vec{T}, \bar{b} : \mathbf{ch}^o[] \vdash \bar{a}\langle\vec{x}\rangle.\bar{b}\langle\rangle : \diamond$.

6 Related Work

Logical Studies of π-calculi. There is a considerable amount of studies on connections between process calculi and linear logic. Here we divide these studies into two classes. These classes are substantially different; for example, one regards the formula $A \otimes B$ as a type for processes with two "ports" of type A and B, whereas the other as the session-type $!A.B$. Our work is more closely related to the former than the latter, but some interesting coincidence to the latter kind of studies can also be found.

The former class of research dates back to the work by Abramsky [1] and Bellin and Scott [5], where they discovered that π-calculus processes can encode proof-nets of classical linear logic. Later, Abramsky et al. [2] introduced the *interaction categories* to give a semantic description of a CCS-like process calculus. In their work, they observed that the compact closed structure is important to capture the strong expressive power of process calculi.

A tighter connection between π-calculus and proof-nets was recently presented by Honda and Laurent [19]. They showed that an **i**/**o**-typed π-calculus corresponds to *polarised proof-nets*, and introduced the notion of *extended reduction* for the π-calculus to simulate cut-elimination. The π-calculus used in this work is very similar to π_F in terms of syntax and reduction. Their calculus is asynchronous, does not allow non-replicated inputs, and requires **i**/**o**-separation. Furthermore, the extended reduction is almost the same as the rules (E-Beta) and (E-GC) except for the side conditions. A significant difference compared to our work is that their calculus is *local* [28,49], reflecting the fact that the corresponding logic is polarised.

Our work is inspired by these studies. The idea of **i**/**o**-separation can already be found in the work by Bellin and Scott and the use of compact closed category is motivated by the study of interaction category. It is worth mentioning here that the design of π_F is also influenced by the calculus introduced by Laird [22], although it is not a logical study but categorical (see below).

The latter approach started with the Curry-Howard correspondences between session-typed π-calculi and linear logic established by Caires, Pfenning and Toninho [8,9] and subsequently by Wadler [48]. These correspondences are exact in the sense that every process has a corresponding proof, and vice versa. As a consequence, processes of the calculi inherit good properties of linear logic proofs such as termination and confluence of cut-elimination. In terms of process calculi, process of these calculi do not fall into deadlock or race condition. This can be seen as a serious restriction of expressive power [3,26,48].

Several extensions to increase the expressiveness of these calculi have been proposed and studied. Interestingly, ideas behind some of these extensions are related to our work, in particular to Sect. 5 discussing the multicut rule [2] and the axiom $! \cong ?$. Atkey et al. [3] studied *CP* [48] with the multicut rule and $! \cong ?$ and discussed how these extensions increase the expressiveness of the calculus, at the cost of losing some good properties of CP. Dardha and Gay [10] studied another extension of CP with multicut, keeping the calculus deadlock-free by an elaborated type system.

Balzer and Pfenning [4] proposed a session-typed calculus with shared (mutable) resources, inspired by linear-non-linear adjunction [6].

Categorical Semantics of π-calculi. The idea of using a closed Freyd category to model the π-calculus is strongly inspired by Laird [22]. He introduced the *distributive-closed Freyd category* to describe abstract properties of a game-semantic model of the asynchronous π-calculus and showed that distributive-closed Freyd categories with some additional structures suffice to interpret the asynchronous π-calculus. The additional structures are specific to his game model and not completely axiomatised.[7] Our notion of compact closed Freyd category might be seen as a reformulation of his idea, obtained by filtering out some structures difficult to axiomatise and by strengthening some others to make axioms simpler. A significant difference is that our categorical model does not deal with non-replicated inputs, which we think is essential for a simple axiomatisation.

Another approach for categorical semantics of the π-calculus has been the presheaf based approach [12,44]. These studies gave particular categories that nicely handles the nominal aspects of the π-calculus; these studies, however, do not aim for a correspondence between a categorical structure and the π-calculus.

Higher-Order Calculi with Channels. Besides the λ_{ch}-calculus, there are numbers of functional languages augmented by communication channels, from theoretical ones [13,25,46,48] to practical languages [34,38].

On the practical side, Concurrent ML (CML) [38], among others, is a well-developed higher-order concurrent language. CML has primitives to create channels and threads, and primitives to send and accept values through channels.

[7] A list of properties in [22] does not seem to be complete. We could not prove some claims in the paper only from these properties, but with ones specific to his model.

Since our λ_{ch}-calculus can create (non-linear) channels and send values via channels, the λ_{ch}-calculus can be seen as a core calculus of CML despite its origin in categorical semantics. The major difference between CML and the λ_{ch}-calculus is that communications in CML are synchronous whereas communications in the λ_{ch}-calculus are asynchronous.

On the theoretical side, session-typed functional languages have been actively studied [13,25,46,48]. Notably, some of these languages [25,46,48] are built upon the Curry-Howard foundation between linear logic and session-typed processes. It might be interesting to investigate whether we can relate these languages and the λ_{ch}-calculus through the lens of Curry-Howard-Lambek correspondence.

Higher-Order vs. First-Order π-calculus. A number of translations from higher-order languages to the π-calculus have been developed [39,40,42,45,47] since Milner [29] presented the encodings of the λ-calculus into the π-calculus. The basic idea shared by these studies is to transform $\lambda x.M$ to a process $!a(x,p).P$ that receives the argument x together with a name p where the rest of the computation will be transmitted. In our framework, this idea is described as the isomorphism $A \Rightarrow B \cong A \otimes B^* \Rightarrow I$.

Among others, the translation from AHOπ to Lπ [42] is the closest to our translation from the λ_{ch}-calculus to the π_F-calculus. Sangiorgi [41] observed that Milner's translation can be established via the translation of AHOπ by applying the CPS transformation to the λ-calculus. This observation also applies to our translation. That is, we can obtain Milner's translation by combining CPS transformation and the compilation of the λ_{ch}-calculus.

7 Conclusion and Future Work

We have introduced an **i**/**o**-typed π-calculus (π_F-calculus) as well as the categorical counterpart of π_F-calculus (compact closed Freyd category) and showed the categorical type theory correspondence between them. The correspondence was established by regarding the π-calculus as a higher-order programming language, introducing the **i**/**o**-separation, and introducing the η-rule, a rule that explains the mismatch between behavioural equivalences and categorical models.

As an application of our semantic framework we introduced a higher-order calculus λ_{ch}-calculus "equivalent" to the π_F-calculus. We have demonstrated that translations between λ_{ch}-calculus and π_F-calculus can be derived by a simple semantic argument, and showed that the translation from λ_{ch} to π_F is a generalisation of the translation from AHOπ to Lπ given by Sangiorgi [42].

There are three main directions for future work. First, further investigation on the η-rule is indispensable. We plan to construct a categorical model of the π_F-calculus with an additional constant that captures barbed congruence. Revealing the relationship between locality and the η-rule is another important problem. Second, the operational properties of the λ_{ch}-calculus and its relation to the equational theory needs a further investigation. Third, finding the logical counterpart of compact closed Freyd category to establish a proper Curry-Howard-Lambek correspondence is an interesting future work.

Acknowledgement. We would like to thank Naoki Kobayashi, Masahito Hasegawa and James Laird for discussions, and anonymous referees for valuable comments. This work was supported by JSPS KAKENHI Grant Number 15H05706 and 16K16004.

References

1. Abramsky, S.: Proofs as processes. Theor. Comput. Sci. **135**(1), 5–9 (1994)
2. Abramsky, S., Gay, S.J., Nagarajan, R.: Interaction categories and the foundations of typed concurrent programming. In: Proceedings of the NATO Advanced Study Institute on Deductive Program Design, Marktoberdorf, Germany, pp. 35–113 (1996)
3. Atkey, R., Lindley, S., Morris, J.G.: Conflation confers concurrency. In: A List of Successes That Can Change the World - Essays Dedicated to Philip Wadler on the Occasion of His 60th Birthday, pp. 32–55 (2016)
4. Balzer, S., Pfenning, F.: Manifest sharing with session types. PACMPL **1**(ICFP), 37:1–37:29 (2017)
5. Bellin, G., Scott, P.J.: On the π-calculus and linear logic. Theor. Comput. Sci. **135**(1), 11–65 (1994)
6. Benton, P.N.: A mixed linear and non-linear logic: proofs, terms and models. In: Pacholski, L., Tiuryn, J. (eds.) CSL 1994. LNCS, vol. 933, pp. 121–135. Springer, Heidelberg (1995). https://doi.org/10.1007/BFb0022251
7. Boreale, M.: On the expressiveness of internal mobility in name-passing calculi. Theor. Comput. Sci. **195**(2), 205–226 (1998)
8. Caires, L., Pfenning, F.: Session types as intuitionistic linear propositions. In: Gastin, P., Laroussinie, F. (eds.) CONCUR 2010. LNCS, vol. 6269, pp. 222–236. Springer, Heidelberg (2010). https://doi.org/10.1007/978-3-642-15375-4_16
9. Caires, L., Pfenning, F., Toninho, B.: Linear logic propositions as session types. Math. Struct. Comput. Sci. **26**(3), 367–423 (2016)
10. Dardha, O., Gay, S.J.: A new linear logic for deadlock-free session-typed processes. In: Baier, C., Dal Lago, U. (eds.) FoSSaCS 2018. LNCS, vol. 10803, pp. 91–109. Springer, Cham (2018). https://doi.org/10.1007/978-3-319-89366-2_5
11. de Nicola, R., Hennessy, M.C.B.: Testing equivalences for processes. In: Diaz, J. (ed.) ICALP 1983. LNCS, vol. 154, pp. 548–560. Springer, Heidelberg (1983). https://doi.org/10.1007/BFb0036936
12. Fiore, M.P., Moggi, E., Sangiorgi, D.: A fully abstract model for the π-calculus. Inf. Comput. **179**(1), 76–117 (2002)
13. Gay, S.J., Vasconcelos, V.T.: Linear type theory for asynchronous session types. J. Funct. Program. **20**(1), 19–50 (2010)
14. Girard, J.: Linear logic. Theor. Comput. Sci. **50**, 1–102 (1987)
15. Hasegawa, M.: From linear logic to cyclic sharing. Lecture slides, Linearity (2018)
16. Hayashi, S.: Adjunction of semifunctors: categorical structures in nonextensional lambda calculus. Theor. Comput. Sci. **41**, 95–104 (1985)
17. Hoare, C.A.R.: Communicating Sequential Processes. Prentice-Hall, Upper Saddle River (1985)
18. Honda, K.: Types for dyadic interaction. In: Best, E. (ed.) CONCUR 1993. LNCS, vol. 715, pp. 509–523. Springer, Heidelberg (1993). https://doi.org/10.1007/3-540-57208-2_35
19. Honda, K., Laurent, O.: An exact correspondence between a typed pi-calculus and polarised proof-nets. Theor. Comput. Sci. **411**(22–24), 2223–2238 (2010)

20. Honda, K., Vasconcelos, V.T., Kubo, M.: Language primitives and type discipline for structured communication-based programming. In: Hankin, C. (ed.) ESOP 1998. LNCS, vol. 1381, pp. 122–138. Springer, Heidelberg (1998). https://doi.org/10.1007/BFb0053567
21. Kelly, G.M., Laplaza, M.L.: Coherence for compact closed categories. J. Pure Appl. Algebra **19**, 193–213 (1980)
22. Laird, J.: A game semantics of the asynchronous π-calculus. In: Abadi, M., de Alfaro, L. (eds.) CONCUR 2005. LNCS, vol. 3653, pp. 51–65. Springer, Heidelberg (2005). https://doi.org/10.1007/11539452_8
23. Lambek, J., Scott, P.J.: Introduction to Higher-Order Categorical Logic, vol. 7. Cambridge University Press, New York (1988)
24. Levy, P.B., Power, J., Thielecke, H.: Modelling environments in call-by-value programming languages. Inf. Comput. **185**(2), 182–210 (2003)
25. Lindley, S., Morris, J.G.: A semantics for propositions as sessions. In: Vitek, J. (ed.) ESOP 2015. LNCS, vol. 9032, pp. 560–584. Springer, Heidelberg (2015). https://doi.org/10.1007/978-3-662-46669-8_23
26. Mazza, D.: The true concurrency of differential interaction nets. Math. Struct. Comput. Sci. **28**(7), 1097–1125 (2018)
27. Melliès, P.A.: Categorical semantics of linear logic. Panoramas et syntheses **27**, 15–215 (2009)
28. Merro, M.: Locality in the π-calculus and applications to distributed objects. Ph.D. thesis, École Nationale Supérieure des Mines de Paris (2000)
29. Milner, R.: Functions as processes. Math. Struct. Comput. Sci. **2**(2), 119–141 (1992)
30. Milner, R., Parrow, J., Walker, D.: A calculus of mobile processes, I. Inf. Comput. **100**(1), 1–40 (1992)
31. Milner, R., Parrow, J., Walker, D.: A calculus of mobile processes, II. Inf. Comput. **100**(1), 41–77 (1992)
32. Milner, R., Sangiorgi, D.: Barbed bisimulation. In: Kuich, W. (ed.) ICALP 1992. LNCS, vol. 623, pp. 685–695. Springer, Heidelberg (1992). https://doi.org/10.1007/3-540-55719-9_114
33. Moggi, E.: Computational lambda-calculus and monads. In: Proceedings of the Fourth Annual Symposium on Logic in Computer Science (LICS 1989), Pacific Grove, California, USA, 5–8 June 1989, pp. 14–23 (1989)
34. Peyton Jones, S.L., Gordon, A.D., Finne, S.: Concurrent Haskell. In: Conference Record of POPL 1996: The 23rd ACM SIGPLAN-SIGACT Symposium on Principles of Programming Languages, Papers Presented at the Symposium, St. Petersburg Beach, Florida, USA, 21–24 January 1996, pp. 295–308 (1996)
35. Pierce, B.C., Sangiorgi, D.: Typing and subtyping for mobile processes. Math. Struct. Comput. Sci. **6**(5), 409–453 (1996)
36. Power, J., Robinson, E.: Premonoidal categories and notions of computation. Math. Struct. Comput. Sci. **7**(5), 453–468 (1997)
37. Power, J., Thielecke, H.: Closed Freyd- and κ-categories. In: Wiedermann, J., van Emde Boas, P., Nielsen, M. (eds.) ICALP 1999. LNCS, vol. 1644, pp. 625–634. Springer, Heidelberg (1999). https://doi.org/10.1007/3-540-48523-6_59
38. Reppy, J.H.: CML: a higher-order concurrent language. In: Proceedings of the ACM SIGPLAN 1991 Conference on Programming Language Design and Implementation (PLDI), Toronto, Ontario, Canada, 26–28 June 1991, pp. 293–305 (1991)
39. Sangiorgi, D.: Expressing mobility in process algebras: first-order and higher-order paradigms. Ph.D. thesis, University of Edinburgh, UK (1993)

40. Sangiorgi, D.: π-Calculus, internal mobility, and agent-passing calculi. Theor. Comput. Sci. **167**(1&2), 235–274 (1996)
41. Sangiorgi, D.: From λ to π; or, rediscovering continuations. Math. Struct. Comput. Sci. **9**(4), 367–401 (1999)
42. Sangiorgi, D.: Asynchronous process calculi: the first- and higher-order paradigms. Theor. Comput. Sci. **253**(2), 311–350 (2001)
43. Sangiorgi, D., Walker, D.: The π-calculus—A Theory of Mobile Processes. Cambridge University Press, New York (2001)
44. Stark, I.: A fully abstract domain model for the π-calculus. In: Proceedings, 11th Annual IEEE Symposium on Logic in Computer Science, New Brunswick, New Jersey, USA, 27–30 July 1996, pp. 36–42 (1996)
45. Toninho, B., Caires, L., Pfenning, F.: Functions as session-typed processes. In: Birkedal, L. (ed.) FoSSaCS 2012. LNCS, vol. 7213, pp. 346–360. Springer, Heidelberg (2012). https://doi.org/10.1007/978-3-642-28729-9_23
46. Toninho, B., Caires, L., Pfenning, F.: Higher-order processes, functions, and sessions: a monadic integration. In: Felleisen, M., Gardner, P. (eds.) ESOP 2013. LNCS, vol. 7792, pp. 350–369. Springer, Heidelberg (2013). https://doi.org/10.1007/978-3-642-37036-6_20
47. Turner, D.N.: The polymorphic Pi-calculus: theory and implementation. Ph.D. thesis, University of Edinburgh, UK (1996)
48. Wadler, P.: Propositions as sessions. J. Funct. Program. **24**(2–3), 384–418 (2014)
49. Yoshida, N.: Minimality and separation results on asynchronous mobile processes - representability theorems by concurrent combinators. Theor. Comput. Sci. **274**(1–2), 231–276 (2002)

5

Effectful Normal Form Bisimulation

Ugo Dal Lago[1,2(✉)] and Francesco Gavazzo[1,2(✉)]

[1] University of Bologna, Bologna, Italy
[2] Inria Sophia Antipolis, Sophia Antipolis Cedex, France
ugo.dallago@unibo.it, francesco.gavazzo@gmail.com

Abstract. Normal form bisimulation, also known as *open* bisimulation, is a coinductive technique for higher-order program equivalence in which programs are compared by looking at their essentially infinitary tree-like normal forms, i.e. at their Böhm or Lévy-Longo trees. The technique has been shown to be useful not only when proving metatheorems about λ-calculi and their semantics, but also when looking at concrete examples of terms. In this paper, we show that there is a way to generalise normal form bisimulation to calculi with algebraic effects, *à la* Plotkin and Power. We show that some mild conditions on monads and relators, which have already been shown to guarantee effectful applicative bisimilarity to be a congruence relation, are enough to prove that the obtained notion of bisimilarity, which we call *effectful normal form bisimilarity*, is a congruence relation, and thus sound for contextual equivalence. Additionally, contrary to applicative bisimilarity, normal form bisimilarity allows for enhancements of the bisimulation proof method, hence proving a powerful reasoning principle for effectful programming languages.

1 Introduction

The study of program equivalence has always been one of the central tasks of programming language theory: giving satisfactory definitions and methodologies for it can be fruitful in contexts like program verification and compiler optimisation design, but also helps in understanding the *nature* of the programming language at hand. This is particularly true when dealing with higher-order languages, in which giving satisfactory notions of program equivalence is well-known to be hard. Indeed, the problem has been approached in many different ways. One can define program equivalence through denotational semantics, thus relying on a model. One could also proceed following the route traced by Morris [51], and define programs to be *contextually* equivalent when they behave the same in every context, this way taking program equivalence as the *largest* adequate congruence.

Both these approaches have their drawbacks, the first one relying on the existence of a (not too coarse) denotational model, the latter quantifying over all contexts, and thus making concrete proofs of equivalence hard. Among the

Thanks to the ANR projects 14CE250005 ELICA and 16CE250011 REPAS.

many alternative techniques the research community has been proposing along the years, one can cite logical relations and applicative bisimilarity [1,4,8], both based on the idea that equivalent higher-order terms should behave the same when fed with any (pair of related) inputs. This way, terms are compared mimicking any possible action a discriminating context could possibly perform on the tested terms. In other words, the universal quantification on all possible contexts, although not *explicitly* present, is anyway *implicitly* captured by the bisimulation or logical game.

Starting from the pioneering work by Böhm, another way of defining program equivalence has been proved extremely useful not only when giving metatheorems about λ-calculi and programming languages, but also when proving concrete programs to be (contextually) equivalent. What we are referring to, of course, is the notion of a *Böhm tree* of a λ-term e (see [5] for a formal definition), which is a possibly infinite tree representing the *head normal* h form of e, if e has one, but also analyzing the arguments to the head variable of h in a coinductive way. The celebrated Böhm Theorem, also known as Separation Theorem [11], stipulates that two terms are contextually equivalent *if and only if* their respective (appropriately η-equated) Böhm trees are the same.

The notion of equivalence induced by Böhm trees can be characterised without any reference to trees, by means of a suitable bisimilarity relation [37,65]. Additionally, Böhm trees can also be defined when λ-terms are *not* evaluated to their *head* normal form, like in the classical theory of λ-calculus, but to their *weak head* normal form (like in the call-by-name [37,65]), or to their *eager* normal form (like in the call-by-value λ-calculus [38]). In both cases, the notion of program equivalence one obtains by comparing the syntactic structure of trees, admits an elegant coinductive characterisation as a suitable bisimilarity relation. The family of bisimilarity relations thus obtained goes under the generic name of *normal form bisimilarity*.

Real world functional programming languages, however, come equipped not only with higher-order functions, but also with *computational effects*, turning them into *impure* languages in which functions cannot be seen merely as turning an input to an output. This requires switching to a new model, which cannot be the usual, pure, λ-calculus. Indeed, program equivalence in effectful λ-calculi [49,56] have been studied by way of denotational semantics [18,20,31], logical relations [10,14], applicative bisimilarity [13,16,36], and normal form bisimilarity [20,41]. While the denotational semantics, logical relation semantics, and applicative bisimilarity of effectful calculi have been studied in the abstract [15,25,30], the same cannot be said about normal form bisimilarity. Particularly relevant for our purposes is [15], where a notion of applicative bisimilarity for generic algebraic effects, called *effectful applicative bisimilarity*, based on the (standard) notion of a monad, and on the (less standard) notion of a *relator* [71] or *lax extension* [6,26], is introduced.

Intuitively, a relator is an abstraction axiomatising the structural properties of relation lifting operations. This way, relators allow for an abstract description of the possible ways a relation between programs can be lifted to a relation between (the results of) effectful computations, the latter being described throughout monads and algebraic operations. Several concrete notions of program equivalence, such as pure, nondeterministic and probabilistic applicative bisimilarity [1,16,36,52] can be analysed using relators. Additionally, besides their prime role in the study of effectful applicative bisimilarity, relators have also been used to study logic-based equivalences [67] and applicative distances [23] for languages with generic algebraic effects.

The main contribution of [15] consists in devising a set of axioms on monads and relators (summarised in the notions of a *Σ-continuous monad* and a *Σ-continuous relator*) which are both satisfied by many concrete examples, and that abstractly guarantee that the associated notion of applicative bisimilarity is a congruence.

In this paper, we show that an abstract notion of normal form (bi)simulation can indeed be given for calculi with algebraic effects, thus defining a theory analogous to [15]. Remarkably, we show that the defining axioms of Σ-continuous monads and Σ-continuous relators guarantee the resulting notion of normal form (bi)similarity to be a (pre)congruence relation, thus enabling compositional reasoning about program equivalence and refinement. Given that these axioms have already been shown to hold in many relevant examples of calculi with effects, our work shows that there is a way to "cook up" notions of *effectful* normal form bisimulation *without* having to reprove congruence of the obtained notion of program equivalence: this comes somehow for free. Moreover, this holds both when call-by-name and call-by-value program evaluation is considered, although in this paper we will mostly focus on the latter, since the call-by-value reduction strategy is more natural in presence of computational effects[1].

Compared to (effectful) applicative bisimilarity, as well as to other standard operational techniques—such as contextual and CIU equivalence [47,51], or logical relations [55,61]—(effectful) normal form bisimilarity has the major advantage of being an *intensional* program equivalence, equating programs according to the syntactic structure of their (possibly infinitary) normal forms. As a consequence, in order to deem two programs as normal form bisimilar, it is sufficient to test them in isolation, i.e. independently of their interaction with the environment. This way, we obtain easier proofs of equivalence between (effectful) programs. Additionally, normal form bisimilarity allows for enhancements of the bisimulation proof method [60], hence qualifying as a powerful and effective tool for program equivalence.

Intensionality represents a major difference between normal form bisimilarity and applicative bisimilarity, where the environment interacts with the tested programs by passing them arbitrary input arguments (thus making applicative bisimilarity an *extensional* notion of program equivalence). Testing programs in isolation has, however, its drawbacks. In fact, although we prove effectful normal form bisimilarity to be a sound proof technique for (effectful) applicative bisim-

[1] Besides, as we will discuss in Sect. 6.4, the formal analysis of call-by-name normal form bisimilarity strictly follows the corresponding (more challenging) analysis of call-by-value normal form bisimilarity.

ilarity (and thus for contextual equivalence), full abstraction fails, as already observed in the case of the pure λ-calculus [3,38] (nonetheless, it is worth mentioning that full abstraction results are known to hold for calculi with a rich expressive power [65,68]).

In light of these observations, we devote some energy to studying some concrete examples which highlight the weaknesses of applicative bisimilarity, on the one hand, and the strengths of normal form bisimilarity, on the other hand.

This paper is structured as follows. In Sect. 2 we informally discuss examples of (pairs of) programs which are operational equivalent, but whose equivalence cannot be readily established using standard operational methods. Throughout this paper, we will show how effectful normal form bisimilarity allows for handy proofs of such equivalences. Section 3 is dedicated to mathematical preliminaries, with a special focus on (selected) examples of monads and algebraic operations. In Sect. 4 we define our vehicle calculus Λ_Σ, an untyped λ-calculus enriched with algebraic operations, to which we give call-by-value monadic operational semantics. Section 5 introduces relators and their main properties. In Sect. 6 we introduce *effectful eager normal form (bi)similarity*, the call-by-value instantiation of effectful normal form (bi)similarity, and its main metatheoretical properties. In particular, we prove effectful eager normal form (bi)similarity to be a (pre)congruence relation (Theorem 2) included in effectful applicative (bi)similarity (Proposition 5). Additionally, we prove soundness of eager normal bisimulation up-to context (Theorem 3), a powerful enhancement of the bisimulation proof method that allows for handy proof of program equivalence. Finally, in Sect. 6.4 we briefly discuss how to modify our theory to deal with call-by-name calculi.

2 From Applicative to Normal Form Bisimilarity

In this section, some examples of (pairs of) programs which can be shown equivalent by effectful normal form bisimilarity will be provided, giving evidence on the flexibility and strength of the proposed technique. We will focus on examples drawn from fixed point theory, simply because these, being infinitary in nature, are quite hard to be dealt with "finitary" techniques like contextual equivalence or applicative bisimilarity.

Example 1. Our first example comes from the ordinary theory of pure, untyped λ-calculus. Let us consider Curry's and Turing's call-by-value fixed point combinators Y and Z:

$$Y \triangleq \lambda y.\Delta\Delta, \qquad Z \triangleq \Theta\Theta, \qquad \Delta \triangleq \lambda x.y(\lambda z.xxz), \qquad \Theta \triangleq \lambda x.\lambda y.y(\lambda z.xxyz).$$

It is well known that Y and Z are contextually equivalent, although proving such an equivalence from first principles is doomed to be hard. For that reason, one usually looks at proof techniques for contextual equivalence. Here we consider applicative bisimilarity [1]. As in the pure λ-calculus applicative bisimilarity coincides with the intersection of applicative similarity and its converse, for the sake of the argument we discuss which difficulties one faces when trying to prove Z to be applicatively similar to Y.

Let us try to construct an applicative simulation $\mathcal{R}$ relating Y and Z. Clearly we need to have $(Y, Z) \in \mathcal{R}$. Since Y evaluates to $\lambda y.\Delta\Delta$, and Z evaluates to $\lambda y.y(\lambda z.\Theta\Theta yz)$, in order for $\mathcal{R}$ to be an applicative simulation, we need to show that for any value v, $(\Delta[v/y]\Delta[v/y], v(\lambda z.\Theta\Theta vz)) \in \mathcal{R}$. Since the result of the evaluation of $\Delta[v/y]\Delta[v/y]$ is the same of $v(\lambda z.\Delta[v/y]\Delta[v/y]z)$, we have reached a point in which we are stuck: in order to ensure $(Y, Z) \in \mathcal{R}$, we need to show that $(v(\lambda z.\Delta[v/y]\Delta[v/y]z), v(\lambda z.\Theta\Theta vz)) \in \mathcal{R}$. However, the value v being provided by the environment, no information on it is available. That is, we have no information on how v tests its input program. In particular, given any context $\mathcal{C}[-]$, we can consider the value $\lambda x.\mathcal{C}[x]$, meaning that proving Y and Z to be applicatively bisimilar is almost as hard as proving them to be contextually equivalent from first principles.

As we will see, proving Z to be normal form similar to Y is straightforward, since in order to test $\lambda y.\Delta\Delta$ and $\lambda y.y(\lambda z.\Theta\Theta yz)$, we simply test their subterms $\Delta\Delta$ and $y(\lambda z.\Theta\Theta yz)$, thus not allowing the environment to influence computations.

Example 2. Our next example is a refinement of Example 1 to a probabilistic setting, as proposed in [66] (but in a call-by-name setting). We consider a variation of Turing's call-by-value fixed point combinator which, at any iteration, can probabilistically decide whether to start another iteration (following the pattern of the standard Turing's fixed point combinator) or to turn for good into Y, where Y and Δ are defined as in Example 1:

$$Z \triangleq \Theta\Theta, \qquad \Theta \triangleq \lambda x.\lambda y.(y(\lambda z.\Delta\Delta z) \textbf{ or } y(\lambda z.xxyz)).$$

Notice that the constructor **or** behaves as a (fair) probabilistic choice operator, hence acting as an effect producer. It is natural to ask whether these new versions of Y and Z are still equivalent. However, following insights from previous example, it is not hard to see the equivalence between Y and Z cannot be readily proved by means of standard operational methods such as probabilistic contextual equivalence [16], probabilistic CIU equivalence and logical relations [10], and probabilistic applicative bisimilarity [13,16]. All the aforementioned techniques require to test programs in a given environment (such as a whole context or an input argument), and are thus ineffective in handling fixed point combinators such as Y and Z.

We will give an elementary proof of the equivalence between Y and Z in Example 17, and a more elegant proof relying on a suitable *up-to context* technique in Example 18. In [66], the call-by-name counterparts of Y and Z are proved to be equivalent using probabilistic environmental bisimilarity. The notion of an environmental bisimulation [63] involves both an environment storing pairs of terms played during the bisimulation game, and a clause universally quantifying over pairs of terms in the evaluation context closure of such an environment[2], thus making environmental bisimilarity a rather heavy technique to use. Our proof of the equivalence of Y and Z is simpler: in fact, our notion of effectful normal form bisimulation does not involve any universal quantification over all possible closed function arguments (like applicative bisimilarity), or their evaluation context closure (like environmental bisimilarity), or closed instantiation of uses (like CIU equivalence).

Example 3. Our third example concerns call-by-name calculi and shows how our notion of normal form bisimilarity can handle even intricate recursion schemes. We consider the following argument-switching probabilistic fixed point combinators:

$$P \triangleq AA, \qquad A \triangleq \lambda x.\lambda y.\lambda z.(y(xxyz) \textbf{ or } z(xxzy)),$$
$$Q \triangleq BB, \qquad B \triangleq \lambda x.\lambda y.\lambda z.(y(xxzy) \textbf{ or } z(xxyz)).$$

We easily see that P and Q satisfy the following (informal) program equations:

$$Pef = e(Pef) \textbf{ or } f(Pfe), \qquad Qef = e(Qfe) \textbf{ or } f(Qef).$$

Again, proving the equivalence between P and Q using applicative bisimilarity is problematic. In fact, testing the applicative behaviour of P and Q requires to reason about the behaviour of e.g. $e(Pef)$, which in turn requires to reason about the (arbitrary) term e, on which no information is provided. The (essentially infinitary) normal forms of P and Q, however, can be proved to be essentially the same by reasoning about the syntactical structure of P and Q. Moreover, our *up-to context* technique enables an elegant and concise proof of the equivalence between P and Q (Sect. 6.4).

Example 4. Our last example discusses the use of the cost monad as an *instrument* to facilitate a more intensional analysis of programs. In fact, we can use the ticking operation **tick** to perform cost analysis. For instance, we can consider the following variation of Curry's and Turing's fixed point combinator of Example 1, obtained by adding the operation symbol **tick** after every λ-abstraction.

$$Y \triangleq \lambda y.\textbf{tick}(\Delta\Delta), \qquad \Delta \triangleq \lambda x.\textbf{tick}(y(\lambda z.\textbf{tick}(xxz))),$$
$$Z \triangleq \Theta\Theta, \qquad \Theta \triangleq \lambda x.\textbf{tick}(\lambda y.\textbf{tick}(y(\lambda z.\textbf{tick}(xxyz)))).$$

Every time a β-redex $(\lambda x.\textbf{tick}(e))v$ is reduced, the ticking operation **tick** increases an imaginary cost counter of a unit. Using ticking, we can provide a more intensional analysis of the relationship between Y and Z, along the lines of Sands' improvement theory [62].

[2] Meaning that two terms e_1, e_2 are tested for their applicative behaviour against all terms of the form $E[e], E[e']$, for any pair of terms (e, e') stored in the environment.

3 Preliminaries: Monads and Algebraic Operations

In this section we recall some basic definitions and results needed in the rest of the paper. Unfortunately, there is no hope to be comprehensive, and thus we assume the reader to be familiar with basic domain theory [2] (in particular with the notions of ω-complete (pointed) partial order—ω-cppo, for short—monotone, and continuous functions), basic order theory [19], and basic category theory [46]. Additionally, we assume the reader to be acquainted with the notion of a Kleisli triple [46] $\mathbb{T} = \langle T, \eta, -^{\dagger} \rangle$. As it is customary, we use the notation $f^{\dagger} : TX \to TY$ for the Kleisli extension of $f : X \to TY$, and reserve the letter η to denote the unit of $\mathbb{T}$. Due to their equivalence, oftentimes we refer to Kleisli triples as monads.

Concerning notation, we try to follow [46] and [2], with the only exception that we use the notation $(x_n)_n$ to denote an ω-chain $x_0 \sqsubseteq \cdots \sqsubseteq x_n \sqsubseteq \cdots$ in a domain $(X, \sqsubseteq, \bot)$. The notation $\mathbb{T} = \langle T, \eta, -^{\dagger} \rangle$ for an arbitrary Kleisli triple is standard, but it is not very handy when dealing with multiple monads at the same time. To fix this issue, we sometimes use the notation $\mathbb{T} = \langle T, \mathrm{T}, -^{\mathbb{T}} \rangle$ to denote a Kleisli triple. Additionally, when unambiguous we omit subscripts. Finally, we denote by Set the category of sets and functions, and by Rel the category of sets and relations. We reserve the symbol 1 to denote the identity function. Unless explicitly stated, we assume functors (and monads) to be functors (and monads) on Set. As a consequence, we write *functors* to refer to endofunctors on Set.

We use monads to give operational semantics to our calculi. Following Moggi [49,50], we model notions of computation as monads, meaning that we use monads as mathematical models of the kind of (side) effects computations may produce. The following are examples of monads modelling relevant notions of computation. Due to space constraints, we omit several interesting examples such as the output, the exception, and the nondeterministic/powerset monad, for which the reader is referred to e.g. [50,73].

Example 5 (Partiality). Partial computations are modelled by the partiality (also called maybe) monad $\mathbb{M} = \langle M, \mathrm{M}, -^{\mathbb{M}} \rangle$. The carrier MX of $\mathbb{M}$ is defined as $\{\mathit{just}\ x \mid x \in X\} \cup \{\bot\}$, where $\bot$ is a special symbol denoting divergence. The unit and Kleisli extension of $\mathbb{M}$ are defined as follows:

$$\mathrm{M}(x) \triangleq \mathit{just}\ x, \qquad f^{\mathbb{M}}(\mathit{just}\ x) \triangleq f(x), \qquad f^{\mathbb{M}}(\bot) \triangleq \bot.$$

Example 6 (Probabilistic Nondeterminism). In this example we assume sets to be countable[3]. The (discrete) distribution monad $\mathbb{D} = \langle D, \mathrm{D}, -^{\mathbb{D}} \rangle$ has carrier $\mathbb{D}X \triangleq \{\mu : X \to [0,1] \mid \sum_x \mu(x) = 1\}$, whereas the maps D and $-^{\mathbb{D}}$ are defined as follows (where $y \neq x$):

$$\mathrm{D}(x)(x) \triangleq 1, \qquad \mathrm{D}(x)(y) \triangleq 0, \qquad f^{\mathbb{D}}(\mu)(y) \triangleq \textstyle\sum_{x \in X} \mu(x) \cdot f(x)(y).$$

[3] Although this is not strictly necessary, for simplicity we work with distributions over countable sets only, as the sets of values and normal forms are countable.

Oftentimes, we write a distribution μ as a weighted formal sum. That is, we write μ as the sum[4] $\sum_{i \in I} p_i \cdot x_i$ such that $\mu(x) = \sum_{x_i = x} p_i$. $\mathbb{D}$ models probabilistic total computations, according to the rationale that a (total) probabilistic program evaluates to a distribution over values, the latter describing the possible results of the evaluation. Finally, we model probabilistic partial computations using the monad $\mathbb{DM} = \langle DM, \text{DM}, -^{\mathbb{DM}} \rangle$. The carrier of $\mathbb{DM}$ is defined as $DMX \triangleq D(MX)$, whereas the unit DM is defined in the obvious way. For $f : X \to DMY$, define:

$$f^{\mathbb{DM}}(\mu)(y) \triangleq \sum_{x \in X} \mu(just\ x) \cdot f(x)(y) + \mu(\bot) \cdot \text{D}(\bot)(y).$$

It is easy to see that $\mathbb{DM}$ is isomorphic to the subdistribution monad.

Example 7 (Cost). The cost (also known as ticking or improvement [62]) monad $\mathbb{C} = \langle C, \text{C}, -^{\mathbb{C}} \rangle$ has carrier $CX \triangleq M(\mathbb{N} \times X)$. The unit of $\mathbb{C}$ is defined as $\text{C}(x) \triangleq just\ (0, x)$, whereas Kleisli extension is defined as follows:

$$f^{\mathbb{C}}(\chi) \triangleq \begin{cases} \bot & \text{if } \chi = \bot, \text{ or } \chi = just\ (n, x) \text{ and } f(x) = \bot \\ just\ (n+m, y) & \text{if } \chi = just\ (n, x) \text{ and } f(x) = just\ (m, y). \end{cases}$$

The cost monad is used to model the cost of (partial) computations. An element of the form $just\ (n, x)$ models the result of a computation outputting the value x with cost n (the latter being an abstract notion that can be instantiated to e.g. the number of reduction steps performed). Partiality is modelled as the element $\bot$, according to the rationale that we can assume all divergent computations to have the same cost, so that such information need not be explicitly written (for instance, measuring the number of reduction steps performed, we would have that divergent computations all have cost ∞).

Example 8 (Global states). Let $\mathcal{L}$ be a set of public location names. We assume the content of locations to be encoded as families of values (such as numerals or booleans) and denote the collection of such values as $\mathcal{V}$. A store (or state) is a function $\sigma : \mathcal{L} \to \mathcal{V}$. We write S for the set of stores $\mathcal{V}^{\mathcal{L}}$. The global state monad $\mathbb{G} = \langle G, \text{G}, -^{\mathbb{G}} \rangle$ has carrier $GX \triangleq (X \times S)^S$, whereas G and $-^{\mathbb{G}}$ are defined by:

$$\text{G}(x)(\sigma) \triangleq (x, \sigma), \qquad f^{\mathbb{G}}(\alpha)(\sigma) \triangleq f(x')(\sigma'),$$

where $\alpha(\sigma) = (x', \sigma')$. It is straightforward to see that we can combine the global state monad with the partiality monad, obtaining the monad $\mathbb{M} \otimes \mathbb{G}$ whose carrier is $(M \otimes G)X \triangleq M(X \times S)^S$. In a similar fashion, we see that we can combine the global state monad with $\mathbb{DM}$ and $\mathbb{C}$, as we are going to see in Remark 1.

Remark 1. The monads $\mathbb{DM}$ and $\mathbb{M} \otimes \mathbb{G}$ of Example 6 and Example 8, respectively, are instances of two general constructions, namely the *sum* and *tensor* of effects [28]. Although these operations are defined on Lawvere theories [29, 40], here we can rephrase them in terms of monads as follows.

[4] For simplicity, we write only those p_is such that $p_i > 0$.

Proposition 1. *Given a monad* $\mathbb{T} = \langle T, \text{T}, -^{\mathbb{T}} \rangle$, *define the* sum $\mathbb{TM}$ *of* $\mathbb{T}$ *and* $\mathbb{M}$ *and the* tensor $\mathbb{T} \otimes \mathbb{G}$ *of* $\mathbb{T}$ *and* $\mathbb{G}$, *as the triples* $\langle TM, \text{TM}, -^{\mathbb{TM}} \rangle$ *and* $\langle T \otimes G, \text{T} \otimes \text{G}, -^{\mathbb{T}\otimes\mathbb{G}} \rangle$, *respectively. The carriers of the triples are defined as* $TMX \triangleq T(MX)$ *and* $(T \otimes G)X \triangleq T(S \times X)^S$, *whereas the maps* TM *and* T ⊗ G *are defined as* $\text{TM}_X \triangleq \text{T}_{MX} \circ \text{M}_X$ *and* $(\text{T} \otimes \text{G})_X \triangleq \mathsf{curry}\ \text{T}_{S \times X}$, *respectively. Finally, define:*

$$f^{\mathbb{TM}} \triangleq (f_M)^{\mathbb{T}}, \qquad f^{\mathbb{T}\otimes\mathbb{G}}(\alpha)(\sigma) \triangleq (\mathsf{uncurry}\ f)^{\mathbb{T}}(\alpha)(\sigma),$$

where, for a function $f : X \to TMY$ *we define* $f_M : MX \to TMY$ *as* $f_M(\bot) \triangleq \text{T}_{MX}(\bot)$, $f_M(just\ x) \triangleq f(x)$, *and* curry *and* uncurry *are defined as usual. Then* $\mathbb{TM}$ *and* $\mathbb{T} \otimes \mathbb{G}$ *are monads.*

Proving Proposition 1 is a straightforward exercise (the reader can also consult [28]). We notice that tensoring $\mathbb{G}$ with $\mathbb{DM}$ we obtain a monad for probabilistic imperative computations, whereas tensoring $\mathbb{G}$ with $\mathbb{C}$ we obtain a monad for imperative computations with cost.

3.1 Algebraic Operations

Monads provide an elegant way to structure effectful computations. However, they do not offer any actual effect constructor. Following Plotkin and Power [56–58], we use *algebraic operations* as effect producers. From an operational perspective, algebraic operations are those operations whose behaviour is independent of their continuations or, equivalently, of the environment in which they are evaluated. Intuitively, that means that e.g. $E[e_1\ \mathbf{or}\ e_2]$ is operationally equivalent to $E[e_1]$ **or** $E[e_2]$, for any evaluation context E. Examples of algebraic operations are given by (binary) nondeterministic and probabilistic choices as well as primitives for rising exceptions and output operations.

Syntactically, algebraic operations are given via a signature Σ consisting of a set of operation symbols (uninterpreted operations) together with their arity (i.e. their number of operands). Semantically, operation symbols are interpreted as algebraic operations on monads. To any n-ary operation symbol[5] $(\mathbf{op} : n) \in \Sigma$ and any set X we associate a map $[\![\mathbf{op}]\!]_X : (TX)^n \to TX$ (so that we equip TX with a Σ-algebra structure [12]) such that $f^\dagger$ is Σ-algebra morphism, meaning that for any $f : X \to TY$, and elements $\mathfrak{x}_1, \ldots, \mathfrak{x}_n \in TX$ we have $[\![\mathbf{op}]\!]_Y(f^\dagger(\mathfrak{x}_1), \ldots, f^\dagger(\mathfrak{x}_n)) = f^\dagger([\![\mathbf{op}]\!]_X(\mathfrak{x}_1, \ldots, \mathfrak{x}_n))$.

Example 9. The partiality monad $\mathbb{M}$ usually comes with no operation, as the possibility of divergence is an implicit feature of any Turing complete language. However, it is sometimes useful to add an explicit divergence operation (for instance, in strongly normalising calculi). For that, we consider the signature $\Sigma_{\mathbb{M}} \triangleq \{\underline{\Omega} : 0\}$. Having arity zero, the operation $\underline{\Omega}$ acts as a constant, and has semantics $[\![\underline{\Omega}]\!] = \bot$. Since $f^{\mathbb{M}}(\bot) = \bot$, we see that $\underline{\Omega}$ in indeed an algebraic operation on $\mathbb{M}$.

---

[5] Here **op** denotes the operation symbol, whereas $n \geq 0$ denotes its arity.

For the distribution monad $\mathbb{D}$ we define the signature $\Sigma_{\mathbb{D}} \triangleq \{\mathbf{or} : 2\}$. The intended semantics of a program e_1 **or** e_2 is to evaluate to e_i ($i \in \{1,2\}$) with probability 0.5. The interpretation of **or** is defined by $[\![\mathbf{or}]\!](\mu,\nu)(x) \triangleq 0.5 \cdot \mu(x) + 0.5 \cdot \nu(x)$. It is easy to see that **or** is an algebraic operation on $\mathbb{D}$, and that it trivially extends to $\mathbb{DM}$.

Finally, for the cost monad $\mathbb{C}$ we define the signature $\Sigma_{\mathbb{C}} \triangleq \{\mathbf{tick} : 1\}$. The intended semantics of **tick** is to add a unit to the cost counter:

$$[\![\mathbf{tick}]\!](\bot) \triangleq \bot, \qquad [\![\mathbf{tick}]\!](just\ (n,x)) \triangleq just\ (n+1,x).$$

The framework we have just described works fine for modelling operations with finite arity, but does not allow to handle operations with infinitary arity. This is witnessed, for instance, by imperative calculi with global stores, where it is natural to have operations of the form $\mathbf{get}_\ell(x.k)$ with the following intended semantics: $\mathbf{get}_\ell(x.k)$ reads the content of the location ℓ, say it is a value v, and continue as $k[v/x]$. In order to take such operations into account, we follow [58] and work with generalised operations.

A *generalised operation* (operation, for short) on a set X is a function $\omega : P \times X^I \to X$. The set P is called the *parameter set* of the operation, whereas the (index) set I is called the *arity* of the operation. A generalised operation $\omega : P \times X^I \to X$ thus takes as arguments a parameter p (such as a location name) and a map $\kappa : I \to X$ giving for each index $i \in I$ the argument $\kappa(i)$ to pass to ω. Syntactically, generalised operations are given via a signature Σ consisting of a set of elements of the form $\mathbf{op} : P \rightsquigarrow I$ (the latter being nothing but a notation denoting that the operation symbols **op** has parameter set P and index set I). Semantically, an interpretation of an operation symbol $\mathbf{op} : P \rightsquigarrow I$ on a monad $\mathbb{T}$ associates to any set X a map $[\![\mathbf{op}]\!]_X : P \times (TX)^I \to TX$ such that for any $f : X \to TY$, $p \in P$, and $\kappa : I \to TX$:

$$f^\dagger([\![\mathbf{op}]\!]_X(p,\kappa)) = [\![\mathbf{op}]\!]_Y(p, f^\dagger \circ \kappa).$$

If $\mathbb{T}$ comes with an interpretation for operation symbols in Σ, we say that $\mathbb{T}$ is *Σ-algebraic.*

It is easy to see by taking the one-element set $1 = \{*\}$ as parameter set and a finite set as arity set, generalised operations subsume finitary operations. For simplicity, we use the notation $\mathbf{op} : n$ in place of $\mathbf{op} : 1 \rightsquigarrow n$, and write $\mathbf{op}(x_1, \ldots, x_n)$ in place of $\mathbf{op}(*, n \mapsto x_n)$.

Example 10. For the global state monad we consider the signature $\Sigma_{\mathbb{G}} \triangleq \{\mathbf{set}_\ell : \mathcal{V} \rightsquigarrow 1, \mathbf{get}_\ell : 1 \rightsquigarrow \mathcal{V} \mid \ell \in \mathcal{L}\}$. From a computational perspective, such operations are used to build programs of the form $\mathbf{set}_\ell(v,e)$ and $\mathbf{get}_\ell(x.e)$. The former stores the value v in the location ℓ and continues as e, whereas the latter reads the content of the location ℓ, say it is v, and continue as $e[v/x]$. Here e is used as the description of a function κ_e from values to terms defined by $\kappa_e(v) \triangleq e[v/x]$. The interpretation of the new operations on $\mathbb{G}$ is standard:

$$[\![\mathbf{set}_\ell]\!](v,\alpha)(\sigma) = \alpha(\sigma[\ell := v]), \qquad [\![\mathbf{get}_\ell]\!](\kappa)(\sigma) = \kappa(\sigma(\ell))(\sigma).$$

Straightforward calculations show that indeed $\mathbf{set}_\ell$ and $\mathbf{get}_\ell$ are algebraic operations on $\mathbb{G}$. Moreover, such operations can be easily extended to the partial global state monad $\mathbb{M} \otimes \mathbb{G}$ as well as to the probabilistic (partial) global store monad $\mathbb{DM} \otimes \mathbb{G}$. These extensions share a common pattern, which is nothing but an instance of the tensor of effects. In fact, given a $\Sigma_{\mathbb{T}}$-algebraic monad $\mathbb{T}$ we can define the signature $\Sigma_{\mathbb{T}\otimes\mathbb{G}}$ as $\Sigma_{\mathbb{T}} \cup \Sigma_{\mathbb{G}}$, and observe that the $\mathbb{T} \otimes \mathbb{G}$ is $\Sigma_{\mathbb{T}\otimes\mathbb{G}}$-algebraic. We refer the reader to [28] for details. Here we simply notice that we can define the interpretation $[\![\mathbf{op}]\!]^{\mathbb{T}\otimes\mathbb{G}}$ of $\mathbf{op} : P \rightsquigarrow \mathcal{V}$ on $\mathbb{T} \otimes \mathbb{G}$ as $[\![\mathbf{op}]\!]^{\mathbb{T}\otimes\mathbb{G}}_X(p, \kappa)(\sigma) \triangleq [\![\mathbf{op}]\!]^{\mathbb{T}}_{S\times X}(p, v \mapsto \kappa(v)(\sigma))$, where $[\![\mathbf{op}]\!]^{\mathbb{T}}$ is the interpretation of $\mathbf{op}$ on $\mathbb{T}$ (the interpretations of $\mathbf{set}_\ell$ and $\mathbf{get}_\ell$ are straightforward).

Monads and algebraic operations provide mathematical abstractions to structure and produce effectful computations. However, in order to give operational semantics to, e.g., probabilistic calculi [17] we need monads to account for infinitary computational behaviours. We thus look at *Σ-continuous monads.*

Definition 1. *A Σ-algebraic monad $\mathbb{T} = \langle T, \eta, -^\dagger\rangle$ is Σ-*continuous *(cf. [24]) if to any set X is associated an order $\sqsubseteq_X$ and an element $\bot_X \in TX$ such that $\langle TX, \sqsubseteq_X, \bot_X\rangle$ is an ω-cppo, and for all $(\mathbf{op} : P \rightsquigarrow I) \in \Sigma$, $f, f_n, g : X \to TY$, $\kappa, \kappa_n, \nu : I \to TX$, $\chi, \chi_n, y \in TX$, we have $f^\dagger(\bot) = \bot$ and:*

$$\begin{aligned} \kappa \sqsubseteq \nu &\implies [\![\mathbf{op}]\!](p, \kappa) \sqsubseteq [\![\mathbf{op}]\!](p, \nu) & [\![\mathbf{op}]\!](p, \textstyle\bigsqcup_n \kappa_n) &= \textstyle\bigsqcup_n [\![\mathbf{op}]\!](p, \kappa_n) \\ f \sqsubseteq g &\implies f^\dagger \sqsubseteq g^\dagger & (\textstyle\bigsqcup_n f_n)^\dagger &= \textstyle\bigsqcup_n f_n^\dagger \\ \chi \sqsubseteq y &\implies f^\dagger(\chi) \sqsubseteq f^\dagger(y) & f^\dagger(\textstyle\bigsqcup_n \chi_n) &= \textstyle\bigsqcup_n f^\dagger(\chi_n). \end{aligned}$$

When clear from the context, we will omit subscripts in $\bot_X$ and $\sqsubseteq_X$.

Example 11. The monads $\mathbb{M}$, $\mathbb{DM}$, $\mathbb{GM}$, and $\mathbb{C}$ are Σ-continuous. The order on MX and $\mathbb{C}$ is the flat ordering $\sqsubseteq$ defined by $\chi \sqsubseteq y \overset{\triangle}{\iff} \chi = \bot$ or $\chi = y$, whereas the order on DMX is defined by $\mu \sqsubseteq \nu \overset{\triangle}{\iff} \forall x \in X.\ \mu(just\ x) \leq \nu(just\ x)$. Finally, the order on GMX is defined pointwise from the flat ordering on $M(X \times S)$.

Having introduced the notion of a Σ-continuous monad, we can now define our vehicle calculus Λ_Σ and its monadic operational semantics.

4 A Computational Call-by-value Calculus with Algebraic Operations

In this section we define the calculus Λ_Σ. Λ_Σ is an untyped λ-calculus parametrised by a signature of operation symbols, and corresponds to the coarse-grain [44] version of the calculus studied in [15]. Formally, terms of Λ_Σ are defined by the following grammar, where x ranges over a countably infinite set of variables and $\mathbf{op}$ is a generalised operation symbol in Σ.

$$e ::= x \mid \lambda x.e \mid ee \mid \mathbf{op}(p, x.e).$$

A value is either a variable or a λ-abstraction. We denote by Λ the collection of terms and by $\mathcal{V}$ the collection of values of Λ_Σ. For an operation symbol $\mathbf{op} : P \rightsquigarrow I$, we assume that set I to be encoded by some subset of $\mathcal{V}$ (using e.g. Church's encoding). In particular, in a term of the form $\mathbf{op}(p, x.e)$, e acts as a function in the variable x that takes as input a value. Notice also how parameters $p \in P$ are part of the syntax. For simplicity, we ignore the specific subset of values used to encode elements of I, and simply write $\mathbf{op} : P \rightsquigarrow \mathcal{V}$ for operation symbols in Σ.

We adopt standard syntactical conventions as in [5] (notably the so-called variable convention). The notion of a free (resp. bound) variable is defined as usual (notice that the variable x is bound in $\mathbf{op}(p, x.e)$). As it is customary, we identify terms up to renaming of bound variables and say that a term is closed if it has no free variables (and that it is open, otherwise). Finally, we write $f[e/x]$ for the capture-free substitution of the term e for all free occurrences of x in f. In particular, $\mathbf{op}(p, x'.f)[e/x]$ is defined as $\mathbf{op}(p, x'.f[e/x])$.

Before giving Λ_Σ call-by-value operational semantics, it is useful to remark a couple of points. First of all, testing terms according to their (possibly infinitary) normal forms obviously requires to work with open terms. Indeed, in order to inspect the *intensional* behaviour of a value $\lambda x.e$, one has to inspect the intensional behaviour of e, which is an open term. As a consequence, contrary to the usual practice, we give operational semantics to both *open* and *closed* terms. Actually, the very distinction between open and closed terms is not that meaningful in this context, and thus we simply speak of terms. Second, we notice that *values* constitute a syntactic category defined independently of the operational semantics of the calculus: values are just variables and λ-abstractions. However, giving operational semantics to arbitrary terms we are interested in richer collections of irreducible expressions, i.e. expressions that cannot be simplified any further. Such collections will be different accordingly to the operational semantics adopted. For instance, in a call-by-name setting it is natural to regard the term $x((\lambda x.x)v)$ as a terminal expression (being it a head normal form), whereas in a call-by-value setting $x((\lambda x.x)v)$ can be further simplified to xv, which in turn should be regarded as a terminal expression.

We now give Λ_Σ a monadic *call-by-value* operational semantics [15], postponing the definition of monadic *call-by-name* operational semantics to Sect. 6.4. Recall that a (call-by-value) evaluation context [22] is a term with a single hole $[-]$ defined by the following grammar, where $e \in \Lambda$ and $v \in \mathcal{V}$:

$$E ::= [-] \;\big|\; Ee \;\big|\; vE.$$

We write $E[e]$ for the term obtained by substituting the term e for the hole $[-]$ in E.

Following [38], we define a *stuck term* as a term of the form $E[xv]$. Intuitively, a stuck term is an expression whose evaluation is stuck. For instance, the term $e \triangleq y(\lambda x.x)$ is stuck. Obviously, e is not a value, but at the same time it cannot be simplified any further, as y is a variable, and not a λ-abstraction. Following this intuition, we define the collection $\mathcal{E}$ of *eager normal forms* (enfs hereafter) as the collection of values and stuck terms. We let letters $s, t, \ldots$ range over elements in $\mathcal{E}$.

Lemma 1. *Any term e is either a value v, or can be uniquely decomposed as either $E[vw]$ or $E[\mathbf{op}(p, x.f)]$.*

Operational semantics of Λ_Σ is defined with respect to a Σ-continuous monad $\mathbb{T} = \langle T, \eta, -^\dagger \rangle$ relying on Lemma 1. More precisely, we define a *call-by-value* evaluation function $[\![-]\!]$ mapping each term to an element in $T\mathcal{E}$. For instance, evaluating a probabilistic term e we obtain a distribution over eager normal forms (plus bottom), the latter being either values (meaning that the evaluation of e terminates) or stuck terms (meaning that the evaluation of e went stuck at some point).

Definition 2. *Define the $\mathbb{N}$-indexed family of maps $[\![-]\!]_n : \Lambda \to T\mathcal{E}$ as follows:*

$$\begin{aligned}
[\![e]\!]_0 &\triangleq \bot, \\
[\![v]\!]_{n+1} &\triangleq \eta(v), \\
[\![E[xv]]\!]_{n+1} &\triangleq \eta(E[xv]), \\
[\![E[(\lambda x.e)v]]\!]_{n+1} &\triangleq [\![E[e[v/x]]]\!]_n, \\
[\![E[\mathbf{op}(p, x.e)]\!]_{n+1} &\triangleq [\![\mathbf{op}]\!]_{\mathcal{E}}(p, v \mapsto [\![E[e[v/x]]]\!]_n).
\end{aligned}$$

The monad $\mathbb{T}$ being Σ-continuous, we see that the sequence $([\![e]\!]_n)_n$ forms an ω-chain in $T\mathcal{E}$, so that we can define $[\![e]\!]$ as $\bigsqcup_n [\![e]\!]_n$. Moreover, exploiting Σ-continuity of $\mathbb{T}$ we see that $[\![-]\!]$ is continuous.

We compare the behaviour of terms of Λ_Σ relying on the notion of an *effectful eager normal form (bi)simulation*, the extension of eager normal form (bi)simulation [38] to calculi with algebraic effects. In order to account for effectful behaviours, we follow [15] and parametrise our notions of equivalence and refinement by *relators* [6,71].

5 Relators

The notion of a *relator* for a functor T (on Set) [71] (also called *lax extension* of T [6]) is a construction lifting a relation $\mathcal{R}$ between two sets X and Y to a relation $\Gamma\mathcal{R}$ between TX and TY. Besides their applications in categorical topology [6] and coalgebra [71], relators have been recently used to study notions of applicative bisimulation [15], logic-based equivalence [67], and bisimulation-based distances [23] for λ-calculi extended with algebraic effects. Moreover, several forms of monadic lifting [25,32] resembling relators have been used to study abstract notions of logical relations [55,61].

Before defining relators formally, it is useful to recall some background notions on (binary) relations. The reader is referred to [26] for further details. We denote by Rel the category of sets and relations, and use the notation $\mathcal{R} : X \nrightarrow Y$ for a relation $\mathcal{R}$ between sets X and Y. Given relations $\mathcal{R} : X \nrightarrow Y$ and

$\mathcal{S} : Y \nrightarrow Z$, we write $\mathcal{S} \circ \mathcal{R} : X \nrightarrow Z$ for their composition, and $\mathsf{I}_X : X \nrightarrow X$ for the identity relation on X. Finally, we recall that for all sets X, Y, the hom-set $\mathsf{Rel}(X, Y)$ has a complete lattice structure, meaning that we can define relations both inductively and coinductively.

Given a relation $\mathcal{R} : X \nrightarrow Y$, we denote by $\mathcal{R}^\circ : Y \nrightarrow X$ its dual (or opposite) relations and by $-_\circ : \mathsf{Set} \to \mathsf{Rel}$ the graph functor mapping each function $f : X \to Y$ to its graph $f_\circ : X \nrightarrow Y$. The functor $-_\circ$ being faithful, we will often write $f : X \to Y$ in place of $f_\circ : X \nrightarrow Y$. It is useful to keep in mind the pointwise reading of relations of the form $g^\circ \circ \mathcal{S} \circ f$, for a relation $\mathcal{S} : Z \nrightarrow W$ and functions $f : X \to Z$, $g : Y \to W$:

$$(g^\circ \circ \mathcal{S} \circ f)(x, y) = \mathcal{S}(f(x), g(y)).$$

Given $\mathcal{R} : X \nrightarrow Y$, we can thus express a generalised monotonicity condition in a pointfree fashion using the inclusion $\mathcal{R} \subseteq g^\circ \circ \mathcal{S} \circ f$. Finally, since we are interested in preorder and equivalence relations, we recall that a relation $\mathcal{R} : X \nrightarrow X$ is reflexive if $\mathsf{I}_X \subseteq \mathcal{R}$, transitive if $\mathcal{R} \circ \mathcal{R} \subseteq \mathcal{R}$, and symmetric if $\mathcal{R} \subseteq \mathcal{R}^\circ$. We can now define relators formally.

Definition 3. *A* relator *for a functor T (on* Set*) is a set-indexed family of maps $(\mathcal{R} : X \nrightarrow Y) \mapsto (\Gamma\mathcal{R} : TX \nrightarrow TY)$ satisfying conditions* (rel 1)–(rel 4)*. We say that Γ is* conversive *if it additionally satisfies condition* (rel 5).

$$\mathsf{I}_{TX} \subseteq \Gamma(\mathsf{I}_X), \tag{rel 1}$$
$$\Gamma\mathcal{S} \circ \Gamma\mathcal{R} \subseteq \Gamma(\mathcal{S} \circ \mathcal{R}), \tag{rel 2}$$
$$Tf \subseteq \Gamma f, \quad (Tf)^\circ \subseteq \Gamma f^\circ, \tag{rel 3}$$
$$\mathcal{R} \subseteq \mathcal{S} \implies \Gamma\mathcal{R} \subseteq \Gamma\mathcal{S}, \tag{rel 4}$$
$$\Gamma(\mathcal{R}^\circ) = (\Gamma\mathcal{R})^\circ. \tag{rel 5}$$

Conditions (rel 1), (rel 2), and (rel 4) are rather standard[6]. As we will see, condition (rel 4) makes the defining functional of (bi)simulation relations monotone, whereas conditions (rel 1) and (rel 2) make notions of (bi)similarity reflexive and transitive. Similarly, condition (rel 5) makes notions of bisimilarity symmetric. Condition (rel 3), which actually consists of two conditions, states that relators behave as expected when acting on (graphs of) functions. In [15,43] a kernel preservation condition is required in place of (rel 3). Such a condition is also known as *stability* in [27]. Stability requires the equality $\Gamma(g^\circ \circ \mathcal{R} \circ f) = (Tg)^\circ \circ \Gamma\mathcal{R} \circ Tf$ to hold. It is easy to see that a relator always satisfies stability (see Corollary III.1.4.4 in [26]).

Relators provide a powerful abstraction of notions of 'relation lifting', as witnessed by the numerous examples of relators we are going to discuss. However, before discussing such examples, we introduce the notion of a *relator for a monad* or *lax extension of a monad.* In fact, since we modelled computational effects as monads, it seems natural to define the notion of a relator for a *monad* (and not just for a functor).

[6] Notice that since $\mathsf{I} = (1)_\circ$ we can derive condition (rel 1) from condition (rel 3).

Definition 4. *Let $\mathbb{T} = \langle T, \eta, -^{\dagger} \rangle$ be a monad, and Γ be a relator for T. We say that Γ is a relator for $\mathbb{T}$ if it satisfies the following conditions:*

$$\mathcal{R} \subseteq \eta_Y^{\circ} \circ \Gamma\mathcal{R} \circ \eta_X, \qquad \text{(rel 7)}$$

$$\mathcal{R} \subseteq g^{\circ} \circ \Gamma\mathcal{S} \circ f \implies \Gamma\mathcal{R} \subseteq (g^{\dagger})^{\circ} \circ \Gamma\mathcal{S} \circ f^{\dagger}. \qquad \text{(rel 8)}$$

Finally, we observe that the collection of relators is closed under specific operations (see [43]).

Proposition 2. *Let T, U be functors, and let UT denote their composition. Moreover, let Γ, Δ be relators for T and U, respectively, and $\{\Gamma_i\}_{i \in I}$ be a family of relators for T. Then:*

1. *The map $\Delta\Gamma$ defined by $\Delta\Gamma\mathcal{R} \triangleq \Delta(\Gamma\mathcal{R})$ is a relator for UT.*
2. *The maps $\bigwedge_{i \in I} \Gamma_i$ and Γ° defined by $(\bigwedge_{i \in I} \Gamma_i)\mathcal{R} \triangleq \bigcap_{i \in I} \Gamma_i\mathcal{R}$ and $\Gamma^{\circ}\mathcal{R} \triangleq (\Gamma\mathcal{R}^{\circ})^{\circ}$, respectively, are relators for T.*
3. *Additionally, if Γ is a relator for a monad $\mathbb{T}$, then so are $\bigwedge_{i \in I} \Gamma_i$ and Γ°.*

Example 12. For the partiality monad $\mathbb{M}$ we define the set-indexed family of maps $\hat{\mathbb{M}} : \mathsf{Rel}(X, Y) \to \mathsf{Rel}(MX, MY)$ as:

$$\chi \, \hat{\mathbb{M}}\mathcal{R} \, y \overset{\triangle}{\iff} (\chi = \bot) \vee (\exists x \in X.\ \exists y \in Y.\ \chi = \mathit{just}\ x \wedge y = \mathit{just}\ y \wedge x \,\mathcal{R}\, y).$$

The mapping $\hat{\mathbb{M}}$ describes the structure of the usual *simulation* clause for partial computations, whereas $\mathbb{M}^{\circ}$ describes the corresponding *co-simulation* clause. It is easy to see that $\hat{\mathbb{M}}$ is a relator for $\mathbb{M}$. By Proposition 2, the map $\hat{\mathbb{M}} \wedge \hat{\mathbb{M}}^{\circ}$ is a conversive relator for $\mathbb{M}$. It is immediate to see that the latter relator describes the structure of the usual *bisimulation* clause for partial computations.

Example 13. For the distribution monad we define the relator $\hat{\mathbb{D}}$ relying on the notion of a *coupling* and results from optimal transport [72]. Recall that a *coupling* for $\mu \in D(X)$ and $\nu \in D(Y)$ a is a joint distribution $\omega \in D(X \times Y)$ such that: $\mu = \sum_{y \in Y} \omega(-, y)$ and $\nu = \sum_{x \in X} \omega(x, -)$. We denote the set of couplings of μ and ν by $\Omega(\mu, \nu)$. Define the (set-indexed) map $\hat{\mathbb{D}} : \mathsf{Rel}(X, Y) \to \mathsf{Rel}(DX, DY)$ as follows:

$$\mu \, \hat{\mathbb{D}}\mathcal{R} \, \nu \overset{\triangle}{\iff} (\exists \omega \in \Omega(\mu, \nu).\ \forall x, y.\ \omega(x, y) > 0 \implies x \,\mathcal{R}\, y).$$

We can show that $\hat{\mathbb{D}}$ is a relator for $\mathbb{D}$ relying on *Strassen's Theorem* [69], which shows that $\hat{\mathbb{D}}$ can be characterised universally (i.e. using an universal quantification).

Theorem 1 (Strassen's Theorem [69]**).** *For all $\mu \in DX$, $\nu \in DY$, and $\mathcal{R} : X \nrightarrow Y$, we have: $\mu \, \hat{\mathbb{D}}\mathcal{R} \, \nu \iff \forall \mathcal{X} \subseteq X.\ \mu(\mathcal{X}) \leq \nu(\mathcal{R}[\mathcal{X}])$.*

As a corollary of Theorem 1, we see that $\hat{\mathbb{D}}$ describes the defining clause of Larsen-Skou bisimulation for Markov chains (based on full distributions) [34]. Finally, we observe that $\hat{\mathbb{DM}} \triangleq \hat{\mathbb{D}}\hat{\mathbb{M}}$ is a relator for $\mathbb{DM}$.

Example 14. For relations $\mathcal{R} : X \nrightarrow Y, \mathcal{S} : X' \nrightarrow Y'$, let $\mathcal{R}\times\mathcal{S} : X\times X' \nrightarrow Y\times Y'$ be defined as $(\mathcal{R}\times\mathcal{S})((x,x'),(y,y')) \overset{\triangle}{\iff} \mathcal{R}(x,y)\wedge\mathcal{S}(x',y')$. We define the relator $\hat{\mathbb{C}} : \mathsf{Rel}(X,Y) \to \mathsf{Rel}(CX,CY)$ for the cost monad $\mathbb{C}$ as $\hat{\mathbb{C}}\mathcal{R} \triangleq \hat{\mathbb{M}}(\geq \times \mathcal{R})$, where $\geq$ denotes the opposite of the natural ordering on $\mathbb{N}$. It is straightforward to see that $\hat{\mathbb{C}}$ is indeed a relator for $\mathbb{C}$. The use of the opposite of the natural order in the definition of $\hat{\mathbb{C}}$ captures the idea that we use $\hat{\mathbb{C}}$ to measure complexity. Notice that $\hat{\mathbb{C}}$ describes Sands' simulation clause for program improvement [62].

Example 15. For the global state monad $\mathbb{G}$ we define the map $\hat{\mathbb{G}} : \mathsf{Rel}(X,Y) \to \mathsf{Rel}(GX,GY)$ as $\alpha\, \hat{\mathbb{G}}\mathcal{R}\, \beta \overset{\triangle}{\iff} \forall\sigma \in S.\ \alpha(\sigma)\ (\mathsf{I}_S \times \mathcal{R})\ \beta(\sigma)$. It is straightforward to see that $\hat{\mathbb{G}}$ is a relator for $\mathbb{G}$.

It is not hard to see that we can extend $\hat{\mathbb{G}}$ to relators for $\mathbb{M}\otimes\mathbb{G}$, $\mathbb{DM}\otimes\mathbb{G}$, and $\mathbb{C}\otimes\mathbb{G}$. In fact, Proposition 1 extends to relators.

Proposition 3. *Given a monad* $\mathbb{T} = \langle T, \mathrm{T}, -^{\mathrm{T}}\rangle$ *and a relator* $\hat{\mathbb{T}}$ *for* $\mathbb{T}$, *define the sum* $\mathbb{T}\hat{\mathbb{M}}$ *of* $\hat{\mathbb{T}}$ *and* $\hat{\mathbb{M}}$ *as* $\hat{\mathbb{T}}\hat{\mathbb{M}}$. *Additionally, define the tensor* $\widehat{\mathbb{T}\otimes\mathbb{G}}$ *of* $\hat{\mathbb{T}}$ *and* $\hat{\mathbb{G}}$ *by* $\alpha\, (\widehat{\mathbb{T}\otimes\mathbb{G}})\mathcal{R}\, \beta$ *if an only if* $\forall\sigma.\ \alpha(\sigma)\, \hat{\mathbb{T}}(\mathsf{I}_S \times \mathcal{R})\, \beta(\sigma)$. *Then* $\mathbb{T}\hat{\mathbb{M}}$ *is a relator for* $\mathbb{TM}$, *and* $(\widehat{\mathbb{T}\otimes\mathbb{G}})$ *is a relator for* $\mathbb{T}\otimes\mathbb{G}$.

Finally, we require relators to properly interact with the Σ-continuous structure of monads.

Definition 5. *Let* $\mathbb{T} = \langle T, \eta, -^{\dagger}\rangle$ *be a* Σ*-continuous monad and* Γ *be relator for* $\mathbb{T}$. *We say that* Γ *is* Σ-continuous *if it satisfies the following clauses—called the* inductive conditions*—for any* ω*-chain* $(\mathfrak{x}_n)_n$ *in* TX, *element* $y \in TY$, *elements* $\mathfrak{x}, \mathfrak{x}' \in TX$, *and relation* $\mathcal{R} : X \nrightarrow Y$.

$$\bot\, \Gamma\mathcal{R}\, y, \quad \mathfrak{x} \sqsubseteq \mathfrak{x}', \mathfrak{x}'\, \Gamma\mathcal{R}\, y \implies \mathfrak{x}\, \Gamma\mathcal{R}\, y, \quad \forall n.\ \mathfrak{x}_n\, \Gamma\mathcal{R}\, y \implies \bigsqcup_n \mathfrak{x}_n\, \Gamma\mathcal{R}\, y.$$

The relators $\hat{\mathbb{M}}$, $\hat{\mathbb{DM}}$, $\hat{\mathbb{C}}$, $\widehat{\mathbb{M}\otimes\mathbb{G}}$, $\widehat{\mathbb{DM}\otimes\mathbb{G}}$, $\widehat{\mathbb{C}\otimes\mathbb{G}}$ are all Σ-continuous. The reader might have noticed that we have not imposed any condition on how relators should interact with algebraic operations. Nonetheless, it would be quite natural to require a relator Γ to satisfy condition (rel 9) below, for all operation symbol $\mathbf{op} : P \rightsquigarrow I \in \Sigma$, maps $\kappa, \nu : I \to TX$, parameter $p \in P$, and relation $\mathcal{R}$.

$$\forall i \in I.\ \kappa(i)\, \Gamma\mathcal{R}\, \nu(i) \implies [\![\mathbf{op}]\!](p,\kappa)\, \Gamma\mathcal{R}\, [\![\mathbf{op}]\!](p,\nu) \qquad \text{(rel 9)}$$

Remarkably, if $\mathbb{T}$ is Σ-algebraic, then any relator for $\mathbb{T}$ satisfies (rel 9) (cf. [15]).

Proposition 4. *Let* $\mathbb{T} = \langle T, \eta, -^{\dagger}\rangle$ *be a* Σ*-algebraic monad, and let* Γ *be a relator for* $\mathbb{T}$. *Then* Γ *satisfies condition* (rel 9).

Having defined relators and their basic properties, we now introduce the notion of an effectful eager normal form (bi)simulation.

6 Effectful Eager Normal Form (Bi)simulation

In this section we tacitly assume a Σ-continuous monad $\mathbb{T} = \langle T, \eta, -^\dagger \rangle$ and a Σ-continuous relator Γ for it be fixed. Σ-continuity of Γ is not required for defining effectful eager normal form (bi)simulation, but it is crucial to prove that the induced notion of similarity and bisimilarity are precongruence and congruence relations, respectively.

Working with effectful calculi, it is important to distinguish between relations over *terms* and relations over *eager normal forms*. For that reason we will work with pairs of relations of the form $(\mathcal{R}_\Lambda : \Lambda \nrightarrow \Lambda, \mathcal{R}_\mathcal{E} : \mathcal{E} \nrightarrow \mathcal{E})$, which we call λ-term relations (or term relations, for short). We use letters $\mathcal{R}, \mathcal{S}, \ldots$ to denote term relations. The collection of λ-term relations (i.e. $\mathsf{Rel}(\Lambda, \Lambda) \times \mathsf{Rel}(\mathcal{E}, \mathcal{E})$) inherits a complete lattice structure from $\mathsf{Rel}(\Lambda, \Lambda)$ and $\mathsf{Rel}(\mathcal{E}, \mathcal{E})$ pointwise, hence allowing λ-term relations to be defined both inductively and coinductively. We use these properties to define our notion of effectful eager normal form similarity.

Definition 6. *A term relation $\mathcal{R} = (\mathcal{R}_\Lambda : \Lambda \nrightarrow \Lambda, \mathcal{R}_\mathcal{E} : \mathcal{E} \nrightarrow \mathcal{E})$ is an* effectful eager normal form simulation *with respect to Γ (hereafter enf-simulation, as Γ will be clear from the context) if the following conditions hold, where in condition* (enf 4) $z \notin FV(E) \cup FV(E')$.

$$e \mathcal{R}_\Lambda f \implies [\![e]\!] \, \Gamma \mathcal{R}_\mathcal{E} \, [\![f]\!], \tag{enf 1}$$

$$x \mathcal{R}_\mathcal{E} s \implies s = x, \tag{enf 2}$$

$$\lambda x.e \, \mathcal{R}_\mathcal{E} \, s \implies \exists f.\ s = \lambda x.f \wedge e \mathcal{R}_\Lambda f, \tag{enf 3}$$

$$E[xv] \, \mathcal{R}_\mathcal{E} \, s \implies \exists E', v'.\ s = E'[xv'] \wedge v \mathcal{R}_\mathcal{E} v' \wedge \exists z.\ E[z] \, \mathcal{R}_\Lambda \, E'[z]. \tag{enf 4}$$

We say that relation $\mathcal{R}$ respects enfs *if it satisfies conditions* (enf 2)–(enf 4).

Definition 6 is quite standard. Clause (enf 1) is morally the same clause on terms used to define effectful applicative similarity in [15]. Clauses (enf 2) and (enf 3) state that whenever two enfs are related by $\mathcal{R}_\mathcal{E}$, then they must have the same outermost syntactic structure, and their subterms must be pairwise related. For instance, if $\lambda x.e \, \mathcal{R}_\mathcal{E} \, s$ holds, then s must the a λ-abstraction, i.e. an expression of the form $\lambda x.f$, and e and f must be related by $\mathcal{R}_\Lambda$.

Clause (enf 4) is the most interesting one. It states that whenever $E[xv] \mathcal{R}_\mathcal{E} s$, then s must be a stuck term $E'[xv']$, for some evaluation context E' and value v'. Notice that $E[xv]$ and s must have the same 'stuck variable' x. Additionally, v and v' must be related by $\mathcal{R}_\mathcal{E}$, and E and E' must be properly related too. The idea is that to see whether E and E' are related, we replace the stuck expressions xv, xv' with a fresh variable z, and test $E[z]$ and $E'[z]$ (thus resuming the evaluation process). We require $E[z] \, \mathcal{R}_\mathcal{E} \, E'[z]$ to hold, for *some* fresh variable z. The choice of the variable does not really matter, provided it is fresh. In fact, as we will see, effectful eager normal form similarity $\preceq^\mathsf{E}$ is substitutive and reflexive. In particular, if $E[z] \preceq^\mathsf{E}_\mathcal{E} E'[z]$ holds, then $E[y] \preceq^\mathsf{E}_\mathcal{E} E'[y]$ holds as well, for any variable $y \notin FV(E) \cup FV(E')$.

Notice that Definition 6 does not involve any universal quantification. In particular, enfs are tested by inspecting their syntactic structure, thus making the definition of an enf-simulation somehow 'local': terms are tested in isolation and not via their interaction with the environment. This is a major difference with e.g. applicative (bi)simulation, where the environment interacts with λ-abstractions by passing them arbitrary (closed) values as arguments.

Definition 6 induces a functional $\mathcal{R} \mapsto [\mathcal{R}]$ on the complete lattice $\mathsf{Rel}(\Lambda, \Lambda) \times \mathsf{Rel}(\mathcal{E}, \mathcal{E})$, where $[\mathcal{R}] = ([\mathcal{R}]_{\Lambda}, [\mathcal{R}]_{\mathcal{E}})$ is defined as follows (here $\mathsf{I}_{\mathcal{X}}$ denotes the identity relation on variables, i.e. the set of pairs of the form (x, x)):

$$[\mathcal{R}]_{\Lambda} \triangleq \{(e, f) \mid [\![e]\!] \, \Gamma\mathcal{R}_{\mathcal{E}} \, [\![f]\!]\}$$
$$[\mathcal{R}]_{\mathcal{E}} \triangleq \mathsf{I}_{\mathcal{X}} \cup \{(\lambda x.e, \lambda x.f) \mid e \, \mathcal{R}_{\Lambda} \, f\},$$
$$\cup \{(E[xv], E'[xv']) \mid v \, \mathcal{R}_{\mathcal{E}} \, v' \wedge \exists z \notin FV(E) \cup FV(E').\ E[z] \, \mathcal{R}_{\Lambda} \, E'[z]\}.$$

It is easy to see that a term relation $\mathcal{R}$ is an enf-simulation if and only if $\mathcal{R} \subseteq [\mathcal{R}]$. Notice also that although $[\mathcal{R}]_{\mathcal{E}}$ always contains the identity relation on variables, $\mathcal{R}_{\mathcal{E}}$ does not have to: the empty relation $(\emptyset, \emptyset)$ is an enf-simulation. Finally, since relators are monotone (condition (rel 4)), $\mathcal{R} \mapsto [\mathcal{R}]$ is monotone too. As a consequence, by Knaster-Tarski Theorem [70], it has a greatest fixed point which we call *effectful eager normal form similarity* with respect to Γ (hereafter enf-similarity) and denote by $\preceq^{\mathsf{E}} = (\preceq^{\mathsf{E}}_{\Lambda}, \preceq^{\mathsf{E}}_{\mathcal{E}})$. Enf-similarity is thus the largest enf-simulation with respect to Γ. Moreover, $\preceq^{\mathsf{E}}$ being defined coinductively, it comes with an associated coinduction proof principle stating that if a term relation $\mathcal{R}$ is an enf-simulation, then it is contained in $\preceq^{\mathsf{E}}$. Symbolically: $\mathcal{R} \subseteq [\mathcal{R}] \implies \mathcal{R} \subseteq \preceq^{\mathsf{E}}$.

Example 16. We use the coinduction proof principle to show that $\preceq^{\mathsf{E}}$ contains the β-rule, viz. $(\lambda x.e)v \preceq^{\mathsf{E}}_{\Lambda} e[v/x]$. For that, we simply observe that the term relation $(\{((\lambda x.e)v, e[v/x])\}, \mathsf{I}_{\mathcal{E}})$ is an enf-simulation. Indeed, $[\![(\lambda x.e)v]\!] = [\![e[v/x]]\!]$, so that by (rel 1) we have $[\![(\lambda x.e)v]\!] \, \Gamma\mathsf{I}_{\mathcal{E}} \, [\![e[v/x]]\!]$.

Finally, we define effectful eager normal form *bisimilarity.*

Definition 7. *A term relation $\mathcal{R}$ is an* effectful eager normal form bisimulation *with respect to Γ (enf-bisimulation, for short) if it is a* symmetric *enf-simulation.* Eager normal bisimilarity *with respect to Γ (enf-bisimilarity, for short) $\simeq^{\mathsf{E}}$ is the largest symmetric enf-simulation. In particular, enf-bisimilarity (with respect to Γ) coincides with enf-similarity with respect to $\Gamma \wedge \Gamma^{\circ}$.*

Example 17. We show that the probabilistic call-by-value fixed point combinators Y and Z of Example 2 are enf-bisimilar. In light of Proposition 5, this allows us to conclude that Y and Z are applicatively bisimilar, and thus contextually equivalent [15]. Let us consider the relator $\hat{\mathbb{DM}}$ for probabilistic partial computations. We show $Y \simeq^{\mathsf{E}}_{\Lambda} Z$ by coinduction, proving that the symmetric closure of the term relation $\mathcal{R} = (\mathcal{R}_{\Lambda}, \mathcal{R}_{\mathcal{E}})$ defined as follows is an enf-simulation:

$$\mathcal{R}_{\Lambda} \triangleq \{(Y, Z), (\Delta\Delta z, Zyz), (\Delta\Delta, y(\lambda z.\Delta\Delta z) \textbf{ or } y(\lambda z.Zyz))\} \cup \mathsf{I}_{\Lambda}$$
$$\mathcal{R}_{\mathcal{E}} \triangleq \{(y(\lambda z.\Delta\Delta z), y(\lambda z.Zyz)), (\lambda z.\Delta\Delta z, \lambda z.Zyz), (\lambda y.\Delta\Delta, \lambda y.(y(\lambda z.\Delta\Delta z) \textbf{ or } y(\lambda z.Zyz))), (y(\lambda z.\Delta\Delta z)z, y(\lambda z.Zyz)z)\} \cup \mathsf{I}_{\mathcal{E}}.$$

The term relation $\mathcal{R}$ is obtained from the relation $\{(Y, Z)\}$ by progressively adding terms and enfs according to clauses (enf 1)–(enf 4) in Definition 6. Checking that $\mathcal{R}$ is an enf-simulation is straightforward. As an illustrative example, we prove that $\Delta\Delta z \, \mathcal{R}_{\Lambda} \, Zyz$ implies $[\![\Delta\Delta z]\!] \, \hat{\mathbb{DM}}(\mathcal{R}_{\mathcal{E}}) \, [\![Zyz]\!]$. The latter amounts to show:

$$\big(1 \cdot just\ y(\lambda z.\Delta\Delta z)z\big) \, \hat{\mathbb{DM}}(\mathcal{R}_{\mathcal{E}}) \, \big(\frac{1}{2} \cdot just\ y(\lambda z.\Delta\Delta z)z + \frac{1}{2} \cdot just\ y(\lambda z.Zyz)z\big),$$

where, as usual, we write distributions as weighted formal sums. To prove the latter, it is sufficient to find a suitable coupling of $[\![\Delta\Delta z]\!]$ and $[\![Zyz]\!]$. Define the distribution $\omega \in D(M\mathcal{E} \times M\mathcal{E})$ as follows:

$$\omega(just\ y(\lambda z.\Delta\Delta z)z, just\ y(\lambda z.\Delta\Delta z)z) = \frac{1}{2},$$
$$\omega(just\ y(\lambda z.\Delta\Delta z)z, just\ y(\lambda z.Zyz)z) = \frac{1}{2},$$

and assigning zero to all other pairs in $M\mathcal{E} \times M\mathcal{E}$. Obviously ω is a coupling of $[\![\Delta\Delta z]\!]$ and $[\![Zyz]\!]$. Additionally, we see that $\omega(\chi, y)$ implies $\chi \, \hat{\mathbb{M}}\mathcal{R}_{\mathcal{E}} \, y$, since both $y(\lambda z.\Delta\Delta z)z \, \mathcal{R}_{\mathcal{E}} \, y(\lambda z.\Delta\Delta z)z$, and $y(\lambda z.\Delta\Delta z)z \, \mathcal{R}_{\mathcal{E}} \, y(\lambda z.Zyz)z$ hold.

As already discussed in Example 2, the operational equivalence between Y and Z is an example of an equivalence that cannot be readily established using standard operational methods—such as CIU equivalence or applicative bisimilarity—but whose proof is straightforward using enf-bisimilarity. Additionally, Theorem 3 will allow us to reduce the size of $\mathcal{R}$, thus minimising the task of checking that our relation is indeed an enf-bisimulation. To the best of the authors' knowledge, the probabilistic instance of enf-(bi)similarity is the first example of a *probabilistic eager normal form (bi)similarity* in the literature.

6.1 Congruence and Precongruence Theorems

In order for $\preceq^{\mathsf{E}}$ and $\simeq^{\mathsf{E}}$ to qualify as good notions of program refinement and equivalence, respectively, they have to allow for compositional reasoning. Roughly speaking, a term relation $\mathcal{R}$ is compositional if the validity of the relationship $\mathcal{C}[e] \, \mathcal{R} \, \mathcal{C}[e']$ between compound terms $\mathcal{C}[e], \mathcal{C}[e']$ follows from the validity of the relationship $e \, \mathcal{R} \, e'$ between the subterms e, e'. Mathematically, the notion of compositionality is formalised throughout the notion of *compatibility*, which directly leads to the notions of a precongruence and congruence relation. In this section we prove that $\preceq^{\mathsf{E}}$ and $\simeq^{\mathsf{E}}$ are substitutive precongruence and congruence

$$\frac{}{x \,\mathcal{R}^{\mathsf{sc}}_{\mathcal{E}}\, x}\ (\mathsf{sc\text{-}var}) \qquad \frac{e \,\mathcal{R}_{\mathsf{x}}\, e'}{e \,\mathcal{R}^{\mathsf{sc}}_{\mathsf{x}}\, e'}\ (\mathsf{sc\text{-}\downarrow}) \qquad \frac{s \,\mathcal{R}^{\mathsf{sc}}_{\mathcal{E}}\, s'}{s \,\mathcal{R}^{\mathsf{sc}}_{\Lambda}\, s'}\ (\mathsf{sc\text{-}to\text{-}\lambda})$$

$$\frac{e \,\mathcal{R}^{\mathsf{sc}}_{\Lambda}\, f}{\lambda x.e \,\mathcal{R}^{\mathsf{sc}}_{\mathcal{E}}\, \lambda x.f}\ (\mathsf{sc\text{-}abs}) \qquad \frac{e_i \,\mathcal{R}^{\mathsf{sc}}_{\Lambda}\, e'_i}{e_1 e_2 \,\mathcal{R}^{\mathsf{sc}}_{\Lambda}\, e'_1 e'_2}\ (\mathsf{sc\text{-}app}) \qquad \frac{e \,\mathcal{R}^{\mathsf{sc}}_{\Lambda}\, f}{\mathbf{op}(p, x.e) \,\mathcal{R}^{\mathsf{sc}}_{\Lambda}\, \mathbf{op}(p, x.f)}\ (\mathsf{sc\text{-}op})$$

$$\frac{v \,\mathcal{R}^{\mathsf{sc}}_{\mathcal{E}}\, v' \quad w \,\mathcal{R}^{\mathsf{sc}}_{\mathcal{E}}\, w'}{v[w/x] \,\mathcal{R}^{\mathsf{sc}}_{\mathcal{E}}\, v'[w'/x]}\ (\mathsf{sc\text{-}subst\text{-}val}) \qquad \frac{e \,\mathcal{R}^{\mathsf{sc}}_{\Lambda}\, e' \quad v \,\mathcal{R}^{\mathsf{sc}}_{\mathcal{E}}\, v'}{e[v/x] \,\mathcal{R}^{\mathsf{sc}}_{\Lambda}\, e'[v'/x]}\ (\mathsf{sc\text{-}subst})$$

$$\frac{E[z] \,\mathcal{R}^{\mathsf{sc}}_{\Lambda}\, E'[z] \quad v \,\mathcal{R}^{\mathsf{sc}}_{\mathcal{E}}\, v'}{E[xv] \,\mathcal{R}^{\mathsf{sc}}_{\mathcal{E}}\, E[xv']}\ (\mathsf{sc\text{-}stuck}) \qquad \frac{E[z] \,\mathcal{R}^{\mathsf{sc}}_{\Lambda}\, E'[z] \quad e \,\mathcal{R}^{\mathsf{sc}}_{\Lambda}\, e'}{E[e] \,\mathcal{R}^{\mathsf{sc}}_{\Lambda}\, E'[e']}\ (\mathsf{sc\text{-}ectx})$$

Fig. 1. Compatible and substitutive closure construction.

relations, that is preorder and equivalence relations closed under term constructors of Λ_Σ and substitution, respectively. To prove such results, we generalise Lassen's relational construction for the pure call-by-name λ-calculus [37]. Such a construction has been previously adapted to the *pure* call-by-value λ-calculus (and its extension with delimited and abortive control operators) in [9], whereas Lassen has proved compatibility of pure eager normal form bisimilarity via a CPS translation [38]. Both those proofs rely on syntactical properties of the calculus (mostly expressed using suitable small-step semantics), and thus seem to be hardly adaptable to effectful calculi. On the contrary, our proofs rely on the properties of relators, thereby making our results and techniques more modular and thus valid for a large class of effects.

We begin proving precongruence of enf-similarity. The central tool we use to prove the wished precongruence theorem is the so-called *(substitutive) context closure* [37] $\mathcal{R}^{\mathsf{sc}}$ of a term relation $\mathcal{R}$, which is inductively defined by the rules in Fig. 1, where $\mathsf{x} \in \{\Lambda, \mathcal{E}\}$, $i \in \{1, 2\}$, and $z \notin FV(E) \cup FV(E')$.

We easily see that $\mathcal{R}^{\mathsf{sc}}$ is the smallest term relation that contains $\mathcal{R}$, it is closed under language constructors of Λ_Σ (a property known as *compatibility* [5]), and it is closed under the substitution operation (a property known as *substitutivity* [5]). As a consequence, we say that a term relation $\mathcal{R}$ is a *substitutive compatible* relation if $\mathcal{R}^{\mathsf{sc}} \subseteq \mathcal{R}$ (and thus $\mathcal{R} = \mathcal{R}^{\mathsf{sc}}$). If, additionally, $\mathcal{R}$ is a preorder (resp. equivalence) relation, then we say that $\mathcal{R}$ is a *substitutive precongruence* (resp. *substitutive congruence*) relation.

We are now going to prove that if $\mathcal{R}$ is an enf-simulation, then so is $\mathcal{R}^{\mathsf{sc}}$. In particular, we will infer that $(\preceq^{\mathsf{E}})^{\mathsf{sc}}$ is a enf-simulation, and thus it is contained in $\preceq^{\mathsf{E}}$, by coinduction.

Lemma 2 (Main Lemma). *If $\mathcal{R}$ be an enf-simulation, then so is $\mathcal{R}^{\mathsf{sc}}$.*

Proof (sketch). The proof is long and non-trivial. Due to space constraints here we simply give some intuitions behind it. First, a routine proof by induction shows that since $\mathcal{R}$ respects enfs, then so does $\mathcal{R}^{\mathsf{sc}}$. Next, we wish to prove that $e \,\mathcal{R}^{\mathsf{sc}}_{\Lambda}\, f$ implies $[\![e]\!] \,\Gamma\mathcal{R}^{\mathsf{sc}}_{\mathcal{E}}\, [\![f]\!]$. Since Γ is inductive, the latter follows if for any $n \geq 0$, $e \mathcal{R}^{\mathsf{SC}}_{\Lambda} f$ implies $[\![e]\!]_n \, \Gamma\mathcal{R}^{\mathsf{SC}}_{\mathcal{E}} \, [\![f]\!]$. We prove the latter implication by lexicographic induction on (1) the natural number n and (2) the derivation $e \mathcal{R}^{\mathsf{SC}}_{\Lambda} f$. The case for $n = 0$ is trivial (since Γ is inductive). The remaining cases are nontrivial, and are handled observing that $[\![E[e]]\!] = (s \mapsto [\![E[s]]\!])^{\dagger}[\![e]\!]$ and $[\![e[v/x]]\!]_n \sqsubseteq [\![-[v/x]]\!]^{\dagger}_n [\![e]\!]_n$. Both these identities allow us to apply condition (rel 8) to simplify proof obligations (usually relying on part (2) of the induction hypothesis as well). This scheme is iterated until we reach either an enf (in which case we are done by condition (rel 7)) or a pair of expressions on which we can apply part (1) of the induction hypothesis.

Theorem 2. *Enf-similarity (resp. bisimilarity) is a substitutive precongruence (resp. congruence) relation.*

Proof. We show that enf-similarity is a substitutive precongruence relation. By Lemma 2, it is sufficient to show that $\preceq^{\mathsf{E}}$ is a preorder. This follows by coinduction, since the term relations I and $\preceq^{\mathsf{E}} \circ \preceq^{\mathsf{E}}$ are enf-simulations (the proofs make use of conditions (rel 1) and (rel 2), as well as of substitutivity of $\preceq^{\mathsf{E}}$).

Finally, we show that enf-bisimilarity is a substitutive congruence relation. Obviously $\simeq^{\mathsf{E}}$ is an equivalence relation, so that it is sufficient to prove $(\simeq^{\mathsf{E}})^{\mathsf{SC}} \subseteq \simeq^{\mathsf{E}}$. That directly follows by coinduction relying on Lemma 2, provided that $(\simeq^{\mathsf{E}})^{\mathsf{SC}}$ is symmetric. An easy inspection of the rules in Fig. 1 reveals that $\mathcal{R}^{\mathsf{SC}}$ is symmetric, whenever $\mathcal{R}$ is.

6.2 Soundness for Effectful Applicative (Bi)similarity

Theorem 2 qualifies enf-bisimilarity and enf-similarity as good candidate notions of program equivalence and refinement for Λ_{Σ}, at least from a structural perspective. However, we gave motivations for such notions looking at specific examples where effectful applicative (bi)similarity is ineffective. It is then natural to ask whether enf-(bi)similarity can be used as a proof technique for effectful applicative (bi)similarity.

Here we give a formal comparison between enf-(bi)similarity and effectful applicative (bi)similarity, as defined in [15]. First of all, we rephrase the notion of an effectful applicative (bi)simulation of [15] to our calculus Λ_{Σ}. For that, we use the following notational convention. Let $\Lambda_0, \mathcal{V}_0$ denote the collections of closed terms and closed values, respectively. We notice that if $e \in \Lambda_0$, then $[\![e]\!] \in T\mathcal{V}_0$. As a consequence, $[\![-]\!]$ induces a closed evaluation function $|-| : \Lambda_0 \to T\mathcal{V}_0$ characterised by the identity $[\![-]\!] \circ \iota = T\iota \circ |-|$, where $\iota : \mathcal{V}_0 \hookrightarrow \mathcal{E}$ is the obvious inclusion map. We can thus phrase the definition of effectful applicative similarity (with respect to a relator Γ) as follows.

Definition 8. *A term relation* $\mathcal{R} = (\mathcal{R}_{\Lambda_0} : \Lambda_0 \nrightarrow \Lambda_0, \mathcal{R}_{\mathcal{V}_0} : \mathcal{V}_0 \nrightarrow \mathcal{V}_0)$ *is an effectful applicative simulation with respect to* Γ *(applicative simulation, for short) if:*

$$e \, \mathcal{R}_{\Lambda_0} \, f \implies |e| \, \Gamma\mathcal{R}_{\mathcal{V}_0} \, |f|, \qquad \text{(app 1)}$$

$$\lambda x.e \, \mathcal{R}_{\mathcal{V}_0} \, \lambda x.f \implies \forall v \in \mathcal{V}_0.\ e[v/x] \, \mathcal{R}_{\Lambda_0} \, f[v/x]. \qquad \text{(app 2)}$$

As usual, we can define effectful applicative similarity with respect to Γ (applicative similarity, for short), denoted by $\preceq_0^{\mathsf{A}} = (\preceq_{\Lambda_0}^{\mathsf{A}}, \preceq_{\mathcal{V}_0}^{\mathsf{A}})$, coinductively as the largest applicative simulation. Its associated coinduction proof principle states that if a relation is an applicative simulation, then it is contained in applicative similarity. Finally, we extend $\preceq_0^{\mathsf{A}}$ to arbitrary terms by defining the relation $\preceq^{\mathsf{A}} = (\preceq_\Lambda^{\mathsf{A}}, \preceq_\mathcal{V}^{\mathsf{A}})$ as follows: let e, f, w, u be terms and values with free variables among $\bar{x} = x_1, \ldots, x_n$. We let $\bar{v}$ range over n-ary sequences of closed values $v_1, \ldots, v_n$. Define:

$$e \preceq_\Lambda^{\mathsf{A}} f \stackrel{\triangle}{\iff} \forall \bar{v}.\ e[\bar{v}/\bar{x}] \preceq_{\Lambda_0}^{\mathsf{A}} f[\bar{v}/\bar{x}], \qquad w \preceq_\Lambda^{\mathsf{A}} u \stackrel{\triangle}{\iff} \forall \bar{v}.\ w[\bar{v}/\bar{x}] \preceq_{\Lambda_0}^{\mathsf{A}} u[\bar{v}/\bar{x}].$$

The following result states that enf-similarity is a sound proof technique for applicative similarity.

Proposition 5. *Enf-similarity $\preceq^{\mathsf{E}}$ is included in applicative similarity $\preceq^{\mathsf{A}}$.*

Proof. Let $\preceq^{\mathsf{C}} = (\preceq_\Lambda^{\mathsf{C}}, \preceq_\mathcal{V}^{\mathsf{C}})$ denote enf-similarity restricted to closed terms and values. We first show that $\preceq^{\mathsf{C}}$ is an applicative simulation, from which follows, by coinduction, that it is included in $\preceq_0^{\mathsf{A}}$. It is easy to see that $\preceq^{\mathsf{C}}$ satisfies condition (app 2). In order to prove that it also satisfies condition (app 1), we have to show that for all $e, f \in \Lambda_\circ$, $e \preceq_\Lambda^{\mathsf{C}} f$ implies $|e|\ \Gamma\preceq_\mathcal{V}^{\mathsf{C}} |f|$. Since $e \preceq_\Lambda^{\mathsf{C}} f$ obviously implies $\iota(e) \preceq_\Lambda^{\mathsf{E}} \iota(f)$, by (enf 1) we infer $[\![\iota(e)]\!]\ \Gamma\preceq_\mathcal{V}^{\mathsf{E}} [\![\iota(f)]\!]$, and thus $T\iota|e|\ \Gamma\preceq_\mathcal{V}^{\mathsf{E}} T\iota|f|$. By stability of Γ, the latter implies $|e|\ \Gamma(\iota^\circ \circ \preceq_\mathcal{E} \circ \iota)\ |f|$, and thus the wished thesis, since $\iota^\circ \circ \preceq_\mathcal{E} \circ \iota$ is nothing but $\preceq_\mathcal{V}^{\mathsf{C}}$. Finally, we show that for all terms e, f, if $e \preceq_\Lambda^{\mathsf{E}} f$, then $e \preceq_\Lambda^{\mathsf{A}} f$ (a similar result holds *mutatis mutandis* for values, so that we can conclude $\preceq^{\mathsf{E}} \subseteq \preceq^{\mathsf{A}}$). Indeed, suppose $FV(e) \cup FV(f) \subseteq \bar{x}$, then by substitutivity of $\preceq^{\mathsf{E}}$ we have that $e \preceq_\Lambda^{\mathsf{E}} f$ implies $e[\bar{v}/\bar{x}] \preceq_\Lambda^{\mathsf{E}} f[\bar{v}/\bar{x}]$, for all closed values $\bar{v}$ (notice that since we are substituting *closed* values, sequential and simultaneous substitution coincide). That essentially means $e[\bar{v}/\bar{x}] \preceq_\Lambda^{\mathsf{C}} f[\bar{v}/\bar{x}]$, and thus $e[\bar{v}/\bar{x}] \preceq_{\Lambda_0}^{\mathsf{A}} f[\bar{v}/\bar{x}]$. We thus conclude $e \preceq_\Lambda^{\mathsf{A}} f$.

Since in [15] it is shown that effectful applicative similarity (resp. bisimilarity) is contained in effectful contextual approximation (resp. equivalence), Proposition 5 gives the following result.

Corollary 1. *Enf-similarity and enf-bisimilarity are sound proof techniques for contextual approximation and equivalence, respectively.*

Although sound, enf-bisimilarity is *not* fully abstract for applicative bisimilarity. In fact, as already observed in [38], in the pure λ-calculus enf-bisimilarity is strictly finer than applicative bisimilarity (and thus strictly finer than contextual equivalence too). For instance, the terms xv and $(\lambda y.xv)(xv)$ are obviously applicatively bisimilar but not enf-bisimilar.

6.3 Eager Normal Form (Bi)simulation Up-to Context

The up-to context technique [37,60,64] is a refinement of the coinduction proof principle of enf-(bi)similarity that allows for handier proofs of equivalence and refinement between terms. When exhibiting a candidate enf-(bi)simulation relation $\mathcal{R}$, it is desirable for $\mathcal{R}$ to be as small as possible, so to minimise the task of verifying that $\mathcal{R}$ is indeed an enf-(bi)simulation.

The motivation behind such a technique can be easily seen looking at Example 17, where we showed the equivalence between the probabilistic fixed point combinators Y and Z working with relations containing several administrative pairs of terms. The presence of such pairs was forced by Definition 7, although they appear somehow unnecessary in order to convince that Y and Z exhibit the same operational behaviour.

Enf-(bi)simulation up-to context is a refinement of enf-(bi)simulation that allows to check that a relation $\mathcal{R}$ behaves as an enf-(bi)simulation relation up to its substitutive and compatible closure.

Definition 9. *A term relation* $\mathcal{R} = (\mathcal{R}_\Lambda : \Lambda \nrightarrow \Lambda, \mathcal{R}_\mathcal{E} : \mathcal{E} \nrightarrow \mathcal{E})$ *is an* effectful eager normal form simulation up-to context with respect to Γ *(enf-simulation up-to context, hereafter) if satisfies the following conditions, where in condition* (up-to 4) $z \notin FV(E) \cup FV(E')$.

$$e\,\mathcal{R}_\Lambda\,f \implies [\![e]\!]\,\Gamma\mathcal{R}_\mathcal{E}^{\mathsf{SC}}\,[\![f]\!], \qquad \text{(up-to 1)}$$

$$x\,\mathcal{R}_\mathcal{E}\,s \implies s = x, \qquad \text{(up-to 2)}$$

$$\lambda x.e\,\mathcal{R}_\mathcal{E}\,s \implies \exists f.\ s = \lambda x.f \wedge e\,\mathcal{R}_\Lambda^{\mathsf{SC}}\,f, \qquad \text{(up-to 3)}$$

$$E[xv]\,\mathcal{R}_\mathcal{E}\,s \implies \exists E', v'.\ s = E'[xv'] \wedge v\,\mathcal{R}_\mathcal{E}^{\mathsf{SC}}\,v' \wedge \exists z.\ E[z]\,\mathcal{R}_\Lambda^{\mathsf{SC}}\,E'[z]. \qquad \text{(up-to 4)}$$

In order for the up-to context technique to be sound, we need to show that every enf-simulation up-to context is contained in enf-similarity. This is a direct consequence of the following variation of Lemma 2.

Lemma 3. *If* $\mathcal{R}$ *is a enf-simulation up-to context, then* $\mathcal{R}^{\mathsf{SC}}$ *is a enf-simulation.*

Proof. The proof is structurally identical to the one of Lemma 2, where we simply observe that wherever we use the assumption that $\mathcal{R}$ is an enf-simulation, we can use the weaker assumption that $\mathcal{R}$ is an enf-simulation up-to context.

In particular, since by Lemma 2 we have that $\preceq^{\mathsf{E}} = (\preceq^{\mathsf{E}})^{\mathsf{SC}}$, we see that enf-similarity is an enf-simulation up-to context. Additionally, by Lemma 3 it is the largest such. Since the same result holds for enf-bisimilarity and enf-bisimilarity up-to context, we have the following theorem.

Theorem 3. *Enf-similarity is the largest enf-simulation up-to context, and enf-bisimilarity is the largest enf-bisimulation up-to context.*

Example 18. We apply Theorem 3 to simplify the proof of the equivalence between Y and Z given in Example 17. In fact, it is sufficient to show that the symmetric closure of term relation $\mathcal{R}$ defined below is an enf-bisimulation up-to context.

$$\mathcal{R}_\Lambda \triangleq \{(Y, Z), (\Delta\Delta z, Zyz), (\Delta\Delta, y(\lambda z.\Delta\Delta z) \textbf{ or } y(\lambda z.Zyz))\}, \qquad \mathcal{R}_\mathcal{E} \triangleq \mathsf{I}_\mathcal{E}.$$

Example 19. Recall the fixed point combinators with ticking operations Y and Z of Example 4. Let us consider the relator $\hat{\mathbb{C}}$. It is not hard to see that Y and Z are not enf-bisimilar (that is because the ticking operation is evaluated at different moments, so to speak). Nonetheless, once we pass them a variable x_0 as argument, we have $Zx_0 \preceq^{\mathsf{E}}_{\Lambda} Yx_0$. For, observe that the term relation $\mathcal{R}$ defined below is an enf-simulation up-context.

$$\mathcal{R}_{\Lambda} \triangleq \{(Yx_0, Zx_0), (\mathbf{tick}(\Delta[x_0/y]\Delta[x_0/y]z), \mathbf{tick}(\Theta\Theta x_0 z))\}, \qquad \mathcal{R}_{\mathcal{E}} = \emptyset.$$

Intuitively, Y executes a tick first, and then proceeds iterating the evaluation of $\Delta[x_0/y]\Delta[x_0/y]$, the latter involving two tickings only. On the contrary, Z proceeds by recursively call itself, hence involving three tickings at any iteration, so to speak. Since $\preceq^{\mathsf{E}}$ is substitutive, for any value v we have $Zv \preceq^{\mathsf{E}} Yv$.

Theorem 3 makes enf-(bi)similarity an extremely powerful proof technique for program equivalence/refinement, especially because it is yet unknown whether there exist *sound* up-to context techniques for applicative (bi)similarity [35].

6.4 Weak Head Normal Form (Bi)simulation

So far we have focused on call-by-value calculi, since in presence of effects the call-by-value evaluation strategy seems the more natural one. Nonetheless, our framework can be easily adapted to deal with call-by-name calculi too. In this last section we spend some words on *effectful weak head normal form (bi)similarity* (whnf-(bi)similarity, for short). The latter is nothing but the call-by-name counterpart of enf-(bi)similarity. The main difference between enf-(bi)similarity and whnf-(bi)similarity relies on the notion of an evaluation context (and thus of a stuck term). In fact, in a call-by-name setting, Λ_{Σ} evaluation contexts are expressions of the form $[-]e_1 \cdots e_n$, which are somehow simpler than their call-by-value counterparts. Such a simplicity is reflected in the definition of whnf-(bi)similarity, which allows to prove *mutatis mutandis* all results proved for enf-(bi)similarity (such results are, without much of a surprise, actually easier to prove).

We briefly expand on that. The collection of weak head normal forms (whnfs, for short) $\mathcal{W}$ is defined as the union of $\mathcal{V}$ and the collection of stuck terms, the latter being expressions of the form $xe_1 \cdots e_n$. The evaluation function of Definition 2 now maps terms to elements in $T\mathcal{W}$, and it is essentially obtained modifying Definition 2 defining $[\![E[xe]]\!]_{n+1} \triangleq \eta(E[xe])$ and $[\![E[(\lambda x.f)e]]\!]_{n+1} \triangleq [\![E[f[e/x]]]\!]_n$. The notion of a whnf-(bi)simulation (and thus the notions of whnf-(bi)similarity) is obtained modifying Definition 6 accordingly. In particular, clauses (enf 2) and (enf 4) are replaced by the following clause, where we use the notation $\mathcal{R} = (\mathcal{R}_{\Lambda} : \Lambda \nrightarrow \Lambda, \mathcal{R}_{\mathcal{W}} : \mathcal{W} \nrightarrow \mathcal{W})$ to denote a (call-by-name) λ-term relation.

$$xe_0 \cdots e_k \,\mathcal{R}_{\mathcal{W}}\, s \implies \exists f_0, \ldots, f_k.\ s = xf_0 \cdots f_k \wedge \forall i.\ e_i \,\mathcal{R}_{\Lambda}\, f_i.$$

A straightforward modifications of the rules in Fig. 1 allows to prove an analogous of Lemma 2 for whnf-simulations, and thus to conclude (pre)congruence properties of whnf-(bi)similarity. Additionally, such results generalise to whnf-(bi)simulation up to-context, the latter being defined according to Definition 9, so that we have an analogous of Theorem 3 as well. The latter allows to infer the equivalence of the argument-switching fixed point combinators of Example 3, simply by noticing that the symmetric closure of the term relation $\mathcal{R} = (\{(P, Q), (Pyz, Qzy), (Pzy, Qyz)\}, \emptyset)$ is a whnf-bisimulation up-to context.

Finally, it is straightforward to observe that whnf-(bi)similarity is included in the call-by-name counterpart of effectful applicative (bi)similarity, but that the inclusion is strict. In fact, the (pure λ-calculus) terms xx and $x(\lambda y.xy)$ are applicatively bisimilar, but not whnf-bisimilar.

7 Related Work

Normal form (bi)similarity has been originally introduced for the call-by-name λ-calculus in [65], where it was called *open bisimilarity*. Open bisimilarity provides a coinductive characterisation of Lévy-Longo tree equivalence [42,45,53], and has been shown to coincide with the equivalence (notably weak bisimilarity) induced by Milner's encoding of the λ-calculus into the π-calculus [48].

In [37] normal form bisimilarity relations characterising both Böhm and Lévy-Longo tree equivalences have been studied by purely operational means, providing new congruence proofs of the aforementioned tree equivalences based on suitable relational constructions. Such results have been extended to the call-by-value λ-calculus in [38], where the so-called *eager normal form bisimilarity* is introduced. The latter is shown to coincide with the Lévy-Longo tree equivalence induced by a suitable CPS translation [54], and thus to be a congruence relation. An elementary proof of congruence properties of eager normal form bisimilarity is given in [9], where Lassen's relational construction [37] is extended to the call-by-value λ-calculus, as well as its extensions with delimited and abortive control operators. Finally, following [65], eager normal form bisimilarity has been recently characterised as the equivalence induced by a suitable encoding of the (call-by-value) λ-calculus in the π-calculus [21].

Concerning effectful extensions of normal form bisimilarity, our work seems to be rather new. In fact, normal form bisimilarity has been studied for *deterministic* extensions of the λ-calculus with specific *non*-algebraic effects, notably control operators [9], as well as control and state [68] (where full abstraction of the obtained notion of normal form bisimilarity is proved). The only extension of normal form bisimilarity to an algebraic effect the authors are aware of, is given in [39], where normal form bisimilarity is studied for a *nondeterministic call-by-name* λ-calculus. However, we should mention that contrary to normal form bisimilarity, both nondeterministic [20] and probabilistic [41] extensions of Böhm tree equivalence have been investigated (although none of them employ, to the best of the authors' knowledge, coinductive techniques).

8 Conclusion

This paper shows that effectful normal form bisimulation is indeed a powerful methodology for program equivalence. Interestingly, the proof of congruence for normal form bisimilarity can be given just once, without the necessity of redoing it for every distinct notion of algebraic effect considered. This relies on the fact that the underlying monad and relator are Σ-continuous, something which has already been proved for many distinct notions of effects [15].

Topics for further work are plentiful. First of all, a natural question is whether the obtained notion of bisimilarity coincides with contextual equivalence. This is known *not* to hold in the deterministic case [37,38], but to hold in presence of control and state [68], which offer the environment the necessary discriminating power. Is there any (sufficient) condition on effects guaranteeing full abstraction of normal form bisimilarity? This is an intriguing question we are currently investigating. In fact, contrary to applicative bisimilarity (which is known to be unsound in presence of non-algebraic effects [33], such as local states), the syntactic nature of normal form bisimilarity seems to be well-suited for languages combining both algebraic and non-algebraic effects.

Another interesting topic for future research, is investigating whether normal form bisimilarity can be extended to languages having both algebraic operations and effect handlers [7,59].

References

1. Abramsky, S.: The lazy lambda calculus. In: Turner, D. (ed.) Research Topics in Functional Programming, pp. 65–117. Addison Wesley, Boston (1990)
2. Abramsky, S., Jung, A.: Domain theory. In: Handbook of Logic in Computer Science, pp. 1–168. Clarendon Press (1994)
3. Abramsky, S., Ong, C.L.: Full abstraction in the lazy lambda calculus. Inf. Comput. **105**(2), 159–267 (1993)
4. Appel, A., McAllester, D.: An indexed model of recursive types for foundational proof-carrying code. ACM Trans. Program. Lang. Syst. **23**(5), 657–683 (2001)
5. Barendregt, H.: The lambda calculus: its syntax and semantics. In: Studies in Logic and the Foundations of Mathematics. North-Holland (1984)
6. Barr, M.: Relational algebras. Lect. Notes Math. **137**, 39–55 (1970)
7. Bauer, A., Pretnar, M.: Programming with algebraic effects and handlers. J. Log. Algebr. Meth. Program. **84**(1), 108–123 (2015)
8. Benton, N., Kennedy, A., Beringer, L., Hofmann, M.: Relational semantics for effect-based program transformations: higher-order store. In: Proceedings of PPDP 2009, pp. 301–312 (2009)
9. Biernacki, D., Lenglet, S., Polesiuk, P.: Proving soundness of extensional normal-form bisimilarities. Electr. Notes Theor. Comput. Sci. **336**, 41–56 (2018)
10. Bizjak, A., Birkedal, L.: Step-indexed logical relations for probability. In: Pitts, A. (ed.) FoSSaCS 2015. LNCS, vol. 9034, pp. 279–294. Springer, Heidelberg (2015). https://doi.org/10.1007/978-3-662-46678-0_18
11. Böhm, C.: Alcune proprietà delle forme $\beta\eta$-normali del λk-calcolo. Pubblicazioni dell'Istituto per le Applicazioni del Calcolo **696** (1968)

12. Burris, S., Sankappanavar, H.: A Course in Universal Algebra. Graduate Texts in Mathematics. Springer, New York (1981)
13. Crubillé, R., Dal Lago, U.: On probabilistic applicative bisimulation and call-by-value λ-Calculi. In: Shao, Z. (ed.) ESOP 2014. LNCS, vol. 8410, pp. 209–228. Springer, Heidelberg (2014). https://doi.org/10.1007/978-3-642-54833-8_12
14. Culpepper, R., Cobb, A.: Contextual equivalence for probabilistic programs with continuous random variables and scoring. In: Yang, H. (ed.) ESOP 2017. LNCS, vol. 10201, pp. 368–392. Springer, Heidelberg (2017). https://doi.org/10.1007/978-3-662-54434-1_14
15. Dal Lago, U., Gavazzo, F., Levy, P.: Effectful applicative bisimilarity: monads, relators, and Howe's method. In: Proceedings of LICS 2017, pp. 1–12 (2017)
16. Dal Lago, U., Sangiorgi, D., Alberti, M.: On coinductive equivalences for higher-order probabilistic functional programs. In: Proceedings of POPL 2014, pp. 297–308 (2014)
17. Dal Lago, U., Zorzi, M.: Probabilistic operational semantics for the lambda calculus. RAIRO - Theor. Inf. Appl. **46**(3), 413–450 (2012)
18. Danos, V., Harmer, R.: Probabilistic game semantics. ACM Trans. Comput. Logic **3**(3), 359–382 (2002)
19. Davey, B., Priestley, H.: Introduction to Lattices and Order. Cambridge University Press, Cambridge (1990)
20. De Liguoro, U., Piperno, A.: Non deterministic extensions of untyped lambda-calculus. Inf. Comput. **122**(2), 149–177 (1995)
21. Durier, A., Hirschkoff, D., Sangiorgi, D.: Eager functions as processes. In: Proceedings of the 33rd Annual ACM/IEEE Symposium on Logic in Computer Science, LICS 2018, pp. 364–373 (2018)
22. Felleisen, M., Hieb, R.: The revised report on the syntactic theories of sequential control and state. Theor. Comput. Sci. **103**(2), 235–271 (1992)
23. Gavazzo, F.: Quantitative behavioural reasoning for higher-order effectful programs: applicative distances. In: Proceedings of the 33rd Annual ACM/IEEE Symposium on Logic in Computer Science, LICS 2018, Oxford, UK, 09–12 July 2018, pp. 452–461 (2018)
24. Goguen, J.A., Thatcher, J.W., Wagner, E.G., Wright, J.B.: Initial algebra semantics and continuous algebras. J. ACM **24**(1), 68–95 (1977)
25. Goubault-Larrecq, J., Lasota, S., Nowak, D.: Logical relations for monadic types. Math. Struct. Comput. Sci. **18**(6), 1169–1217 (2008)
26. Hofmann, D., Seal, G., Tholen, W. (eds.): Monoidal Topology. A Categorical Approach to Order, Metric, and Topology. No. 153 in Encyclopedia of Mathematics and its Applications. Cambridge University Press (2014)
27. Hughes, J., Jacobs, B.: Simulations in coalgebra. Theor. Comput. Sci. **327**(1–2), 71–108 (2004)
28. Hyland, M., Plotkin, G.D., Power, J.: Combining effects: sum and tensor. Theor. Comput. Sci. **357**(1–3), 70–99 (2006)
29. Hyland, M., Power, J.: The category theoretic understanding of universal algebra: Lawvere theories and monads. Electr. Notes Theor. Comput. Sci. **172**, 437–458 (2007)
30. Johann, P., Simpson, A., Voigtländer, J.: A generic operational metatheory for algebraic effects. In: Proceedings of LICS 2010, pp. 209–218. IEEE Computer Society (2010)
31. Jones, C.: Probabilistic non-determinism. Ph.D. thesis, University of Edinburgh, UK (1990)

32. Katsumata, S., Sato, T.: Preorders on monads and coalgebraic simulations. In: Pfenning, F. (ed.) FoSSaCS 2013. LNCS, vol. 7794, pp. 145–160. Springer, Heidelberg (2013). https://doi.org/10.1007/978-3-642-37075-5_10
33. Koutavas, V., Levy, P.B., Sumii, E.: From applicative to environmental bisimulation. Electr. Notes Theor. Comput. Sci. **276**, 215–235 (2011)
34. Larsen, K.G., Skou, A.: Bisimulation through probabilistic testing. In: Proceedings of POPL 1989, pp. 344–352 (1989)
35. Lassen, S.: Relational reasoning about contexts. In: Gordon, A.D., Pitts, A.M. (eds.) Higher Order Operational Techniques in Semantics, pp. 91–136 (1998)
36. Lassen, S.: Relational reasoning about functions and nondeterminism. Ph.D. thesis, Department of Computer Science, University of Aarhus, May 1998
37. Lassen, S.B.: Bisimulation in untyped lambda calculus: Böhm trees and bisimulation up to context. Electr. Notes Theor. Comput. Sci. **20**, 346–374 (1999)
38. Lassen, S.B.: Eager normal form bisimulation. In: Proceedings of LICS 2005, pp. 345–354 (2005)
39. Lassen, S.B.: Normal form simulation for McCarthy's Amb. Electr. Notes Theor. Comput. Sci. **155**, 445–465 (2006)
40. Lawvere, W.F.: Functorial semantics of algebraic theories. Ph.D. thesis (2004)
41. Leventis, T.: Probabilistic Böhm trees and probabilistic separation. In: Proceedings of LICS (2018)
42. Levy, J.-J.: An algebraic interpretation of the λβK-calculus and a labelled λ-calculus. In: Böhm, C. (ed.) λ-Calculus and Computer Science Theory. LNCS, vol. 37, pp. 147–165. Springer, Heidelberg (1975). https://doi.org/10.1007/BFb0029523
43. Levy, P.B.: Similarity quotients as final coalgebras. In: Hofmann, M. (ed.) FoSSaCS 2011. LNCS, vol. 6604, pp. 27–41. Springer, Heidelberg (2011). https://doi.org/10.1007/978-3-642-19805-2_3
44. Levy, P., Power, J., Thielecke, H.: Modelling environments in call-by-value programming languages. Inf. Comput. **185**(2), 182–210 (2003)
45. Longo, G.: Set-theoretical models of lambda calculus: theories, expansions, isomorphisms. Ann. Pure Appl. Logic **24**, 153–188 (1983)
46. Mac Lane, S.: Categories for the Working Mathematician. GTM, vol. 5. Springer, New York (1971). https://doi.org/10.1007/978-1-4612-9839-7
47. Mason, I.A., Talcott, C.L.: Equivalence in functional languages with effects. J. Funct. Program. **1**(3), 287–327 (1991)
48. Milner, R.: Functions as processes. Math. Struct. Comput. Sci. **2**(2), 119–141 (1992)
49. Moggi, E.: Computational lambda-calculus and monads. In: Proceedings of LICS 1989, pp. 14–23. IEEE Computer Society (1989)
50. Moggi, E.: Notions of computation and monads. Inf. Comput. **93**(1), 55–92 (1991)
51. Morris, J.: Lambda calculus models of programming languages. Ph.D. thesis, MIT (1969)
52. Ong, C.L.: Non-determinism in a functional setting. In: Proceedings of LICS 1993, pp. 275–286. IEEE Computer Society (1993)
53. Ong, C.: The lazy lambda calculus: an investigation into the foundations of functional programming. University of London, Imperial College of Science and Technology (1988)
54. Plotkin, G.: Call-by-name, call-by-value and the lambda-calculus. Theoret. Comput. Sci. **1**(2), 125–159 (1975)
55. Plotkin, G.: Lambda-definability and logical relations. Technical report SAI-RM-4. University of Edinburgh, School of A.I. (1973)

56. Plotkin, G., Power, J.: Adequacy for algebraic effects. In: Honsell, F., Miculan, M. (eds.) FoSSaCS 2001. LNCS, vol. 2030, pp. 1–24. Springer, Heidelberg (2001). https://doi.org/10.1007/3-540-45315-6_1
57. Plotkin, G., Power, J.: Notions of computation determine monads. In: Nielsen, M., Engberg, U. (eds.) FoSSaCS 2002. LNCS, vol. 2303, pp. 342–356. Springer, Heidelberg (2002). https://doi.org/10.1007/3-540-45931-6_24
58. Plotkin, G.D., Power, J.: Algebraic operations and generic effects. Appl. Categorical Struct. **11**(1), 69–94 (2003)
59. Plotkin, G.D., Pretnar, M.: Handling algebraic effects. Logical Methods Comput. Sci. **9**(4), 1–36 (2013)
60. Pous, D., Sangiorgi, D.: Enhancements of the bisimulation proof method. In: Sangiorgi, D., Rutten, J. (eds.) Advanced Topics in Bisimulation and Coinduction. Cambridge University Press, New York (2012)
61. Reynolds, J.: Types, abstraction and parametric polymorphism. In: IFIP Congress, pp. 513–523 (1983)
62. Sands, D.: Improvement theory and its applications. In: Gordon, A.D., Pitts, A.M. (eds.) Higher Order Operational Techniques in Semantics, pp. 275–306. Publications of the Newton Institute, Cambridge University Press (1998)
63. Sangiorgi, D., Kobayashi, N., Sumii, E.: Environmental bisimulations for higher-order languages. ACM Trans. Program. Lang. Syst. **33**(1), 5:1–5:69 (2011)
64. Sangiorgi, D.: A theory of bisimulation for the ϕ-calculus. In: Best, E. (ed.) CONCUR 1993. LNCS, vol. 715, pp. 127–142. Springer, Heidelberg (1993). https://doi.org/10.1007/3-540-57208-2_10
65. Sangiorgi, D.: The lazy lambda calculus in a concurrency scenario. Inf. Comput. **111**(1), 120–153 (1994)
66. Sangiorgi, D., Vignudelli, V.: Environmental bisimulations for probabilistic higher-order languages. In: Proceedings of POPL 2016, pp. 595–607 (2016)
67. Simpson, A., Voorneveld, N.: Behavioural equivalence via modalities for algebraic effects. In: Ahmed, A. (ed.) ESOP 2018. LNCS, vol. 10801, pp. 300–326. Springer, Cham (2018). https://doi.org/10.1007/978-3-319-89884-1_11
68. Støvring, K., Lassen, S.B.: A complete, co-inductive syntactic theory of sequential control and state. In: Proceedings of POPL 2007, pp. 161–172 (2007)
69. Strassen, V.: The existence of probability measures with given marginals. Ann. Math. Statist. **36**(2), 423–439 (1965)
70. Tarski, A.: A lattice-theoretical fixpoint theorem and its applications. Pacific J. Math. **5**(2), 285–309 (1955)
71. Thijs, A.: Simulation and fixpoint semantics. Rijksuniversiteit Groningen (1996)
72. Villani, C.: Optimal Transport: Old and New. Grundlehren der mathematischen Wissenschaften. Springer, Heidelberg (2008). https://doi.org/10.1007/978-3-540-71050-9
73. Wadler, P.: Monads for functional programming. In: Program Design Calculi, Proceedings of the NATO Advanced Study Institute on Program Design Calculi, Marktoberdorf, Germany, 28 July – 9 August 1992, pp. 233–264 (1992)

6

A Static Higher-Order Dependency Pair Framework

Carsten Fuhs[1(✉)] and Cynthia Kop[2(✉)]

[1] Department of Computer Science and Information Systems, Birkbeck, University of London, London, UK
carsten@dcs.bbk.ac.uk
[2] Department of Software Science, Radboud University Nijmegen, Nijmegen, The Netherlands
c.kop@cs.ru.nl

Abstract. We revisit the static dependency pair method for proving termination of higher-order term rewriting and extend it in a number of ways: (1) We introduce a new rewrite formalism designed for general applicability in termination proving of higher-order rewriting, Algebraic Functional Systems with Meta-variables. (2) We provide a syntactically checkable soundness criterion to make the method applicable to a large class of rewrite systems. (3) We propose a modular dependency pair *framework* for this higher-order setting. (4) We introduce a fine-grained notion of *formative* and *computable* chains to render the framework more powerful. (5) We formulate several existing and new termination proving techniques in the form of processors within our framework.

The framework has been implemented in the (fully automatic) higher-order termination tool WANDA.

1 Introduction

Term rewriting [3,48] is an important area of logic, with applications in many different areas of computer science [4,11,18,23,25,36,41]. *Higher-order* term rewriting – which extends the traditional *first-order* term rewriting with higher-order types and binders as in the λ-calculus – offers a formal foundation of functional programming and a tool for equational reasoning in higher-order logic. A key question in the analysis of both first- and higher-order term rewriting is *termination*; both for its own sake, and as part of confluence and equivalence analysis.

In first-order term rewriting, a hugely effective method for proving termination (both manually and automatically) is the *dependency pair (DP) approach* [2]. This approach has been extended to the *DP framework* [20,22], a highly modular methodology which new techniques for proving termination *and non-termination* can easily be plugged into in the form of *processors*.

In higher-order rewriting, two DP approaches with distinct costs and benefits are used: *dynamic* [31,45] and *static* [6,32–34,44,46] DPs. Dynamic DPs are more broadly applicable, yet static DPs often enable more powerful analysis techniques. Still, neither approach has the modularity and extendability of the DP framework, nor can they be used to prove non-termination. Also, these approaches consider different styles of higher-order rewriting, which means that for all results certain language features are not available.

In this paper, we address these issues for the *static* DP approach by extending it to a full higher-order *dependency pair framework* for both termination and non-termination analysis. For broad applicability, we introduce a new rewriting formalism, *AFSMs*, to capture several flavours of higher-order rewriting, including *AFSs* [26] (used in the annual Termination Competition [50]) and *pattern HRSs* [37,39] (used in the annual Confluence Competition [10]). To show the versatility and power of this methodology, we define various processors in the framework – both adaptations of existing processors from the literature and entirely new ones.

Detailed Contributions. We reformulate the results of [6,32,34,44,46] into a DP framework for AFSMs. In doing so, we instantiate the applicability restriction of [32] by a very liberal syntactic condition, and add two new flags to track properties of DP problems: one completely new, one from an earlier work by the authors for the *first-order* DP framework [16]. We give eight *processors* for reasoning in our framework: four translations of techniques from static DP approaches, three techniques from first-order or dynamic DPs, and one completely new.

This is a *foundational* paper, focused on defining a general theoretical framework for higher-order termination analysis using dependency pairs rather than questions of implementation. We have, however, implemented most of these results in the fully automatic termination analysis tool WANDA [28].

Related Work. There is a vast body of work in the first-order setting regarding the DP approach [2] and framework [20,22,24]. We have drawn from the ideas in these works for the core structure of the higher-order framework, but have added some new features of our own and adapted results to the higher-order setting.

There is no true higher-order DP *framework* yet: both static and dynamic approaches actually lie halfway between the original "DP approach" of first-order rewriting and a full DP framework as in [20,22]. Most of these works [30–32,34,46] prove "non-loopingness" or "chain-freeness" of a set $\mathcal{P}$ of DPs through a number of theorems. Yet, there is no concept of *DP problems*, and the set $\mathcal{R}$ of rules cannot be altered. They also fix assumptions on dependency chains – such as minimality [34] or being "tagged" [31] – which frustrate extendability and are more naturally dealt with in a DP framework using flags.

The static DP approach for higher-order term rewriting is discussed in, e.g., [34,44,46]. The approach is limited to *plain function passing (PFP)* systems. The definition of PFP has been made more liberal in later papers, but always concerns the position of higher-order variables in the left-hand sides of rules. These works include non-pattern HRSs [34,46], which we do not consider, but do not employ formative rules or meta-variable conditions, or consider non-termination, which we do. Importantly, they do not consider strictly positive inductive types, which could be used to significantly broaden the PFP restriction. Such types *are* considered in an early paper which defines a variation of static higher-order dependency pairs [6] based on a computability closure [7,8]. However, this work carries different restrictions (e.g., DPs must be type-preserving and not introduce fresh variables) and considers only one analysis technique (reduction pairs).

Definitions of DP approaches for *functional programming* also exist [32,33], which consider applicative systems with ML-style polymorphism. These works also employ a much broader, semantic definition than PFP, which is actually more general than the syntactic restriction we propose here. However, like the static approaches for term rewriting, they do not truly exploit the computability [47] properties inherent in this restriction: it is only used for the initial generation of dependency pairs. In the present work, we will take advantage of our exact computability notion by introducing a `computable` flag that can be used by the computable subterm criterion processor (Theorem 63) to handle benchmark systems that would otherwise be beyond the reach of static DPs. Also in these works, formative rules, meta-variable conditions and non-termination are not considered.

Regarding *dynamic* DP approaches, a precursor of the present work is [31], which provides a halfway framework (methodology to prove "chain-freeness") for dynamic DPs, introduces a notion of formative rules, and briefly translates a basic form of static DPs to the same setting. Our formative *reductions* consider the shape of reductions rather than the rules they use, and they can be used as a flag in the framework to gain additional power in other processors. The adaptation of static DPs in [31] was very limited, and did not for instance consider strictly positive inductive types or rules of functional type.

For a more elaborate discussion of both static and dynamic DP approaches in the literature, we refer to [31] and the second author's PhD thesis [29].

Organisation of the Paper. Section 2 introduces higher-order rewriting using AFSMs and recapitulates computability. In Sect. 3 we impose restrictions on the input AFSMs for which our framework is soundly applicable. In Sect. 4 we define static DPs for AFSMs, and derive the key results on them. Section 5 formulates the DP framework and a number of DP processors for existing and new termination proving techniques. Section 6 concludes. Detailed proofs for all results in this paper and an experimental evaluation are available in a technical report [17]. In addition, many of the results have been informally published in the second author's PhD thesis [29].

2 Preliminaries

In this section, we first define our notation by introducing the AFSM formalism. Although not one of the standards of higher-order rewriting, AFSMs combine features from various forms of higher-order rewriting and can be seen as a form of IDTSs [5] which includes application. We will finish with a definition of *computability*, a technique often used for higher-order termination methods.

2.1 Higher-Order Term Rewriting Using AFSMs

Unlike first-order term rewriting, there is no single, unified approach to higher-order term rewriting, but rather a number of similar but not fully compatible systems aiming to combine term rewriting and typed λ-calculi. For generality, we will use *Algebraic Functional Systems with Meta-variables*: a formalism which admits translations from the main formats of higher-order term rewriting.

Definition 1 (Simple types). *We fix a set $\mathcal{S}$ of* sorts*. All sorts are simple types, and if σ, τ are simple types, then so is $\sigma \to \tau$.*

We let $\to$ be right-associative. Note that all types have a unique representation in the form $\sigma_1 \to \ldots \to \sigma_m \to \iota$ with $\iota \in \mathcal{S}$.

Definition 2 (Terms and meta-terms). *We fix disjoint sets $\mathcal{F}$ of* function symbols*, $\mathcal{V}$ of* variables *and $\mathcal{M}$ of* meta-variables*, each symbol equipped with a type. Each meta-variable is additionally equipped with a natural number. We assume that both $\mathcal{V}$ and $\mathcal{M}$ contain infinitely many symbols of all types. The set $\mathcal{T}(\mathcal{F}, \mathcal{V})$ of* terms *over $\mathcal{F}, \mathcal{V}$ consists of expressions s where $s : \sigma$ can be derived for some type σ by the following clauses:*

(V) $x : \sigma$ if $x : \sigma \in \mathcal{V}$ (@) $s\ t : \tau$ if $s : \sigma \to \tau$ and $t : \sigma$
(F) $\mathtt{f} : \sigma$ if $\mathtt{f} : \sigma \in \mathcal{F}$ (Λ) $\lambda x.s : \sigma \to \tau$ if $x : \sigma \in \mathcal{V}$ and $s : \tau$

Meta-terms *are expressions whose type can be derived by those clauses and:*

(M) $Z\langle s_1, \ldots, s_k\rangle : \sigma_{k+1} \to \ldots \to \sigma_m \to \iota$
if $Z : (\sigma_1 \to \ldots \to \sigma_k \to \ldots \to \sigma_m \to \iota,\ k) \in \mathcal{M}$ and $s_1 : \sigma_1, \ldots, s_k : \sigma_k$

The λ binds variables as in the λ-calculus; unbound variables are called free*, and $FV(s)$ is the set of free variables in s. Meta-variables cannot be bound; we write $FMV(s)$ for the set of meta-variables occurring in s. A meta-term s is called* closed *if $FV(s) = \emptyset$ (even if $FMV(s) \neq \emptyset$). Meta-terms are considered modulo α-conversion. Application (@) is left-associative; abstractions (Λ) extend as far to the right as possible. A meta-term s* has type *σ if $s : \sigma$; it* has base type *if $\sigma \in \mathcal{S}$. We define $\mathsf{head}(s) = \mathsf{head}(s_1)$ if $s = s_1\ s_2$, and $\mathsf{head}(s) = s$ otherwise.*

A (meta-)term s has a sub-(meta-)term *t, notation $s \trianglerighteq t$, if either $s = t$ or $s \triangleright t$, where $s \triangleright t$ if (a) $s = \lambda x.s'$ and $s' \trianglerighteq t$, (b) $s = s_1\ s_2$ and $s_2 \trianglerighteq t$ or (c) $s = s_1\ s_2$ and $s_1 \trianglerighteq t$. A (meta-)term s has a* fully applied sub-(meta-)term *t, notation $s \blacktriangleright\!\!\!\!\underline{\ \ } t$, if either $s = t$ or $s \blacktriangleright t$, where $s \blacktriangleright t$ if (a) $s = \lambda x.s'$ and $s' \blacktriangleright\!\!\!\!\underline{\ \ } t$, (b) $s = s_1\ s_2$ and $s_2 \blacktriangleright\!\!\!\!\underline{\ \ } t$ or (c) $s = s_1\ s_2$ and $s_1 \blacktriangleright t$ (so if $s = x\ s_1\ s_2$, then x and $x\ s_1$ are not fully applied subterms, but s and both s_1 and s_2 are).*

For $Z : (\sigma, k) \in \mathcal{M}$, we call k the arity *of Z, notation $arity(Z)$.*

Clearly, all fully applied subterms are subterms, but not all subterms are fully applied. Every term s has a form $t\ s_1 \cdots s_n$ with $n \geq 0$ and $t = \mathsf{head}(s)$ a variable, function symbol, or abstraction; in meta-terms t may also be a meta-variable application $F\langle s_1, \ldots, s_k\rangle$. *Terms* are the objects that we will rewrite; *meta-terms* are used to define rewrite rules. Note that all our terms (and meta-terms) are, by definition, well-typed. For rewriting, we will employ *patterns*:

Definition 3 (Patterns). *A meta-term is a* pattern *if it has one of the forms* $Z\langle x_1, \ldots, x_k\rangle$ *with all* x_i *distinct variables;* $\lambda x.\ell$ *with* $x \in \mathcal{V}$ *and* ℓ *a pattern; or* $a\ \ell_1 \cdots \ell_n$ *with* $a \in \mathcal{F} \cup \mathcal{V}$ *and all* ℓ_i *patterns* $(n \geq 0)$.

In rewrite rules, we will use meta-variables for *matching* and variables only with *binders*. In terms, variables can occur both free and bound, and meta-variables cannot occur. Meta-variables originate in very early forms of higher-order rewriting (e.g., [1,27]), but have also been used in later formalisms (e.g., [8]). They strike a balance between matching modulo β and syntactic matching. By using meta-variables, we obtain the same expressive power as with Miller patterns [37], but do so without including a reversed β-reduction as part of matching.

Notational Conventions: We will use x, y, z for variables, X, Y, Z for meta-variables, b for symbols that could be variables or meta-variables, $\mathtt{f}, \mathtt{g}, \mathtt{h}$ or more suggestive notation for function symbols, and s, t, u, v, q, w for (meta-)terms. Types are denoted σ, τ, and ι, κ are sorts. We will regularly overload notation and write $x \in \mathcal{V}$, $\mathtt{f} \in \mathcal{F}$ or $Z \in \mathcal{M}$ without stating a type (or minimal arity). For meta-terms $Z\langle\rangle$ we will usually omit the brackets, writing just Z.

Definition 4 (Substitution). *A* meta-substitution *is a type-preserving function* γ *from variables and meta-variables to meta-terms. Let the* domain *of* γ *be given by:* $\mathtt{dom}(\gamma) = \{(x : \sigma) \in \mathcal{V} \mid \gamma(x) \neq x\} \cup \{(Z : (\sigma, k)) \in \mathcal{M} \mid \gamma(Z) \neq \lambda y_1 \ldots y_k.Z\langle y_1, \ldots, y_k\rangle\}$*; this domain is allowed to be infinite. We let* $[b_1 := s_1, \ldots, b_n := s_n]$ *denote the meta-substitution* γ *with* $\gamma(b_i) = s_i$ *and* $\gamma(z) = z$ *for* $(z : \sigma) \in \mathcal{V} \setminus \{b_1, \ldots, b_n\}$*, and* $\gamma(Z) = \lambda y_1 \ldots y_k.Z\langle y_1, \ldots, y_k\rangle$ *for* $(Z : (\sigma, k)) \in \mathcal{M} \setminus \{b_1, \ldots, b_n\}$*. We assume there are infinitely many variables* x *of all types such that (a)* $x \notin \mathtt{dom}(\gamma)$ *and (b) for all* $b \in \mathtt{dom}(\gamma)$*:* $x \notin FV(\gamma(b))$.

A substitution *is a meta-substitution mapping everything in its domain to terms. The result* $s\gamma$ *of applying a meta-substitution* γ *to a term* s *is obtained by:*

$$\begin{array}{llll} x\gamma = \gamma(x) & \text{if } x \in \mathcal{V} & (s\ t)\gamma = (s\gamma)\ (t\gamma) & \\ \mathtt{f}\gamma = \mathtt{f} & \text{if } \mathtt{f} \in \mathcal{F} & (\lambda x.s)\gamma = \lambda x.(s\gamma) & \text{if } \gamma(x) = x \wedge x \notin \bigcup_{y \in \mathtt{dom}(\gamma)} FV(\gamma(y)) \end{array}$$

For meta-terms, the result $s\gamma$ *is obtained by the clauses above and:*

$$\begin{array}{rcll} Z\langle s_1, \ldots, s_k\rangle\gamma &=& \gamma(Z)\langle s_1\gamma, \ldots, s_k\gamma\rangle & \text{if } Z \notin \mathtt{dom}(\gamma) \\ Z\langle s_1, \ldots, s_k\rangle\gamma &=& \gamma(Z)\langle\langle s_1\gamma, \ldots, s_k\gamma\rangle\rangle & \text{if } Z \in \mathtt{dom}(\gamma) \\ (\lambda x_1 \ldots x_k.s)\langle\langle t_1, \ldots, t_k\rangle\rangle &=& s[x_1 := t_1, \ldots, x_k := t_k] & \\ (\lambda x_1 \ldots x_n.s)\langle\langle t_1, \ldots, t_k\rangle\rangle &=& s[x_1 := t_1, \ldots, x_n := t_n]\ t_{n+1} \cdots t_k & \text{if } n < k \\ && & \text{and } s \text{ is not an abstraction} \end{array}$$

Note that for fixed k, any term has exactly one of the two forms above ($\lambda x_1 \ldots x_n.s$ with $n < k$ and s not an abstraction, or $\lambda x_1 \ldots x_k.s$).

Essentially, applying a meta-substitution that has meta-variables in its domain combines a substitution with (possibly several) β-steps. For example, we have that: $\mathtt{deriv}\ (\lambda x.\mathtt{sin}\ (F\langle x\rangle))[F := \lambda y.\mathtt{plus}\ y\ x]$ equals $\mathtt{deriv}\ (\lambda z.\mathtt{sin}\ (\mathtt{plus}\ z\ x))$. We also have: $X\langle \mathtt{0}, \mathtt{nil}\rangle[X := \lambda x.\mathtt{map}\ (\lambda y.x)]$ equals $\mathtt{map}\ (\lambda y.\mathtt{0})\ \mathtt{nil}$.

Definition 5 (Rules and rewriting). *Let $\mathcal{F}, \mathcal{V}, \mathcal{M}$ be fixed sets of function symbols, variables and meta-variables respectively. A* rule *is a pair $\ell \Rightarrow r$ of closed meta-terms of the same type such that ℓ is a pattern of the form $\mathtt{f}\ \ell_1 \cdots \ell_n$ with $\mathtt{f} \in \mathcal{F}$ and $FMV(r) \subseteq FMV(\ell)$. A set of rules $\mathcal{R}$ defines a rewrite relation $\Rightarrow_{\mathcal{R}}$ as the smallest monotonic relation on terms which includes:*

(Rule) $\ell\delta \quad \Rightarrow_{\mathcal{R}} \quad r\delta \quad$ *if $\ell \Rightarrow r \in \mathcal{R}$ and $\mathtt{dom}(\delta) = FMV(\ell)$*

(Beta) $(\lambda x.s)\ t \quad \Rightarrow_{\mathcal{R}} \quad s[x := t]$

We say $s \Rightarrow_\beta t$ if $s \Rightarrow_{\mathcal{R}} t$ is derived using a (Beta) step. A term s is terminating *under $\Rightarrow_{\mathcal{R}}$ if there is no infinite reduction $s = s_0 \Rightarrow_{\mathcal{R}} s_1 \Rightarrow_{\mathcal{R}} \dots$, is* in normal form *if there is no t such that $s \Rightarrow_{\mathcal{R}} t$, and is* β-normal *if there is no t with $s \Rightarrow_\beta t$. Note that we are allowed to reduce at any position of a term, even below a λ. The relation $\Rightarrow_{\mathcal{R}}$ is terminating if all terms over $\mathcal{F}, \mathcal{V}$ are terminating. The set $\mathcal{D} \subseteq \mathcal{F}$ of* defined symbols *consists of those $(\mathtt{f} : \sigma) \in \mathcal{F}$ such that a rule $\mathtt{f}\ \ell_1 \cdots \ell_n \Rightarrow r$ exists; all other symbols are called* constructors.

Note that $\mathcal{R}$ is allowed to be infinite, which is useful for instance to model polymorphic systems. Also, right-hand sides of rules do not have to be in β-normal form. While this is rarely used in practical examples, non-β-normal rules may arise through transformations, and we lose nothing by allowing them.

Example 6. Let $\mathcal{F} \supseteq \{\mathtt{0} : \mathtt{nat},\ \mathtt{s} : \mathtt{nat} \to \mathtt{nat},\ \mathtt{nil} : \mathtt{list}, \mathtt{cons} : \mathtt{nat} \to \mathtt{list} \to \mathtt{list},\ \mathtt{map} : (\mathtt{nat} \to \mathtt{nat}) \to \mathtt{list} \to \mathtt{list}\}$ and consider the following rules $\mathcal{R}$:

$$\mathtt{map}\ (\lambda x.Z\langle x\rangle)\ \mathtt{nil} \Rightarrow \mathtt{nil}$$
$$\mathtt{map}\ (\lambda x.Z\langle x\rangle)\ (\mathtt{cons}\ H\ T) \Rightarrow \mathtt{cons}\ Z\langle H\rangle\ (\mathtt{map}\ (\lambda x.Z\langle x\rangle)\ T)$$

Then $\mathtt{map}\ (\lambda y.\mathtt{0})\ (\mathtt{cons}\ (\mathtt{s}\ \mathtt{0})\ \mathtt{nil}) \Rightarrow_{\mathcal{R}} \mathtt{cons}\ \mathtt{0}\ (\mathtt{map}\ (\lambda y.\mathtt{0})\ \mathtt{nil}) \Rightarrow_{\mathcal{R}} \mathtt{cons}\ \mathtt{0}\ \mathtt{nil}$. Note that the bound variable y does not need to occur in the body of $\lambda y.\mathtt{0}$ to match $\lambda x.Z\langle x\rangle$. However, a term like $\mathtt{map}\ \mathtt{s}\ (\mathtt{cons}\ \mathtt{0}\ \mathtt{nil})$ *cannot* be reduced, because $\mathtt{s}$ does not instantiate $\lambda x.Z\langle x\rangle$. We could alternatively consider the rules:

$$\mathtt{map}\ Z\ \mathtt{nil} \Rightarrow \mathtt{nil}$$
$$\mathtt{map}\ Z\ (\mathtt{cons}\ H\ T) \Rightarrow \mathtt{cons}\ (Z\ H)\ (\mathtt{map}\ Z\ T)$$

Where the system before had $(Z : (\mathtt{nat} \to \mathtt{nat}, 1)) \in \mathcal{M}$, here we assume $(Z : (\mathtt{nat} \to \mathtt{nat}, 0)) \in \mathcal{M}$. Thus, rather than meta-variable application $Z\langle H\rangle$ we use explicit application $Z\ H$. Then $\mathtt{map}\ \mathtt{s}\ (\mathtt{cons}\ \mathtt{0}\ \mathtt{nil}) \Rightarrow_{\mathcal{R}} \mathtt{cons}\ (\mathtt{s}\ \mathtt{0})\ (\mathtt{map}\ \mathtt{s}\ \mathtt{nil})$. However, we will often need explicit β-reductions; e.g., $\mathtt{map}\ (\lambda y.\mathtt{0})\ (\mathtt{cons}\ (\mathtt{s}\ \mathtt{0})\ \mathtt{nil}) \Rightarrow_{\mathcal{R}} \mathtt{cons}\ ((\lambda y.\mathtt{0})\ (\mathtt{s}\ \mathtt{0}))\ (\mathtt{map}\ (\lambda y.\mathtt{0})\ \mathtt{nil}) \Rightarrow_\beta \mathtt{cons}\ \mathtt{0}\ (\mathtt{map}\ (\lambda y.\mathtt{0})\ \mathtt{nil})$.

Definition 7 (AFSM). *An* AFSM *is a tuple $(\mathcal{F}, \mathcal{V}, \mathcal{M}, \mathcal{R})$ of a signature and a set of rules built from meta-terms over $\mathcal{F}, \mathcal{V}, \mathcal{M}$; as types of relevant variables and meta-variables can always be derived from context, we will typically just refer to the AFSM $(\mathcal{F}, \mathcal{R})$. An AFSM implicitly defines the abstract reduction system $(\mathcal{T}(\mathcal{F}, \mathcal{V}), \Rightarrow_{\mathcal{R}})$: a set of terms and a rewrite relation on this set. An AFSM is terminating if $\Rightarrow_{\mathcal{R}}$ is terminating (on all terms in $\mathcal{T}(\mathcal{F}, \mathcal{V})$).*

Discussion: The two most common formalisms in termination analysis of higher-order rewriting are *algebraic functional systems* [26] (AFSs) and *higher-order rewriting systems* [37,39] (HRSs). AFSs are very similar to our AFSMs, but use variables for matching rather than meta-variables; this is trivially translated to the AFSM format, giving rules where all meta-variables have arity 0, like the "alternative" rules in Example 6. HRSs use matching modulo β/η, but the common restriction of *pattern HRSs* can be directly translated into AFSMs, provided terms are β-normalised after every reduction step. Even without this β-normalisation step, termination of the obtained AFSM implies termination of the original HRS; for second-order systems, termination is equivalent. AFSMs can also naturally encode CRSs [27] and several applicative systems (cf. [29, Chapter 3]).

Example 8 (Ordinal recursion). A running example is the AFSM $(\mathcal{F}, \mathcal{R})$ with $\mathcal{F} \supseteq \{\mathtt{0} : \mathtt{ord},\ \mathtt{s} : \mathtt{ord} \to \mathtt{ord}, \mathtt{lim} : (\mathtt{nat} \to \mathtt{ord}) \to \mathtt{ord},\ \mathtt{rec} : \mathtt{ord} \to \mathtt{nat} \to (\mathtt{ord} \to \mathtt{nat} \to \mathtt{nat}) \to ((\mathtt{nat} \to \mathtt{ord}) \to (\mathtt{nat} \to \mathtt{nat}) \to \mathtt{nat}) \to \mathtt{nat}\}$ and $\mathcal{R}$ given below. As all meta-variables have arity 0, this can be seen as an AFS.

$$\begin{aligned} \mathtt{rec}\ \mathtt{0}\ K\ F\ G &\Rightarrow K \\ \mathtt{rec}\ (\mathtt{s}\ X)\ K\ F\ G &\Rightarrow F\ X\ (\mathtt{rec}\ X\ K\ F\ G) \\ \mathtt{rec}\ (\mathtt{lim}\ H)\ K\ F\ G &\Rightarrow G\ H\ (\lambda m.\mathtt{rec}\ (H\ m)\ K\ F\ G) \end{aligned}$$

Observant readers may notice that by the given constructors, the type nat in Example 8 is not inhabited. However, as the given symbols are only a subset of $\mathcal{F}$, additional symbols (such as constructors for the nat type) may be included. The presence of additional function symbols does not affect termination of AFSMs:

Theorem 9 (Invariance of termination under signature extensions). *For an AFSM $(\mathcal{F}, \mathcal{R})$ with $\mathcal{F}$ at most countably infinite, let $\mathtt{funs}(\mathcal{R}) \subseteq \mathcal{F}$ be the set of function symbols occurring in some rule of $\mathcal{R}$. Then $(\mathcal{T}(\mathcal{F}, \mathcal{V}), \Rightarrow_{\mathcal{R}})$ is terminating if and only if $(\mathcal{T}(\mathtt{funs}(\mathcal{R}), \mathcal{V}), \Rightarrow_{\mathcal{R}})$ is terminating.*

Proof. Trivial by replacing all function symbols in $\mathcal{F} \setminus \mathtt{funs}(\mathcal{R})$ by corresponding variables of the same type. □

Therefore, we will typically only state the types of symbols occurring in the rules, but may safely assume that infinitely many symbols of all types are present (which for instance allows us to select unused constructors in some proofs).

2.2 Computability

A common technique in higher-order termination is Tait and Girard's *computability* notion [47]. There are several ways to define computability predicates; here we follow, e.g., [5,7–9] in considering *accessible meta-terms* using strictly positive inductive types. The definition presented below is adapted from these works, both to account for the altered formalism and to introduce (and obtain termination of) a relation $\Rrightarrow_C$ that we will use in the "computable subterm criterion processor" of Theorem 63 (a termination criterion that allows us to handle systems that would otherwise be beyond the reach of static DPs). This allows for a minimal presentation that avoids the use of ordinals that would otherwise be needed to obtain $\Rrightarrow_C$ (see, e.g., [7,9]).

To define computability, we use the notion of an *RC-set*:

Definition 10. *A* set of reducibility candidates, *or* RC-set, *for a rewrite relation $\Rightarrow_{\mathcal{R}}$ of an AFSM is a set I of base-type terms s such that: every term in I is terminating under $\Rightarrow_{\mathcal{R}}$; I is closed under $\Rightarrow_{\mathcal{R}}$ (so if $s \in I$ and $s \Rightarrow_{\mathcal{R}} t$ then $t \in I$); if $s = x\ s_1 \cdots s_n$ with $x \in \mathcal{V}$ or $s = (\lambda x.u)\ s_0 \cdots s_n$ with $n \geq 0$, and for all t with $s \Rightarrow_{\mathcal{R}} t$ we have $t \in I$, then $s \in I$ (for any $u, s_0, \dots, s_n \in \mathcal{T}(\mathcal{F}, \mathcal{V})$).*

We define I-computability for an RC-set I by induction on types. For $s \in \mathcal{T}(\mathcal{F}, \mathcal{V})$, we say that s is I-computable if either s is of base type and $s \in I$; or $s : \sigma \to \tau$ and for all $t : \sigma$ that are I-computable, $s\ t$ is I-computable.

The traditional notion of computability is obtained by taking for I the set of all terminating base-type terms. Then, a term s is computable if and only if (a) s has base type and is terminating; or (b) $s : \sigma \to \tau$ and for all computable $t : \sigma$ the term $s\ t$ is computable. This choice is simple but, for reasoning, not ideal: we do not have a property like: "if $\mathtt{f}\ s_1 \cdots s_n$ is computable then so is each s_i". Such a property would be valuable to have for generalising termination proofs from first-order to higher-order rewriting, as it allows us to use computability where the first-order proof uses termination. While it is not possible to define a computability notion with this property alongside case (b) (as such a notion would not be well-founded), we can come *close* to this property by choosing a different set for I. To define this set, we will use the notion of *accessible arguments*, which is used for the same purpose also in the *General Schema* [8], the *Computability Path Ordering* [9], and the *Computability Closure* [7].

Definition 11 (Accessible arguments). *We fix a quasi-ordering $\succeq^{\mathcal{S}}$ on $\mathcal{S}$ with well-founded strict part $\succ^{\mathcal{S}} := \succeq^{\mathcal{S}} \setminus \preceq^{\mathcal{S}}$.[1] For a type $\sigma \equiv \sigma_1 \to \ldots \to \sigma_m \to \kappa$ (with $\kappa \in \mathcal{S}$) and sort ι, let $\iota \succeq^{\mathcal{S}}_{+} \sigma$ if $\iota \succeq^{\mathcal{S}} \kappa$ and $\iota \succ^{\mathcal{S}}_{-} \sigma_i$ for all i, and let $\iota \succ^{\mathcal{S}}_{-} \sigma$ if $\iota \succ^{\mathcal{S}} \kappa$ and $\iota \succeq^{\mathcal{S}}_{+} \sigma_i$ for all i.[2]*

For $\mathtt{f} : \sigma_1 \to \ldots \to \sigma_m \to \iota \in \mathcal{F}$, let $Acc(\mathtt{f}) = \{i \mid 1 \leq i \leq m \wedge \iota \succeq^{\mathcal{S}}_{+} \sigma_i\}$. For $x : \sigma_1 \to \ldots \to \sigma_m \to \iota \in \mathcal{V}$, let $Acc(x) = \{i \mid 1 \leq i \leq m \wedge \sigma_i$ has the form $\tau_1 \to \ldots \to \tau_n \to \kappa$ with $\iota \succeq^{\mathcal{S}} \kappa\}$. We write $s \trianglerighteq_{\mathsf{acc}} t$ if either $s = t$, or $s = \lambda x.s'$ and $s' \trianglerighteq_{\mathsf{acc}} t$, or $s = a\ s_1 \cdots s_n$ with $a \in \mathcal{F} \cup \mathcal{V}$ and $s_i \trianglerighteq_{\mathsf{acc}} t$ for some $i \in Acc(a)$ with $a \notin FV(s_i)$.

With this definition, we will be able to define a set C such that, roughly, s is C-computable if and only if (a) $s : \sigma \to \tau$ and $s\ t$ is C-computable for all C-computable t, or (b) s has base type, is terminating, and if $s = \mathtt{f}\ s_1 \cdots s_m$ then s_i is C-computable for all *accessible* i (see Theorem 13 below). The reason that $Acc(x)$ for $x \in \mathcal{V}$ is different is proof-technical: computability of $\lambda x.x\ s_1 \cdots s_m$

[1] Well-foundedness is immediate if $\mathcal{S}$ is finite, but we have not imposed that requirement.

[2] Here $\iota \succeq^{\mathcal{S}}_{+} \sigma$ corresponds to "ι occurs only positively in σ" in [5,8,9].

implies the computability of more arguments s_i than computability of $\mathtt{f}\ s_1 \cdots s_m$ does, since x can be instantiated by anything.

Example 12. Consider a quasi-ordering $\succeq^{\mathcal{S}}$ such that $\mathtt{ord} \succ^{\mathcal{S}} \mathtt{nat}$. In Example 8, we then have $\mathtt{ord} \succeq^{\mathcal{S}}_{+} \mathtt{nat} \to \mathtt{ord}$. Thus, $1 \in Acc(\mathtt{lim})$, which gives $\mathtt{lim}\ H \trianglerighteq_{\mathsf{acc}} H$.

Theorem 13. *Let $(\mathcal{F},\mathcal{R})$ be an AFSM. Let $\mathtt{f}\ s_1 \cdots s_m \Rrightarrow_I s_i\ t_1 \cdots t_n$ if both sides have base type, $i \in Acc(\mathtt{f})$, and all t_j are I-computable. There is an RC-set C such that $C = \{s \in \mathcal{T}(\mathcal{F},\mathcal{V}) \mid s$ has base type $\wedge$ s is terminating under $\Rightarrow_{\mathcal{R}} \cup \Rrightarrow_C \wedge$ if $s \Rightarrow^*_{\mathcal{R}} \mathtt{f}\ s_1 \cdots s_m$ then s_i is C-computable for all $i \in Acc(\mathtt{f})\}$.*

Proof (sketch). Note that we cannot *define* C as this set, as the set relies on the notion of C-computability. However, we *can* define C as the fixpoint of a monotone function operating on RC-sets. This follows the proof in, e.g., [8,9]. □

The complete proof is available in [17, Appendix A].

3 Restrictions

The termination methodology in this paper is restricted to AFSMs that satisfy certain limitations: they must be *properly applied* (a restriction on the number of terms each function symbol is applied to) and *accessible function passing* (a restriction on the positions of variables of a functional type in the left-hand sides of rules). Both are syntactic restrictions that are easily checked by a computer (mostly; the latter requires a search for a sort ordering, but this is typically easy).

3.1 Properly Applied AFSMs

In *properly applied AFSMs*, function symbols are assigned a certain, minimal number of arguments that they must always be applied to.

Definition 14. *An AFSM $(\mathcal{F},\mathcal{R})$ is* properly applied *if for every $\mathtt{f} \in \mathcal{D}$ there exists an integer k such that for all rules $\ell \Rightarrow r \in \mathcal{R}$: (1) if $\ell = \mathtt{f}\ \ell_1 \cdots \ell_n$ then $n = k$; and (2) if $r \trianglerighteq \mathtt{f}\ r_1 \cdots r_n$ then $n \geq k$. We denote $minar(\mathtt{f}) = k$.*

That is, every occurrence of a function symbol in the *right-hand* side of a rule has at least as many arguments as the occurrences in the *left-hand* sides of rules. This means that partially applied functions are often not allowed: an AFSM with rules such as $\mathtt{double}\ X \Rightarrow \mathtt{plus}\ X\ X$ and $\mathtt{doublelist}\ L \Rightarrow \mathtt{map}\ \mathtt{double}\ L$ is not properly applied, because $\mathtt{double}$ is applied to one argument in the left-hand side of some rule, and to zero in the right-hand side of another.

This restriction is not as severe as it may initially seem since partial applications can be replaced by λ-abstractions; e.g., the rules above can be made properly applied by replacing the second rule by: $\mathtt{doublelist}\ L \Rightarrow \mathtt{map}\ (\lambda x.\mathtt{double}\ x)\ L$. By using η-expansion, we can transform any AFSM to satisfy this restriction:

Definition 15 ($\mathcal{R}^{\uparrow}$). *Given a set of rules $\mathcal{R}$, let their* η-expansion *be given by* $\mathcal{R}^{\uparrow} = \{(\ell\ Z_1 \cdots Z_m)\uparrow^{\eta} \Rightarrow (r\ Z_1 \cdots Z_m)\uparrow^{\eta} \mid \ell \Rightarrow r \in \mathcal{R}$ *with* $r : \sigma_1 \to \ldots \to \sigma_m \to \iota$, $\iota \in \mathcal{S}$, *and* $Z_1, \ldots, Z_m$ *fresh meta-variables*$\}$, *where*

- $s\uparrow^{\eta} = \lambda x_1 \ldots x_m.\overline{s}\ (x_1\uparrow^{\eta}) \cdots (x_m\uparrow^{\eta})$ *if s is an application or element of* $\mathcal{V} \cup \mathcal{F}$, *and* $s\uparrow^{\eta} = \overline{s}$ *otherwise;*
- $\overline{\mathtt{f}} = \mathtt{f}$ *for* $\mathtt{f} \in \mathcal{F}$ *and* $\overline{x} = x$ *for* $x \in \mathcal{V}$, *while* $\overline{Z\langle s_1, \ldots, s_k\rangle} = Z\langle \overline{s_1}, \ldots, \overline{s_k}\rangle$ *and* $\overline{(\lambda x.s)} = \lambda x.(s\uparrow^{\eta})$ *and* $\overline{s_1\ s_2} = \overline{s_1}\ (s_2\uparrow^{\eta})$.

Note that $\ell\uparrow^{\eta}$ is a pattern if ℓ is. By [29, Thm. 2.16], a relation $\Rightarrow_{\mathcal{R}}$ is terminating if $\Rightarrow_{\mathcal{R}^{\uparrow}}$ is terminating, which allows us to transpose any methods to prove termination of properly applied AFSMs to all AFSMs.

However, there is a caveat: this transformation can introduce non-termination in some special cases, e.g., the terminating rule $\mathtt{f}\ X \Rightarrow \mathtt{g}\ \mathtt{f}$ with $\mathtt{f} : \mathsf{o} \to \mathsf{o}$ and $\mathtt{g} : (\mathsf{o} \to \mathsf{o}) \to \mathsf{o}$, whose η-expansion $\mathtt{f}\ X \Rightarrow \mathtt{g}\ (\lambda x.(\mathtt{f}\ x))$ is non-terminating. Thus, for a properly applied AFSM the methods in this paper apply directly. For an AFSM that is not properly applied, we can use the methods to prove *termination* (but not non-termination) by first η-expanding the rules. Of course, if this analysis leads to a *counterexample* for termination, we may still be able to verify whether this counterexample applies in the original, untransformed AFSM.

Example 16. Both AFSMs in Example 6 and the AFSM in Example 8 are properly applied.

Example 17. Consider an AFSM $(\mathcal{F}, \mathcal{R})$ with $\mathcal{F} \supseteq \{\mathtt{sin}, \mathtt{cos} : \mathtt{real} \to \mathtt{real}, \mathtt{times} : \mathtt{real} \to \mathtt{real} \to \mathtt{real}, \mathtt{deriv} : (\mathtt{real} \to \mathtt{real}) \to \mathtt{real} \to \mathtt{real}\}$ and $\mathcal{R} = \{\mathtt{deriv}\ (\lambda x.\mathtt{sin}\ F\langle x\rangle) \Rightarrow \lambda y.\mathtt{times}\ (\mathtt{deriv}\ (\lambda x.F\langle x\rangle)\ y)\ (\mathtt{cos}\ F\langle y\rangle)\}$. Although the one rule has a functional output type ($\mathtt{real} \to \mathtt{real}$), this AFSM is properly applied, with `deriv` having always at least 1 argument. Therefore, we do not need to use $\mathcal{R}^{\uparrow}$. However, if $\mathcal{R}$ were to additionally include some rules that did not satisfy the restriction (such as the `double` and `doublelist` rules above), then η-expanding *all* rules, including this one, would be necessary. We have: $\mathcal{R}^{\uparrow} = \{\mathtt{deriv}\ (\lambda x.\mathtt{sin}\ F\langle x\rangle)\ Y \Rightarrow (\lambda y.\mathtt{times}\ (\mathtt{deriv}\ (\lambda x.F\langle x\rangle)\ y)\ (\mathtt{cos}\ F\langle y\rangle))\ Y\}$. Note that the right-hand side of the η-expanded `deriv` rule is not β-normal.

3.2 Accessible Function Passing AFSMs

In *accessible function passing* AFSMs, variables of functional type may not occur at arbitrary places in the left-hand sides of rules: their positions are restricted using the sort ordering $\succeq^{\mathcal{S}}$ and accessibility relation $\trianglerighteq_{\mathsf{acc}}$ from Definition 11.

Definition 18 (Accessible function passing). *An AFSM $(\mathcal{F}, \mathcal{R})$ is* accessible function passing (AFP) *if there exists a sort ordering $\succeq^{\mathcal{S}}$ following Definition 11 such that: for all* $\mathtt{f}\ \ell_1 \cdots \ell_n \Rightarrow r \in \mathcal{R}$ *and all* $Z \in FMV(r)$: *there are variables* $x_1, \ldots, x_k$ *and some i such that* $\ell_i \trianglerighteq_{\mathsf{acc}} Z\langle x_1, \ldots, x_k\rangle$.

The key idea of this definition is that computability of each ℓ_i implies computability of all meta-variables in r. This excludes cases like Example 20 below. Many common examples satisfy this restriction, including those we saw before:

Example 19. Both systems from Example 6 are AFP: choosing the sort ordering $\succeq^{\mathcal{S}}$ that equates $\mathtt{nat}$ and $\mathtt{list}$, we indeed have $\mathtt{cons}\ H\ T \trianglerighteq_{\mathsf{acc}} H$ and $\mathtt{cons}\ H\ T \trianglerighteq_{\mathsf{acc}} T$ (as $Acc(\mathtt{cons}) = \{1,2\}$) and both $\lambda x.Z\langle x\rangle \trianglerighteq_{\mathsf{acc}} Z\langle x\rangle$ and $Z \trianglerighteq_{\mathsf{acc}} Z$. The AFSM from Example 8 is AFP because we can choose $\mathtt{ord} \succ^{\mathcal{S}} \mathtt{nat}$ and have $\mathtt{lim}\ H \trianglerighteq_{\mathsf{acc}} H$ following Example 12 (and also $\mathtt{s}\ X \trianglerighteq_{\mathsf{acc}} X$ and $K \trianglerighteq_{\mathsf{acc}} K$, $F \trianglerighteq_{\mathsf{acc}} F$, $G \trianglerighteq_{\mathsf{acc}} G$). The AFSM from Example 17 is AFP, because $\lambda x.\mathtt{sin}\ F\langle x\rangle \trianglerighteq_{\mathsf{acc}} F\langle x\rangle$ for any $\succeq^{\mathcal{S}}$: $\lambda x.\mathtt{sin}\ F\langle x\rangle \trianglerighteq_{\mathsf{acc}} F\langle x\rangle$ because $\mathtt{sin}\ F\langle x\rangle \trianglerighteq_{\mathsf{acc}} F\langle x\rangle$ because $1 \in Acc(\mathtt{sin})$.

In fact, *all* first-order AFSMs (where all fully applied sub-meta-terms of the left-hand side of a rule have base type) are AFP via the sort ordering $\succeq^{\mathcal{S}}$ that equates all sorts. Also (with the same sort ordering), an AFSM $(\mathcal{F},\mathcal{R})$ is AFP if, for all rules $\mathtt{f}\ \ell_1 \cdots \ell_k \Rightarrow r \in \mathcal{R}$ and all $1 \leq i \leq k$, we can write: $\ell_i = \lambda x_1 \ldots x_{n_i}.\ell'$ where $n_i \geq 0$ and all fully applied sub-meta-terms of ℓ' have base type.

This covers many practical systems, although for Example 8 we need a non-trivial sort ordering. Also, there are AFSMs that cannot be handled with *any* $\succeq^{\mathcal{S}}$.

Example 20 (Encoding the untyped λ-calculus). Consider an AFSM with $\mathcal{F} \supseteq \{\mathtt{ap} : \mathtt{o} \rightarrow \mathtt{o} \rightarrow \mathtt{o},\ \mathtt{lm} : (\mathtt{o} \rightarrow \mathtt{o}) \rightarrow \mathtt{o}\}$ and $\mathcal{R} = \{\mathtt{ap}\ (\mathtt{lm}\ F) \Rightarrow F\}$ (note that the only rule has type $\mathtt{o} \rightarrow \mathtt{o}$). This AFSM is not accessible function passing, because $\mathtt{lm}\ F \trianglerighteq_{\mathsf{acc}} F$ cannot hold for any $\succeq^{\mathcal{S}}$ (as this would require $\mathtt{o} \succ^{\mathcal{S}} \mathtt{o}$).

Note that this example is also not terminating. With $t = \mathtt{lm}\ (\lambda x.\mathtt{ap}\ x\ x)$, we get this self-loop as evidence: $\mathtt{ap}\ t\ t\ \Rightarrow_{\mathcal{R}} (\lambda x.\mathtt{ap}\ x\ x)\ t \Rightarrow_{\beta} \mathtt{ap}\ t\ t$.

Intuitively: in an accessible function passing AFSM, meta-variables of a higher type may occur only in "safe" places in the left-hand sides of rules. Rules like the ones in Example 20, where a higher-order meta-variable is lifted out of a base-type term, are not admitted (unless the base type is greater than the higher type).

In the remainder of this paper, we will refer to a *properly applied, accessible function passing* AFSM as a PA-AFP AFSM.

Discussion: This definition is strictly more liberal than the notions of "plain function passing" in both [34] and [46] as adapted to AFSMs. The notion in [46] largely corresponds to AFP if $\succeq^{\mathcal{S}}$ equates all sorts, and the HRS formalism guarantees that rules are properly applied (in fact, all fully applied sub-meta-terms of both left- and right-hand sides of rules have base type). The notion in [34] is more restrictive. The current restriction of PA-AFP AFSMs lets us handle examples like ordinal recursion (Example 8) which are not covered by [34,46]. However, note that [34,46] consider a different formalism, which does take rules whose left-hand side is not a pattern into account (which we do not consider). Our restriction also quite resembles the "admissible" rules in [6] which are defined using a pattern computability closure [5], but that work carries additional restrictions.

In later work [32,33], Kusakari extends the static DP approach to forms of polymorphic functional programming, with a very liberal restriction: the definition is parametrised with an *arbitrary* RC-set and corresponding accessibility ("safety") notion. Our AFP restriction is actually an instance of this condition (although a more liberal one than the example RC-set used in [32,33]). We have chosen a specific instance because it allows us to use dedicated techniques for the RC-set; for example, our *computable subterm criterion processor* (Theorem 63).

4 Static Higher-Order Dependency Pairs

To obtain sufficient criteria for both termination and non-termination of AFSMs, we will now transpose the definition of static dependency pairs [6,33,34,46] to AFSMs. In addition, we will add the new features of *meta-variable conditions*, *formative reductions*, and *computable chains*. Complete versions of all proof sketches in this section are available in [17, Appendix B].

Although we retain the first-order terminology of dependency *pairs*, the setting with meta-variables makes it more suitable to define DPs as *triples*.

Definition 21 ((Static) Dependency Pair). *A* dependency pair (DP) *is a triple* $\ell \Rrightarrow p\ (A)$*, where* ℓ *is a closed pattern* $\mathtt{f}\ \ell_1 \cdots \ell_k$*,* p *is a closed meta-term* $\mathtt{g}\ p_1 \cdots p_n$*, and* A *is a set of* meta-variable conditions*: pairs* $Z : i$ *indicating that* Z *regards its* i^{th} *argument. A DP is* conservative *if* $FMV(p) \subseteq FMV(\ell)$.

A substitution γ respects *a set of meta-variable conditions* A *if for all* $Z : i$ *in* A *we have* $\gamma(Z) = \lambda x_1 \ldots x_j.t$ *with either* $i > j$*, or* $i \leq j$ *and* $x_i \in FV(t)$*. DPs will be used only with substitutions that respect their meta-variable conditions.*

For $\ell \Rrightarrow p\ (\emptyset)$ *(so a DP whose set of meta-variable conditions is empty), we often omit the third component and just write* $\ell \Rrightarrow p$.

Like the first-order setting, the static DP approach employs *marked function symbols* to obtain meta-terms whose instances cannot be reduced at the root.

Definition 22 (Marked symbols). *Let* $(\mathcal{F}, \mathcal{R})$ *be an AFSM. Define* $\mathcal{F}^\sharp := \mathcal{F} \uplus \{\mathtt{f}^\sharp : \sigma \mid \mathtt{f} : \sigma \in \mathcal{D}\}$*. For a meta-term* $s = \mathtt{f}\ s_1 \cdots s_k$ *with* $\mathtt{f} \in \mathcal{D}$ *and* $k = minar(\mathtt{f})$*, we let* $s^\sharp = \mathtt{f}^\sharp\ s_1 \cdots s_k$*; for* s *of other forms* $s^\sharp$ *is not defined.*

Moreover, we will consider *candidates*. In the first-order setting, candidate terms are subterms of the right-hand sides of rules whose root symbol is a defined symbol. Intuitively, these subterms correspond to function calls. In the current setting, we have to consider also meta-variables as well as rules whose right-hand side is not β-normal (which might arise for instance due to η-expansion).

Definition 23 (β-reduced-sub-meta-term, $\unrhd_\beta$, $\unrhd_A$). *A meta-term* s *has a fully applied* β-reduced-sub-meta-term t *(shortly,* BRSMT*), notation* $s \unrhd_\beta t$*, if there exists a set of meta-variable conditions* A *with* $s \unrhd_A t$*. Here* $s \unrhd_A t$ *holds if:*

- $s = t$*, or*
- $s = \lambda x.u$ *and* $u \unrhd_A t$*, or*

- $s = (\lambda x.u)\ s_0 \cdots s_n$ *and some* $s_i \trianglerighteq_A t$, *or* $u[x := s_0]\ s_1 \cdots s_n \trianglerighteq_A t$, *or*
- $s = a\ s_1 \cdots s_n$ *with* $a \in \mathcal{F} \cup \mathcal{V}$ *and some* $s_i \trianglerighteq_A t$, *or*
- $s = Z\langle t_1, \ldots, t_k\rangle\ s_1 \cdots s_n$ *and some* $s_i \trianglerighteq_A t$, *or*
- $s = Z\langle t_1, \ldots, t_k\rangle\ s_1 \cdots s_n$ *and* $t_i \trianglerighteq_A t$ *for some* $i \in \{1, \ldots, k\}$ *with* $(Z : i) \in A$.

Essentially, $s \trianglerighteq_A t$ means that t can be reached from s by taking β-reductions at the root and "subterm"-steps, where $Z : i$ is in A whenever we pass into argument i of a meta-variable Z. BRSMTs are used to generate *candidates*:

Definition 24 (Candidates). *For a meta-term s, the set* $\mathsf{cand}(s)$ *of* candidates of s *consists of those pairs t (A) such that (a) t has the form* $\mathtt{f}\ s_1 \cdots s_k$ *with* $\mathtt{f} \in \mathcal{D}$ *and* $k = minar(\mathtt{f})$, *and (b) there are* $s_{k+1}, \ldots, s_n$ *(with* $n \geq k$*) such that* $s \trianglerighteq_A t\ s_{k+1} \cdots s_n$, *and (c) A is minimal: there is no subset* $A' \subsetneq A$ *with* $s \trianglerighteq_{A'} t$.

Example 25. In AFSMs where all meta-variables have arity 0 and the right-hand sides of rules are β-normal, the set $\mathsf{cand}(s)$ for a meta-term s consists exactly of the pairs t $(\emptyset)$ where t has the form $\mathtt{f}\ s_1 \cdots s_{minar(\mathtt{f})}$ and t occurs as part of s. In Example 8, we thus have $\mathsf{cand}(G\ H\ (\lambda m.\mathtt{rec}\ (H\ m)\ K\ F\ G)) = \{\mathtt{rec}\ (H\ m)\ K\ F\ G\ (\emptyset)\}$.

If some of the meta-variables *do* take arguments, then the meta-variable conditions matter: candidates of s are pairs t (A) where A contains exactly those pairs $Z : i$ for which we pass through the ith argument of Z to reach t in s.

Example 26. Consider an AFSM with the signature from Example 8 but a rule using meta-variables with larger arities:

$$\begin{array}{c}\mathtt{rec}\ (\mathtt{lim}\ (\lambda n.H\langle n\rangle))\ K\ (\lambda x.\lambda n.F\langle x, n\rangle)\ (\lambda f.\lambda g.G\langle f, g\rangle) \Rrightarrow \\ G\langle \lambda n.H\langle n\rangle,\ \lambda m.\mathtt{rec}\ H\langle m\rangle\ K\ (\lambda x.\lambda n.F\langle x, n\rangle)\ (\lambda f.\lambda g.G\langle f, g\rangle)\rangle\end{array}$$

The right-hand side has one candidate:

$$\mathtt{rec}\ H\langle m\rangle\ K\ (\lambda x.\lambda n.F\langle x, n\rangle)\ (\lambda f.\lambda g.G\langle f, g\rangle)\ (\{G : 2\})$$

The original static approaches define DPs as pairs $\ell^\sharp \Rrightarrow p^\sharp$ where $\ell \Rightarrow r$ is a rule and p a subterm of r of the form $\mathtt{f}\ r_1 \cdots r_m$ – as their rules are built using terms, not meta-terms. This can set variables bound in r free in p. In the current setting, we use candidates with their meta-variable conditions and implicit β-steps rather than subterms, and we replace such variables by meta-variables.

Definition 27 (*SDP*). *Let s be a meta-term and $(\mathcal{F}, \mathcal{R})$ be an AFSM. Let $metafy(s)$ denote s with all free variables replaced by corresponding meta-variables. Now* $SDP(\mathcal{R}) = \{\ell^\sharp \Rrightarrow metafy(p^\sharp)\ (A) \mid \ell \Rightarrow r \in \mathcal{R} \wedge p\ (A) \in \mathsf{cand}(r)\}$.

Although static DPs always have a pleasant form $\mathtt{f}^\sharp\ \ell_1 \cdots \ell_k \Rrightarrow \mathtt{g}^\sharp\ p_1 \cdots p_n\ (A)$ (as opposed to the *dynamic* DPs of, e.g., [31], whose right-hand sides can have a meta-variable at the head, which complicates various techniques in the framework), they have two important complications not present in first-order DPs: the right-hand side p of a DP $\ell \Rrightarrow p\ (A)$ may contain meta-variables that do not occur in the left-hand side ℓ – traditional analysis techniques are not really equipped for this – and the left- and right-hand sides may have different types. In Sect. 5 we will explore some methods to deal with these features.

Example 28. For the non-η-expanded rules of Example 17, the set $SDP(\mathcal{R})$ has one element: $\mathtt{deriv}^\sharp\ (\lambda x.\mathtt{sin}\ F\langle x\rangle) \Rrightarrow \mathtt{deriv}^\sharp\ (\lambda x.F\langle x\rangle)$. (As times and cos are not defined symbols, they do not generate dependency pairs.) The set $SDP(\mathcal{R}^\uparrow)$ for the η-expanded rules is $\{\mathtt{deriv}^\sharp\ (\lambda x.\mathtt{sin}\ F\langle x\rangle)\ Y \Rrightarrow \mathtt{deriv}^\sharp\ (\lambda x.F\langle x\rangle)\ Y\}$. To obtain the relevant candidate, we used the β-reduction step of BRSMTs.

Example 29. The AFSM from Example 8 is AFP following Example 19; here $SDP(\mathcal{R})$ is:

$$\mathtt{rec}^\sharp\ (\mathtt{s}\ X)\ K\ F\ G \Rrightarrow \mathtt{rec}^\sharp\ X\ K\ F\ G\ (\emptyset)$$
$$\mathtt{rec}^\sharp\ (\mathtt{lim}\ H)\ K\ F\ G \Rrightarrow \mathtt{rec}^\sharp\ (H\ M)\ K\ F\ G\ (\emptyset)$$

Note that the right-hand side of the second DP contains a meta-variable that is not on the left. As we will see in Example 64, that is not problematic here.

Termination analysis using dependency pairs importantly considers the notion of a *dependency chain.* This notion is fairly similar to the first-order setting:

Definition 30 (Dependency chain). *Let $\mathcal{P}$ be a set of DPs and $\mathcal{R}$ a set of rules. A (finite or infinite)* $(\mathcal{P},\mathcal{R})$-dependency chain *(or just $(\mathcal{P},\mathcal{R})$-chain) is a sequence $[(\ell_0 \Rrightarrow p_0\ (A_0), s_0, t_0), (\ell_1 \Rrightarrow p_1\ (A_1), s_1, t_1), \ldots]$ where each $\ell_i \Rrightarrow p_i\ (A_i) \in \mathcal{P}$ and all s_i, t_i are terms, such that for all i:*

1. *there exists a substitution γ on domain $FMV(\ell_i) \cup FMV(p_i)$ such that $s_i = \ell_i\gamma$, $t_i = p_i\gamma$ and for all $Z \in \mathtt{dom}(\gamma)$: $\gamma(Z)$ respects A_i;*
2. *we can write $t_i = \mathtt{f}\ u_1 \cdots u_n$ and $s_{i+1} = \mathtt{f}\ w_1 \cdots w_n$ and each $u_j \Rightarrow^*_{\mathcal{R}} w_j$.*

Example 31. In the (first) AFSM from Example 6, we have $SDP(\mathcal{R}) = \{\mathtt{map}^\sharp\ (\lambda x.Z\langle x\rangle)(\mathtt{cons}\ H\ T) \Rrightarrow \mathtt{map}^\sharp\ (\lambda x.Z\langle x\rangle)\ T\}$. An example of a finite dependency chain is $[(\rho, s_1, t_1), (\rho, s_2, t_2)]$ where ρ is the one DP, $s_1 = \mathtt{map}^\sharp\ (\lambda x.\mathtt{s}\ x)\ (\mathtt{cons}\ \mathtt{0}\ (\mathtt{cons}\ (\mathtt{s}\ \mathtt{0})\ (\mathtt{map}\ (\lambda x.x)\ \mathtt{nil})))$ and $t_1 = \mathtt{map}^\sharp\ (\lambda x.\mathtt{s}\ x)\ (\mathtt{cons}\ (\mathtt{s}\ \mathtt{0})\ (\mathtt{map}\ (\lambda x.x)\ \mathtt{nil}))$ and $s_2 = \mathtt{map}^\sharp\ (\lambda x.\mathtt{s}\ x)\ (\mathtt{cons}\ (\mathtt{s}\ \mathtt{0})\ \mathtt{nil})$ and $t_2 = \mathtt{map}^\sharp\ (\lambda x.\mathtt{s}\ x)\ \mathtt{nil}$.

Note that here t_1 reduces to s_2 in a single step ($\mathtt{map}\ (\lambda x.x)\ \mathtt{nil} \Rightarrow_{\mathcal{R}} \mathtt{nil}$).

We have the following key result:

Theorem 32. *Let $(\mathcal{F},\mathcal{R})$ be a PA-AFP AFSM. If $(\mathcal{F},\mathcal{R})$ is non-terminating, then there is an infinite $(SDP(\mathcal{R}),\mathcal{R})$-dependency chain.*

Proof (sketch). The proof is an adaptation of the one in [34], altered for the more permissive definition of *accessible function passing* over *plain function passing* as well as the meta-variable conditions; it also follows from Theorem 37 below. □

By this result we can use dependency pairs to prove termination of a given properly applied and AFP AFSM: if we can prove that there is no infinite $(SDP(\mathcal{R}), \mathcal{R})$-chain, then termination follows immediately. Note, however, that the reverse result does *not* hold: it is possible to have an infinite $(SDP(\mathcal{R}), \mathcal{R})$-dependency chain even for a terminating PA-AFP AFSM.

Example 33. Let $\mathcal{F} \supseteq \{\mathtt{0}, \mathtt{1} : \mathtt{nat}, \mathtt{f} : \mathtt{nat} \to \mathtt{nat}, \mathtt{g} : (\mathtt{nat} \to \mathtt{nat}) \to \mathtt{nat}\}$ and $\mathcal{R} = \{\mathtt{f}\ \mathtt{0} \Rightarrow \mathtt{g}\ (\lambda x.\mathtt{f}\ x), \mathtt{g}\ (\lambda x.F\langle x\rangle) \Rightarrow F\langle \mathtt{1}\rangle\}$. This AFSM is PA-AFP, with $SDP(\mathcal{R}) = \{\mathtt{f}^\sharp\ \mathtt{0} \Rrightarrow \mathtt{g}^\sharp\ (\lambda x.\mathtt{f}\ x),\ \mathtt{f}^\sharp\ \mathtt{0} \Rrightarrow \mathtt{f}^\sharp\ X\}$; the second rule does not cause the addition of any dependency pairs. Although $\Rightarrow_{\mathcal{R}}$ is terminating, there is an infinite $(SDP(\mathcal{R}), \mathcal{R})$-chain $[(\mathtt{f}^\sharp\ \mathtt{0} \Rrightarrow \mathtt{f}^\sharp\ X, \mathtt{f}^\sharp\ \mathtt{0}, \mathtt{f}^\sharp\ \mathtt{0}), (\mathtt{f}^\sharp\ \mathtt{0} \Rrightarrow \mathtt{f}^\sharp\ X, \mathtt{f}^\sharp\ \mathtt{0}, \mathtt{f}^\sharp\ \mathtt{0}), \ldots]$.

The problem in Example 33 is the *non-conservative* DP $\mathtt{f}^\sharp\ \mathtt{0} \Rrightarrow \mathtt{f}^\sharp\ X$, with X on the right but not on the left. Such DPs arise from *abstractions* in the right-hand sides of rules. Unfortunately, abstractions are introduced by the restricted η-expansion (Definition 15) that we may need to make an AFSM properly applied. Even so, often all DPs are conservative, like Examples 6 and 17. There, we do have the inverse result:

Theorem 34. *For any AFSM $(\mathcal{F}, \mathcal{R})$: if there is an infinite $(SDP(\mathcal{R}), \mathcal{R})$-chain $[(\rho_0, s_0, t_0), (\rho_1, s_1, t_1), \ldots]$ with all ρ_i conservative, then $\Rightarrow_{\mathcal{R}}$ is non-terminating.*

Proof (sketch). If $FMV(p_i) \subseteq FMV(\ell_i)$, then we can see that $s_i \Rightarrow_{\mathcal{R}} \cdot \Rightarrow_{\beta}^{*} t_i'$ for some term t_i' of which t_i is a subterm. Since also each $t_i \Rightarrow_{\mathcal{R}}^{*} s_{i+1}$, the infinite chain induces an infinite reduction $s_0 \Rightarrow_{\mathcal{R}}^{+} t_0' \Rightarrow_{\mathcal{R}}^{*} s_1' \Rightarrow_{\mathcal{R}}^{+} t_1'' \Rightarrow_{\mathcal{R}}^{*} \cdots$. □

The core of the dependency pair *framework* is to systematically simplify a set of pairs $(\mathcal{P}, \mathcal{R})$ to prove either absence or presence of an infinite $(\mathcal{P}, \mathcal{R})$-chain, thus showing termination or non-termination as appropriate. By Theorems 32 and 34 we can do so, although with some conditions on the non-termination result. We can do better by tracking certain properties of dependency chains.

Definition 35 (Minimal and Computable chains). *Let $(\mathcal{F}, \mathcal{U})$ be an AFSM and $C_{\mathcal{U}}$ an RC-set satisfying the properties of Theorem 13 for $(\mathcal{F}, \mathcal{U})$. Let $\mathcal{F}$ contain, for every type σ, at least countably many symbols $\mathtt{f} : \sigma$ not used in $\mathcal{U}$.*

A $(\mathcal{P}, \mathcal{R})$-chain $[(\rho_0, s_0, t_0), (\rho_1, s_1, t_1), \ldots]$ is $\mathcal{U}$-computable *if: $\Rightarrow_{\mathcal{U}} \supseteq \Rightarrow_{\mathcal{R}}$, and for all $i \in \mathbb{N}$ there exists a substitution γ_i such that $\rho_i = \ell_i \Rrightarrow p_i\ (A_i)$ with $s_i = \ell_i\gamma_i$ and $t_i = p_i\gamma_i$, and $(\lambda x_1 \ldots x_n.v)\gamma_i$ is $C_{\mathcal{U}}$-computable for all v and B such that $p_i \trianglerighteq_B v$, γ_i respects B, and $FV(v) = \{x_1, \ldots, x_n\}$.*

A chain is minimal *if the strict subterms of all t_i are terminating under $\Rightarrow_{\mathcal{R}}$.*

In the first-order DP framework, *minimal* chains give access to several powerful techniques to prove absence of infinite chains, such as the *subterm criterion* [24] and *usable rules* [22,24]. *Computable* chains go a step further, by building on the computability inherent in the proof of Theorem 32 and the notion of *accessible function passing* AFSMs. In computable chains, we can require that (some of) the subterms of all t_i are *computable* rather than merely *terminating*.

This property will be essential in the *computable subterm criterion processor* (Theorem 63).

Another property of dependency chains is the use of *formative rules*, which has proven very useful for dynamic DPs [31]. Here we go further and consider *formative reductions*, which were introduced for the first-order DP framework in [16]. This property will be essential in the *formative rules processor* (Theorem 58).

Definition 36 (Formative chain, formative reduction). *A $(\mathcal{P},\mathcal{R})$-chain $[(\ell_0 \Rrightarrow p_0\ (A_0), s_0, t_0), (\ell_1 \Rrightarrow p_1\ (A_1), s_1, t_1), \dots]$ is* formative *if for all i, the reduction $t_i \Rightarrow_{\mathcal{R}}^* s_{i+1}$ is ℓ_{i+1}-formative. Here, for a pattern ℓ, substitution γ and term s, a reduction $s \Rightarrow_{\mathcal{R}}^* \ell\gamma$ is* ℓ-formative *if one of the following holds:*

- *ℓ is not a fully extended linear pattern; that is: some meta-variable occurs more than once in ℓ or ℓ has a sub-meta-term $\lambda x.C[Z\langle \boldsymbol{s}\rangle]$ with $x \notin \{\boldsymbol{s}\}$*
- *ℓ is a meta-variable application $Z\langle x_1,\dots,x_k\rangle$ and $s = \ell\gamma$*
- *$s = a\ s_1 \cdots s_n$ and $\ell = a\ \ell_1 \cdots \ell_n$ with $a \in \mathcal{F}^\sharp \cup \mathcal{V}$ and each $s_i \Rightarrow_{\mathcal{R}}^* \ell_i\gamma$ by an ℓ_i-formative reduction*
- *$s = \lambda x.s'$ and $\ell = \lambda x.\ell'$ and $s' \Rightarrow_{\mathcal{R}}^* \ell'\gamma$ by an ℓ'-formative reduction*
- *$s = (\lambda x.u)\ v\ w_1 \cdots w_n$ and $u[x := v]\ w_1 \cdots w_n \Rightarrow_{\mathcal{R}}^* \ell\gamma$ by an ℓ-formative reduction*
- *ℓ is not a meta-variable application, and there are $\ell' \Rightarrow r' \in \mathcal{R}$, meta-variables $Z_1 \dots Z_n$ $(n \geq 0)$ and δ such that $s \Rightarrow_{\mathcal{R}}^* (\ell'\ Z_1 \cdots Z_n)\delta$ by an $(\ell'\ Z_1 \cdots Z_n)$-formative reduction, and $(r'\ Z_1 \cdots Z_n)\delta \Rightarrow_{\mathcal{R}}^* \ell\gamma$ by an ℓ-formative reduction.*

The idea of a formative reduction is to avoid redundant steps: if $s \Rightarrow_{\mathcal{R}}^* \ell\gamma$ by an ℓ-formative reduction, then this reduction takes only the steps needed to obtain an instance of ℓ. Suppose that we have rules $\texttt{plus}\ \texttt{0}\ Y \Rightarrow Y$, $\texttt{plus}\ (\texttt{s}\ X)\ Y \Rightarrow \texttt{s}\ (\texttt{plus}\ X\ Y)$. Let $\ell := \texttt{g}\ \texttt{0}\ X$ and $t := \texttt{plus}\ \texttt{0}\ \texttt{0}$. Then the reduction $\texttt{g}\ t\ t \Rightarrow_{\mathcal{R}} \texttt{g}\ \texttt{0}\ t$ is ℓ-formative: we must reduce the first argument to get an instance of ℓ. The reduction $\texttt{g}\ t\ t \Rightarrow_{\mathcal{R}} \texttt{g}\ t\ \texttt{0} \Rightarrow_{\mathcal{R}} \texttt{g}\ \texttt{0}\ \texttt{0}$ is not ℓ-formative, because the reduction in the second argument does not contribute to the non-meta-variable positions of ℓ. This matters when we consider ℓ as the left-hand side of a rule, say $\texttt{g}\ \texttt{0}\ X \Rightarrow \texttt{0}$: if we reduce $\texttt{g}\ t\ t \Rightarrow_{\mathcal{R}} \texttt{g}\ t\ \texttt{0} \Rightarrow_{\mathcal{R}} \texttt{g}\ \texttt{0}\ \texttt{0} \Rightarrow_{\mathcal{R}} \texttt{0}$, then the first step was redundant: removing this step gives a shorter reduction to the same result: $\texttt{g}\ t\ t \Rightarrow_{\mathcal{R}} \texttt{g}\ \texttt{0}\ t \Rightarrow_{\mathcal{R}} \texttt{0}$. In an infinite reduction, redundant steps may also be postponed indefinitely.

We can now strengthen the result of Theorem 32 with two new properties.

Theorem 37. *Let $(\mathcal{F},\mathcal{R})$ be a* properly applied, accessible function passing *AFSM. If $(\mathcal{F},\mathcal{R})$ is non-terminating, then there is an infinite $\mathcal{R}$-computable formative $(SDP(\mathcal{R}),\mathcal{R})$-dependency chain.*

Proof (sketch). We select a *minimal non-computable (MNC)* term $s := \texttt{f}\ s_1 \cdots s_k$ (where all s_i are $C_{\mathcal{R}}$-computable) and an infinite reduction starting in s. Then we stepwise build an infinite dependency chain, as follows. Since s is non-computable but each s_i terminates (as computability implies termination), there exist a rule

$\mathtt{f}\ \ell_1 \cdots \ell_k \Rightarrow r$ and substitution γ such that each $s_i \Rightarrow^*_{\mathcal{R}} \ell_i\gamma$ and $r\gamma$ is non-computable. We can then identify a candidate t (A) of r such that γ respects A and $t\gamma$ is a MNC subterm of $r\gamma$; we continue the process with $t\gamma$ (or a term at its head). For the *formative* property, we note that if $s \Rightarrow^*_{\mathcal{R}} \ell\gamma$ and u is terminating, then $u \Rightarrow^*_{\mathcal{R}} \ell\delta$ by an ℓ-formative reduction for substitution δ such that each $\delta(Z) \Rightarrow^*_{\mathcal{R}} \gamma(Z)$. This follows by postponing those reduction steps not needed to obtain an instance of ℓ. The resulting infinite chain is $\mathcal{R}$-computable because we can show, by induction on the definition of $\trianglerighteq_{\mathsf{acc}}$, that if $\ell \Rightarrow r$ is an AFP rule and $\ell\gamma$ is a MNC term, then $\gamma(Z)$ is $C_{\mathcal{R}}$-computable for all $Z \in FMV(r)$. □

As it is easily seen that all $C_{\mathcal{U}}$-computable terms are $\Rightarrow_{\mathcal{U}}$-terminating and therefore $\Rightarrow_{\mathcal{R}}$-terminating, every $\mathcal{U}$-computable $(\mathcal{P},\mathcal{R})$-dependency chain is also minimal. The notions of $\mathcal{R}$-computable and formative chains still do not suffice to obtain a true inverse result, however (i.e., to prove that termination implies the absence of an infinite $\mathcal{R}$-computable chain over $SDP(\mathcal{R})$): the infinite chain in Example 33 is $\mathcal{R}$-computable.

To see why the two restrictions that the AFSM must be *properly applied* and *accessible function passing* are necessary, consider the following examples.

Example 38. Consider $\mathcal{F} \supseteq \{\mathtt{fix} : ((\mathsf{o} \rightarrow \mathsf{o}) \rightarrow \mathsf{o} \rightarrow \mathsf{o}) \rightarrow \mathsf{o} \rightarrow \mathsf{o}\}$ and $\mathcal{R} = \{\mathtt{fix}\ F\ X \Rightarrow F\ (\mathtt{fix}\ F)\ X\}$. This AFSM is not properly applied; it is also not terminating, as can be seen by instantiating F with $\lambda y.y$. However, it does not have any static DPs, since $\mathtt{fix}\ F$ is not a candidate. Even if we altered the definition of static DPs to admit a dependency pair $\mathtt{fix}^\sharp\ F\ X \Rrightarrow \mathtt{fix}^\sharp\ F$, this pair could not be used to build an infinite dependency chain.

Note that the problem does not arise if we study the η-expanded rules $\mathcal{R}^\uparrow = \{\mathtt{fix}\,F\,X \Rightarrow F\ (\lambda z.\mathtt{fix}\ F\ z)\ X\}$, as the dependency pair $\mathtt{fix}^\sharp\ F\ X \Rrightarrow \mathtt{fix}^\sharp\ F\ Z$ does admit an infinite chain. Unfortunately, as the one dependency pair does not satisfy the conditions of Theorem 34, we cannot use this to prove non-termination.

Example 39. The AFSM from Example 20 is not accessible function passing, since $Acc(\mathtt{lm}) = \emptyset$. This is good because the set $SDP(\mathcal{R})$ is empty, which would lead us to falsely conclude termination without the restriction.

Discussion: Theorem 37 transposes the work of [34,46] to AFSMs and extends it by using a more liberal restriction, by limiting interest to *formative*, $\mathcal{R}$-*computable* chains, and by including meta-variable conditions. Both of these new properties of chains will support new termination techniques within the DP framework.

The relationship with the works for functional programming [32,33] is less clear: they define a different form of chains suited well to polymorphic systems, but which requires more intricate reasoning for non-polymorphic systems, as DPs can be used for reductions at the head of a term. It is not clear whether there are non-polymorphic systems that can be handled with one and not the other. The notions of formative and $\mathcal{R}$-computable chains are not considered there; meta-variable conditions are not relevant to their λ-free formalism.

5 The Static Higher-Order DP Framework

In first-order term rewriting, the DP *framework* [20] is an extendable framework to prove termination and non-termination. As observed in the introduction, DP analyses in higher-order rewriting typically go beyond the initial DP *approach* [2], but fall short of the full *framework*. Here, we define the latter for static DPs. Complete versions of all proof sketches in this section are in [17, Appendix C].

We have now reduced the problem of termination to non-existence of certain chains. In the DP framework, we formalise this in the notion of a *DP problem*:

Definition 40 (DP problem). *A* DP problem *is a tuple* $(\mathcal{P}, \mathcal{R}, m, f)$ *with* $\mathcal{P}$ *a set of DPs,* $\mathcal{R}$ *a set of rules,* $m \in \{\mathtt{minimal}, \mathtt{arbitrary}\} \cup \{\mathtt{computable}_{\mathcal{U}} \mid$ *any set of rules* $\mathcal{U}\}$*, and* $f \in \{\mathtt{formative}, \mathtt{all}\}$.[3]

A DP problem $(\mathcal{P}, \mathcal{R}, m, f)$ *is* finite *if there exists no infinite* $(\mathcal{P}, \mathcal{R})$*-chain that is* $\mathcal{U}$*-computable if* $m = \mathtt{computable}_{\mathcal{U}}$*, is minimal if* $m = \mathtt{minimal}$*, and is formative if* $f = \mathtt{formative}$*. It is* infinite *if* $\mathcal{R}$ *is non-terminating, or if there exists an infinite* $(\mathcal{P}, \mathcal{R})$*-chain where all DPs used in the chain are conservative.*

To capture the levels of permissiveness in the m *flag, we use a transitive-reflexive relation* $\succeq$ *generated by* $\mathtt{computable}_{\mathcal{U}} \succeq \mathtt{minimal} \succeq \mathtt{arbitrary}$.

Thus, the combination of Theorems 34 and 37 can be rephrased as: an AFSM $(\mathcal{F}, \mathcal{R})$ is terminating if $(\mathit{SDP}(\mathcal{R}), \mathcal{R}, \mathtt{computable}_{\mathcal{R}}, \mathtt{formative})$ is finite, and is non-terminating if $(\mathit{SDP}(\mathcal{R}), \mathcal{R}, m, f)$ is infinite for some $m \in \{\mathtt{computable}_{\mathcal{U}}, \mathtt{minimal}, \mathtt{arbitrary}\}$ and $f \in \{\mathtt{formative}, \mathtt{all}\}$.[4]

The core idea of the DP framework is to iteratively simplify a set of DP problems via *processors* until nothing remains to be proved:

Definition 41 (Processor). *A* dependency pair processor *(or just* processor*) is a function that takes a DP problem and returns either* NO *or a set of DP problems. A processor Proc is* sound *if a DP problem* M *is finite whenever* $\mathit{Proc}(M) \neq$ NO *and all elements of* $\mathit{Proc}(M)$ *are finite. A processor Proc is* complete *if a DP problem* M *is infinite whenever* $\mathit{Proc}(M) =$ NO *or contains an infinite element.*

To prove finiteness of a DP problem M with the DP framework, we proceed analogously to the first-order DP framework [22]: we repeatedly apply sound DP processors starting from M until none remain. That is, we execute the following rough procedure: (1) let $A := \{M\}$; (2) while $A \neq \emptyset$: select a problem $Q \in A$ and a sound processor *Proc* with $\mathit{Proc}(Q) \neq \mathtt{NO}$, and let $A := (A \setminus \{Q\}) \cup \mathit{Proc}(Q)$. If this procedure terminates, then M is a finite DP problem.

[3] Our framework is implicitly parametrised by the signature $\mathcal{F}^\sharp$ used for term formation. As none of the processors we present modify this component (as indeed there is no need to by Theorem 9), we leave it implicit.

[4] The processors in this paper do not *alter* the flag m, but some *require* minimality or computability. We include the $\mathtt{minimal}$ option and the subscript $\mathcal{U}$ for the sake of future generalisations, and for reuse of processors in the *dynamic* approach of [31].

To prove termination of an AFSM $(\mathcal{F}, \mathcal{R})$, we would use as initial DP problem $(\mathit{SDP}(\mathcal{R}), \mathcal{R}, \texttt{computable}_{\mathcal{R}}, \texttt{formative})$, provided that $\mathcal{R}$ is properly applied and accessible function passing (where η-expansion following Definition 15 may be applied first). If the procedure terminates – so finiteness of M is proved by the definition of soundness – then Theorem 37 provides termination of $\Rightarrow_{\mathcal{R}}$.

Similarly, we can use the DP framework to prove infiniteness: (1) let $A := \{M\}$; (2) while $A \neq \texttt{NO}$: select a problem $Q \in A$ and a complete processor *Proc*, and let $A := \texttt{NO}$ if $\mathit{Proc}(Q) = \texttt{NO}$, or $A := (A \setminus \{Q\}) \cup \mathit{Proc}(Q)$ otherwise. For non-termination of $(\mathcal{F}, \mathcal{R})$, the initial DP problem should be $(\mathit{SDP}(\mathcal{R}), \mathcal{R}, m, f)$, where m, f can be any flag (see Theorem 34). Note that the algorithms coincide while processors are used that are both sound *and* complete. In a tool, automation (or the user) must resolve the non-determinism and select suitable processors.

Below, we will present a number of processors within the framework. We will typically present processors by writing "for a DP problem M satisfying X, Y, Z, $\mathit{Proc}(M) = \dots$". In these cases, we let $\mathit{Proc}(M) = \{M\}$ for any problem M not satisfying the given properties. Many more processors are possible, but we have chosen to present a selection which touches on all aspects of the DP framework:

- processors which map a DP problem to NO (Theorem 65), a singleton set (most processors) and a non-singleton set (Theorem 42);
- changing the set $\mathcal{R}$ (Theorems 54, 58) and various flags (Theorem 54);
- using specific values of the f (Theorem 58) and m flags (Theorems 54, 61, 63);
- using term orderings (Theorems 49, 52), a key part of many termination proofs.

5.1 The Dependency Graph

We can leverage reachability information to *decompose* DP problems. In first-order rewriting, a graph structure is used to track which DPs can possibly follow one another in a chain [2]. Here, we define this *dependency graph* as follows.

Definition 42 (Dependency graph). *A DP problem $(\mathcal{P}, \mathcal{R}, m, f)$ induces a graph structure DG, called its* dependency graph, *whose nodes are the elements of $\mathcal{P}$. There is a (directed) edge from ρ_1 to ρ_2 in DG iff there exist s_1, t_1, s_2, t_2 such that $[(\rho_1, s_1, t_1), (\rho_2, s_2, t_2)]$ is a $(\mathcal{P}, \mathcal{R})$-chain with the properties for m, f.*

Example 43. Consider an AFSM with $\mathcal{F} \supseteq \{\mathtt{f} : (\mathtt{nat} \rightarrow \mathtt{nat}) \rightarrow \mathtt{nat} \rightarrow \mathtt{nat}\}$ and $\mathcal{R} = \{\mathtt{f}\ (\lambda x.F\langle x\rangle)\ (\mathtt{s}\ Y) \Rightarrow F\langle \mathtt{f}\ (\lambda x.\mathtt{0})\ (\mathtt{f}\ (\lambda x.F\langle x\rangle)\ Y)\rangle\}$. Let $\mathcal{P} := \mathit{SDP}(\mathcal{R}) =$

$$\left\{\begin{array}{ll} (1)\ \mathtt{f}^\sharp\ (\lambda x.F\langle x\rangle)\ (\mathtt{s}\ Y) \Rrightarrow \mathtt{f}^\sharp\ (\lambda x.\mathtt{0})\ (\mathtt{f}\ (\lambda x.F\langle x\rangle)\ Y) & (\{F : 1\}) \\ (2)\ \mathtt{f}^\sharp\ (\lambda x.F\langle x\rangle)\ (\mathtt{s}\ Y) \Rrightarrow \mathtt{f}^\sharp\ (\lambda x.F\langle x\rangle)\ Y & (\{F : 1\}) \end{array}\right\}$$

The dependency graph of $(\mathcal{P}, \mathcal{R}, \texttt{minimal}, \texttt{formative})$ is:

There is no edge from (1) to itself or (2) because there is no substitution γ such that $(\lambda x.\mathtt{0})\gamma$ can be reduced to a term $(\lambda x.F\langle x\rangle)\delta$ where $\delta(F)$ regards its first argument (as $\Rrightarrow^*_{\mathcal{R}}$ cannot introduce new variables).

In general, the dependency graph for a given DP problem is undecidable, which is why we consider *approximations.*

Definition 44 (Dependency graph approximation [31]**).** *A finite graph G_θ approximates DG if θ is a function that maps the nodes of DG to the nodes of G_θ such that, whenever DG has an edge from ρ_1 to ρ_2, G_θ has an edge from $\theta(\rho_1)$ to $\theta(\rho_2)$. (G_θ may have edges that have no corresponding edge in DG.)*

Note that this definition allows for an *infinite* graph to be approximated by a *finite* one; infinite graphs may occur if $\mathcal{R}$ is infinite (e.g., the union of all simply-typed instances of polymorphic rules).

If $\mathcal{P}$ is finite, we can take a graph approximation $G_{\mathtt{id}}$ with the same nodes as *DG*. A simple approximation may have an edge from $\ell_1 \Rrightarrow p_1$ (A_1) to $\ell_2 \Rrightarrow p_2$ (A_2) whenever both p_1 and ℓ_2 have the form $\mathtt{f}^\sharp\ s_1 \cdots s_k$ for the same $\mathtt{f}$ and k. However, one can also take the meta-variable conditions into account, as we did in Example 43.

Theorem 45 (Dependency graph processor). *The processor $Proc_{G_\theta}$ that maps a DP problem $M = (\mathcal{P}, \mathcal{R}, m, f)$ to $\{(\{\rho \in \mathcal{P} \mid \theta(\rho) \in C_i\}, \mathcal{R}, m, f) \mid 1 \leq i \leq n\}$ if G_θ is an approximation of the dependency graph of M and $C_1, \ldots, C_n$ are the (nodes of the) non-trivial strongly connected components (SCCs) of G_θ, is both sound and complete.*

Proof (sketch). In an infinite $(\mathcal{P}, \mathcal{R})$-chain $[(\rho_0, s_0, t_0), (\rho_1, s_1, t_1), \ldots]$, there is always a path from ρ_i to ρ_{i+1} in DG. Since G_θ is finite, every infinite path in *DG* eventually remains in a cycle in G_θ. This cycle is part of an SCC. □

Example 46. Let $\mathcal{R}$ be the set of rules from Example 43 and G be the graph given there. Then $Proc_G(SDP(\mathcal{R}), \mathcal{R}, \mathtt{computable}_{\mathcal{R}}, \mathtt{formative}) = \{(\{\mathtt{f}^\sharp\ (\lambda x.F\langle x\rangle)\ (\mathtt{s}\ Y) \Rrightarrow \mathtt{f}^\sharp\ (\lambda x.F\langle x\rangle)\ Y\ (\{F : 1\})\}, \mathcal{R}, \mathtt{computable}_{\mathcal{R}}, \mathtt{formative})\}$.

Example 47. Let $\mathcal{R}$ consist of the rules for map from Example 6 along with $\mathtt{f}\ L \Rrightarrow \mathtt{map}\ (\lambda x.\mathtt{g}\ x)\ L$ and $\mathtt{g}\ X \Rrightarrow X$. Then $SDP(\mathcal{R}) = \{(1)\ \mathtt{map}^\sharp\ (\lambda x.Z\langle x\rangle)\ (\mathtt{cons}\ H\ T) \Rrightarrow \mathtt{map}^\sharp\ (\lambda x.Z\langle x\rangle)\ T,\ (2)\ \mathtt{f}^\sharp\ L \Rrightarrow \mathtt{map}^\sharp\ (\lambda x.\mathtt{g}\ x)\ L,\ (3)\ \mathtt{f}^\sharp\ L \Rrightarrow \mathtt{g}^\sharp\ X\}$. DP (3) is not conservative, but it is not on any cycle in the graph approximation $G_{\mathtt{id}}$ obtained by considering head symbols as described above:

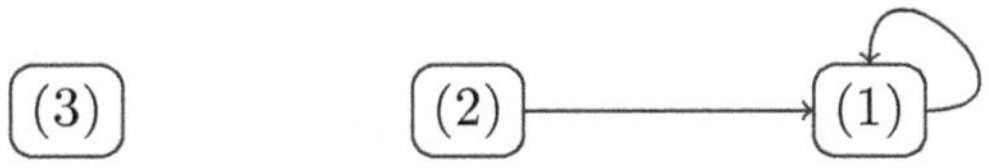

As (1) is the only DP on a cycle, $Proc_{SDP_{G_{\mathtt{id}}}}(SDP(\mathcal{R}), \mathcal{R}, \mathtt{computable}_{\mathcal{R}}, \mathtt{formative}) = \{\ (\{(1)\}, \mathcal{R}, \mathtt{computable}_{\mathcal{R}}, \mathtt{formative})\ \}$.

Discussion: The dependency graph is a powerful tool for simplifying DP problems, used since early versions of the DP approach [2]. Our notion of a dependency graph approximation, taken from [31], strictly generalises the original notion in [2], which uses a graph on the same node set as DG with possibly further edges. One can get this notion here by using a graph $G_{\mathtt{id}}$. The advantage of our definition is that it ensures soundness of the dependency graph processor also for *infinite* sets of DPs. This overcomes a restriction in the literature [34, Corollary 5.13] to dependency graphs without non-cyclic infinite paths.

5.2 Processors Based on Reduction Triples

At the heart of most DP-based approaches to termination proving lie well-founded orderings to delete DPs (or rules). For this, we use *reduction triples* [24,31].

Definition 48 (Reduction triple). *A* reduction triple $(\succsim, \succcurlyeq, \succ)$ *consists of two quasi-orderings* $\succsim$ *and* $\succcurlyeq$ *and a well-founded strict ordering* $\succ$ *on meta-terms such that* $\succsim$ *is monotonic, all of* $\succsim, \succcurlyeq, \succ$ *are meta-stable (that is,* $\ell \succsim r$ *implies* $\ell\gamma \succsim r\gamma$ *if* ℓ *is a closed pattern and* γ *a substitution on domain* $FMV(\ell) \cup FMV(r)$*, and the same for* $\succcurlyeq$ *and* $\succ$*),* $\Rightarrow_\beta \subseteq \succsim$*, and both* $\succsim \circ \succ \subseteq \succ$ *and* $\succcurlyeq \circ \succ \subseteq \succ$*.*

In the first-order DP framework, the reduction pair processor [20] seeks to orient all rules with $\succsim$ and all DPs with either $\succsim$ or $\succ$; if this succeeds, those pairs oriented with $\succ$ may be removed. Using reduction *triples* rather than pairs, we obtain the following extension to the higher-order setting:

Theorem 49 (Basic reduction triple processor). *Let* $M = (\mathcal{P}_1 \uplus \mathcal{P}_2, \mathcal{R}, m, f)$ *be a DP problem. If* $(\succsim, \succcurlyeq, \succ)$ *is a reduction triple such that*

1. *for all* $\ell \Rightarrow r \in \mathcal{R}$*, we have* $\ell \succsim r$*;*
2. *for all* $\ell \Rrightarrow p\ (A) \in \mathcal{P}_1$*, we have* $\ell \succ p$*;*
3. *for all* $\ell \Rrightarrow p\ (A) \in \mathcal{P}_2$*, we have* $\ell \succcurlyeq p$*;*

then the processor that maps M *to* $\{(\mathcal{P}_2, \mathcal{R}, m, f)\}$ *is both sound and complete.*

Proof (sketch). For an infinite $(\mathcal{P}_1 \uplus \mathcal{P}_2, \mathcal{R})$-chain $[(\rho_0, s_0, t_0), (\rho_1, s_1, t_1), \ldots]$ the requirements provide that, for all i: (a) $s_i \succ t_i$ if $\rho_i \in \mathcal{P}_1$; (b) $s_i \succcurlyeq t_i$ if $\rho_i \in \mathcal{P}_2$; and (c) $t_i \succsim s_{i+1}$. Since $\succ$ is well-founded, only finitely many DPs can be in $\mathcal{P}_1$, so a tail of the chain is actually an infinite $(\mathcal{P}_2, \mathcal{R}, m, f)$-chain. □

Example 50. Let $(\mathcal{F}, \mathcal{R})$ be the (non-η-expanded) rules from Example 17, and $SDP(\mathcal{R})$ the DPs from Example 28. From Theorem 49, we get the following ordering requirements:

$$\mathtt{deriv}\ (\lambda x.\mathtt{sin}\ F\langle x\rangle) \succsim \lambda y.\mathtt{times}\ (\mathtt{deriv}\ (\lambda x.F\langle x\rangle)\ y)\ (\mathtt{cos}\ F\langle y\rangle)$$
$$\mathtt{deriv}^\sharp\ (\lambda x.\mathtt{sin}\ F\langle x\rangle) \succ \mathtt{deriv}^\sharp\ (\lambda x.F\langle x\rangle)$$

We can handle both requirements by using a polynomial interpretation $\mathcal{J}$ to $\mathbb{N}$ [15,43], by choosing $\mathcal{J}_{\mathtt{sin}}(n) = n+1$, $\mathcal{J}_{\mathtt{cos}}(n) = 0$, $\mathcal{J}_{\mathtt{times}}(n_1, n_2) = n_1$, $\mathcal{J}_{\mathtt{deriv}}(f) = \mathcal{J}_{\mathtt{deriv}^\sharp}(f) = \lambda n.f(n)$. Then the requirements are evaluated to: $\lambda n.f(n) + 1 \geq \lambda n.f(n)$ and $\lambda n.f(n) + 1 > \lambda n.f(n)$, which holds on $\mathbb{N}$.

Theorem 49 is not ideal since, by definition, the left- and right-hand side of a DP may have different types. Such DPs are hard to handle with traditional techniques such as HORPO [26] or polynomial interpretations [15,43], as these methods compare only (meta-)terms of the same type (modulo renaming of sorts).

Example 51. Consider the toy AFSM with $\mathcal{R} = \{\mathtt{f}\ (\mathtt{s}\ X)\ Y \Rightarrow \mathtt{g}\ X\ Y,\ \mathtt{g}\ X \Rightarrow \lambda z.\mathtt{f}\ X\ z\}$ and $\mathit{SDP}(\mathcal{R}) = \{\mathtt{f}^\sharp\ (\mathtt{s}\ X)\ Y \Rrightarrow \mathtt{g}^\sharp\ X,\ \mathtt{g}^\sharp\ X \Rrightarrow \mathtt{f}^\sharp\ X\ Z\}$. If $\mathtt{f}$ and $\mathtt{g}$ both have a type $\mathtt{nat} \rightarrow \mathtt{nat} \rightarrow \mathtt{nat}$, then in the first DP, the left-hand side has type $\mathtt{nat}$ while the right-hand side has type $\mathtt{nat} \rightarrow \mathtt{nat}$. In the second DP, the left-hand side has type $\mathtt{nat} \rightarrow \mathtt{nat}$ and the right-hand side has type $\mathtt{nat}$.

To be able to handle examples like the one above, we adapt [31, Thm. 5.21] by altering the ordering requirements to have base type.

Theorem 52 (Reduction triple processor). *Let* Bot *be a set* $\{\bot_\sigma : \sigma \mid \sigma \text{ a type}\} \subseteq \mathcal{F}^\sharp$ *of unused constructors,* $M = (\mathcal{P}_1 \uplus \mathcal{P}_2, \mathcal{R}, m, f)$ *a DP problem and* $(\succsim, \succcurlyeq, \succ)$ *a reduction triple such that: (a) for all* $\ell \Rightarrow r \in \mathcal{R}$*, we have* $\ell \succsim r$*; and (b) for all* $\ell \Rrightarrow p\ (A) \in \mathcal{P}_1 \uplus \mathcal{P}_2$ *with* $\ell : \sigma_1 \rightarrow \ldots \rightarrow \sigma_m \rightarrow \iota$ *and* $p : \tau_1 \rightarrow \ldots \rightarrow \tau_n \rightarrow \kappa$ *we have, for fresh meta-variables* $Z_1 : \sigma_1, \ldots, Z_m : \sigma_m$*:*

- $\ell\ Z_1 \cdots Z_m \succ p\ \bot_{\tau_1} \cdots \bot_{\tau_n}$ *if* $\ell \Rrightarrow p\ (A) \in \mathcal{P}_1$
- $\ell\ Z_1 \cdots Z_m \succcurlyeq p\ \bot_{\tau_1} \cdots \bot_{\tau_n}$ *if* $\ell \Rrightarrow p\ (A) \in \mathcal{P}_2$

Then the processor that maps M *to* $\{(\mathcal{P}_2, \mathcal{R}, m, f)\}$ *is both sound and complete.*

Proof (sketch). If $(\succsim, \succcurlyeq, \succ)$ is such a triple, then for $R \in \{\succcurlyeq, \succ\}$ define R' as follows: for $s : \sigma_1 \rightarrow \ldots \rightarrow \sigma_m \rightarrow \iota$ and $t : \tau_1 \rightarrow \ldots \rightarrow \tau_n \rightarrow \kappa$, let $s\ R'\ t$ if for all $u_1 : \sigma_1, \ldots, u_m : \sigma_m$ there exist $w_1 : \tau_1, \ldots, w_n : \tau_n$ such that $s\ u_1 \cdots u_m\ R\ t\ w_1 \cdots w_n$. Now apply Theorem 49 with the triple $(\succsim, \succcurlyeq', \succ')$. □

Here, the elements of Bot take the role of minimal terms for the ordering. We use them to flatten the type of the right-hand sides of ordering requirements, which makes it easier to use traditional methods to generate a reduction triple.

While $\succ$ and $\succcurlyeq$ may still have to orient meta-terms of distinct types, these are always *base* types, which we could collapse to a single sort. The only relation required to be monotonic, $\succsim$, regards pairs of meta-terms of the *same* type. This makes it feasible to apply orderings like HORPO or polynomial interpretations.

Both the basic and non-basic reduction triple processor are difficult to use for *non-conservative* DPs, which generate ordering requirements whose right-hand side contains a meta-variable not occurring on the left. This is typically difficult for traditional techniques, although possible to overcome, by choosing triples that do not regard such meta-variables (e.g., via an argument filtering [35,46]):

Example 53. We apply Theorem 52 on the DP problem $(SDP(\mathcal{R}), \mathcal{R}, \texttt{computable}_{\mathcal{R}}, \texttt{formative})$ of Example 51. This gives for instance the following ordering requirements:

$$\begin{array}{cc} \texttt{f}\ (\texttt{s}\ X)\ Y \succsim \texttt{g}\ X\ Y & \texttt{f}^\sharp\ (\texttt{s}\ X)\ Y \succ \texttt{g}^\sharp\ X\ \bot_{\texttt{nat}} \\ \texttt{g}\ X \succsim \lambda z.\texttt{f}\ X\ z & \texttt{g}^\sharp\ X\ Y \succcurlyeq \texttt{f}^\sharp\ X\ Z \end{array}$$

The right-hand side of the last DP uses a meta-variable Z that does not occur on the left. As neither $\succ$ nor $\succcurlyeq$ are required to be monotonic (only $\succsim$ is), function symbols do not have to regard all their arguments. Thus, we can use a polynomial interpretation $\mathcal{J}$ to $\mathbb{N}$ with $\mathcal{J}_{\bot_{\texttt{nat}}} = 0$, $\mathcal{J}_{\texttt{s}}(n) = n + 1$ and $\mathcal{J}_{\texttt{h}}(n_1, n_2) = n_1$ for $\texttt{h} \in \{\texttt{f}, \texttt{f}^\sharp, \texttt{g}, \texttt{g}^\sharp\}$. The ordering requirements then translate to $X + 1 \geq X$ and $\lambda y.X \geq \lambda z.X$ for the rules, and $X + 1 > X$ and $X \geq X$ for the DPs. All these inequalities on $\mathbb{N}$ are clearly satisfied, so we can remove the first DP. The remaining problem is quickly dispersed with the dependency graph processor.

5.3 Rule Removal Without Search for Orderings

While processors often simplify only $\mathcal{P}$, they can also simplify $\mathcal{R}$. One of the most powerful techniques in first-order DP approaches that can do this are *usable rules*. The idea is that for a given set $\mathcal{P}$ of DPs, we only need to consider a *subset* $UR(\mathcal{P}, \mathcal{R})$ of $\mathcal{R}$. Combined with the dependency graph processor, this makes it possible to split a large term rewriting system into a number of small problems.

In the higher-order setting, simple versions of usable rules have also been defined [31,46]. We can easily extend these definitions to AFSMs:

Theorem 54. *Given a DP problem* $M = (\mathcal{P}, \mathcal{R}, m, f)$ *with* $m \succeq \texttt{minimal}$ *and* $\mathcal{R}$ *finite, let* $UR(\mathcal{P}, \mathcal{R})$ *be the smallest subset of* $\mathcal{R}$ *such that:*

- *if a symbol* $\texttt{f}$ *occurs in the right-hand side of an element of* $\mathcal{P}$ *or* $UR(\mathcal{P}, \mathcal{R})$, *and there is a rule* $\texttt{f}\ \ell_1 \cdots \ell_k \Rightarrow r$, *then this rule is also in* $UR(\mathcal{P}, \mathcal{R})$;
- *if there exists* $\ell \Rightarrow r \in \mathcal{R}$ *or* $\ell \Rrightarrow r\ (A) \in \mathcal{P}$ *such that* $r \trianglerighteq F\langle s_1, \ldots, s_k\rangle\ t_1 \cdots t_n$ *with* $s_1, \ldots, s_k$ *not all distinct variables or with* $n > 0$, *then* $UR(\mathcal{P}, \mathcal{R}) = \mathcal{R}$.

Then the processor that maps M *to* $\{(\mathcal{P}, UR(\mathcal{P}, \mathcal{R}), \texttt{arbitrary}, \texttt{all})\}$ *is sound.*

For the proof we refer to the very similar proofs in [31,46].

Example 55. For the set $SDP(\mathcal{R})$ of the ordinal recursion example (Examples 8 and 29), all rules are usable due to the occurrence of $H\ M$ in the second DP. For the set $SDP(\mathcal{R})$ of the map example (Examples 6 and 31), there are no usable rules, since the one DP contains no defined function symbols or applied meta-variables.

This higher-order processor is much less powerful than its first-order version: if any DP or usable rule has a sub-meta-term of the form $F\ s$ or $F\langle s_1, \ldots, s_k\rangle$ with $s_1, \ldots, s_k$ not all distinct variables, then *all* rules are usable. Since applying a higher-order meta-variable to some argument is extremely common in higher-order rewriting, the technique is usually not applicable. Also, this processor imposes a heavy price on the flags: minimality (at least) is required, but is lost; the formative flag is also lost. Thus, usable rules are often combined with reduction triples to temporarily disregard rules, rather than as a way to permanently remove rules.

To address these weaknesses, we consider a processor that uses similar ideas to usable rules, but operates from the *left-hand* sides of rules and DPs rather than the right. This adapts the technique from [31] that relies on the new *formative* flag. As in the first-order case [16], we use a semantic characterisation of formative rules. In practice, we then work with over-approximations of this characterisation, analogous to the use of dependency graph approximations in Theorem 45.

Definition 56. *A function FR that maps a pattern ℓ and a set of rules $\mathcal{R}$ to a set $FR(\ell, \mathcal{R}) \subseteq \mathcal{R}$ is a* formative rules approximation *if for all s and γ: if $s \Rightarrow^*_{\mathcal{R}} \ell\gamma$ by an ℓ-formative reduction, then this reduction can be done using only rules in $FR(\ell, \mathcal{R})$.*

We let $FR(\mathcal{P}, \mathcal{R}) = \bigcup\{FR(\ell_i, \mathcal{R}) \mid \mathtt{f}\ \ell_1 \cdots \ell_n \Rrightarrow p\,(A) \in \mathcal{P} \wedge 1 \leq i \leq n\}$.

Thus, a formative rules approximation is a subset of $\mathcal{R}$ that is *sufficient* for a formative reduction: if $s \Rightarrow^*_{\mathcal{R}} \ell\gamma$, then $s \Rightarrow^*_{FR(\ell,\mathcal{R})} \ell\gamma$. It is allowed for there to exist other formative reductions that do use additional rules.

Example 57. We define a simple formative rules approximation: (1) $FR(Z, \mathcal{R}) = \emptyset$ if Z is a meta-variable; (2) $FR(\mathtt{f}\ \ell_1 \cdots \ell_m, \mathcal{R}) = FR(\ell_1, \mathcal{R}) \cup \cdots \cup FR(\ell_m, \mathcal{R})$ if $\mathtt{f} : \sigma_1 \to \ldots \to \sigma_m \to \iota$ and no rules have type ι; (3) $FR(s, \mathcal{R}) = \mathcal{R}$ otherwise. This is a formative rules approximation: if $s \Rightarrow^*_{\mathcal{R}} Z\gamma$ by a Z-formative reduction, then $s = Z\gamma$, and if $s \Rightarrow^*_{\mathcal{R}} \mathtt{f}\ \ell_1 \cdots \ell_m$ and no rules have the same output type as s, then $s = \mathtt{f}\ s_1 \cdots s_m$ and each $s_i \Rightarrow^*_{\mathcal{R}} \ell_i\gamma$ (by an ℓ_i-formative reduction).

The following result follows directly from the definition of formative rules.

Theorem 58 (Formative rules processor). *For a formative rules approximation FR, the processor $Proc_{FR}$ that maps a DP problem $(\mathcal{P}, \mathcal{R}, m, \mathtt{formative})$ to $\{(\mathcal{P}, FR(\mathcal{P}, \mathcal{R}), m, \mathtt{formative})\}$ is both sound and complete.*

Proof (sketch). A processor that only removes rules (or DPs) is always complete. For soundness, if the chain is formative then each step $t_i \Rightarrow^*_{\mathcal{R}} s_{i+1}$ can be replaced by $t_i \Rightarrow^*_{FR(\mathcal{P},\mathcal{R})} s_{i+1}$. Thus, the chain can be seen as a $(\mathcal{P}, FR(\mathcal{P}, \mathcal{R}))$-chain. □

Example 59. For our ordinal recursion example (Examples 8 and 29), *none* of the rules are included when we use the approximation of Example 57 since all rules have output type $\mathtt{ord}$. Thus, $Proc_{FR}$ maps $(SDP(\mathcal{R}), \mathcal{R}, \mathtt{computable}_{\mathcal{R}}, \mathtt{formative})$ to $(SDP(\mathcal{R}), \emptyset, \mathtt{computable}_{\mathcal{R}}, \mathtt{formative})$. *Note:* this example can also be completed without formative rules (see Example 64). Here we illustrate that, even with a simple formative rules approximation, we can often delete all rules of a given type.

Formative rules are introduced in [31], and the definitions can be adapted to a more powerful formative rules approximation than the one sketched in Example 59. Several examples and deeper intuition for the first-order setting are given in [16].

5.4 Subterm Criterion Processors

Reduction triple processors are powerful, but they exert a computational price: we must orient all rules in $\mathcal{R}$. The subterm criterion processor allows us to remove DPs without considering $\mathcal{R}$ at all. It is based on a *projection function* [24], whose higher-order counterpart [31, 34, 46] is the following:

Definition 60. *For $\mathcal{P}$ a set of DPs, let* $\mathtt{heads}(\mathcal{P})$ *be the set of all symbols* $\mathtt{f}$ *that occur as the head of a left- or right-hand side of a DP in $\mathcal{P}$. A* projection function *for $\mathcal{P}$ is a function $\nu : \mathtt{heads}(\mathcal{P}) \to \mathbb{N}$ such that for all DPs $\ell \Rrightarrow p\ (A) \in \mathcal{P}$, the function $\overline{\nu}$ with $\overline{\nu}(\mathtt{f}\ s_1 \cdots s_n) = s_{\nu(\mathtt{f})}$ is well-defined both for ℓ and for p.*

Theorem 61 (Subterm criterion processor). *The processor $Proc_{\mathtt{subcrit}}$ that maps a DP problem $(\mathcal{P}_1 \uplus \mathcal{P}_2, \mathcal{R}, m, f)$ with $m \succeq \mathtt{minimal}$ to $\{(\mathcal{P}_2, \mathcal{R}, m, f)\}$ if a projection function ν exists such that $\overline{\nu}(\ell) \rhd \overline{\nu}(p)$ for all $\ell \Rrightarrow p\ (A) \in \mathcal{P}_1$ and $\overline{\nu}(\ell) = \overline{\nu}(p)$ for all $\ell \Rrightarrow p\ (A) \in \mathcal{P}_2$, is sound and complete.*

Proof (sketch). If the conditions are satisfied, every infinite $(\mathcal{P}, \mathcal{R})$-chain induces an infinite $\unrhd \cdot \Rightarrow_{\mathcal{R}}^*$ sequence that starts in a strict subterm of t_1, contradicting minimality unless all but finitely many steps are equality. Since every occurrence of a pair in $\mathcal{P}_1$ results in a strict $\rhd$ step, a tail of the chain lies in $\mathcal{P}_2$. □

Example 62. Using $\nu(\mathtt{map}^\sharp) = 2$, $Proc_{\mathtt{subcrit}}$ maps the DP problem $(\{(1)\}, \mathcal{R}, \mathtt{computable}_{\mathcal{R}}, \mathtt{formative})$ from Example 47 to $\{(\emptyset, \mathcal{R}, \mathtt{computable}_{\mathcal{R}}, \mathtt{formative})\}$.

The subterm criterion can be strengthened, following [34, 46], to also handle DPs like the one in Example 28. Here, we focus on a new idea. For *computable* chains, we can build on the idea of the subterm criterion to get something more.

Theorem 63 (Computable subterm criterion processor). *The processor $Proc_{\mathtt{statcrit}}$ that maps a DP problem $(P_1 \uplus \mathcal{P}_2, \mathcal{R}, \mathtt{computable}_{\mathcal{U}}, f)$ to $\{(\mathcal{P}_2, \mathcal{R}, \mathtt{computable}_{\mathcal{U}}, f)\}$ if a projection function ν exists such that $\overline{\nu}(\ell) \sqsupset \overline{\nu}(p)$ for all $\ell \Rrightarrow p\ (A) \in \mathcal{P}_1$ and $\overline{\nu}(\ell) = \overline{\nu}(p)$ for all $\ell \Rrightarrow p\ (A) \in \mathcal{P}_2$, is sound and complete. Here, $\sqsupset$ is the relation on base-type terms with $s \sqsupset t$ if $s \neq t$ and (a) $s \unrhd_{\mathtt{acc}} t$ or (b) a meta-variable Z exists with $s \unrhd_{\mathtt{acc}} Z\langle x_1, \ldots, x_k\rangle$ and $t = Z\langle t_1, \ldots, t_k\rangle\ s_1 \cdots s_n$.*

Proof (sketch). By the conditions, every infinite $(\mathcal{P}, \mathcal{R})$-chain induces an infinite $(\Rrightarrow_{C_{\mathcal{U}}} \cup \Rrightarrow_{\beta})^* \cdot \Rightarrow_{\mathcal{R}}^*$ sequence (where $C_{\mathcal{U}}$ is defined following Theorem 13). This contradicts computability unless there are only finitely many inequality steps. As pairs in $\mathcal{P}_1$ give rise to a strict decrease, they may occur only finitely often. □

Example 64. Following Examples 8 and 29, consider the projection function ν with $\nu(\mathtt{rec}^\sharp) = 1$. As $\mathtt{s}\ X \unrhd_{\mathtt{acc}} X$ and $\mathtt{lim}\ H \unrhd_{\mathtt{acc}} H$, both $\mathtt{s}\ X \sqsupset X$ and $\mathtt{lim}\ H \sqsupset H\ M$ hold. Thus $Proc_{\mathtt{statc}}(\mathcal{P}, \mathcal{R}, \mathtt{computable}_{\mathcal{R}}, \mathtt{formative}) = \{(\emptyset, \mathcal{R}, \mathtt{computable}_{\mathcal{R}}, \mathtt{formative})\}$. By the dependency graph processor, the AFSM is terminating.

The computable subterm criterion processor fundamentally relies on the new $\mathtt{computable}_{\mathcal{U}}$ flag, so it has no counterpart in the literature so far.

5.5 Non-termination

While (most of) the processors presented so far are complete, none of them can actually return NO. We have not yet implemented such a processor; however, we can already provide a general specification of a *non-termination processor.*

Theorem 65 (Non-termination processor). *Let $M = (\mathcal{P}, \mathcal{R}, m, f)$ be a DP problem. The processor that maps M to* NO *if it determines that a sufficient criterion for non-termination of $\Rightarrow_{\mathcal{R}}$ or for existence of an infinite conservative $(\mathcal{P}, \mathcal{R})$-chain according to the flags m and f holds is sound and complete.*

Proof. Obvious. □

This is a very general processor, which does not tell us *how* to determine such a sufficient criterion. However, it allows us to conclude non-termination as part of the framework by identifying a suitable infinite chain.

Example 66. If we can find a finite $(\mathcal{P}, \mathcal{R})$-chain $[(\rho_0, s_0, t_0), \dots, (\rho_n, s_n, t_n)]$ with $t_n = s_0\gamma$ for some substitution γ which uses only conservative DPs, is formative if $f = \mathtt{formative}$ and is $\mathcal{U}$-computable if $m = \mathtt{computable}_{\mathcal{U}}$, such a chain is clearly a sufficient criterion: there is an infinite chain $[(\rho_0, s_0, t_0), \dots, (\rho_0, s_0\gamma, t_0\gamma), \dots, (\rho_0, s_0\gamma\gamma, t_0\gamma\gamma), \dots]$. If $m = \mathtt{minimal}$ and we find such a chain that is however not minimal, then note that $\Rightarrow_{\mathcal{R}}$ is non-terminating, which also suffices.

For example, for a DP problem $(\mathcal{P}, \mathcal{R}, \mathtt{minimal}, \mathtt{all})$ with $\mathcal{P} = \{\mathtt{f}^\sharp\ F\ X \Rrightarrow \mathtt{g}^\sharp\ (F\ X),\ \mathtt{g}^\sharp\ X \Rrightarrow \mathtt{f}^\sharp\ \mathtt{h}\ X\}$, there is a finite dependency chain: $[(\mathtt{f}^\sharp\ F\ X \Rrightarrow \mathtt{g}^\sharp\ (F\ X),\ \mathtt{f}^\sharp\,\mathtt{h}\,x,\ \mathtt{g}^\sharp\ (\mathtt{h}\ x)),\ \ (\mathtt{g}^\sharp\ X \Rrightarrow \mathtt{f}^\sharp\,\mathtt{h}\,X,\ \mathtt{g}^\sharp\ (\mathtt{h}\ x),\ \mathtt{f}^\sharp\,\mathtt{h}\,(\mathtt{h}\ x))]$. As $\mathtt{f}^\sharp\,\mathtt{h}\,(\mathtt{h}\ x)$ is an instance of $\mathtt{f}^\sharp\ \mathtt{h}\ x$, the processor maps this DP problem to NO.

To instantiate Theorem 65, we can borrow non-termination criteria from first-order rewriting [13,21,42], with minor adaptions to the typed setting. Of course, it is worthwhile to also investigate dedicated higher-order non-termination criteria.

6 Conclusions and Future Work

We have built on the static dependency pair approach [6,33,34,46] and formulated it in the language of the DP *framework* from first-order rewriting [20,22]. Our formulation is based on AFSMs, a dedicated formalism designed to make termination proofs transferrable to various higher-order rewriting formalisms.

This framework has two important additions over existing higher-order DP approaches in the literature. First, we consider not only arbitrary and minimally non-terminating dependency chains, but also minimally *non-computable* chains; this is tracked by the $\mathtt{computable}_{\mathcal{U}}$ flag. Using the flag, a dedicated processor allows us to efficiently handle rules like Example 8. This flag has no counterpart in the first-order setting. Second, we have generalised the idea of formative rules in [31] to a notion of formative *chains*, tracked by a `formative` flag. This makes it possible to define a corresponding processor that permanently removes rules.

Implementation and Experiments. To provide a strong formal groundwork, we have presented several processors in a general way, using semantic definitions of, e.g., the dependency graph approximation and formative rules rather than syntactic definitions using functions like *TCap* [21]. Even so, most parts of the DP framework for AFSMs have been implemented in the open-source termination prover WANDA [28], alongside a dynamic DP framework [31] and a mechanism to delegate some ordering constraints to a first-order tool [14]. For reduction triples, polynomial interpretations [15] and a version of HORPO [29, Ch. 5] are used. To solve the constraints arising in the search for these orderings, and also to determine sort orderings (for the accessibility relation) and projection functions (for the subterm criteria), WANDA employs an external SAT-solver. WANDA has won the higher-order category of the International Termination Competition [50] four times. In the International Confluence Competition [10], the tools ACPH [40] and CSI^ho [38] use WANDA as their "oracle" for termination proofs on HRSs.

We have tested WANDA on the *Termination Problems Data Base* [49], using AProVE [19] and MiniSat [12] as back-ends. When no additional features are enabled, WANDA proves termination of 124 (out of 198) benchmarks with static DPs, versus 92 with only a search for reduction orderings; a 34% increase. When all features except static DPs are enabled, WANDA succeeds on 153 benchmarks, versus 166 with also static DPs; an 8% increase, or alternatively, a 29% decrease in failure rate. The full evaluation is available in [17, Appendix D].

Future Work. While the static and the dynamic DP approaches each have their own strengths, there has thus far been little progress on a *unified* approach, which could take advantage of the syntactic benefits of both styles. We plan to combine the present work with the ideas of [31] into such a unified DP framework.

In addition, we plan to extend the higher-order DP framework to rewriting with *strategies*, such as implicit β-normalisation or strategies inspired by functional programming languages like OCaml and Haskell. Other natural directions are dedicated automation to detect non-termination, and reducing the number of term constraints solved by the reduction triple processor via a tighter integration with usable and formative rules with respect to argument filterings.

References

1. Aczel, P.: A general Church-Rosser theorem. Unpublished Manuscript, University of Manchester (1978)
2. Arts, T., Giesl, J.: Termination of term rewriting using dependency pairs. Theor. Comput. Sci. **236**(1–2), 133–178 (2000). https://doi.org/10.1016/S0304-3975(99)00207-8
3. Baader, F., Nipkow, F.: Term Rewriting and All That. Cambridge University Press, Cambridge (1998)
4. Bachmair, L., Ganzinger, H.: Rewrite-based equational theorem proving with selection and simplification. J. Logic Comput. **4**(3), 217–247 (1994). https://doi.org/10.1093/logcom/4.3.217

5. Blanqui, F.: Termination and confluence of higher-order rewrite systems. In: Bachmair, L. (ed.) RTA 2000. LNCS, vol. 1833, pp. 47–61. Springer, Heidelberg (2000). https://doi.org/10.1007/10721975_4
6. Blanqui, F.: Higher-order dependency pairs. In: Proceedings of the WST 2006 (2006)
7. Blanqui, F.: Termination of rewrite relations on λ-terms based on Girard's notion of reducibility. Theor. Comput. Sci. **611**, 50–86 (2016). https://doi.org/10.1016/j.tcs.2015.07.045
8. Blanqui, F., Jouannaud, J., Okada, M.: Inductive-data-type systems. Theor. Comput. Sci. **272**(1–2), 41–68 (2002). https://doi.org/10.1016/S0304-3975(00)00347-9
9. Blanqui, F., Jouannaud, J., Rubio, A.: The computability path ordering. Logical Methods Comput. Sci. **11**(4) (2015). https://doi.org/10.2168/LMCS-11(4:3)2015
10. Community. The International Confluence Competition (CoCo) (2018). http://project-coco.uibk.ac.at/
11. Dershowitz, N., Kaplan, S.: Rewrite, rewrite, rewrite, rewrite, rewrite. In: Conference Record of the Sixteenth Annual ACM Symposium on Principles of Programming Languages, Austin, Texas, USA, 11–13 January 1989, pp. 250–259. ACM Press (1989). https://doi.org/10.1145/75277.75299
12. Eén, N., Sörensson, N.: An extensible SAT-solver. In: Giunchiglia, E., Tacchella, A. (eds.) SAT 2003. LNCS, vol. 2919, pp. 502–518. Springer, Heidelberg (2004). https://doi.org/10.1007/978-3-540-24605-3_37
13. Emmes, F., Enger, T., Giesl, J.: Proving non-looping non-termination automatically. In: Gramlich, B., Miller, D., Sattler, U. (eds.) IJCAR 2012. LNCS (LNAI), vol. 7364, pp. 225–240. Springer, Heidelberg (2012). https://doi.org/10.1007/978-3-642-31365-3_19
14. Fuhs, C., Kop, C.: Harnessing first order termination provers using higher order dependency pairs. In: Tinelli, C., Sofronie-Stokkermans, V. (eds.) FroCoS 2011. LNCS (LNAI), vol. 6989, pp. 147–162. Springer, Heidelberg (2011). https://doi.org/10.1007/978-3-642-24364-6_11
15. Fuhs, C., Kop, C.: Polynomial interpretations for higher-order rewriting. In: Tiwari, A. (ed.) 23rd International Conference on Rewriting Techniques and Applications (RTA 2012) , RTA 2012. LIPIcs, vol. 15, Nagoya, Japan, 28 May–2 June 2012. pp. 176–192. Schloss Dagstuhl - Leibniz-Zentrum fuer Informatik (2012). https://doi.org/10.4230/LIPIcs.RTA.2012.176
16. Fuhs, C., Kop, C.: First-order formative rules. In: Dowek, G. (ed.) RTA 2014. LNCS, vol. 8560, pp. 240–256. Springer, Cham (2014). https://doi.org/10.1007/978-3-319-08918-8_17
17. Fuhs, C., Kop, C.: A static higher-order dependency pair framework (extended version). Technical report arXiv:1902.06733 [cs.LO], CoRR (2019)
18. Fuhs, C., Kop, C., Nishida, N.: Verifying procedural programs via constrained rewriting induction. ACM Trans. Comput. Logic **18**(2), 14:1–14:50 (2017). https://doi.org/10.1145/3060143
19. Giesl, J., et al.: Analyzing program termination and complexity automatically with AProVE. J. Autom. Reasoning **58**(1), 3–31 (2017). https://doi.org/10.1007/s10817-016-9388-y
20. Giesl, J., Thiemann, R., Schneider-Kamp, P.: The dependency pair framework: combining techniques for automated termination proofs. In: Baader, F., Voronkov, A. (eds.) LPAR 2005. LNCS (LNAI), vol. 3452, pp. 301–331. Springer, Heidelberg (2005). https://doi.org/10.1007/978-3-540-32275-7_21

21. Giesl, J., Thiemann, R., Schneider-Kamp, P.: Proving and disproving termination of higher-order functions. In: Gramlich, B. (ed.) FroCoS 2005. LNCS (LNAI), vol. 3717, pp. 216–231. Springer, Heidelberg (2005). https://doi.org/10.1007/11559306_12
22. Giesl, J., Thiemann, R., Schneider-Kamp, P., Falke, S.: Mechanizing and improving dependency pairs. J. Autom. Reasoning **37**(3), 155–203 (2006). https://doi.org/10.1007/s10817-006-9057-7
23. Haftmann, F., Nipkow, T.: Code generation via higher-order rewrite systems. In: Blume, M., Kobayashi, N., Vidal, G. (eds.) FLOPS 2010. LNCS, vol. 6009, pp. 103–117. Springer, Heidelberg (2010). https://doi.org/10.1007/978-3-642-12251-4_9
24. Hirokawa, N., Middeldorp, A.: Tyrolean termination tool: techniques and features. Inf. Comput. **205**(4), 474–511 (2007). https://doi.org/10.1016/j.ic.2006.08.010
25. Hoe, J.C., Arvind: Hardware synthesis from term rewriting systems. In: Silveira, L.M., Devadas, S., Reis, R. (eds.) VLSI: Systems on a Chip. IFIPAICT, vol. 34, pp. 595–619. Springer, Boston (2000). https://doi.org/10.1007/978-0-387-35498-9_52
26. Jouannaud, J., Rubio, A.: The higher-order recursive path ordering. In: 14th Annual IEEE Symposium on Logic in Computer Science, Trento, Italy, 2–5 July 1999, pp. 402–411. IEEE Computer Society (1999). https://doi.org/10.1109/LICS.1999.782635
27. Klop, J., Oostrom, V.V., Raamsdonk, F.V.: Combinatory reduction systems: introduction and survey. Theor. Comput. Sci. **121**(1–2), 279–308 (1993). https://doi.org/10.1016/0304-3975(93)90091-7
28. Kop, C.: WANDA - a higher-order termination tool. http://wandahot.sourceforge.net/
29. Kop, C.: Higher order termination. Ph.D. thesis, VU Amsterdam (2012)
30. Kop, C., van Raamsdonk, F.: Higher order dependency pairs for algebraic functional systems. In: Schmidt-Schauß, M. (ed.) Proceedings of the 22nd International Conference on Rewriting Techniques and Applications, RTA 2011. LIPIcs, vol. 10, Novi Sad, Serbia, 30 May–1 June 2011, pp. 203–218. Schloss Dagstuhl - Leibniz-Zentrum fuer Informatik (2011). https://doi.org/10.4230/LIPIcs.RTA.2011.203
31. Kop, C., van Raamsdonk, F.: Dynamic dependency pairs for algebraic functional systems. Logical Methods Comput. Sci. **8**(2), 10:1–10:51 (2012). https://doi.org/10.2168/LMCS-8(2:10)2012
32. Kusakari, K.: Static dependency pair method in rewriting systems for functional programs with product, algebraic data, and ML-polymorphic types. IEICE Trans. **96-D**(3), 472–480 (2013). https://doi.org/10.1587/transinf.E96.D.472
33. Kusakari, K.: Static dependency pair method in functional programs. IEICE Trans. Inf. Syst. **E101.D**(6), 1491–1502 (2018). https://doi.org/10.1587/transinf.2017FOP0004
34. Kusakari, K., Isogai, Y., Sakai, M., Blanqui, F.: Static dependency pair method based on strong computability for higher-order rewrite systems. IEICE Trans. Inf. Syst. **92**(10), 2007–2015 (2009). https://doi.org/10.1587/transinf.E92.D.2007
35. Kusakari, K., Nakamura, M., Toyama, Y.: Argument filtering transformation. In: Nadathur, G. (ed.) PPDP 1999. LNCS, vol. 1702, pp. 47–61. Springer, Heidelberg (1999). https://doi.org/10.1007/10704567_3
36. Meadows, C.A.: Applying formal methods to the analysis of a key management protocol. J. Comput. Secur. **1**(1), 5–36 (1992). https://doi.org/10.3233/JCS-1992-1102

37. Miller, D.: A logic programming language with lambda-abstraction, function variables, and simple unification. J. Logic Comput. **1**(4), 497–536 (1991). https://doi.org/10.1093/logcom/1.4.497
38. Nagele, J.: CoCo 2018 participant: CSI^ho 0.2 (2018). http://project-coco.uibk.ac.at/2018/papers/csiho.pdf
39. Nipkow, T.: Higher-order critical pairs. In: Proceedings of the Sixth Annual Symposium on Logic in Computer Science (LICS 1991), Amsterdam, The Netherlands, 15–18 July 1991, pp. 342–349. IEEE Computer Society (1991). https://doi.org/10.1109/LICS.1991.151658
40. Onozawa, K., Kikuchi, K., Aoto, T., Toyama, Y.: ACPH: system description for CoCo 2017 (2017). http://project-coco.uibk.ac.at/2017/papers/acph.pdf
41. Otto, C., Brockschmidt, M., von Essen, C., Giesl, J.: Automated termination analysis of Java Bytecode by term rewriting. In: Lynch, C. (ed.) Proceedings of the 21st International Conference on Rewriting Techniques and Applications, RTA 2010. LIPIcs, vol. 6, Edinburgh, Scottland, UK, 11–13 July 2010, pp. 259–276. Schloss Dagstuhl - Leibniz-Zentrum fuer Informatik (2010). https://doi.org/10.4230/LIPIcs.RTA.2010.259
42. Payet, É.: Loop detection in term rewriting using the eliminating unfoldings. Theor. Comput. Sci. **403**(2–3), 307–327 (2008). https://doi.org/10.1016/j.tcs.2008.05.013
43. van de Pol, J.: Termination of higher-order rewrite systems. Ph.D. thesis, University of Utrecht (1996)
44. Sakai, M., Kusakari, K.: On dependency pair method for proving termination of higher-order rewrite systems. IEICE Trans. Inf. Syst. **E88-D**(3), 583–593 (2005)
45. Sakai, M., Watanabe, Y., Sakabe, T.: An extension of the dependency pair method for proving termination of higher-order rewrite systems. IEICE Trans. Inf. Syst. **E84-D**(8), 1025–1032 (2001)
46. Suzuki, S., Kusakari, K., Blanqui, F.: Argument filterings and usable rules in higher-order rewrite systems. IPSJ Trans. Program. **4**(2), 1–12 (2011)
47. Tait, W.: Intensional interpretation of functionals of finite type. J. Symbolic Logic **32**(2), 187–199 (1967)
48. Terese: Term Rewriting Systems. Cambridge Tracts in Theoretical Computer Science, vol. 55. Cambridge University Press, Cambridge (2003)
49. Wiki: Termination Problems DataBase (TPDB). http://termination-portal.org/wiki/TPDB
50. Wiki: The International Termination Competition (TermComp) (2018). http://termination-portal.org/wiki/Termination_Competition

7

Types by Need

Beniamino Accattoli[1], Giulio Guerrieri[2(✉)], and Maico Leberle[1]

[1] Inria & LIX, École Polytechnique, UMR 7161, Palaiseau, France
{beniamino.accattoli,maico-carlos.leberle}@inria.fr
[2] Department of Computer Science, University di Bath, Bath, UK
g.guerrieri@bath.ac.uk

Abstract. A cornerstone of the theory of λ-calculus is that intersection types characterise termination properties. They are a flexible tool that can be adapted to various notions of termination, and that also induces adequate denotational models.

Since the seminal work of de Carvalho in 2007, it is known that multi types (*i.e.* non-idempotent intersection types) refine intersection types with quantitative information and a strong connection to linear logic. Typically, type derivations provide bounds for evaluation lengths, and minimal type derivations provide exact bounds.

De Carvalho studied call-by-name evaluation, and Kesner used his system to show the termination equivalence of call-by-need and call-by-name. De Carvalho's system, however, cannot provide exact bounds on call-by-need evaluation lengths.

In this paper we develop a new multi type system for call-by-need. Our system produces exact bounds and induces a denotational model of call-by-need, providing the first tight quantitative semantics of call-by-need.

1 Introduction

Duplications and erasures have always been considered as key phenomena in the λ-calculus—the λI-calculus, where erasures are forbidden, is an example of this. The advent of linear logic [38] gave them a new, prominent logical status. Forbidding erasure and duplication enables single-use resources, i.e. linearity, but limits expressivity, as every computation terminates in linear time. Their controlled reintroduction via the non-linear modality ! recovers the full expressive power of cut-elimination and allows a fine analysis of resource consumption. Duplication and erasure are therefore the key ingredients for logical expressivity, and—via Curry-Howard—for the expressivity of the λ-calculus. They are also essential to understand evaluation strategies.

In a λ-term there can be many β-redexes, that is, places where β-reduction can be applied. In this sense, the λ-calculus is non-deterministic. Non-determinism does not affect the result of evaluation, if any, but it affects whether evaluation terminates, and in how many steps. There are two natural deterministic evaluation strategies, *call-by-name* (shortened to CbN) and *call-by-value* (CbV), which have dual behaviour with respect to duplication and erasure.

Call-by-Name = Silly Duplication + Wise Erasure. CbN *never* evaluates arguments of β-redexes before the redexes themselves. As a consequence, it never evaluates in subterms that will be erased. This is wise, and makes CbN a *normalising strategy*, that is, a strategy that reaches a result whenever one exists[1]. A second consequence is that if the argument of the redex is duplicated then it may be evaluated more than once. This is silly, as it repeats work already done.

Call-by-Value = Wise Duplication + Silly Erasure. CbV, on the other hand, *always* evaluates arguments of β-redexes before the redexes themselves. Consequently, arguments are not re-evaluated—this is wise with respect to duplication—but they are also evaluated when they are going to be erased. For instance, on $t := (\lambda x.\lambda y.y)\Omega$, where Ω is the famous looping λ-term, CbV evaluation diverges (it keeps evaluating Ω) while CbN converges in one β-step (simply erasing Ω). This CbV treatment of erasure is clearly as silly as the duplicated work of CbN.

Call-by-Need = Wise Duplication + Wise Erasure. It is natural to try to combine the advantages of both CbN and CbV. The strategy that is wise with respect to both duplications and erasures is usually called *call-by-need* (CbNeed), it was introduced by Wadsworth [57], and dates back to the '70s. Despite being at the core of Haskell, one of the most-used functional programming languages, and—in its strong variant—being at work in the kernel of Coq as designed by Barras [16], the theory of CbNeed is much less developed than that of CbN or CbV.

One of the reasons for this is that it cannot be defined inside the λ-calculus without some hacking. Manageable presentations of CbNeed indeed require first-class sharing and micro-step operational semantics where variable occurrences are replaced one at a time (when needed), and not all at once as in the λ-calculus. Another reason is the less natural logical interpretation.

Linear Logic, Names, Values, and Needs. CbN and CbV have neat interpretations in linear logic. They correspond to two different representations of intuitionistic logic in linear logic, based on two different representations of implication[2].

The logical interpretation of CbNeed—studied by Maraist et al. in [47]—is less neat than those of CbN and CbV. Within linear logic, CbNeed is usually understood as corresponding to the CbV representation where erasures are generalised to all terms, not only those under the scope of a ! modality. So, it is seen as a sort of *affine* CbV. Such an interpretation however is unusual, because it does not match exactly with cut-elimination in linear logic, as for CbN and CbV.

Call-by-Need, Abstractly. The main theorem of the theory of CbNeed is that it is termination equivalent to CbN, that is, on a fixed term, CbNeed evaluation terminates if and only if CbN evaluation terminates, and, moreover, they essentially

---

[1] If a term t admits both converging and diverging evaluation sequences then the diverging sequences occur in erasable subterms of t, which is why CbN avoids them.

[2] The CbN translation maps $A \Rightarrow B$ to $(!A^{\text{CbN}}) \multimap B^{\text{CbN}}$, while the CbV maps it to $!A^{\text{CbV}} \multimap !B^{\text{CbV}}$, or equivalently to $!(A^{\text{CbV}} \multimap B^{\text{CbV}})$.

produce the same result (up to some technical details that are irrelevant here). This is due to the fact that both strategies avoid silly divergent sequences such as that of $(\lambda x.\lambda y.y)\Omega$. Termination equivalence is an abstract theorem stating that CbNeed erases as wisely as CbN. Curiously, in the literature there are no abstract theorems reflecting the dual fact that CbNeed duplicates as wisely as CbV—we provide one, as a side contribution of this paper.

Call-by-Need and Denotational Semantics. CbNeed is then usually considered as a CbV optimisation of CbN. In particular, every denotational model of CbN is also a model of CbNeed, and adequacy—that is the fact that the denotation of t is not degenerated if and only if t terminates—transfers from CbN to CbNeed.

Denotational semantics is invariant by evaluation, and so is insensitive to evaluation lengths by definition. It then seems that denotational semantics cannot distinguish between CbN and CbNeed. The aim of this paper is, somewhat counter-intuitively, to separate CbN and CbNeed semantically. We develop a type system whose type judgements induce a model—this is typical of *intersection* type systems—and whose type derivations provide exact bounds for CbNeed evaluation—this is usually obtained via *non-idempotent* intersection types. Unsurprisingly, the design of the type system requires a delicate mix of erasure and duplication and builds on the linear logic understanding of CbN and CbV.

Multi Types. Our typing framework is given by *multi types*, which is an alternative name for *non-idempotent intersection types*[3]. Multi types characterise termination properties exactly as intersection types, having moreover the advantages that they are closely related to (the relational semantics of) linear logic, their type derivations provide quantitative information about evaluation lengths, and the proof techniques are simpler—no need for the reducibility method.

The seminal work of de Carvalho [23] (appeared in 2007 but unpublished until 2018, see also [22]) showed how to use multi types to obtain exact bounds on evaluation lengths in CbN. Ehrhard adapted multi types to CbV [34], and very recently Accattoli and Guerrieri adapted de Carvalho's study of exact bounds to Ehrhard's system and CbV evaluation [8]. Kesner used de Carvalho's CbN multi types to obtain a simple proof that CbNeed is termination equivalent to CbN [40] (first proved with other techniques by Maraist, Odersky, and Wadler [48] and Ariola and Felleisen [11] in the nineties), and then Kesner and coauthors continued exploring the theory of CbNeed via CbN multi types [14,15,42].

Kesner's use of CbN multi types to study CbNeed is *qualitative*, as it deals with termination and not with exact bounds. For a *quantitative* study of CbNeed, de Carvalho's CbN system cannot really be informative: CbN multi types provide bounds for CbNeed which cannot be exact because they already provide exact bounds for CbN, which generally takes more steps than CbNeed.

[3] The new terminology is due to the fact that a non-idempotent intersection $A \wedge A \wedge B \wedge C$ can be seen as a multi-set $[A, A, B, C]$.

Multi Types by Need. In this paper we provide the first multi type system characterising CbNeed termination and whose minimal type derivations provide *exact* bounds for CbNeed evaluation lengths. The design of the type system is delicate, as we explain in Sect. 6. One of the key points is that, in contrast to Ehrhard's system for CbV [34], multi types for CbNeed cannot be directly extracted by the relational semantics of linear logic, given that CbNeed does not have a clean representation in it. A by-product of our work is a new denotational semantics of CbNeed, the first one to precisely reflect its quantitative properties.

Beyond the result itself, the paper tries to stress how the key ingredients of our type system are taken from those for CbN and CbV and combined together. To this aim, we first present multi types for CbN and CbV, and only then we proceed to build the CbNeed system and prove its properties.

Along the way, we also prove the missing fundamental property of CbNeed, that is, that it duplicates as efficiently as CbV. The result dualizes the termination equivalence of CbN and CbNeed, which shows that CbNeed erases as wisely as CbN. *Careful*: the CbV system is correct but of course not complete with respect to CbNeed, because CbNeed may normalise when CbV diverges. The proof of the result is straightforward, because of our presentations of CbV and CbNeed. We adopt a liberal, non-deterministic formulation of CbV, and assuming (without loss of generality, see [1]) that garbage collection is always postponed. These two ingredients turn CbNeed into a fragment of CbV, obtaining the new fundamental result as a corollary of correctness of CbV multi types for CbV evaluation.

Technical Development. The paper is extremely uniform, technically speaking. The three evaluations are presented as strategies of Accattoli and Kesner's Linear Substitution Calculus (shortened to LSC) [1,6], a calculus with a simple but expressive form of explicit sharing. The LSC is strongly related to linear logic [2], and provides a neat and manageable presentation of CbNeed, introduced by Accattoli, Barenbaum, and Mazza in [3], and further developed by various authors in [4,5,10,14,15,40,42]. Our type systems count evaluation steps by annotating typing rules in the *exact* same way, and the proofs of correctness and completeness all follow the *exact* same structure. While the results for CbN are very minor variations with respect to those in the literature [7,23], those for CbV are the first ones with respect to a presentation of CbV with sharing.

As it is standard for CbNeed, we restrict our study to closed terms and weak evaluation (that is, out of abstractions). The main consequence of this fact is that normal forms are particularly simple (sometimes called *answers* in the literature). Compared with other recent works dealing with exact bounds such as Accattoli, Graham-Lengrand, and Kesner [7] and Accattoli and Guerrieri [8] the main difference is that the size of normal forms is not taken into account by type derivations. This is because of the simple notions of normal forms in the closed and weak case, and not because the type systems are not accurate.

Related Work About CbNeed. Call-by-need was introduced by Wadsworth [57] in the '70s. In the '90s, it was first reformulated as operational semantics by

Launchbury [46], Maraist, Odersky, and Wadler [48], and Ariola and Felleisen [11,12], and then implemented by Sestoft [55] and further studied by Kutzner and Schmidt-Schauß [45]. More recent papers are Garcia, Lumsdaine, and Sabry [36], Ariola, Herbelin, and Saurin [13], Chang and Felleisen [26], Danvy and Zerny [29], Downen et al. [33], Pédrot and Saurin [53], and Balabonski et al. [14].

Related Work About Multi Types. Intersection types are a standard tool to study λ-calculi—see Coppo and Dezani [27,28], Pottinger [54], and Krivine [44]. Non-idempotent intersection types, *i.e.* multi types, were first considered by Gardner [37], and then by Kfoury [43], Neergaard and Mairson [50], and de Carvalho [23]—a survey is Bucciarelli, Kesner, and Ventura [20].

Many recent works rely on multi types or relational semantics to study properties of programs and proofs. Beyond the cited ones, Diaz-Caro, Manzonetto, and Pagani [32], Carraro and Guerrieri [21], Ehrhard and Guerrieri [35], and Guerrieri [39] deal with CbV, while Bernadet and Lengrand [17], de Carvalho, Pagani, and Tortora de Falco [24] provide exact bounds. Further related work is by Bucciarelli, Ehrhard, and Manzonetto [18], de Carvalho and Tortora de Falco [25], Tsukada and Ong [56], Kesner and Vial [41], Piccolo, Paolini and Ronchi Della Rocca [52], Ong [51], Mazza, Pellissier, and Vial [49], Bucciarelli, Kesner and Ronchi Della Rocca [19]—this list is not exhaustive.

Proofs. Proofs are omitted. They can be found in the technical report [9].

2 Closed λ-Calculi

In this section we define the CbN, CbV, and CbNeed evaluation strategies. We present them in the context of the Accattoli and Kesner's *linear substitution calculus* (LSC) [1,6]. We mainly follow the uniform presentation of these strategies given by Accattoli, Barenbaum, and Mazza [3]. The only difference is that we adopt a non-deterministic presentation of CbV, subsuming both the left-to-right and the right-to-left strategies in [3], that makes our results slightly more general. Such a non-determinism is harmless: not only CbV evaluation is confluent, it even has the diamond property, so that all evaluations have the same length. Moreover, the non-deterministic presentation, together with the postponement of erasing steps discussed below, allows us to see CbNeed as a fragment of CbV, which shall provide a free proof that CbNeed duplicates as wisely as CbV.

Terms and Contexts. The set of terms $\Lambda_{\mathtt{lsc}}$ of the LSC is given by the grammar below, where $t[x{\leftarrow}s]$ is an *explicit substitution* (shortened to ES), that is a more compact notation for $\mathtt{let}\ x = s\ \mathtt{in}\ t$ (intuitively, "t where x will be substituted by s"). Both $\lambda x.t$ and $t[x{\leftarrow}s]$ bind x in t, with the usual notion of α-equivalence.

$$\text{LSC TERMS} \quad t, s, u ::= x \mid v \mid ts \mid t[x{\leftarrow}s] \qquad \text{LSC VALUES} \quad v ::= \lambda x.t$$

The set $\mathtt{fv}(t)$ of *free* variables of a term t is defined as expected, in particular, $\mathtt{fv}(t[x{\leftarrow}s]) := (\mathtt{fv}(t)\setminus\{x\})\cup\mathtt{fv}(s)$. A term t is *closed* if $\mathtt{fv}(t) = \emptyset$, *open* otherwise. As usual, terms are identified up to α-equivalence.

Contexts are terms with exactly one occurrence of the *hole* $\langle\cdot\rangle$, an additional constant. We shall use many different contexts. The most general ones are *weak contexts* W (i.e. not under abstractions). The (evaluation) contexts C, V and E—used to define CbN, CbV and CbNeed evaluation strategies, respectively—are special cases of weak contexts (in fact, CbV contexts coincide with weak contexts, the consequences of that are discussed on p. 8). To define evaluation strategies, *substitution contexts* (*i.e.* lists of explicit substitutions) also play a role.

WEAK CONTEXTS	$W ::= \langle\cdot\rangle \mid Wt \mid W[x\leftarrow t] \mid tW \mid t[x\leftarrow W]$
SUBSTITUTION CONTEXTS	$S ::= \langle\cdot\rangle \mid S[x\leftarrow t]$
CBN CONTEXTS	$C ::= \langle\cdot\rangle \mid Ct \mid C[x\leftarrow t]$
CBV CONTEXTS	$V ::= W$
CBNEED CONTEXTS	$E ::= \langle\cdot\rangle \mid Et \mid E[x\leftarrow t] \mid E\langle\langle x\rangle\rangle[x\leftarrow E']$

We write $W\langle t\rangle$ for the term obtained by replacing the hole $\langle\cdot\rangle$ in context W by the term t. This *plugging* operation, as usual with contexts, can capture variables—for instance $((\langle\cdot\rangle t)[x\leftarrow s])\langle x\rangle = (xt)[x\leftarrow s]$. We write $W\langle\langle t\rangle\rangle$ when we want to stress that the context W does not capture the free variables of t.

Micro-step Semantics. The rewriting rules decompose the usual small-step semantics for λ-calculi, by *substituting linearly* one variable occurrence at the time, and only when such an occurrence is in evaluation position. We emphasise this fact saying that we adopt a *micro-step semantics.* We now give the definitions, examples of evaluation sequences follow right next.

Formally, a micro-step semantics is defined by first giving its *root-steps* and then taking the closure of root-steps under suitable contexts.

MULTIPLICATIVE ROOT-STEP	$S\langle\lambda x.t\rangle s \mapsto_{\mathtt{m}} S\langle t[x\leftarrow s]\rangle$
EXPONENTIAL CBN ROOT-STEP	$C\langle\langle x\rangle\rangle[x\leftarrow t] \mapsto_{\mathsf{e}_{\mathrm{cbn}}} C\langle\langle t\rangle\rangle[x\leftarrow t]$
EXPONENTIAL CBV ROOT-STEP	$V\langle\langle x\rangle\rangle[x\leftarrow S\langle v\rangle] \mapsto_{\mathsf{e}_{\mathrm{cbv}}} S\langle V\langle\langle v\rangle\rangle[x\leftarrow v]\rangle$
EXPONENTIAL CBNEED ROOT-STEP	$E\langle\langle x\rangle\rangle[x\leftarrow S\langle v\rangle] \mapsto_{\mathsf{e}_{\mathrm{need}}} S\langle E\langle\langle v\rangle\rangle[x\leftarrow v]\rangle$

where, in the root-step $\mapsto_{\mathtt{m}}$ (resp. $\mapsto_{\mathsf{e}_{\mathrm{cbv}}}$; $\mapsto_{\mathsf{e}_{\mathrm{need}}}$), if $S := [y_1\leftarrow s_1]\ldots[y_n\leftarrow s_n]$ for some $n \in \mathbb{N}$, then $\mathtt{fv}(s)$ (resp. $\mathtt{fv}(V\langle\langle x\rangle\rangle)$; $\mathtt{fv}(E\langle\langle x\rangle\rangle)$) and $\{y_1,\ldots,y_n\}$ are disjoint. This condition can always be fulfilled by α-equivalence.

The *evaluation strategies* $\rightarrow_{\mathrm{cbn}}$ for CbN, $\rightarrow_{\mathrm{cbv}}$ for CbV, and $\rightarrow_{\mathrm{need}}$ for CbNeed, are defined as the closure of root-steps under CbN, CbV and CbNeed evaluation contexts, respectively (so, all evaluation strategies do not reduce under abstractions, since all such contexts are weak):

CbN	CbV	CbNeed
$\to_{\mathtt{m}_{\text{cbn}}} := C\langle\mapsto_{\mathtt{m}}\rangle$	$\to_{\mathtt{m}_{\text{cbv}}} := V\langle\mapsto_{\mathtt{m}}\rangle$	$\to_{\mathtt{m}_{\text{need}}} := E\langle\mapsto_{\mathtt{m}}\rangle$
$\to_{\mathtt{e}_{\text{cbn}}} := C\langle\mapsto_{\mathtt{e}_{\text{cbn}}}\rangle$	$\to_{\mathtt{e}_{\text{cbv}}} := V\langle\mapsto_{\mathtt{e}_{\text{cbv}}}\rangle$	$\to_{\mathtt{e}_{\text{need}}} := E\langle\mapsto_{\mathtt{e}_{\text{need}}}\rangle$
$\to_{\text{cbn}} := C\langle\mapsto_{\mathtt{m}} \cup \mapsto_{\mathtt{e}_{\text{cbn}}}\rangle$	$\to_{\text{cbv}} := V\langle\mapsto_{\mathtt{m}} \cup \mapsto_{\mathtt{e}_{\text{cbv}}}\rangle$	$\to_{\text{need}} := E\langle\mapsto_{\mathtt{m}} \cup \mapsto_{\mathtt{e}_{\text{need}}}\rangle$

where the notation $\to := W\langle\mapsto\rangle$ means that, given a root-step $\mapsto$, the evaluation $\to$ is defined as follows: $t \to s$ if and only if there are terms t' and s' and a context W such that $t = W\langle t'\rangle$ and $s = W\langle s'\rangle$ and $t' \mapsto s'$.

Note that evaluations $\to_{\text{cbn}}$, $\to_{\text{cbv}}$ and $\to_{\text{need}}$ can equivalently be defined as $\to_{\mathtt{m}_{\text{cbn}}} \cup \to_{\mathtt{e}_{\text{cbn}}}$, $\to_{\mathtt{m}_{\text{cbn}}} \cup \to_{\mathtt{e}_{\text{cbv}}}$ and $\to_{\mathtt{m}_{\text{need}}} \cup \to_{\mathtt{e}_{\text{need}}}$, respectively.

Given an evaluation sequence $d\colon t \to^*_{\text{cbn}} s$ we note with $|d|$ the length of d, and with $|d|_{\mathtt{m}}$ and $|d|_{\mathtt{e}}$ the number of multiplicative and exponential steps in d, respectively—and similarly for $\to_{\text{cbv}}$ and $\to_{\text{need}}$.

Erasing Steps. The reader may be surprised by our evaluation strategies, as none of them includes erasing steps, despite the absolute relevance of erasures pointed out in the introduction. There are no contradictions: in the LSC—in contrast to the λ-calculus—erasing steps can always be postponed (see [1]), and so they are often simply omitted. This is actually close to programming language practice, as the garbage collector acts asynchronously with respect to the evaluation flow. For the sake of clarity let us spell out the erasing rules—they shall nonetheless be ignored in the rest of the paper. In CbN and CbNeed every term is erasable, so the root erasing step takes the following form

$$t[x\leftarrow s] \mapsto_{\mathtt{gc}} t \qquad \text{if } x \notin \mathtt{fv}(t)$$

and it is then closed by weak evaluation contexts.

In CbV only values are erasable; so, the root erasing step in CbV is:

$$t[x\leftarrow S\langle v\rangle] \mapsto_{\mathtt{gc}} S\langle t\rangle \qquad \text{if } x \notin \mathtt{fv}(t)$$

and it is then closed by weak evaluation contexts.

Example 1. A good example to observe the differences between CbN, CbV, and CbNeed is given by the term $t := ((\lambda x.\lambda y.xx)(II))(II)$ where $I := \lambda z.z$ is the identity combinator. In CbN, it evaluates with 5 multiplicative steps and 5 exponential steps, as follows:

$$\begin{array}{ll}
t \to_{\mathtt{m}_{\text{cbn}}} (\lambda y.xx)[x\leftarrow II](II) & \to_{\mathtt{m}_{\text{cbn}}} (xx)[y\leftarrow II][x\leftarrow II] \\
\to_{\mathtt{e}_{\text{cbn}}} ((II)x)[y\leftarrow II][x\leftarrow II] & \to_{\mathtt{m}_{\text{cbn}}} (z[z\leftarrow I]x)[y\leftarrow II][x\leftarrow II] \\
\to_{\mathtt{e}_{\text{cbn}}} (I[z\leftarrow I]x)[y\leftarrow II][x\leftarrow II] & \to_{\mathtt{m}_{\text{cbn}}} w[w\leftarrow x][z\leftarrow I][y\leftarrow II][x\leftarrow II] \\
\to_{\mathtt{e}_{\text{cbn}}} x[w\leftarrow x][z\leftarrow I][y\leftarrow II][x\leftarrow II] & \to_{\mathtt{e}_{\text{cbn}}} (II)[w\leftarrow x][z\leftarrow I][y\leftarrow II][x\leftarrow II] \\
\to_{\mathtt{m}_{\text{cbn}}} x'[x'\leftarrow I][w\leftarrow x][z\leftarrow I][y\leftarrow II][x\leftarrow II] & \to_{\mathtt{e}_{\text{cbn}}} I[x'\leftarrow I][w\leftarrow x][z\leftarrow I][y\leftarrow II][x\leftarrow II]
\end{array}$$

In CbV, t evaluates with 5 multiplicative steps and 5 exponential steps, for instance from right to left, as follows:

$$
\begin{array}{ll}
t \to_{\mathtt{m}_{\mathrm{cbv}}} (\lambda x.\lambda y.xx)(II)(z[z{\leftarrow}I]) & \to_{\mathtt{e}_{\mathrm{cbv}}} (\lambda x.\lambda y.xx)(II)(I[z{\leftarrow}I]) \\
\to_{\mathtt{m}_{\mathrm{cbv}}} (\lambda x.\lambda y.xx)(w[w{\leftarrow}I])(I[z{\leftarrow}I]) & \to_{\mathtt{e}_{\mathrm{cbv}}} (\lambda x.\lambda y.xx)(I[w{\leftarrow}I])(I[z{\leftarrow}I]) \\
\to_{\mathtt{m}_{\mathrm{cbv}}} (\lambda y.xx)[x{\leftarrow}I[w{\leftarrow}I]](I[z{\leftarrow}I]) & \to_{\mathtt{m}_{\mathrm{cbv}}} (xx)[y{\leftarrow}I[z{\leftarrow}I]][x{\leftarrow}I[w{\leftarrow}I]] \\
\to_{\mathtt{e}_{\mathrm{cbv}}} (xI)[y{\leftarrow}I[z{\leftarrow}I]][x{\leftarrow}I][w{\leftarrow}I] & \to_{\mathtt{e}_{\mathrm{cbv}}} (II)[y{\leftarrow}I[z{\leftarrow}I]][x{\leftarrow}I][w{\leftarrow}I] \\
\to_{\mathtt{m}_{\mathrm{cbv}}} x'[x'{\leftarrow}I][y{\leftarrow}I[z{\leftarrow}I]][x{\leftarrow}I][w{\leftarrow}I] & \to_{\mathtt{e}_{\mathrm{cbv}}} I[x'{\leftarrow}I][y{\leftarrow}I[z{\leftarrow}I]][x{\leftarrow}I][w{\leftarrow}I]
\end{array}
$$

Note that the fact that CbN and CbV take the same number of steps is by chance, as they reduce different redexes: CbN never reduce the unneeded redex II associated to y, but it reduces twice the needed II redex associated to x, while CbV reduces both, but each one only once.

In CbNeed, t evaluates in 4 multiplicative steps and 4 exponential steps.

$$
\begin{array}{ll}
t \to_{\mathtt{m}_{\mathrm{need}}} (\lambda y.xx)[x{\leftarrow}II](II) & \to_{\mathtt{m}_{\mathrm{need}}} (xx)[y{\leftarrow}II][x{\leftarrow}II] \\
\to_{\mathtt{m}_{\mathrm{need}}} (xx)[y{\leftarrow}II][x{\leftarrow}z[z{\leftarrow}I]] & \to_{\mathtt{e}_{\mathrm{need}}} (xx)[y{\leftarrow}II][x{\leftarrow}I[z{\leftarrow}I]] \\
\to_{\mathtt{e}_{\mathrm{need}}} (Ix)[y{\leftarrow}II][x{\leftarrow}I][z{\leftarrow}I] & \to_{\mathtt{m}_{\mathrm{need}}} (w[w{\leftarrow}x])[y{\leftarrow}II][x{\leftarrow}I][z{\leftarrow}I] \\
\to_{\mathtt{e}_{\mathrm{need}}} w[w{\leftarrow}I][y{\leftarrow}II][x{\leftarrow}I][z{\leftarrow}I] & \to_{\mathtt{e}_{\mathrm{need}}} I[w{\leftarrow}I][y{\leftarrow}II][x{\leftarrow}I][z{\leftarrow}I]
\end{array}
$$

CbV Diamond Property. CbV contexts coincide with weak ones. As a consequence, our presentation of CbV is non-deterministic, as for instance one can have

$$x[x{\leftarrow}I](y[y{\leftarrow}I]) \;{}_{\mathtt{m}_{\mathrm{cbv}}}{\leftarrow}\; (II)(y[y{\leftarrow}I]) \to_{\mathtt{e}_{\mathrm{cbv}}} (II)(I[y{\leftarrow}I])$$

but it is easily seen that diagrams can be closed in exactly one step (if the two reducts are different). For instance,

$$x[x{\leftarrow}I](y[y{\leftarrow}I]) \to_{\mathtt{e}_{\mathrm{cbv}}} x[x{\leftarrow}I](I[y{\leftarrow}I]) \;{}_{\mathtt{m}_{\mathrm{cbv}}}{\leftarrow}\; (II)(I[y{\leftarrow}I])$$

Moreover, the kind of steps is preserved, as the example illustrates. This is an instance of the strong form of confluence called *diamond property.* A consequence is that either all evaluation sequences normalise or all diverge, and if they normalise they have all the same length and the same number of steps of each kind. Roughly, the diamond property is a form of relaxed determinism. In particular, it makes sense to talk about the number of multiplicative/exponential steps to normal form, independently of the evaluation sequence. The proof of the property is an omitted routine check of diagrams.

Normal Forms. We use two predicates to characterise normal forms, one for both CbN and CbNeed normal forms, for which ES can contain whatever term, and one for CbV normal forms, where ES can only contain normal terms:

$$
\frac{}{\mathsf{normal}(\lambda x.t)} \qquad \frac{\mathsf{normal}(t)}{\mathsf{normal}(t[x{\leftarrow}s])} \qquad \frac{}{\mathsf{normal}_{\mathrm{cbv}}(\lambda x.t)} \qquad \frac{\mathsf{normal}_{\mathrm{cbv}}(t) \quad \mathsf{normal}_{\mathrm{cbv}}(s)}{\mathsf{normal}_{\mathrm{cbv}}(t[x{\leftarrow}s])}
$$

Proposition 1 (Syntactic characterization of closed normal forms). *Let t be a closed term.*

1. CbN and CbNeed*: For* $\mathsf{r} \in \{\text{cbn}, \text{need}\}$*,* t *is* r*-normal if and only if* $\mathsf{normal}(t)$*.*
2. CbV*:* t *is* cbv*-normal if and only if* $\mathsf{normal}_{\text{cbv}}(t)$*.*

The simple structure of normal forms is the main point where the restriction to closed calculi plays a role in this paper.

From the syntactic characterization of normal forms (Proposition 1) it follows immediately that among closed terms, normal forms for CbN and CbNeed coincide, while normal forms for CbV are a subset of them. Such a subset is proper since the closed term $I[x{\leftarrow}\delta\delta]$ (where $I := \lambda z.z$ and $\delta := \lambda y.yy$) is normal for CbN and CbNeed but not for CbV (and it cannot normalise in CbV).

3 Preliminaries About Multi Types

In this section we define basic notions about multi types, type contexts, and (type) judgements that are shared by the three typing systems of the paper.

Multi-sets. The type systems are based on two layers of types, defined in a mutually recursive way, *linear types* L and finite *multi-sets* M of linear types. The intuition is that a linear type L corresponds to a single use of a term, and that an argument t is typed with a multi-set M of n linear types if it is going to end up (at most) n times in evaluation position, with respect to the strategy associated with the type system. The three systems differ on the definition of linear types, that is therefore not specified here, while all adopt the same notion of finite multi-set M of linear types (named *multi type*), that we now introduce:

$$\text{MULTI TYPES} \qquad M, N ::= [L_i]_{i \in J} \quad \text{(for any finite set } J\text{)}$$

where $[\ldots]$ denotes the multi-set constructor. The empty multi-set $[\,]$ (the multi type obtained for $J = \emptyset$) is called *empty (multi) type* and denoted by the special symbol $\mathbf{0}$. An example of multi-set is $[L, L, L']$, that contains two occurrences of L and one occurrence of L'. Multi-set union is noted $\uplus$.

Type Contexts. A *type context* Γ is a (total) map from variables to multi types such that only finitely many variables are not mapped to $\mathbf{0}$. The *domain* of Γ is the set $\mathtt{dom}(\Gamma) := \{x \mid \Gamma(x) \neq \mathbf{0}\}$. The type context Γ is *empty* if $\mathtt{dom}(\Gamma) = \emptyset$.

Multi-set union $\uplus$ is extended to type contexts point-wise, *i.e.* $(\Gamma \uplus \Pi)(x) := \Gamma(x) \uplus \Pi(x)$ for each variable x. This notion is extended to a finite family of type contexts as expected, so that $\biguplus_{i \in J} \Gamma_i$ denotes a finite union of type contexts—it stands for the empty context when $J = \emptyset$. A type context Γ is denoted by $x_1 : M_1, \ldots, x_n : M_n$ (for some $n \in \mathbb{N}$) if $\mathtt{dom}(\Gamma) \subseteq \{x_1, \ldots, x_n\}$ and $\Gamma(x_i) = M_i$ for all $1 \leq i \leq n$. Given two type contexts Γ and Π such that $\mathtt{dom}(\Gamma) \cap \mathtt{dom}(\Pi) = \emptyset$, the type context Γ, Π is defined by $(\Gamma, \Pi)(x) := \Gamma(x)$ if $x \in \mathtt{dom}(\Gamma)$, $(\Gamma, \Pi)(x) := \Pi(x)$ if $x \in \mathtt{dom}(\Pi)$, and $(\Gamma, \Pi)(x) := \mathbf{0}$ otherwise.

$$\frac{}{x\!:\![L] \vdash^{(0,1)} x\!:\!L}\ \mathsf{ax} \qquad \frac{}{\vdash^{(0,0)} \lambda x.t\!:\!\mathsf{normal}}\ \mathsf{normal}$$

$$\frac{\Gamma, x\!:\!M \vdash^{(m,e)} t\!:\!L}{\Gamma \vdash^{(m,e)} \lambda x.t\!:\!M \multimap L}\ \mathsf{fun} \qquad \frac{(\Pi_i \vdash^{(m_i,e_i)} t\!:\!L_i)_{i\in J}}{\biguplus_{i\in J} \Pi_i \vdash^{(\Sigma_{i\in J} m_i, \Sigma_{i\in J} e_i)} t\!:\![L_i]_{i\in J}}\ \mathsf{many}$$

$$\frac{\Gamma \vdash^{(m,e)} t\!:\!M \multimap L \quad \Pi \vdash^{(m',e')} s\!:\!M}{\Gamma \uplus \Pi \vdash^{(m+m'+1,e+e')} ts\!:\!L}\ \mathsf{app} \qquad \frac{\Gamma, x\!:\!M \vdash^{(m,e)} t\!:\!L \quad \Pi \vdash^{(m',e')} s\!:\!M}{\Gamma \uplus \Pi \vdash^{(m+m',e+e')} t[x\leftarrow s]\!:\!L}\ \mathsf{ES}$$

Fig. 1. Type system for CbN evaluation

Judgements. Type judgements are of the form $\Gamma \vdash^{(m,e)} t\!:\!L$ or $\Gamma \vdash^{(m,e)} t\!:\!M$ (noted also $\vdash^{(m,e)} t\!:\!L$ and $\vdash^{(m,e)} t\!:\!M$, respectively, when Γ is the empty context), where the *indices* m and e are natural numbers whose intended meaning is that t evaluates to normal form in m multiplicative steps and e exponential steps, with respect to the evaluation strategy associated with the type system.

To make clear in which type systems the judgement is derived, we write $\Phi \triangleright_{\mathrm{cbn}} \Gamma \vdash^{(m,e)} t\!:\!L$ if Φ is a derivation in the CbN system ending in the judgement $\Gamma \vdash^{(m,e)} t\!:\!L$, and similarly for CbV and CbNeed.

4 Types by Name

In this section we introduce the CbN multi type system, together with intuitions about multi types. We also prove that derivations provide exact bounds on CbN evaluation sequences, and define the induced denotational model.

CbN Types. The system is essentially a reformulation of de Carvalho's system R [23], itself being a type-based presentation of the relational model of the CbN λ-calculus induced by relational model of linear logic via the CbN translation of λ-calculus into linear logic. Definitions:

- CbN *linear types* are given by the following grammar:

  CBN LINEAR TYPES $\qquad L, L' ::= \mathsf{normal} \mid M \multimap L$

  Multi(-sets) types are defined as in Sect. 3, relatively to CbN linear types. Note the linear constant normal (used to type abstractions, which are normal terms): it plays a crucial role in our quantitative analysis of CbN evaluation.
- The CbN *typing rules* are in Fig. 1.
- The many *rule*: it has as many premises as the elements in the (possibly empty) set of indices J. When $J = \emptyset$, the rule has no premises, and it types t with the empty multi type $\mathbf{0}$. The many rule is needed to derive the right premises of the rules app and ES, that have a multi type M on their right-hand side. Essentially, it corresponds to the promotion rule of linear logic, that, in the CbN representation of the λ-calculus, is indeed used for typing the right subterm of applications and the content of explicit substitutions.

– The *size* of a derivation $\Phi \triangleright_{\text{cbn}} \Gamma \vdash^{(m,e)} t : L$ is the sum $m + e$ of the indices. A quick look to the typing rules shows that indices on typing judgements are not needed, as m can be recovered as the number of app rules, and e as the number of ax rules. It is however handy to note them explicitly.

Subtleties and Easy Facts. Let us overview some facts about our presentation of the type system.

1. *Introduction and destruction of multi-sets*: multi-set are introduced on the right by the many rule and on the left by ax. Moreover, on the left they are summed by app and ES.
2. *Vacuous abstractions*: the abstraction rule fun can always abstract a variable x; note that if $M = \mathbf{0}$, then $\Gamma, x : M$ is equal to Γ.
3. *Relevance*: No weakening is allowed in axioms. An easy induction on type derivations shows that

Lemma 1 (Type contexts and variable occurrences for CbN). *Let* $\Phi \triangleright_{\text{cbn}} \Gamma \vdash^{(m,e)} t : L$ *be a derivation. If* $x \notin \mathtt{fv}(t)$ *then* $x \notin \mathtt{dom}(\Gamma)$.

Lemma 1 implies that derivations of closed terms have empty type context. Note that there can be free variables of t not in $\mathtt{dom}(\Gamma)$: the ones only occurring in subterms not touched by the evaluation strategy.

Key Ingredients. Two key points of the CbN system that play a role in the design of the CbNeed one in Sect. 6 are:

1. *Erasable terms and* $\mathbf{0}$: the empty multi type $\mathbf{0}$ is the type of erasable terms. Indeed, abstractions that erase their argument—whose paradigmatic example is $\lambda x.y$—can only be typed with $\mathbf{0} \multimap L$, because of Lemma 1. Note that in CbN every term—even diverging ones—can be typed with $\mathbf{0}$ by rule many (taking 0 premises), because, correctly, in CbN every term can be erased.
2. *Adequacy and linear types*: all CbN typing rules but many assign linear types. And many is used only as right premise of the rules app and ES, to derive M. It is with respect to linear types, in fact, that the adequacy of the system is going to be proved: a term is CbN normalising if and only if it is typable with a linear type, given by Theorems 1 and 2 below.

Tight Derivations. A term may have several derivations, indexed by different pairs (m, e). They always provide upper bounds on CbN evaluation lengths. The interesting aspect of our type systems, however, is that there is a simple description of a class of derivations that provide *exact* bounds for these quantities, as we shall show. Their definition relies on the normal type constant.

Definition 1 (Tight derivations for CbN). *A derivation* $\Phi \triangleright_{\text{cbn}} \Gamma \vdash^{(m,e)} t : L$ *is* tight *(for CbN) if* $L = \mathsf{normal}$ *and* Γ *is empty.*

Example 2. Let us return to the term $t := ((\lambda x.\lambda y.xx)(II))(II)$ used in Example 1 for explaining the difference in reduction lengths among the different strategies. We now give a derivation for it in the CbN type system.

First, let us shorten normal to n. Then, we define Φ as the following derivation for the subterm $\lambda x.\lambda y.xx$ of t:

$$
\dfrac{
  \dfrac{
    \dfrac{}{x:[[\mathsf{n}]\multimap\mathsf{n}]\vdash^{(0,1)} x:[\mathsf{n}]\multimap\mathsf{n}}\,\mathsf{ax}
    \qquad
    \dfrac{\dfrac{}{x:[\mathsf{n}]\vdash^{(0,1)} x:\mathsf{n}}\,\mathsf{ax}}{x:[\mathsf{n}]\vdash^{(0,1)} x:[\mathsf{n}]}\,\mathsf{many}
  }{
    \dfrac{x:[\mathsf{n},[\mathsf{n}]\multimap\mathsf{n}]\vdash^{(1,2)} xx:\mathsf{n}}{x:[\mathsf{n},[\mathsf{n}]\multimap\mathsf{n}]\vdash^{(1,2)} \lambda y.xx:\mathbf{0}\multimap\mathsf{n}}\,\mathsf{fun}
  }\,\mathsf{app}
}{
  \vdash^{(1,2)} \lambda x.\lambda y.xx:[\mathsf{n},[\mathsf{n}]\multimap\mathsf{n}]\multimap(\mathbf{0}\multimap\mathsf{n})
}\,\mathsf{fun}
$$

Now, we need two derivations for II, one of type n, given by Ψ as follows

$$
\dfrac{
  \dfrac{\dfrac{}{z:[\mathsf{n}]\vdash^{(0,1)} z:\mathsf{n}}\,\mathsf{ax}}{\vdash^{(0,1)} \lambda z.z:[\mathsf{n}]\multimap\mathsf{n}}\,\mathsf{fun}
  \qquad
  \dfrac{\dfrac{}{\vdash^{(0,0)} \lambda w.w:\mathsf{n}}\,\mathsf{normal}}{\vdash^{(0,0)} \lambda w.w:[\mathsf{n}]}\,\mathsf{many}
}{
  \vdash^{(1,1)} II:\mathsf{n}
}\,\mathsf{app}
$$

and one of type $[\mathsf{n}]\multimap\mathsf{n}$, given by Ξ as follows

$$
\dfrac{
  \dfrac{\dfrac{}{z:[[\mathsf{n}]\multimap\mathsf{n}]\vdash^{(0,1)} z:[\mathsf{n}]\multimap\mathsf{n}}\,\mathsf{ax}}{\vdash^{(0,1)} \lambda z.z:[[\mathsf{n}]\multimap\mathsf{n}]\multimap([\mathsf{n}]\multimap\mathsf{n})}\,\mathsf{fun}
  \qquad
  \dfrac{\dfrac{\dfrac{}{w:[\mathsf{n}]\vdash^{(0,1)} w:\mathsf{n}}\,\mathsf{ax}}{\vdash^{(0,1)} \lambda w.w:[\mathsf{n}]\multimap\mathsf{n}}\,\mathsf{fun}}{\vdash^{(0,1)} \lambda w.w:[[\mathsf{n}]\multimap\mathsf{n}]}\,\mathsf{many}
}{
  \vdash^{(1,2)} II:[\mathsf{n}]\multimap\mathsf{n}
}\,\mathsf{app}
$$

Finally, we put Φ, Ψ and Ξ together in the following derivation Θ for $t = (s(II))(II)$, where $s := \lambda x.\lambda y.xx$ and $\mathsf{n}^{[\mathsf{n}]} := [\mathsf{n}]\multimap\mathsf{n}$

$$
\dfrac{
  \dfrac{
    \begin{array}{c}\vdots\,\Phi\\ \vdash^{(1,2)} s:[\mathsf{n},\mathsf{n}^{[\mathsf{n}]}]\multimap(\mathbf{0}\multimap\mathsf{n})\end{array}
    \qquad
    \dfrac{
      \begin{array}{c}\vdots\,\Psi\\ \vdash^{(1,1)} II:\mathsf{n}\end{array}
      \quad
      \begin{array}{c}\vdots\,\Xi\\ \vdash^{(1,2)} II:\mathsf{n}^{[\mathsf{n}]}\end{array}
    }{\vdash^{(2,3)} II:[\mathsf{n},\mathsf{n}^{[\mathsf{n}]}]}\,\mathsf{many}
  }{\vdash^{(4,5)} s(II):\mathbf{0}\multimap\mathsf{n}}\,\mathsf{app}
  \qquad
  \dfrac{}{\vdash^{(0,0)} II:\mathbf{0}}\,\mathsf{many}
}{
  \vdash^{(5,5)} (s(II))(II):\mathsf{n}
}\,\mathsf{app}
$$

Note that Θ is a tight derivation and the indices $(5,5)$ correspond to the number of $\mathtt{m}_{\mathrm{cbn}}$-steps and $\mathtt{e}_{\mathrm{cbn}}$-steps, respectively, from t to its cbn-normal form, as shown in Example 1. Theorem 1 below shows that this is not by chance: tight derivations for CbN are minimal and provide exact bounds to evaluation lengths in CbN.

The next two subsections prove the two halves of the properties of the CbN type system, namely correctness and completeness.

4.1 CbN Correctness

Correctness is the fact that *every typable term is CbN normalising.* In our setting it comes with additional quantitative information: the indices m and e of a derivation $\Phi \triangleright_{\text{cbn}} \Gamma \vdash^{(m,e)} t : L$ provide upper bounds on the length of the CbN evaluation of t, that are exact when the derivation is tight.

The proof technique is standard. Moreover, the correctness theorems for CbV and CbNeed in the next sections follow *exactly* the same structure. The proof relies on a quantitative subject reduction property showing that m decreases by *exactly one* at each $\mathtt{m}_{\text{cbn}}$-step, and similarly for e and $\mathtt{e}_{\text{cbn}}$-steps. In turn, subject reduction relies on a linear substitution lemma. Last, correctness for *tight* derivations requires a further property of normal forms.

Let us point out that correctness is stated with respect to closed terms only, but the auxiliary results have to deal with open terms, since they are proved by inductions (over predicates defined by induction) over the structure of terms.

Linear Substitution. The linear substitution lemma states that substituting over a variable occurrence as in the exponential rule consumes exactly one linear type and decreases of one the exponential index e.

Lemma 2 (CbN linear substitution). *If $\Phi \triangleright_{\text{cbn}} \Gamma, x : M \vdash^{(m,e)} C\langle\langle x\rangle\rangle : L$ then there is a splitting $M = [L'] \uplus N$ such that for every derivation $\Psi \triangleright_{\text{cbn}} \Pi \vdash^{(m',e')} t : L'$ there is a derivation $\Phi' \triangleright_{\text{cbn}} \Gamma \uplus \Pi, x : N \vdash^{(m+m',e+e'-1)} C\langle\langle t\rangle\rangle : L$.*

The proof is by induction over CbN evaluation contexts.

Quantitative Subject Reduction. A key point of multi types is that the size of type derivations shrinks after every evaluation step, which is what allows to bound evaluation lengths. Remarkably, the size (defined as the sum of the indices) shrinks by exactly 1 at every evaluation step.

Proposition 2 (Quantitative subject reduction for CbN). *Let $\Phi \triangleright_{\text{cbn}} \Gamma \vdash^{(m,e)} t : L$ be a derivation.*

1. Multiplicative*: if $t \to_{\mathtt{m}_{\text{cbn}}} s$ then $m \geq 1$ and there exists a derivation $\Psi \triangleright_{\text{cbn}} \Gamma \vdash^{(m-1,e)} s : L$.*
2. Exponential*: if $t \to_{\mathtt{e}_{\text{cbn}}} s$ then $e \geq 1$ and there exists a derivation $\Psi \triangleright_{\text{cbn}} \Gamma \vdash^{(m,e-1)} s : L$.*

The proof is by induction on $t \to_{\mathtt{m}_{\text{cbn}}} s$ and $t \to_{\mathtt{e}_{\text{cbn}}} s$, using the linear substitution lemma for the root exponential step.

Tightness and Normal Forms. Since the indices are always non-negative, quantitative subject reduction (Proposition 2) implies that they bound evaluation lengths. The bound is not necessarily exact, as derivations of normal forms can have strictly positive indices. If they are tight, however, they are indexed by $(0, 0)$, as we now show. The proof of this fact (by induction on the predicate normal) requires a slightly different statement, for the induction to go through.

Proposition 3 (normal **typing of normal forms for CbN).** *Let t be such that* $\mathsf{normal}(t)$*, and* $\Phi \triangleright_{\text{cbn}} \Gamma \vdash^{(m,e)} t : \mathsf{normal}$ *be a derivation. Then Γ is empty, and so Φ is tight, and $m = e = 0$.*

The Tight Correctness Theorem. The theorem is then proved by a straightforward induction on the evaluation length relying on quantitative subject reduction (Proposition 2) for the inductive case, and the properties of tight typings for normal forms (Proposition 3) for the base case.

Theorem 1 (CbN tight correctness). *Let t be a closed term. If $\Phi \triangleright_{\text{cbn}} \vdash^{(m,e)} t : L$ then there is s such that $d\colon t \rightarrow^*_{\text{cbn}} s$, with* $\mathsf{normal}(s)$*, $|d|_{\mathtt{m}} \leq m$ and $|d|_{\mathtt{e}} \leq e$. Moreover, if Φ is tight then $|d|_{\mathtt{m}} = m$ and $|d|_{\mathtt{e}} = e$.*

Note that Theorem 1 implicitly states that tight derivations have *minimal* size among derivations.

4.2 CbN Completeness

Completeness is the fact that *every CbN normalising term has a (tight) type derivation.* As for correctness, the completeness theorem is always obtained via three intermediate steps, dual to those for correctness.

Normal Forms. The first step is to prove (by induction on the predicate normal) that every normal form is typable, and is actually typable with a tight derivation.

Proposition 4 (Normal forms are tightly typable for CbN). *Let t be such that* $\mathsf{normal}(t)$*. Then there is tight derivation $\Phi \triangleright_{\text{cbn}} \vdash^{(0,0)} t : \mathsf{normal}$.*

Linear Removal. In order to prove subject expansion, we have to first show that typability can also be pulled back along substitutions, via a linear removal lemma dual to the linear substitution lemma.

Lemma 3 (Linear removal for CbN). *Let $\Phi \triangleright_{\text{cbn}} \Gamma, x : M \vdash^{(m,e)} C\langle\langle s\rangle\rangle : L$, where $x \notin \mathtt{fv}(s)$. Then there exist*
- *a linear type L' and two type contexts Γ' and Π,*
- *a derivation $\Phi' \triangleright_{\text{cbn}} \Gamma' \vdash^{(m',e')} s : L'$, and*
- *a derivation $\Psi \triangleright_{\text{cbn}} \Pi, x : M \uplus [L'] \vdash^{(m'',e'')} C\langle\langle x\rangle\rangle : L$*

such that
- Type contexts*: $\Gamma = \Gamma' \uplus \Pi$.*
- Indices*: $(m, e) = (m' + m'', e' + e'' - 1)$.*

Quantitative Subject Expansion. This property is the dual of subject reduction.

Proposition 5 (Quantitative subject expansion for CbN). *Let $\Phi \triangleright_{\text{cbn}} \Gamma \vdash^{(m,e)} s : L$ be a derivation.*
1. Multiplicative*: if $t \rightarrow_{\mathtt{m}_{\text{cbn}}} s$ then there is a derivation $\Psi \triangleright_{\text{cbn}} \Gamma \vdash^{(m+1,e)} t : L$.*
2. Exponential*: if $t \rightarrow_{\mathtt{e}_{\text{cbn}}} s$ then there is a derivation $\Psi \triangleright_{\text{cbn}} \Gamma \vdash^{(m,e+1)} t : L$.*

The proof is by induction on $t \rightarrow_{\mathtt{m}_{\text{cbn}}} s$ and $t \rightarrow_{\mathtt{e}_{\text{cbn}}} s$, using the linear removal lemma for the root exponential step.

The Tight Completeness Theorem. The theorem is proved by a straightforward induction on the evaluation length relying on quantitative subject expansion (Proposition 5) in the inductive case, and the existence of tight typings for normal forms (Proposition 4) in the base case.

Theorem 2 (CbN tight completeness). *Let t be a closed term. If $d : t \to^*_{\mathrm{cbn}} s$ and* $\mathsf{normal}(s)$ *then there is a tight derivation* $\Phi \triangleright_{\mathrm{cbn}} \vdash^{(|d|_{\mathtt{m}},|d|_{\mathtt{e}})} t : \mathsf{normal}$.

Back to Erasing Steps. Our system can be easily adapted to measure also garbage collection steps (the CbN erasing rule is just before Example 1). First, a new, third index g on judgements is necessary. Second, one needs to distinguish the erasing and non-erasing cases of the app and ES rules, discriminated by the $\mathbf{0}$ type. For instance, the ES rules are (the app rules are similar):

$$\frac{\Gamma \vdash^{(m,e,g)} t : L \quad \Gamma(x) = \mathbf{0}}{\Gamma \vdash^{(m,e,g+1)} t[x{\leftarrow}s] : L}\ \mathsf{ES}_{\mathrm{gc}} \qquad \frac{\Gamma, x : M \vdash^{(m,e,g)} t : L \quad \Pi \vdash^{(m',e',g')} s : M \quad M \neq \mathbf{0}}{\Gamma \uplus \Pi \vdash^{(m+m',e+e',g+g')} t[x{\leftarrow}s] : L}\ \mathsf{ES}$$

The right premise of rule $\mathsf{ES}_{\mathrm{gc}}$ has been removed because the only way to introduce $\mathbf{0}$ is via a many rule with no premises. The index g bounds to the number of erasing steps. In the closed case, however, the bound cannot be, in general, exact. Variables typed with $\mathbf{0}$ by Γ do not exactly match variables not appearing in the typed term (that is the condition triggering the erasing step), because a variable typed with $\mathbf{0}$ may appear in the body of abstractions typed with the normal rule, as such bodies are not typed.

It is reasonable to assume that exact bounds for erasing steps can only by provided by a type system characterising strong evaluation, whose typing rules have to inspect abstraction bodies. These erasing typing rules are nonetheless going to play a role in the design of the CbNeed system in Sect. 6.

4.3 CbN Model

The idea to build the denotational model from the multi type system is that the interpretation (or semantics) of a term is simply the set of its type assignments, *i.e.* the set of its derivable types together with their type contexts. More precisely, let t be a term and $x_1, \ldots, x_n$ (with $n \geq 0$) be pairwise distinct variables. If $\mathtt{fv}(t) \subseteq \{x_1, \ldots, x_n\}$, we say that the list $\vec{x} = (x_1, \ldots, x_n)$ is *suitable for t*. If $\vec{x} = (x_1, \ldots, x_n)$ is suitable for t, the (*relational*) *semantics of t for $\vec{x}$* is

$$[\![t]\!]^{\mathrm{CbN}}_{\vec{x}} := \{((M_1, \ldots, M_n), L) \mid \exists \Phi \triangleright_{\mathrm{cbn}} x_1 : M_1, \ldots, x_n : M_n \vdash^{(m,e)} t : L\}.$$

Subject reduction (Proposition 2) and expansion (Proposition 5) guarantee that the semantics $[\![t]\!]^{\mathrm{CbN}}_{\vec{x}}$ of t (for *any* term t, possibly open) is *invariant* by CbN evaluation. Correctness (Theorem 1) and completeness (Theorem 2) guarantee that, given a *closed* term t, its interpretation $[\![t]\!]^{\mathrm{CbN}}_{\vec{x}}$ is non-empty if and only if t is CbN normalisable, that is, they imply that relational semantics is *adequate*.

$$\frac{}{x : M \vdash^{(0,1)} x : M}\ \mathsf{ax} \qquad \frac{\Gamma \vdash^{(m,e)} t : [N \multimap M] \quad \Pi \vdash^{(m',e')} s : N}{\Gamma \uplus \Pi \vdash^{(m+m'+1,e+e')} ts : M}\ \mathsf{app}$$

$$\frac{\Gamma, x : N \vdash^{(m,e)} t : M}{\Gamma \vdash^{(m,e)} \lambda x.t : N \multimap M}\ \mathsf{fun} \qquad \frac{(\Pi_i \vdash^{(m_i,e_i)} \lambda x.t : L_i)_{i\in J}}{\biguplus_{i\in J} \Pi_i \vdash^{(\Sigma_{i\in J} m_i, \Sigma_{i\in J} e_i)} \lambda x.t : [L_i]_{i\in J}}\ \mathsf{many}$$

$$\frac{\Gamma, x : N \vdash^{(m,e)} t : M \quad \Pi \vdash^{(m',e')} s : N}{\Gamma \uplus \Pi \vdash^{(m+m',e+e')} t[x{\leftarrow}s] : M}\ \mathsf{ES}$$

Fig. 2. Type system for CbV evaluation.

In fact, adequacy also holds with respect to open terms. The issue in that case is that the characterisation of tight derivations is more involved, see Accattoli, Graham-Lengrand and Kesner's [7]. Said differently, weaker correctness and completeness theorems without exact bounds also hold in the open case. The same is true for the CbV and CbNeed systems of the next sections.

5 Types by Value

Here we introduce Ehrhard's CbV multi type system [34] adapted to our presentation of CbV in the LSC, and prove its properties. The system is similar, and yet in many aspects dual, to the CbN one, in particular the grammar of types is different. Linear types for CbV are defined by:

CbV linear types $\qquad L, L' ::= M \multimap N$

Multi(-sets) types are defined as in Sect. 3, relatively to CbV linear types. Note that linear types now have a multi type both as source and as target, and that the normal constant is absent—in CbV, its role is played by $\mathbf{0}$.

The typing rules are in Fig. 2. It is a type-based presentation of the relational model of the CbV λ-calculus induced by relational model of linear logic via the CbV translation of λ-calculus into linear logic. Some remarks:

- *Right-hand types*: all rules but fun assign a multi type to the term on the right-hand side, and not a linear type as in CbN.
- *Abstractions and* many: the many rule has a restricted form with respect to the CbN one, it can only be applied to abstractions, that in turn are the only terms that can be typed with a linear type.
- *Indices*: note as the indices are however incremented (on ax and app) and summed (in many and ES) exactly as in the CbN system.

Intuitions: The Empty Type $\mathbf{0}$. The empty multi-set type $\mathbf{0}$ plays a special role in CbV. As in CbN, it is the type of terms that can be erased, but, in contrast to CbN, not every term is erasable in CbV.

In the CbN multi type system every term, even a diverging one, is typable with $\mathbf{0}$. On the one hand, this is correct, because in CbN every term can be erased, and erased terms can also be divergent, because they are never evaluated. On the other hand, adequacy is formulated with respect to non-empty types: a term terminates if and only if it is typable with a non-empty type.

In CbV, instead, terms have to be evaluated before being erased; and, of course, their evaluation has to terminate. Thus, terminating terms and erasable terms coincide. Since the multi type system is meant to characterise terminating terms, in CbV a term is typable if and only if it is typable with $\mathbf{0}$, as we shall prove in this section. Then the empty type is not a degenerate type excluded for adequacy from the interesting types of a term, as in CbN, it rather is *the* type, characterising (adequate) typability altogether. And this is also the reason for the absence of the constant normal—one way to see it is that in CbV $\mathsf{normal} = \mathbf{0}$.

Note that, in particular, in a type judgement $\Gamma \vdash t : M$ the type context Γ may give the empty type to a variable x occurring in t, as for instance in the axiom $x:\mathbf{0} \vdash x:\mathbf{0}$—this may seem very strange to people familiar with CbN multi types. We hope that instead, according to the provided intuition that $\mathbf{0}$ is the type of termination, it would rather seem natural.

Definition 2 (Tight derivation for CbV). *A derivation* $\Phi \triangleright_{\mathrm{cbv}} \Gamma \vdash^{(m,e)} t : M$ *is* tight *(for CbV) if* $M = \mathbf{0}$ *and* Γ *is empty.*

Example 3. Let's consider again the term $t := ((\lambda x.\lambda y.xx)(II))(II)$ of Example 1 (where $I := \lambda z.z$), for which a CbN tight derivation was given in Example 2, and let us type it in the CbV system with a tight derivation.

We define the following derivation Φ_1 for the subterm $s := \lambda x.\lambda y.xx$ of t

$$\dfrac{\dfrac{\dfrac{\dfrac{\dfrac{\dfrac{}{x:[\mathbf{0}\multimap\mathbf{0}]\vdash^{(0,1)} x:[\mathbf{0}\multimap\mathbf{0}]}\,\mathsf{ax} \qquad \dfrac{}{x:\mathbf{0}\vdash^{(0,1)} x:\mathbf{0}}\,\mathsf{ax}}{x:[\mathbf{0}\multimap\mathbf{0}]\vdash^{(1,2)} xx:\mathbf{0}}\,\mathsf{app}}{x:[\mathbf{0}\multimap\mathbf{0}]\vdash^{(1,2)} \lambda y.xx:\mathbf{0}\multimap\mathbf{0}}\,\mathsf{fun}}{x:[\mathbf{0}\multimap\mathbf{0}]\vdash^{(1,2)} \lambda y.xx:[\mathbf{0}\multimap\mathbf{0}]}\,\mathsf{many}}{\vdash^{(1,2)} s:[\mathbf{0}\multimap\mathbf{0}]\multimap[\mathbf{0}\multimap\mathbf{0}]}\,\mathsf{fun}}{\vdash^{(1,2)} s:[[\mathbf{0}\multimap\mathbf{0}]\multimap[\mathbf{0}\multimap\mathbf{0}]]}\,\mathsf{many}$$

Note that $[\mathbf{0}\multimap\mathbf{0}] \uplus \mathbf{0} = [\mathbf{0}\multimap\mathbf{0}]$, which explains the shape of the type context in the conclusion of the app rule. Next, we define the derivation Φ_2 as follows

$$\dfrac{\dfrac{\dfrac{\dfrac{}{z:[\mathbf{0}\multimap\mathbf{0}]\vdash^{(0,1)} z:[\mathbf{0}\multimap\mathbf{0}]}\,\mathsf{ax}}{\vdash^{(0,1)} \lambda z.z:[\mathbf{0}\multimap\mathbf{0}]\multimap[\mathbf{0}\multimap\mathbf{0}]}\,\mathsf{fun}}{\vdash^{(0,1)} \lambda z.z:[[\mathbf{0}\multimap\mathbf{0}]\multimap[\mathbf{0}\multimap\mathbf{0}]]}\,\mathsf{many} \qquad \dfrac{\dfrac{\dfrac{}{w:\mathbf{0}\vdash^{(0,1)} w:\mathbf{0}}\,\mathsf{ax}}{\vdash^{(0,1)} \lambda w.w:\mathbf{0}\multimap\mathbf{0}}\,\mathsf{fun}}{\vdash^{(0,1)} \lambda w.w:[\mathbf{0}\multimap\mathbf{0}]}\,\mathsf{many}}{\vdash^{(1,2)} II:[\mathbf{0}\multimap\mathbf{0}]}\,\mathsf{app}$$

and the derivation Φ_3 as follows

$$\dfrac{\dfrac{\dfrac{\dfrac{}{x' : \mathbf{0} \vdash^{(0,1)} x' : \mathbf{0}}\ \mathsf{ax}}{\vdash^{(0,1)} \lambda x'.x' : \mathbf{0} \multimap \mathbf{0}}\ \mathsf{fun}}{\vdash^{(0,1)} \lambda x'.x' : [\mathbf{0} \multimap \mathbf{0}]}\ \mathsf{many} \qquad \dfrac{}{\vdash^{(0,0)} I : \mathbf{0}}\ \mathsf{many}}{\vdash^{(1,1)} II : \mathbf{0}}\ \mathsf{app}$$

Finally, we put Φ_1, Φ_2 and Φ_3 together in the following derivation Φ for t

$$\dfrac{\dfrac{\dfrac{\vdots\ \Phi_1}{\vdash^{(1,2)} s : [[\mathbf{0} \multimap \mathbf{0}] \multimap [\mathbf{0} \multimap \mathbf{0}]]} \qquad \dfrac{\vdots\ \Phi_2}{\vdash^{(1,2)} II : [\mathbf{0} \multimap \mathbf{0}]}}{\vdash^{(3,4)} (\lambda x.\lambda y.xx)(II) : [\mathbf{0} \multimap \mathbf{0}]}\ \mathsf{app} \qquad \dfrac{\vdots\ \Phi_3}{\vdash^{(1,1)} II : \mathbf{0}}}{\vdash^{(5,5)} ((\lambda x.\lambda y.xx)(II))(II) : \mathbf{0}}\ \mathsf{app}$$

Note that Φ is a tight derivation and the indices $(5, 5)$ correspond to the number of $\mathtt{m}_{\text{cbv}}$-steps and $\mathtt{e}_{\text{cbv}}$-steps, respectively, from t to its cbv-normal form, as shown in Example 1. Theorem 3 below shows that this is not by chance: tight derivations for CbV are minimal and provide exact bounds to evaluation lengths in CbV.

Correctness (*i.e.* typability implies normalisability) and *completeness* (*i.e.* normalisability implies typability) of the CbV type system with respect to CbV evaluation (together with quantitative information about evaluation lengths) follow exactly the same pattern of the CbN case, *mutatis mutandis.*

5.1 CbV Correctness

Lemma 4 (CbV linear substitution). *Let $\Phi \triangleright_{\text{cbv}} \Gamma, x : M \vdash^{(m,e)} V\langle\langle x\rangle\rangle : N$ and v be a value. There is a splitting $M = O \uplus P$ such that, for any derivation $\Psi \triangleright_{\text{cbv}} \Pi \vdash^{(m',e')} v : O$, there is a derivation $\Phi' \triangleright_{\text{cbv}} \Gamma \uplus \Pi, x : P \vdash^{(m+m',e+e'-1)} V\langle\langle v\rangle\rangle : N$.*

Proposition 6 (Quantitative subject reduction for CbV). *Let $\Phi \triangleright_{\text{cbv}} \Gamma \vdash^{(m,e)} t : M$ be a derivation.*

1. Multiplicative*: if $t \to_{\mathtt{m}_{\text{cbv}}} t'$ then $m \geq 1$ and there exists a derivation $\Phi' \triangleright_{\text{cbv}} \Gamma \vdash^{(m-1,e)} t' : M$.*
2. Exponential*: if $t \to_{\mathtt{e}_{\text{cbv}}} t'$ then $e \geq 1$ and there exists a derivation $\Phi' \triangleright_{\text{cbv}} \Gamma \vdash^{(m,e-1)} t' : M$.*

Proposition 7 (Tight typings for normal forms for CbV). *Let $\Phi \triangleright_{\text{cbv}} \Gamma \vdash^{(m,e)} t : \mathbf{0}$ be a derivation, with $\mathsf{normal}_{\text{cbv}}(t)$. Then Γ is empty, and so Φ is tight, and $m = e = 0$.*

Theorem 3 (CbV tight correctness). *Let t be a closed term. If $\Phi \triangleright_{\text{cbv}} \Gamma \vdash^{(m,e)} t : M$ then there is s such that $d\colon t \to^{*}_{\text{cbv}} s$, with $\mathsf{normal}_{\text{cbv}}(s)$, $|d|_{\mathtt{m}} \leq m$ and $|d|_{\mathtt{e}} \leq e$. Moreover, if Φ is tight then $|d|_{\mathtt{m}} = m$ and $|d|_{\mathtt{e}} = e$.*

5.2 CbV Completeness

Proposition 8 (Normal forms are tightly typable for CbV). *Let t be such that* $\mathsf{normal}_{\mathrm{cbv}}(t)$. *Then there exists a tight derivation* $\Phi \triangleright_{\mathrm{cbv}} \; \vdash^{(0,0)} t : \mathbf{0}$.

Lemma 5 (Linear removal for CbV). *Let* $\Phi \triangleright_{\mathrm{cbv}} \Gamma, x : M \vdash^{(m,e)} V\langle\langle v \rangle\rangle : N$ *and v be a value, where* $x \notin \mathtt{fv}(v)$. *Then, there exist*
- *a multi type M' and two type contexts Γ' and Π,*
- *a derivation* $\Phi' \triangleright_{\mathrm{cbv}} \Gamma' \vdash^{(m',e')} v : M'$ *and*
- *a derivation* $\Psi \triangleright_{\mathrm{cbv}} \Pi, x : M \uplus M' \vdash^{(m'',e'')} V\langle\langle x \rangle\rangle : N$

such that
- Type contexts: $\Gamma = \Gamma' \uplus \Pi$,
- Indices: $(m, e) = (m' + m'', e' + e'' - 1)$.

Proposition 9 (Quantitative subject expansion for CbV). *Let* $\Phi' \triangleright_{\mathrm{cbv}} \Gamma \vdash^{(m,e)} t' : M$ *be a derivation.*
1. Multiplicative*: if* $t \rightarrow_{\mathtt{m}_{\mathrm{cbv}}} t'$ *then there is a derivation* $\Phi \triangleright_{\mathrm{cbv}} \Gamma \vdash^{(m+1,e)} t : M$.
2. Exponential*: if* $t \rightarrow_{\mathtt{e}_{\mathrm{cbv}}} t'$ *then there is a derivation* $\Phi \triangleright_{\mathrm{cbv}} \Gamma \vdash^{(m,e+1)} t : M$.

Theorem 4 (CbV tight completeness). *Let t be a closed term. If* $d : t \rightarrow^*_{\mathrm{cbv}} s$ *with* $\mathsf{normal}_{\mathrm{cbv}}(s)$, *then there is a tight derivation* $\Phi \triangleright_{\mathrm{cbv}} \; \vdash^{(|d|_{\mathtt{m}},|d|_{\mathtt{e}})} t : \mathbf{0}$.

CbV Model. The interpretation of terms with respect to the CbV system is defined as follows (where $\vec{x} = (x_1, \ldots, x_n)$ is a list of variables suitable for t):

$$[\![t]\!]^{\mathrm{CbV}}_{\vec{x}} := \{((M_1, \ldots, M_n), N) \mid \exists \Phi \triangleright_{\mathrm{cbv}} x_1 : M_1, \ldots, x_n : M_n \vdash^{(m,e)} t : N\}.$$

Note that rule fun assigns a linear type but the interpretation considers only multi types. The *invariance* and the *adequacy* of $[\![t]\!]^{\mathrm{CbV}}_{\vec{x}}$ with respect to CbV evaluation are obtained exactly as for the CbN case.

6 Types by Need

CbNeed as a Blend of CbN and CbV. The multi type system for CbNeed is obtained by carefully blending ingredients from the CbN and CbV ones:
- *Wise erasures from CbN*: in CbN wise erasures are induced by the fact that the empty multi type $\mathbf{0}$ (the type of erasable terms) and the linear type normal (the type of normalisable terms) are distinct and every term is typable with $\mathbf{0}$ by using the many rule with 0 premises. Adequacy is then formulated with respect to (non-empty) linear types.
- *Wise duplications from CbV*: in CbV wise duplications are due to two aspects. First, only abstractions can be collected in multi-sets by rule many. This fact accounts for the evaluation of arguments to normal form—that is, abstractions—before being substituted. Second, terms are typed with multi types instead of linear types. Roughly, this second fact allows the first one to actually work because the argument is reduced once for a whole multi set of types, and not once for each element of the multi set, as in CbN.

$$\frac{}{x\!:\!M \vdash^{(0,1)} x\!:\!M}\;\mathsf{ax} \qquad \frac{\Gamma \vdash^{(m,e)} t\!:\![N \multimap M] \quad \Pi \vdash^{(m',e')} s\!:\!N}{\Gamma \uplus \Pi \vdash^{(m+m'+1,e+e')} ts\!:\!M}\;\mathsf{app}$$

$$\frac{}{\vdash^{(0,0)} t\!:\!\mathbf{0}}\;\mathsf{many}_0 \qquad \frac{(\Pi_i \vdash^{(m_i,e_i)} \lambda x.t\!:\!L_i)_{i\in J} \quad J \neq \emptyset}{\biguplus_{i\in J} \Pi_i \vdash^{(\Sigma_{i\in J} m_i, \Sigma_{i\in J} e_i)} \lambda x.t\!:\![L_i]_{i\in J}}\;\mathsf{many}_{>0}$$

$$\frac{\Gamma, x\!:\!N \vdash^{(m,e)} t\!:\!M}{\Gamma \vdash^{(m,e)} \lambda x.t\!:\!N \multimap M}\;\mathsf{fun} \qquad \frac{\Gamma, x\!:\!N \vdash^{(m,e)} t\!:\!M \quad \Pi \vdash^{(m',e')} s\!:\!N}{\Gamma \uplus \Pi \vdash^{(m+m',e+e')} t[x{\leftarrow}s]\!:\!M}\;\mathsf{ES}$$

$$\frac{}{\vdash^{(0,0)} \lambda x.t\!:\!\mathsf{normal}}\;\mathsf{normal}$$

Fig. 3. Naïve type system for CbNeed evaluation.

It seems then that a type system for CbNeed can easily be obtained by basically adopting the CbV system plus

- separating $\mathbf{0}$ and normal, that is, adding normal to the system;
- modifying the many rule by distinguishing two cases: with 0 premises it can assign $\mathbf{0}$ to whatever term—as in CbN—otherwise it is forced to work on abstractions, as in CbV;
- restricting adequacy to non-empty types.

Therefore, the grammar of linear types is:

$$\text{CbNeed linear types} \qquad L, L' ::= \mathsf{normal} \mid M \multimap N$$

Multi(-sets) types are defined as in Sect. 3, relatively to CbNeed linear types. The rules of this *naïve system* for CbNeed are in Fig. 3.

Issue with the Naïve System. Unfortunately, the naïve system does not work: tight derivations—defined as expected: empty type context and the term typed with [normal]—do not provide exact bounds. The problem is that the naïve blend of ingredients allows derivations of $\mathbf{0}$ with strictly positive indices m and e. Instead, derivations of $\mathbf{0}$ should always have 0 in both indices—as is the case when they are derived with a many_0 rule with 0 premises—because they correspond to terms to be erased, that are not evaluated in CbNeed. For any term t, indeed, one can for instance derive the following derivation Φ:

$$\dfrac{\dfrac{\dfrac{\dfrac{}{\vdash^{(0,0)} x\!:\!\mathbf{0}}\;\mathsf{many}_0}{\vdash^{(0,0)} \lambda x.x\!:\!\mathbf{0} \multimap \mathbf{0}}\;\mathsf{fun}}{\vdash^{(0,0)} \lambda x.x\!:\![\mathbf{0} \multimap \mathbf{0}]}\;\mathsf{many}_{>0} \qquad \dfrac{}{\vdash^{(0,0)} t\!:\!\mathbf{0}}\;\mathsf{many}_0}{\vdash^{(1,0)} (\lambda x.x)t\!:\!\mathbf{0}}\;\mathsf{app}$$

Note that introducing $\vdash^{(0,1)} x:\mathbf{0}$ with rule ax rather than via many_0 (the typing context $x:\mathbf{0}$ is equivalent to the empty type context) would give a derivation with final judgement $\vdash^{(1,1)} (\lambda x.x)t:\mathbf{0}$—thus, the system messes up both indices.

Such bad derivations of $\mathbf{0}$ are not a problem *per se*, because in CbNeed one expects correctness and completeness to hold only for derivations of non-empty multi types. However, they do mess up also derivations of non-empty multi types because they can still appear *inside* tight derivations, as sub-derivations of subterms to be erased; consider for instance:

$$\dfrac{\dfrac{\dfrac{\dfrac{\dfrac{}{\vdash^{(0,0)} I:\mathsf{normal}}\,\mathsf{normal}}{\vdash^{(0,0)} I:[\mathsf{normal}]}\,\mathsf{many}_{>0}}{\vdash^{(0,0)} \lambda y.I:\mathbf{0}\multimap[\mathsf{normal}]}\,\mathsf{fun}}{\vdash^{(0,0)} \lambda y.I:[\mathbf{0}\multimap[\mathsf{normal}]]}\,\mathsf{many}_{>0} \qquad \begin{array}{c}\vdots\,\Phi\\ \vdash^{(1,0)} (\lambda x.x)t:\mathbf{0}\end{array}}{\vdash^{(2,0)} (\lambda y.I)((\lambda x.x)t):[\mathsf{normal}]}\,\mathsf{app}$$

The term normalises in just 1 $\mathtt{m}_{\mathrm{need}}$-step to $I[y{\leftarrow}(\lambda x.x)t]$ but the multiplicative index of the derivation is 2. The mismatch is due to a bad derivation of $\mathbf{0}$ used as right premise of an app rule. Similarly, the induced typing of $I[y{\leftarrow}(\lambda x.x)t]$ is an example of a bad derivation used as right premise of a rule ES:

$$\dfrac{\dfrac{\dfrac{}{\vdash^{(0,0)} I:\mathsf{normal}}\,\mathsf{normal}}{\vdash^{(0,0)} I:[\mathsf{normal}]}\,\mathsf{many}_{>0} \qquad \begin{array}{c}\vdots\,\Phi\\ \vdash^{(1,0)} (\lambda x.x)t:\mathbf{0}\end{array}}{\vdash^{(1,0)} I[y{\leftarrow}(\lambda x.x)t]:[\mathsf{normal}]}\,\mathsf{ES}$$

The Actual Type System. Our solution to such an issue is to modify the system as to avoid derivations of $\mathbf{0}$ to appear as right premises of rules app and ES. We follow the schema of the rules for counting erasing steps given right after Theorem 2.

Therefore, we add two dedicated rules $\mathsf{app}_{\mathrm{gc}}$ and $\mathsf{ES}_{\mathrm{gc}}$, and constrain the right premise of rules app and ES to have a non-empty type. The system is in Fig. 4 and it is based on the same grammar of types of the naïve system. Note that rules many and ax can still introduce $\mathbf{0}$. These $\mathbf{0}$s, however, can no longer mess up the indices of tight derivations, as we are going to show.

Note that the indices m and e are incremented and summed exactly as in the CbN and CbV type systems.

Definition 3 (Tight derivations for CbNeed). *A derivation* $\Phi \rhd_{\mathrm{need}} \Gamma \vdash^{(m,e)} t:M$ *is* tight *(for CbNeed) if* $M = [\mathsf{normal}]$ *and* Γ *is empty.*

Example 4. We return to the term $t := ((\lambda x.\lambda y.xx)(II))(II)$ used in Example 1 and we give it a tight derivation in the CbNeed type system.

Again, we shorten normal to n. Then, we define Ψ as follows

$$
\dfrac{}{x : M \vdash^{(0,1)} x : M}\;\mathsf{ax}
\qquad
\dfrac{}{\vdash^{(0,0)} \lambda x.t : \mathsf{normal}}\;\mathsf{normal}
$$

$$
\dfrac{\Gamma, x : N \vdash^{(m,e)} t : M}{\Gamma \vdash^{(m,e)} \lambda x.t : N \multimap M}\;\mathsf{fun}
\qquad
\dfrac{(\Gamma_i \vdash^{(m_i,e_i)} \lambda x.t : L_i)_{i\in J}}{\biguplus_{i\in J} \Gamma_i \vdash^{(\Sigma_{i\in J} m_i, \Sigma_{i\in J} e_i)} \lambda x.t : [L_i]_{i\in J}}\;\mathsf{many}
$$

$$
\dfrac{\Gamma \vdash^{(m,e)} t : [\mathbf{0} \multimap M]}{\Gamma \vdash^{(m+1,e)} ts : M}\;\mathsf{app}_{\mathrm{gc}}
\qquad
\dfrac{\Gamma \vdash^{(m,e)} t : [N \multimap M] \quad \Pi \vdash^{(m',e')} s : N \quad N \neq \mathbf{0}}{\Gamma \uplus \Pi \vdash^{(m+m'+1,e+e')} ts : M}\;\mathsf{app}
$$

$$
\dfrac{\Gamma \vdash^{(m,e)} t : M \quad \Gamma(x) = \mathbf{0}}{\Gamma \vdash^{(m,e)} t[x\leftarrow s] : M}\;\mathsf{ES}_{\mathrm{gc}}
\qquad
\dfrac{\Gamma, x : N \vdash^{(m,e)} t : M \quad \Pi \vdash^{(m',e')} s : N \quad N \neq \mathbf{0}}{\Gamma \uplus \Pi \vdash^{(m+m',e+e')} t[x\leftarrow s] : M}\;\mathsf{ES}
$$

Fig. 4. Type system for CbNeed evaluation.

$$
\dfrac{\dfrac{\dfrac{\dfrac{\dfrac{\dfrac{}{x : [[\mathsf{n}] \multimap [\mathsf{n}]] \vdash^{(0,1)} x : [[\mathsf{n}] \multimap [\mathsf{n}]]}\;\mathsf{ax} \qquad \dfrac{}{x : [\mathsf{n}] \vdash^{(0,1)} x : [\mathsf{n}]}\;\mathsf{ax}}{x : [\mathsf{n}, [\mathsf{n}] \multimap [\mathsf{n}]] \vdash^{(1,2)} xx : [\mathsf{n}]}\;\mathsf{app}}{x : [\mathsf{n}, [\mathsf{n}] \multimap [\mathsf{n}]] \vdash^{(1,2)} \lambda y.xx : \mathbf{0} \multimap [\mathsf{n}]}\;\mathsf{fun}}{x : [\mathsf{n}, [\mathsf{n}] \multimap [\mathsf{n}]] \vdash^{(1,2)} \lambda y.xx : [\mathbf{0} \multimap [\mathsf{n}]]}\;\mathsf{many}}{\vdash^{(1,2)} \lambda x.\lambda y.xx : [\mathsf{n}, [\mathsf{n}] \multimap [\mathsf{n}]] \multimap [\mathbf{0} \multimap [\mathsf{n}]]}\;\mathsf{fun}}{\vdash^{(1,2)} \lambda x.\lambda y.xx : [[\mathsf{n}, [\mathsf{n}] \multimap [\mathsf{n}]] \multimap [\mathbf{0} \multimap [\mathsf{n}]]]}\;\mathsf{many}
$$

and, shortening $[\mathsf{n}] \multimap [\mathsf{n}]$ to $[\mathsf{n}]^{[\mathsf{n}]}$, we define Θ as follows

$$
\dfrac{\dfrac{\dfrac{\dfrac{}{z : [\mathsf{n}, [\mathsf{n}]^{[\mathsf{n}]}] \vdash^{(0,1)} z : [\mathsf{n}, [\mathsf{n}]^{[\mathsf{n}]}]}\;\mathsf{ax}}{\vdash^{(0,1)} \lambda z.z : [\mathsf{n}, [\mathsf{n}]^{[\mathsf{n}]}] \multimap [\mathsf{n}, [\mathsf{n}]^{[\mathsf{n}]}]}\;\mathsf{fun}}{\vdash^{(0,1)} \lambda z.z : [[\mathsf{n}, [\mathsf{n}]^{[\mathsf{n}]}] \multimap [\mathsf{n}, [\mathsf{n}]^{[\mathsf{n}]}]]}\;\mathsf{many} \qquad \dfrac{\dfrac{}{\vdash^{(0,0)} \lambda w.w : \mathsf{n}}\;\mathsf{normal} \qquad \dfrac{\dfrac{}{w : [\mathsf{n}] \vdash^{(0,1)} w : [\mathsf{n}]}\;\mathsf{ax}}{\vdash^{(0,1)} \lambda w.w : [\mathsf{n}]^{[\mathsf{n}]}}\;\mathsf{fun}}{\vdash^{(0,1)} \lambda w.w : [\mathsf{n}, [\mathsf{n}]^{[\mathsf{n}]}]}\;\mathsf{many}}{\vdash^{(1,2)} II : [\mathsf{n}, [\mathsf{n}]^{[\mathsf{n}]}]}\;\mathsf{app}
$$

Finally, we put Ψ and Θ together in the following derivation Φ for t

$$
\dfrac{\dfrac{\begin{array}{c}\vdots\,\Psi \\ \vdash^{(1,2)} \lambda x.\lambda y.xx : [[\mathsf{n}, [\mathsf{n}]^{[\mathsf{n}]}] \multimap [\mathbf{0} \multimap [\mathsf{n}]]]\end{array} \qquad \begin{array}{c}\vdots\,\Theta \\ \vdash^{(1,2)} II : [\mathsf{n}, [\mathsf{n}]^{[\mathsf{n}]}]\end{array}}{\vdash^{(3,4)} (\lambda x.\lambda y.xx)(II) : [\mathbf{0} \multimap [\mathsf{n}]]}\;\mathsf{app}}{\vdash^{(4,4)} ((\lambda x.\lambda y.xx)(II))(II) : [\mathsf{n}]}\;\mathsf{app}_{\mathrm{gc}}
$$

Note that the indices $(4,4)$ correspond exactly to the number of $\mathtt{m}_{\mathrm{need}}$-steps and $\mathtt{e}_{\mathrm{need}}$-steps, respectively, from t to its need-normal form—as shown in Example 1—and that Φ is a *tight* derivation. Forthcoming Theorem 5 shows once again that this is not by chance: tight derivations for CbNeed are minimal and provides exact bounds to evaluation lengths in CbNeed.

Remarkably, the technical development to prove *correctness* and *completeness* of the CbNeed type system with respect to CbNeed evaluation follows smoothly along the same lines of the two other systems, *mutatis mutandis*.

6.1 CbNeed Correctness

Lemma 6 (CbNeed linear substitution). *Let* $\Phi \triangleright_{\text{need}} \Gamma, x{:}M \vdash^{(m,e)} E\langle\langle x\rangle\rangle{:}N$ *and* v *be a value. There is a splitting* $M = O \uplus P$ *such that for any derivation* $\Psi \triangleright_{\text{need}} \Pi \vdash^{(m',e')} v : O$ *there exists* $\Phi' \triangleright_{\text{need}} \Gamma \uplus \Pi, x : P \vdash^{(m+m',e+e'-1)} E\langle\langle v\rangle\rangle : N$.

Proposition 10 (Quantitative subject reduction for CbNeed). *Let* $\Phi \triangleright_{\text{need}} \Gamma \vdash^{(m,e)} t : M$ *be a derivation such that* $M \neq \mathbf{0}$.
- Multiplicative*: if* $t \to_{\mathtt{m}_{\text{need}}} s$ *then* $m \geq 1$ *and there is a derivation* $\Phi' \triangleright_{\text{need}} \Gamma \vdash^{(m-1,e)} t : M$.
- Exponential*: if* $t \to_{\mathtt{e}_{\text{need}}} s$ *then* $e \geq 1$ *and there exists a derivation* $\Phi' \triangleright_{\text{need}} \Gamma \vdash^{(m,e-1)} t : M$.

Note the condition $M \neq \mathbf{0}$ in the statement of subject reduction, that is in contrast to the CbV system but akin to the CbN one. It is due to the way multi types are used as arguments, via rules ES_{gc} and app_{gc}. The restriction is necessary: the CbNeed type system derives $\vdash^{(0,1)} x[x{\leftarrow}\delta\delta] : \mathbf{0}$, but $x[x{\leftarrow}\delta\delta]$ is not normalising for CbNeed evaluation. And it is expected, as it amounts to the fact that adequacy holds only with respect to non-empty types, as for CbN, and as stressed when introducing the CbNeed type system. The same restriction appears in Theorem 5, Proposition 13 and Theorem 6 below, for the same reason.

Proposition 11 ([normal] typings for normal forms for CbNeed). *Let* $\Phi \triangleright_{\text{need}} \Gamma \vdash^{(m,e)} t : [\mathsf{normal}]$ *be a derivation, with* $\mathsf{normal}(t)$. *Then* Γ *is empty, and so* Φ *is tight, and* $m = e = 0$.

Theorem 5 (CbNeed tight correctness). *Let* t *be a closed term. If* $\Phi \triangleright_{\text{need}} \vdash^{(m,e)} t : M$ *where* $M \neq \mathbf{0}$, *then there is* s *such that* $d \colon t \to^*_{\text{need}} s$, *with* $\mathsf{normal}(s)$, $|d|_{\mathtt{m}} \leq m$ *and* $|d|_{\mathtt{e}} \leq e$. *Moreover, if* Φ *is tight then* $|d|_{\mathtt{m}} = m$ *and* $|d|_{\mathtt{e}} = e$.

6.2 CbNeed Completeness

Proposition 12 (Normal forms are tightly typable for CbNeed). *Let* t *be such that* $\mathsf{normal}(t)$. *Then there is a tight derivation* $\Phi \triangleright_{\text{need}} \vdash^{(0,0)} t : [\mathsf{normal}]$.

Lemma 7 (Linear removal for CbNeed). *Let* $\Phi \triangleright_{\text{need}} \Gamma, x : M \vdash^{(m,e)} E\langle\langle v\rangle\rangle : N$ *be a derivation and* v *be a value, with* $x \notin \mathtt{fv}(v)$. *Then there exist*
- *a multi type* M' *and two type contexts* Γ' *and* Π,
- *a derivation* $\Phi' \triangleright_{\text{need}} \Gamma' \vdash^{(m',e')} v : M'$, *and*
- *a derivation* $\Psi \triangleright_{\text{need}} \Pi, x : M \uplus M' \vdash^{(m'',e'')} E\langle\langle x\rangle\rangle : N$

such that
- Type contexts*:* $\Gamma = \Pi \uplus \Gamma'$.
- Indices*:* $(m, e) = (m' + m'', e' + e'' - 1)$.

Proposition 13 (Quantitative subject expansion for CbNeed). *Let* $\Phi \triangleright_{\text{need}} \Gamma \vdash^{(m,e)} s : M$ *be a derivation such that* $M \neq \mathbf{0}$. *Then,*
- Multiplicative: *if* $t \to_{\mathtt{m}_{\text{need}}} s$ *then there is a derivation* $\Phi' \triangleright_{\text{need}} \Gamma \vdash^{(m+1,e)} t : M$,
- Exponential*: if* $t \to_{\mathtt{e}_{\text{need}}} s$ *then there is a derivation* $\Phi' \triangleright_{\text{need}} \Gamma \vdash^{(m,e+1)} t : M$.

Theorem 6 (CbNeed tight completeness). *Let* t *be a closed term. If* $d\colon t \to^*_{\text{need}} s$ *and* $\mathsf{normal}(s)$ *then there exists a tight derivation* $\Phi \triangleright_{\text{need}} \vdash^{(|d|_{\mathtt{m}},|d|_{\mathtt{e}})} t : [\mathsf{normal}]$.

CbNeed Model. The interpretation $[\![t]\!]^{\text{CbNeed}}_{\vec{x}}$ with respect to the CbNeed system is defined as the set (where $\vec{x} = (x_1, \ldots, x_n)$ is a list of variables suitable for t):

$$\{((M_1, \ldots, M_n), N) \mid \exists \Phi \triangleright_{\text{need}} x_1 : M_1, \ldots, x_n : M_n \vdash^{(m,e)} t : N \text{ and } N \neq \mathbf{0}\}.$$

Note that the right multi type is required to be non-empty. The *invariance* and the *adequacy* of $[\![t]\!]^{\text{CbNeed}}_{\vec{x}}$ with respect to CbNeed evaluation are obtained exactly as for the CbN and CbV cases.

7 A New Fundamental Theorem for Call-by-Need

CbNeed Erases Wisely. In the literature, *the* theorem about CbNeed is the fact that it is operationally equivalent to CbN. This result was first proven independently by two groups, Maraist, Odersky, and Wadler [48], and Ariola and Felleisen [11], in the nineties, using heavy rewriting techniques.

Recently, Kesner gave a much simpler proof via CbN multi types [40]. She uses multi types to first show termination equivalence of CbN and CbNeed, from which she then infers operational equivalence. Termination equivalence means that a given term terminates in CbN if and only if terminates in CbNeed, and it is a consequence of our slogan that *CbN and CbNeed both erase wisely.*

With our terminology and notations, Kesner's result takes the following form.

Theorem 7 (Kesner [40]). *Let* t *be a closed term.*
1. Correctness*: if* $\Phi \triangleright_{\text{cbn}} \vdash^{(m,e)} t : L$ *then there exists* s *such that* $d\colon t \to^*_{\text{need}} s$, $\mathsf{normal}(s)$, $|d|_{\mathtt{m}} \leq m$ *and* $|d|_{\mathtt{e}} \leq e$.
2. Completeness*: if* $d\colon t \to^*_{\text{need}} s$ *and* $\mathsf{normal}(s)$ *then there is* $\Phi \triangleright_{\text{cbn}} \vdash^{(m,e)} t{:}\mathsf{normal}$.

Note that, with respect to the other similar theorems in this paper, the result does not cover tight derivations and it does not provide exact bounds. In fact, the CbN system *cannot* provide exact bounds for CbNeed, because it does provide them for CbN evaluation, that in general is slower than CbNeed. Consider for instance the term t in Example 1 and its CbN tight derivation in Example 2: the derivation provides indices $(5, 5)$ for t (and so t evaluates in 10 CbN steps), but t evaluates in 8 CbNeed steps. Closing such a gap is the main motivation behind this paper, achieved by the CbNeed multi type system in Sect. 6.

CbNeed Duplicates Wisely. Curiously, in the literature there are no dual results showing that CbNeed duplicates as wisely as CbV. One of the reasons is that it is a theorem that does not admit a simple formulation such as operational or termination equivalence, because CbNeed and CbV are not in such relationships. Morally, this is subsumed by the logical interpretation according to which CbNeed corresponds to an affine variant of the linear logic representation of CbV. Yet, it would be nice to have a precise, formal statement establishing that *CbNeed duplicates as wisely as CbV*—we provide it here.

Our result is that the CbV multi type system is correct with respect to CbNeed evaluation. In particular, the indices (m, e) provided by a CbV type derivation provide bounds for CbNeed evaluation lengths. Two important remarks before we proceed with the formal statement:

- *Bounds are not exact*: the indices of a CbV derivation do not generally provide exacts bounds for CbNeed, not even in the case of tight derivations. The reason is that CbNeed does not evaluate unneeded subterms (*i.e.* those typed with $\mathbf{0}$), while CbV does. Consider again the term t of Example 1, for instance, whose CbV tight derivation has indices $(5, 5)$ (and so t evaluates in 10 CbV steps) but it CbNeed evaluates in 8 steps.
- *Completeness cannot hold*: we prove correctness but not completeness simply because the CbV system is not complete with respect to CbNeed evaluation. Consider for instance $(\lambda x.I)\Omega$: it is CbV untypable by Theorem 4, because it is CbV divergent, and yet it is CbNeed normalisable.

CbV Correctness with Respect to CbNeed. Pleasantly, our presentations of CbV and CbNeed make the proof of the result straightforward. It is enough to observe that, since we do not consider garbage collection and we adopt a non-deterministic formulation of CbV, CbNeed is a subsystem of CbV. Formally, if $t \rightarrow_{\text{need}} s$ then $t \rightarrow_{\text{cbv}} s$, as it is easily seen from the definitions (CbNeed reduces only *some* subterms of applications and ES, while CbV reduces *all* such subterms). The result is then a corollary of the correctness theorem for CbV.

Corollary 1 (CbV correctness w.r.t. CbNeed). *Let t be a closed term and $\Phi \triangleright_{\text{cbv}} \ \vdash^{(m,e)} t : M$ be a derivation. Then there exists s such that $d\colon t \rightarrow^*_{\text{need}} s$ and $\mathsf{normal}(s)$, with $|d|_{\mathtt{m}} \leq m$ and $|d|_{\mathtt{e}} \leq e$.*

Since the CbNeed system provides exact bounds (Theorem 5), we obtain that CbNeed duplicates as wisely as CbV, when the comparison makes sense, that is, on CbV normalisable terms.

Corollary 2 (CbNeed duplicates as wisely as CbV). *Let $d\colon t \rightarrow^*_{\text{cbv}} u$ with $\mathsf{normal}_{\text{cbv}}(u)$. Then there is $d'\colon t \rightarrow^*_{\text{need}} s$ with $\mathsf{normal}(s)$ and $|d'|_{\mathtt{m}} \leq |d|_{\mathtt{m}}$ and $|d'|_{\mathtt{e}} \leq |d|_{\mathtt{e}}$.*

8 Conclusions

Contributions. This paper introduces a multi type system for CbNeed evaluation, carefully blending ingredients from multi type systems for CbN and CbV evaluation in the literature. Notably, it is the first type system whose minimal derivations—explicitly characterised—provide exact bounds for evaluation lengths. It also characterises CbNeed termination, and thus its judgements provide an adequate relational semantics.

The technical development is simple, and uniform with respect to those of CbN and CbV multi type systems. The typing rules count evaluation steps following *exactly* the same schema of the CbN and CbV rules. The proofs of correctness and completeness also follow *exactly* the same structure.

A further side contribution of the paper is a new fundamental result of CbNeed, formally stating that it duplicates as wisely as CbV. More precisely, the CbV multi type system is (quantitatively) correct with respect to CbNeed evaluation. Pleasantly, our presentations of CbV and CbNeed provide the result for free. This result dualizes the other fundamental theorem stating that CbNeed erases as wisely as CbN, usually formulated as termination equivalence, and recently re-proved by Kesner using CbN multi types [40].

Future Work. Recently, Barenbaum et al. extended CbNeed to strong evaluation [14], and it is natural to try to extend our type system as well. The definition of the system, in particular the extension of *tight* derivations to that setting, seems however far from being evident. Barembaum, Bonelli, and Mohamed also apply CbN multi types to a CbNeed calculus extended with pattern matching and fixpoints [15], that might be interesting to refine along the lines of our work.

An orthogonal direction is the study of the denotational models of CbNeed. It would be interesting to have a categorical semantics of CbNeed, as well as a categorical way of discriminating our quantitative precise model from the quantitatively lax one given by CbN multi types. It would also be interesting to obtain game semantics of CbNeed, hopefully satisfying a strong correspondence with our multi types in the style of what happens in CbN [30,31,51,56].

A further, unconventional direction is to dualise the inception of the CbNeed type system trying to mix silly duplication from CbN and silly erasure from CbV, obtaining—presumably—a multi types system measuring a perpetual strategy.

Acknowledgements. This work has been partially funded by the ANR JCJC grant COCA HOLA (ANR-16-CE40-004-01) and by the EPSRC grant EP/R029121/1 "Typed Lambda-Calculi with Sharing and Unsharing".

References

1. Accattoli, B.: An abstract factorization theorem for explicit substitutions. In: 23rd International Conference on Rewriting Techniques and Applications (RTA 2012). LIPIcs, vol. 15, pp. 6–21 (2012). https://doi.org/10.4230/LIPIcs.RTA.2012.6
2. Accattoli, B.: Proof nets and the linear substitution calculus. In: Fischer, B., Uustalu, T. (eds.) ICTAC 2018. LNCS, vol. 11187, pp. 37–61. Springer, Cham (2018). https://doi.org/10.1007/978-3-030-02508-3_3
3. Accattoli, B., Barenbaum, P., Mazza, D.: Distilling abstract machines. In: Proceedings of the 19th ACM SIGPLAN International Conference on Functional Programming (ICFP 2014), pp. 363–376 (2014). https://doi.org/10.1145/2628136.2628154

4. Accattoli, B., Barras, B.: Environments and the complexity of abstract machines. In: Proceedings of the 19th International Symposium on Principles and Practice of Declarative Programming (PPDP 2017), pp. 4–16. ACM (2017). https://doi.org/10.1145/3131851.3131855
5. Accattoli, B., Barras, B.: The negligible and yet subtle cost of pattern matching. In: Chang, B.-Y.E. (ed.) APLAS 2017. LNCS, vol. 10695, pp. 426–447. Springer, Cham (2017). https://doi.org/10.1007/978-3-319-71237-6_21
6. Accattoli, B., Bonelli, E., Kesner, D., Lombardi, C.: A nonstandard standardization theorem. In: The 41st Annual Symposium on Principles of Programming Languages (POPL 2014), pp. 659–670. ACM (2014). https://doi.org/10.1145/2535838.2535886
7. Accattoli, B., Graham-Lengrand, S., Kesner, D.: Tight typings and split bounds. PACMPL **2**(ICFP), 94:1–94:30 (2018). https://doi.org/10.1145/3236789
8. Accattoli, B., Guerrieri, G.: Types of fireballs. In: Ryu, S. (ed.) APLAS 2018. LNCS, vol. 11275, pp. 45–66. Springer, Cham (2018). https://doi.org/10.1007/978-3-030-02768-1_3
9. Accattoli, B., Guerrieri, G., Leberle, M.: Types by Need (Extended Version). CoRR abs/1902.05945 (2019)
10. Accattoli, B., Sacerdoti Coen, C.: On the value of variables. Inf. Comput. **255**, 224–242 (2017). https://doi.org/10.1016/j.ic.2017.01.003
11. Ariola, Z.M., Felleisen, M.: The call-by-need lambda calculus. J. Funct. Program. **7**(3), 265–301 (1997)
12. Ariola, Z.M., Felleisen, M., Maraist, J., Odersky, M., Wadler, P.: The call-by-need lambda calculus. In: Conference Record of POPL 1995: 22nd Symposium on Principles of Programming Languages, pp. 233–246. ACM Press (1995). https://doi.org/10.1145/199448.199507
13. Ariola, Z.M., Herbelin, H., Saurin, A.: Classical call-by-need and duality. In: Ong, L. (ed.) TLCA 2011. LNCS, vol. 6690, pp. 27–44. Springer, Heidelberg (2011). https://doi.org/10.1007/978-3-642-21691-6_6
14. Balabonski, T., Barenbaum, P., Bonelli, E., Kesner, D.: Foundations of strong call by need. PACMPL **1**(ICFP), 20:1–20:29 (2017). https://doi.org/10.1145/3110264
15. Barenbaum, P., Bonelli, E., Mohamed, K.: Pattern matching and fixed points: resource types and strong call-by-need: extended abstract. In: Proceedings of the 20th International Symposium on Principles and Practice of Declarative Programming (PPDP 2018), pp. 6:1–6:12. ACM (2018). https://doi.org/10.1145/3236950.3236972
16. Barras, B.: Auto-validation d'un système de preuves avec familles inductives. Ph.D. thesis, Université Paris 7 (1999)
17. Bernadet, A., Graham-Lengrand, S.: Non-idempotent intersection types and strong normalisation. Logical Methods Comput. Sci. **9**(4) (2013). https://doi.org/10.2168/LMCS-9(4:3)2013
18. Bucciarelli, A., Ehrhard, T., Manzonetto, G.: A relational semantics for parallelism and non-determinism in a functional setting. Ann. Pure Appl. Logic **163**(7), 918–934 (2012). https://doi.org/10.1016/j.apal.2011.09.008
19. Bucciarelli, A., Kesner, D., Ronchi Della Rocca, S.: Inhabitation for non-idempotent intersection types. Logical Methods Comput. Sci. **14**(3) (2018). https://doi.org/10.23638/LMCS-14(3:7)2018
20. Bucciarelli, A., Kesner, D., Ventura, D.: Non-idempotent intersection types for the lambda-calculus. Logic J. IGPL **25**(4), 431–464 (2017). https://doi.org/10.1093/jigpal/jzx018

21. Carraro, A., Guerrieri, G.: A semantical and operational account of call-by-value solvability. In: Muscholl, A. (ed.) FoSSaCS 2014. LNCS, vol. 8412, pp. 103–118. Springer, Heidelberg (2014). https://doi.org/10.1007/978-3-642-54830-7_7
22. de Carvalho, D.: Sémantiques de la logique linéaire et temps de calcul. Ph.D. thesis, Université Aix-Marseille II (2007)
23. de Carvalho, D.: Execution time of λ-terms via denotational semantics and intersection types. Math. Struct. Comput. Sci. **28**(7), 1169–1203 (2018). https://doi.org/10.1017/S0960129516000396
24. de Carvalho, D., Pagani, M., Tortora de Falco, L.: A semantic measure of the execution time in linear logic. Theoret. Comput. Sci. **412**(20), 1884–1902 (2011). https://doi.org/10.1016/j.tcs.2010.12.017
25. de Carvalho, D., Tortora de Falco, L.: A semantic account of strong normalization in linear logic. Inf. Comput. **248**, 104–129 (2016). https://doi.org/10.1016/j.ic.2015.12.010
26. Chang, S., Felleisen, M.: The call-by-need lambda calculus, revisited. In: Seidl, H. (ed.) ESOP 2012. LNCS, vol. 7211, pp. 128–147. Springer, Heidelberg (2012). https://doi.org/10.1007/978-3-642-28869-2_7
27. Coppo, M., Dezani-Ciancaglini, M.: A new type assignment for λ-terms. Arch. Math. Log. **19**(1), 139–156 (1978). https://doi.org/10.1007/BF02011875
28. Coppo, M., Dezani-Ciancaglini, M.: An extension of the basic functionality theory for the λ-calculus. Notre Dame J. Formal Logic **21**(4), 685–693 (1980). https://doi.org/10.1305/ndjfl/1093883253
29. Danvy, O., Zerny, I.: A synthetic operational account of call-by-need evaluation. In: 15th International Symposium on Principles and Practice of Declarative Programming (PPDP 2013), pp. 97–108. ACM (2013). https://doi.org/10.1145/2505879.2505898
30. Di Gianantonio, P., Honsell, F., Lenisa, M.: A type assignment system for game semantics. Theor. Comput. Sci. **398**(1–3), 150–169 (2008). https://doi.org/10.1016/j.tcs.2008.01.023
31. Di Gianantonio, P., Lenisa, M.: Innocent game semantics via intersection type assignment systems. In: Computer Science Logic 2013 (CSL 2013). LIPIcs, vol. 23, pp. 231–247 (2013). https://doi.org/10.4230/LIPIcs.CSL.2013.231
32. Díaz-Caro, A., Manzonetto, G., Pagani, M.: Call-by-value non-determinism in a linear logic type discipline. In: Artemov, S., Nerode, A. (eds.) LFCS 2013. LNCS, vol. 7734, pp. 164–178. Springer, Heidelberg (2013). https://doi.org/10.1007/978-3-642-35722-0_12
33. Downen, P., Maurer, L., Ariola, Z.M., Varacca, D.: Continuations, processes, and sharing. In: Proceedings of the 16th International Symposium on Principles and Practice of Declarative Programming (PPDP 2014), pp. 69–80. ACM (2014). https://doi.org/10.1145/2643135.2643155
34. Ehrhard, T.: Collapsing non-idempotent intersection types. In: Computer Science Logic (CSL 2012) - 26th International Workshop/21st Annual Conference of the EACSL. LIPIcs, vol. 16, pp. 259–273 (2012). https://doi.org/10.4230/LIPIcs.CSL.2012.259
35. Ehrhard, T., Guerrieri, G.: The bang calculus: an untyped lambda-calculus generalizing call-by-name and call-by-value. In: Proceedings of the 18th International Symposium on Principles and Practice of Declarative Programming (PPDP 2016), pp. 174–187. ACM (2016). https://doi.org/10.1145/2967973.2968608

36. Garcia, R., Lumsdaine, A., Sabry, A.: Lazy evaluation and delimited control. In: Proceedings of the 36th Symposium on Principles of Programming Languages (POPL 2009), pp. 153–164. ACM (2009). https://doi.org/10.1145/1480881.1480903
37. Gardner, P.: Discovering needed reductions using type theory. In: Hagiya, M., Mitchell, J.C. (eds.) TACS 1994. LNCS, vol. 789, pp. 555–574. Springer, Heidelberg (1994). https://doi.org/10.1007/3-540-57887-0_115
38. Girard, J.Y.: Linear logic. Theoret. Comput. Sci. **50**, 1–102 (1987). https://doi.org/10.1016/0304-3975(87)90045-4
39. Guerrieri, G.: Towards a semantic measure of the execution time in call-by-value lambda-calculus. In: Proceedings of ITRS 2018 (2018, to appear)
40. Kesner, D.: Reasoning about call-by-need by means of types. In: Jacobs, B., Löding, C. (eds.) FoSSaCS 2016. LNCS, vol. 9634, pp. 424–441. Springer, Heidelberg (2016). https://doi.org/10.1007/978-3-662-49630-5_25
41. Kesner, D., Vial, P.: Types as resources for classical natural deduction. In: 2nd International Conference on Formal Structures for Computation and Deduction (FSCD 2017). LIPIcs, vol. 84, pp. 24:1–24:17 (2017). https://doi.org/10.4230/LIPIcs.FSCD.2017.24
42. Kesner, D., Ríos, A., Viso, A.: Call-by-need, neededness and all that. In: Baier, C., Dal Lago, U. (eds.) FoSSaCS 2018. LNCS, vol. 10803, pp. 241–257. Springer, Cham (2018). https://doi.org/10.1007/978-3-319-89366-2_13
43. Kfoury, A.J.: A linearization of the lambda-calculus and consequences. J. Logic Comput. **10**(3), 411–436 (2000). https://doi.org/10.1093/logcom/10.3.411
44. Krivine, J.L.: Lambda-Calculus, Types and Models. Ellis Horwood Series in Computers and Their Applications. Ellis Horwood, Upper Saddle River, NJ, USA (1993)
45. Kutzner, A., Schmidt-Schauß, M.: A non-deterministic call-by-need lambda calculus. In: Proceedings of the Third International Conference on Functional Programming (ICFP 1998), pp. 324–335. ACM (1998). https://doi.org/10.1145/289423.289462
46. Launchbury, J.: A natural semantics for lazy evaluation. In: Conference Record of the Twentieth Annual Symposium on Principles of Programming Languages (POPL 1993), pp. 144–154. ACM Press (1993). https://doi.org/10.1145/158511.158618
47. Maraist, J., Odersky, M., Turner, D.N., Wadler, P.: Call-by-name, call-by-value, call-by-need and the linear lambda calculus. Theor. Comput. Sci. **228**(1–2), 175–210 (1999). https://doi.org/10.1016/S0304-3975(98)00358-2
48. Maraist, J., Odersky, M., Wadler, P.: The call-by-need lambda calculus. J. Funct. Program. **8**(3), 275–317 (1998)
49. Mazza, D., Pellissier, L., Vial, P.: Polyadic approximations, fibrations and intersection types. PACMPL **2**(POPL), 6:1–6:28 (2018). https://doi.org/10.1145/3158094
50. Neergaard, P.M., Mairson, H.G.: Types, potency, and idempotency: why nonlinearity and amnesia make a type system work. In: Proceedings of the Ninth International Conference on Functional Programming (ICFP 2004), pp. 138–149. ACM (2004). https://doi.org/10.1145/1016850.1016871
51. Ong, C.L.: Quantitative semantics of the lambda calculus: some generalisations of the relational model. In: 32nd Annual Symposium on Logic in Computer Science (LICS 2017), pp. 1–12. IEEE Computer Society (2017). https://doi.org/10.1109/LICS.2017.8005064

52. Paolini, L., Piccolo, M., Ronchi Della Rocca, S.: Essential and relational models. Math. Struct. Comput. Sci. **27**(5), 626–650 (2017). https://doi.org/10.1017/S0960129515000316
53. Pédrot, P.-M., Saurin, A.: Classical by-need. In: Thiemann, P. (ed.) ESOP 2016. LNCS, vol. 9632, pp. 616–643. Springer, Heidelberg (2016). https://doi.org/10.1007/978-3-662-49498-1_24
54. Pottinger, G.: A type assignment for the strongly normalizable λ-terms. In: Seldin, J., Hindley, J. (eds.) To H.B. Curry: Essays on Combinatory Logic, Lambda Calculus and Formalism, pp. 561–578. Academic Press, Cambridge (1980)
55. Sestoft, P.: Deriving a lazy abstract machine. J. Funct. Program. **7**(3), 231–264 (1997)
56. Tsukada, T., Ong, C.L.: Plays as resource terms via non-idempotent intersection types. In: Proceedings of the 31st Annual Symposium on Logic in Computer Science (LICS 2016), pp. 237–246. ACM (2016). https://doi.org/10.1145/2933575.2934553
57. Wadsworth, C.P.: Semantics and pragmatics of the lambda-calculus. Ph.D. thesis, University of Oxford (1971). Chapter 4

8

Codata in Action

Paul Downen[1], Zachary Sullivan[1(✉)], Zena M. Ariola[1], and Simon Peyton Jones[2]

[1] University of Oregon, Eugene, USA
{pdownen,zsulliva,ariola}@cs.uoregon.edu
[2] Microsoft Research, Cambridge, UK
simonpj@microsoft.com

Abstract. Computer scientists are well-versed in dealing with data structures. The same cannot be said about their dual: codata. Even though codata is pervasive in category theory, universal algebra, and logic, the use of codata for programming has been mainly relegated to representing infinite objects and processes. Our goal is to demonstrate the benefits of codata as a general-purpose programming abstraction independent of any specific language: eager or lazy, statically or dynamically typed, and functional or object-oriented. While codata is not featured in many programming languages today, we show how codata can be easily adopted and implemented by offering simple inter-compilation techniques between data and codata. We believe codata is a common ground between the functional and object-oriented paradigms; ultimately, we hope to utilize the Curry-Howard isomorphism to further bridge the gap.

Keywords: Codata · Lambda-calculi · Encodings · Curry-Howard · Function programming · Object-oriented programming

1 Introduction

Functional programming enjoys a beautiful connection to logic, known as the Curry-Howard correspondence, or proofs as programs principle [22]; results and notions about a language are translated to those about proofs, and vice-versa [17]. In addition to expressing computation as proof transformations, this connection is also fruitful for education: everybody would understand that the assumption "an x is zero" does not mean "every x is zero," which in turn explains the subtle typing rules for polymorphism in programs. The typing rules for modules are even more cryptic, but knowing that they correspond exactly to the rules for existential quantification certainly gives us more confidence that they are correct! While not everything useful must have a Curry-Howard correspondence, we believe finding these delightful coincidences where the same idea is rediscovered many times in both logic and programming can only be beneficial [42].

P. Downen and Z. M. Ariola—This work is supported by the National Science Foundation under grants CCF-1423617 and CCF-1719158.

One such instance involves *codata*. In contrast with the mystique it has as a programming construct, codata is pervasive in mathematics and logic, where it arises through the lens of duality. The most visual way to view the duality is in the categorical diagrams of sums versus products—the defining arrows go *into* a sum and come *out of* a product—and in algebras versus coalgebras [25]. In proof theory, codata has had an impact on theorem proving [5] and on the foundation of computation via *polarity* [29,45]. Polarity recognizes which of two dialogic actors speaks first: the proponent (who seeks to verify or prove a fact) or the opponent (who seeks to refute the fact).

The two-sided, interactive view appears all over the study of programming languages, where data is concerned about how values are constructed and codata is concerned about how they are used [15]. Sometimes, this perspective is readily apparent, like with session types [7] which distinguish internal choice (a provider's decision) versus external choice (a client's decision). But other occurrences are more obscure, like in the semantics of PCF (*i.e.* the call-by-name λ-calculus with numbers and general recursion). In PCF, the result of evaluating a program must be of a ground type in order to respect the laws of functions (namely η) [32]. This is not due to differences between ground types versus "higher types," but to the fact that data types are *directly observable*, whereas codata types are only *indirectly observable* via their interface.

Clearly codata has merit in theoretical pursuits; we think it has merit in practical ones as well. The main application of codata so far has been for representing infinite objects and coinductive proofs in proof assistants [1,39]. However, we believe that codata also makes for an important general-purpose programming feature. Codata is a bridge between the functional and object-oriented paradigms; a common denominator between the two very different approaches to programming. On one hand, functional languages are typically rich in data types—as many as the programmer wants to define via `data` declarations—but has a paucity of codata types (usually just function types). On the other hand, object-oriented languages are rich in codata types—programmer-defined in terms of classes or interfaces—but a paucity of data types (usually just primitives like booleans and numbers). We illustrate this point with a collection of example applications that arise in both styles of programming, including common encodings, demand-driven programming, abstraction, and Hoare-style reasoning.

While codata types can be seen in the shadows behind many examples of programming—often hand-compiled away by the programmer—not many functional languages have native support for them. To this end, we demonstrate a pair of simple compilation techniques between a typical core functional language (with data types) and one with codata. One direction—based on the well-known visitor pattern from object-oriented programming—simultaneously shows how to extend an object-oriented language with data types (as is done by Scala) and how to compile core functional programs to a more object-oriented setting (*e.g.* targeting a backend like JavaScript or the JVM). The other shows how to add native codata types to functional languages by reducing them to commonly-supported data types and how to compile a "pure" object-oriented style of programming to a functional setting. Both of these techniques are macro-expansions that are not specific to any particular language, as they work with both statically and dynamically typed disciplines, and they preserve the well-typed status of programs without increasing the complexity of the types involved.

Our claim is that codata is a universal programming feature that has been thus-far missing or diminished in today's functional programming languages. This is too bad, since codata is not just a feature invented for the convenience of programmers, but a persistent idea that has sprung up over and over from the study of mathematics, logic, and computation. We aim to demystify codata, and en route, bridge the wide gulf between the functional and object-oriented paradigms. Fortunately, it is easy for most mainstream languages to add or bring out codata today without a radical change to their implementation. But ultimately, we believe that the languages of the future should incorporate *both* data and codata outright. To that end, our contributions are to:

- (Section 2) Illustrate the benefits of codata in both theory and practice: (1) a decomposition of well-known λ-calculus encodings by inverting the priority of construction and destruction; (2) a first-class abstraction mechanism; (3) a method of demand-driven programming; and (4) a static type system for representing Hoare-style invariants on resource use.
- (Section 3) Provide simple transformations for compiling data to codata, and vice-versa, which are appropriate for languages with different evaluation strategies (eager or lazy) and type discipline (static or dynamic).
- (Section 4) Demonstrate various implementations of codata for general-purpose programming in two ways: (1) an extension of Haskell with codata; and (2) a prototype language that compiles to several languages of different evaluation strategies, type disciplines, and paradigms.

2 The Many Faces of Codata

Codata can be used to solve other problems in programming besides representing infinite objects and processes like streams and servers [1, 39]. We start by presenting codata as a merger between theory and practice, whereby *encodings* of data types in an object-oriented style turn out to be a useful intermediate step in the usual encodings of data in the λ-calculus. *Demand-driven programming* is considered a virtue of lazy languages, but codata is a language-independent tool for capturing this programming idiom. Codata exactly captures the essence of *procedural abstraction*, as achieved with λ-abstractions and objects, with a logically founded formalism [16]. Specifying *pre- and post-conditions* of protocols, which is available in some object systems [14], is straightforward with indexed, recursive codata types, *i.e.* objects with guarded methods [40].

2.1 Church Encodings and Object-Oriented Programming

Crucial information structures, like booleans, numbers, and lists can be encoded in the untyped λ-calculus (*a.k.a.* Church encodings) or in the typed polymorphic

λ-calculus (*a.k.a.* Böhm-Berarducci [9] encodings). It is quite remarkable that data structures can be simulated with just first-class, higher-order functions. The downside is that these encodings can be obtuse at first blush, and have the effect of obscuring the original program when *everything* is written with just λs and application. For example, the λ-representation of the boolean value True, the first projection out of a pair, and the constant function K are all expressed as $\lambda x.\lambda y.x$, which is not that immediately evocative of its multi-purpose nature.

Object-oriented programmers have also been representing data structures in terms of objects. This is especially visible in the Smalltalk lineage of languages like Scala, wherein an objective is that everything that can be an object is. As it turns out, the object-oriented features needed to perform this representation technique are *exactly* those of codata. That is because Church-style encodings and object-oriented representations of data all involve *switching focus from the way values are built (i.e. introduced) to the way they are used (i.e. eliminated).*

Consider the representation of Boolean values as an algebraic data type. There may be many ways to use a `Boolean` value. However, it turns out that there is a *most-general* eliminator of `Booleans`: the expression `if b then x else y`. This basic construct can be used to define all the other uses for `Bools`. Instead of focusing on the constructors `True` and `False` let's then focus on this most-general form of `Bool` elimination; this is the essence of the encodings of booleans in terms of objects. In other words, booleans can be thought of as objects that implement a single method: `If`. So that the expression `if b then x else y` would instead be written as (`b.If x y`). We then define the true and false values in terms of their reaction to `If`:

```
true = {If x y → x}          false = {If x y → y}
```

Or alternatively, we can write the same definition using copatterns, popularized for use in the functional paradigm by Abel *et al.* [1] by generalizing the usual pattern-based definition of functions by multiple clauses, as:

```
true.If x y = x              false.If x y = y
```

This works just like equational definitions by pattern-matching in functional languages: the expression to the left of the equals sign is the same as the expression to the right (for any binding of `x` and `y`). Either way, the net result is that (`true.If "yes" "no"`) is `"yes"`, whereas (`false.If "yes" "no"`) is `"no"`.

This covers the object-based presentation of booleans in a dynamically typed language, but how do static types come into play? In order to give a type description of the above boolean objects, we can use the following interface, analogous to a Java interface:

```
codata Bool where If : Bool → (forall a. a → a → a)
```

This declaration is dual to a data declaration in a functional language: data declarations define the types of constructors (which produce values of the data type) and codata declarations define the types of destructors (which consume values of the codata type) like `If`. The reason that the `If` observation introduces its own polymorphic type `a` is because an if-then-else might return any type of result (as long as both branches agree on the type). That way, both the two objects `true` and `false` above are values of the codata type `Bool`.

At this point, the representation of booleans as codata looks remarkably close to the encodings of booleans in the λ-calculus! Indeed, the only difference is that in the λ-calculus we "anonymize" booleans. Since they reply to only one request, that request name can be dropped. We then arrive at the familiar encodings in the polymorphic λ-calculus:

$$Bool = \forall a.a \to a \to a \qquad true = \Lambda a.\lambda x{:}a.\lambda y{:}a.x \qquad false = \Lambda a.\lambda x{:}a.\lambda y{:}a.y$$

In addition, the invocation of the `If` method just becomes ordinary function application; `b.If x y` of type a is written as $b\ a\ x\ y$. Otherwise, the definition and behavior of booleans as either codata types or as polymorphic functions are the same.

This style of inverting the definition of data types—either into specific codata types or into polymorphic functions—is also related to another concept in object-oriented programming. First, consider how a functional programmer would represent a binary `Tree` (with integer-labeled leaves) and a `walk` function that traverses a tree by converting the labels on all leaves and combining the results of sub-trees:

```
data Tree where Leaf   : Int → Tree
                Branch : Tree → Tree → Tree

walk : (Int → a) → (a → a → a) → Tree → a
walk b f (Leaf x)       = b x
walk b f (Branch l r) = f (walk b f l) (walk b f r)
```

The above code relies on pattern-matching on values of the `Tree` data type and higher-order functions `b` and `f` for accumulating the result. Now, how might an object-oriented programmer tackle the problem of traversing a tree-like structure? The *visitor pattern*! With this pattern, the programmer specifies a "visitor" object which contains knowledge of what to do at every node of the tree, and tree objects must be able to accept a visitor with a method that will recursively walk down each subcomponent of the tree. In a pure style—which returns an accumulated result directly instead of using mutable state as a side channel for results—the visitor pattern for a simple binary tree interface will look like:

```
codata TreeVisitor a where
  VisitLeaf   : TreeVisitor a → (Int → a)
  VisitBranch : TreeVisitor a → (a → a → a)

codata Tree where
  Walk : Tree → (forall a. TreeVisitor a → a)

leaf       : Int → Tree
leaf   x   = {Walk v → v.VisitLeaf x}

branch     : Tree → Tree → Tree
branch l r = {Walk v → v.VisitBranch (l.Walk v) (r.Walk v)}
```

And again, we can write this same code more elegantly, without the need to break apart the two arguments across the equal sign with a manual abstraction, using copatterns as:

```
(leaf     x).Walk v = v.VisitLeaf x
(branch l r).Walk v = v.VisitBranch (l.Walk v) (r.Walk v)
```

Notice how the above code is just an object-oriented presentation of the following encoding of binary trees into the polymorphic λ-calculus:

$$\mathit{Tree} = \forall a.\mathit{TreeVisitor}\ a \to a \qquad \mathit{TreeVisitor}\ a = (\mathit{Int} \to a) \times (a \to a \to a)$$

$$\mathit{leaf} : \mathit{Int} \to \mathit{Tree}$$

$$\mathit{leaf}\ (x{:}\mathit{Int}) = \Lambda a.\lambda v{:}\mathit{TreeVisitor}\ a.\ (\mathit{fst}\ v)\ x$$

$$\mathit{branch} : \forall a.\mathit{Tree} \to \mathit{Tree} \to \mathit{Tree}$$

$$\mathit{branch}\ (l{:}\mathit{Tree})\ (r{:}\mathit{Tree}) = \Lambda a.\lambda v{:}\mathit{TreeVisitor}\ a.\ (\mathit{snd}\ v)\ (l\ a\ v)\ (r\ a\ v)$$

The only essential difference between this λ-encoding of trees versus the λ-encoding of booleans above is currying: the representation of the data type *Tree* takes a single product *TreeVisitor a* of the necessary arguments, whereas the data type *Bool* takes the two necessary arguments separately. Besides this easily-converted difference of currying, the usual Böhm-Berarducci encodings shown here correspond to a pure version of the visitor pattern.

2.2 Demand-Driven Programming

In "Why functional programming matters" [23], Hughes motivates the utility of practical functional programming through its excellence in compositionality. When designing programs, one of the goals is to decompose a large problem into several manageable sub-problems, solve each sub-problem in isolation, and then compose the individual parts together into a complete solution. Unfortunately, Hughes identifies some examples of programs which resist this kind of approach.

In particular, numeric algorithms—for computing square roots, derivatives integrals—rely on an infinite sequence of approximations which converge on the true answer only in the limit of the sequence. For these numeric algorithms, the decision on when a particular approximation in the sequence is "close enough" to the real answer lies solely in the eyes of the beholder: only the observer of the answer can say when to stop improving the approximation. As such, standard imperative implementations of these numeric algorithms are expressed as a single, complex loop, which interleaves both the concerns of producing better approximations with the termination decision on when to stop. Even more complex is the branching structure of the classic minimax algorithm from artificial intelligence for searching for reasonable moves in two-player games like chess, which can have an unreasonably large (if not infinite) search space. Here, too, there is difficulty separating generation from selection, and worse there is the intermediate step of pruning out uninteresting sub-trees of the search space (known as alpha-beta pruning). As a result, a standard imperative implementation of minimax is a single, recursive function that combines all the tasks—generation, pruning, estimation, and selection—at once.

Hughes shows how both instances of failed decomposition can be addressed in functional languages through the technique of *demand-driven programming.* In each case, the main obstacle is that the control of how to drive the next step of the algorithm—whether to continue or not—lies with the consumer. The producer of potential approximations and game states, in contrast, should only take over when demanded by the consumer. By giving primary control to the consumer, each of these problems can be decomposed into sensible sub-tasks, and recomposed back together. Hughes uses lazy evaluation, as found in languages like Miranda and Haskell, in order to implement the demand-driven algorithms. However, the downside of relying on lazy evaluation is that it is a whole-language decision: a language is either lazy by default, like Haskell, or not, like OCaml. When working in a strict language, expressing these demand-driven algorithms with manual laziness loses much of their original elegance [33].

In contrast, a language should directly support the capability of yielding control to the consumer independently of the language being strict or lazy; analogously to what happens with lambda abstractions. An abstraction computes on-demand, why is this property relegated to this predefined type only? In fact, the concept of *codata* also has this property. As such, it allows us to describe demand-driven programs in an agnostic way which works just as well in Haskell as in OCaml without any additional modification. For example, we can implement Hughes' demand-driven AI game in terms of codata instead of laziness. To represent the current game state, and all of its potential developments, we can use an arbitrarily-branching tree codata type.

```
codata Tree a where
  Node     : Tree a → a
  Children : Tree a → List (Tree a)
```

The task of generating all potential future boards from the current board state produces one of these tree objects, described as follows (where `moves` of type `Board → List Board` generates a list of possible moves):

```
gameTree : Board → Tree Board
(gameTree b).Node     = b
(gameTree b).Children = map gameTree (moves b)
```

Notice that the tree might be finite, such as in the game of Tic-Tac-Toe. However, it would still be inappropriate to waste resources fully generating all moves before determining which are even worth considering. Fortunately, the fact that the responses of a codata object are only computed when demanded means that the consumer is in full control over how much of the tree is generated, just as in Hughes' algorithm. This fact lets us write the following simplistic `prune` function which cuts off sub-trees at a fixed depth.

```
prune : Int → Tree Board → Tree Board
(prune x t).Node     = t.Node
(prune 0 t).Children = []
(prune x t).Children = map (prune(x-1)) t.Children
```

The more complex alpha-beta pruning algorithm can be written as its own pass, similar to `prune` above. Just like Hughes' original presentation, the evaluation of the best move for the opponent is the composition of a few smaller functions:

```
eval = maximize . maptree score . prune 5 . gameTree
```

What is the difference between this codata version of minimax and the one presented by Hughes that makes use of laziness? They both compute on-demand which makes the game efficient. However, demand-driven code written with codata can be easily ported between strict and lazy languages with only syntactic changes. In other words, codata is a general, portable, programming feature which is the key for compositionality in program design.[1]

2.3 Abstraction Mechanism

In the pursuit of scalable and maintainable program design, the typical followup to composability is abstraction. The basic purpose of abstraction is to hide certain implementation details so that different parts of the code base need not be concerned with them. For example, a large program will usually be organized into several different parts or "modules," some of which may hold general-purpose "library" code and others may be application-specific "clients" of those libraries. Successful abstractions will leverage tools of the programming language in question so that there is a clear interface between libraries and their clients, codifying which details are exposed to the client and which are kept hidden inside the library. A common such detail to hide is the concrete representation of some data type, like strings and collections. Clear abstraction barriers give freedom to both the library implementor (to change hidden details without disrupting any clients) as well as the client (to ignore details not exposed by the interface).

Reynolds [35] identified, and Cook [12] later elaborated on, two different mechanisms to achieve this abstraction: abstract data types and procedural abstraction. Abstract data types are crisply expressed by the Standard ML module system, based on existential types, which serves as a concrete practical touchstone for the notion. Procedural abstraction is pervasively used in object-oriented languages. However, due to the inherent differences among the many languages and the way they express procedural abstraction, it may not be completely clear of what the "essence" is, the way existential types are the essence of modules. *What is the language-agnostic representation of procedural abstraction? Codata!* The combination of observation-based interfaces, message-passing, and dynamic dispatch are exactly the tools needed for procedural abstraction. Other common object-oriented features—like inheritance, subtyping, encapsulation, and mutable state—are orthogonal to this particular abstraction goal. While they may be useful extensions to codata for accomplishing programming tasks, only pure codata itself is needed to represent abstraction.

[1] To see the full code for all the examples of [24] implemented in terms of codata, visit https://github.com/zachsully/codata_examples.

Specifying a codata type is giving an interface—between an implementation and a client—so that instances of the type (implementations) can respond to requests (clients). In fact, method calls are the only way to interact with our objects. As usual, there is no way to "open up" a higher-order function—one example of a codata type—and inspect the way it was implemented. The same intuition applies to all other codata types. For example, Cook's [12] procedural "set" interface can be expressed as a codata type with the following observations:

```
codata Set where
  IsEmpty  : Set → Bool
  Contains : Set → Int → Bool
  Insert   : Set → Int → Set
  Union    : Set → Set → Set
```

Every single object of type `Set` will respond to these observations, which is the only way to interact with it. This abstraction barrier gives us the freedom of defining several different instances of `Set` objects that can all be freely composed with one another. One such instance of `Set` uses a list to keep track of a hidden state of the contained elements (where `elemOf : List Int → Int → Bool` checks if a particular number is an element of the given list, and the operation `fold : (a → b → b) → b → List a → b` is the standard functional fold):

```
finiteSet : List Int → Set
(finiteSet xs).IsEmpty    = xs == []
(finiteSet xs).Contains y = elemOf xs y
(finiteSet xs).Insert   y = finiteSet (y:xs)
(finiteSet xs).Union    s = fold (λx t → t.Insert x) s xs

emptySet = finiteSet []
```

But of course, many other instances of `Set` can also be given. For example, this codata type interface also makes it possible to represent infinite sets like the set `evens` of all even numbers which is defined in terms of the more general `evensUnion` that unions all even numbers with some other set (where the function `isEven : Int → Int` checks if a number is even):

```
evens = evensUnion emptySet

evensUnion : Set → Set
(evensUnion s).IsEmpty    = False
(evensUnion s).Contains y = isEven y || s.Contains y
(evensUnion s).Insert   y = evensUnion (s.Insert y)
(evensUnion s).Union    t = evensUnion (s.Union t)
```

Because of the natural abstraction mechanism provided by codata, different `Set` implementations can interact with each other. For example, we can union a finite set and `evens` together because both definitions of `Union` know nothing of the internal structure of the other `Set`. Therefore, all we can do is apply the observations provided by the `Set` codata type.

While sets of numbers are fairly simplistic, there are many more practical real-world instances of the procedural abstraction provided by codata to be found in object-oriented languages. For example, databases are a good use of abstraction, where basic database queries can be represented as the observations on table objects. A simplified interface to a database table (containing rows of type a) with selection, deletion, and insertion, is given as follows:

```
codata Database a where
  Select : Database a → (a → Bool) → List a
  Delete : Database a → (a → Bool) → Database a
  Insert : Database a → a → Database a
```

On one hand, specific implementations can be given for connecting to and communicating with a variety of different databases—like Postgres, MySQL, or just a simple file system—which are hidden behind this interface. On the other hand, clients can write generic operations independently of any specific database, such as copying rows from one table to another or inserting a row into a list of compatible tables:

```
copy : Database a → Database a → Database a
copy from to = let rows = from.Select(λ_ → True)
               in foldr (λrow db → db.Insert row) to rows

insertAll : List (Database a) → a → List (Database a)
insertAll dbs row = map (λdb → db.Insert row) dbs
```

In addition to abstracting away the details of specific databases, both `copy` and `insertAll` can communicate between completely different databases by just passing in the appropriate object instances, which all have the same generic type. Another use of this generality is for testing. Besides the normal instances of `Database a` which perform permanent operations on actual tables, one can also implement a fictitious *simulation* which records changes only in temporary memory. That way, client code can be seamlessly tested by running and checking the results of simulated database operations that have no external side effects by just passing pure codata objects.

2.4 Representing Pre- and Post-Conditions

The extension of data types with indexes (*a.k.a.* generalized algebraic data types) has proven useful to statically verify a data structure's invariant, like for red-black trees [43]. With indexed data types, the programmer can inform the static type system that a particular value of a data type satisfies some additional conditions by constraining the way in which it was constructed. Unsurprisingly, indexed codata types are dual and allow the creator of an object to constrain the way it is going to be used, thereby adding pre- and post-conditions to the observations of the object. In other words, in a language with type indexes, codata enables the programmer to express more information in its interface.

This additional expressiveness simplifies applications that rely on a type index to guard observations. Thibodeau *et al.* [40] give examples of such programs, including an automaton specification where its transitions correspond to an observation that changes a pre- and post-condition in its index, and a fair resource scheduler where the observation of several resources is controlled by an index tracking the number of times they have been accessed. For concreteness, let's use an indexed codata type to specify safe protocols as in the following example from an object-oriented language with guarded methods:

```
index Raw, Bound, Live

codata Socket i where
  Bind     : Socket Raw   → String → Socket Bound
  Connect  : Socket Bound → Socket Live
  Send     : Socket Live  → String → ()
  Receive  : Socket Live  → String
  Close    : Socket Live  → ()
```

This example comes from DeLine and Fähndrich [14], where they present an extension to C♯ constraining the pre- and post-conditions for method calls. If we have an instance of this `Socket i` interface, then observing it through the above methods can return new socket objects with a different index. The index thereby governs the order in which clients are allowed to apply these methods. A socket will start with the index `Raw`. The only way to use a `Socket Raw` is to `Bind` it, and the only way to use a `Socket Bound` is to `Connect` it. This forces us to follow a protocol when initializing a `Socket`.

Intermezzo 1. This declaration puts one aspect in the hands of the programmer, though. A client can open a socket and never close it, hogging the resource. We can remedy this problem with linear types, which force us to address any loose ends before finishing the program. With linear types, it would be a type error to have a lingering `Live` socket laying around at the end of the program, and a call to `Close` would use it up. Furthermore, linear types would ensure that outdated copies of `Socket` objects cannot be used again, which is especially appropriate for actions like `Bind` which is meant to *transform* a `Raw` socket into a `Bound` one, and likewise for `Connect` which transforms a `Bound` socket into a `Live` one. Even better, enhancing linear types with a more sophisticated notion of ownership—like in the Rust programming language which differentiates a *permanent* transfer of ownership from *temporarily* borrowing it—makes this resource-sensitive interface especially pleasant. Observations like `Bind`, `Connect`, and `Close` which are meant to fully consume the observed object would involve full ownership of the object itself to the method call and effectively replace the old object with the returned one. In contrast, observations like `Send` and `Receive` which are meant to be repeated on the same object would merely borrow the object for the duration of the action so that it could be used again.

3 Inter-compilation of Core Calculi

We saw previously examples of using codata types to replicate well-known encodings of data types into the λ-calculus. Now, let's dive in and show how data and codata types formally relate to one another. In order to demonstrate the relationship, we will consider two small languages that extend the common polymorphic λ-calculus: λ^{data} extends λ with user-defined algebraic data types, and λ^{codata} extends λ with user-defined codata types. In the end, we will find that both of these foundational languages can be inter-compiled into one another. Data can be represented by codata via the visitor pattern ($\mathfrak{V}$). Codata can be represented by data by tabulating the possible answers of objects ($\mathfrak{T}$).

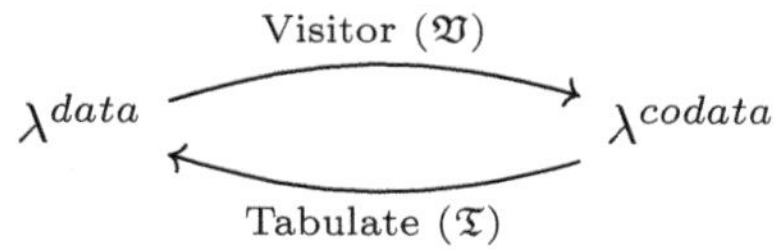

In essence, this demonstrates how to compile programs between the functional and object-oriented paradigms. The $\mathfrak{T}$ direction shows how to extend existing functional languages (like OCaml, Haskell, or Racket) with codata objects without changing their underlying representation. Dually, the $\mathfrak{V}$ direction shows how to compile functional programs with data types into an object-oriented target language (like JavaScript).

Each of the encodings are macro expansions, in the sense that they leave the underlying base λ-calculus constructs of functions, applications, and variables unchanged (as opposed to, for example, continuation-passing style translations). They are defined to operate on untyped terms, but they also preserve typability when given well-typed terms. The naïve encodings preserve the operational semantics of the original term, according to a call-by-name semantics. We also illustrate how the encodings can be modified slightly to correctly simulate the call-by-value operational semantics of the source program. To conclude, we show how the languages and encodings can be generalized to more expressive type systems, which include features like existential types and indexed types (*a.k.a.* generalized algebraic data types and guarded methods).

Notation. We use both an overline $\overline{t}$ and dots $t_1 \ldots$ to indicate a *sequence* of terms t (and likewise for types, variables, *etc.*). The arrow type $\overline{\tau} \to \mathsf{T}$ means $\tau_1 \to \cdots \to \tau_n \to \mathsf{T}$; when n is 0, it is not a function type, *i.e.* just the codomain T. The application $\mathsf{K}\ \overline{t}$ means $(((\mathsf{K}\ t_1)\ \ldots)\ t_n)$; when n is 0, it is not a function application, but the constant K. We write a single step of an operational semantics with the arrow $\mapsto$, and many steps (*i.e.* its reflexive-transitive closure) as $\mapsto\!\!\!\!\to$. Operational steps may occur within an evaluation context E, *i.e.* $t \mapsto t'$ implies that $E[t] \mapsto E[t']$.

3.1 Syntax and Semantics

We present the syntax and semantics of the base language and the two extensions λ^{data} and λ^{codata}. For the sake of simplicity, we keep the languages as minimal as possible to illustrate the main inter-compilations. Therefore, λ^{data} and λ^{codata} do not contain recursion, nested (co)patterns, or indexed types. The extension with recursion is standard, and an explanation of compiling (co)patterns can be found in [11,38,39]. Indexed types are later discussed informally in Sect. 3.6.

Syntax:

$$\text{Type} \ni \quad \tau, \rho ::= a \mid \tau \to \rho \mid \forall a.\, \tau$$
$$\text{Term} \ni t, u, e ::= x \mid t\ u \mid \lambda x.\, e$$

Operational Semantics:

Call-by-name		Call-by-value	
$V ::= x \mid \lambda x.\, e$	$E ::= \Box \mid E\ u$	$V ::= x \mid \lambda x.\, e$	$E ::= \Box \mid E\ u \mid V\ E$
$(\lambda x.\, e)\ u \mapsto e[u/x]$		$(\lambda x.\, e)\ V \mapsto e[V/x]$	

Type System (where $S = t$ for call-by-name and $S = V$ for call-by-value):

$$\frac{x : \tau \in \Gamma}{\Gamma \vdash x : \tau} \qquad \frac{\Gamma \vdash t : \tau \to \rho \quad \Gamma \vdash u : \tau}{\Gamma \vdash t\ u : \rho} \qquad \frac{\Gamma, x : \tau \vdash e : \rho}{\Gamma \vdash \lambda x.\, e : \tau \to \rho}$$

$$\frac{\Gamma, a \vdash S : \tau}{\Gamma \vdash S : \forall a.\, \tau} \qquad \frac{\Gamma \vdash t : \forall a.\tau \quad \Gamma \vdash \rho}{\Gamma \vdash t : \tau[\rho/a]}$$

Fig. 1. Polymorphic λ-calculus: the base language

The Base Language. We will base both our core languages of interest on a common starting point: the polymorphic λ-calculus as shown in Fig. 1.[2] This is the standard simply typed λ-calculus extended with impredicative polymorphism (*a.k.a.* generics). There are only three forms of terms (variables x, applications $t\ u$, and function abstractions $\lambda x.e$) and three forms of types (type variables a, function types $\tau \to \rho$, and polymorphic types $\forall a.\tau$). We keep the type abstraction and instantiation implicit in programs—as opposed to explicit as in System F—for two reasons. First, this more accurately resembles the functional languages in which types are inferred, as opposed to mandatory annotations explicit within the syntax of programs. Second, it more clearly shows how the translations that follow do not rely on first knowing the type of terms, but apply to any untyped term. In other words, the compilation techniques are also appropriate for dynamically typed languages like Scheme and Racket.

Figure 1 reviews both the standard call-by-name and call-by-value operational semantics for the λ-calculus. As usual, the difference between the two is that in call-by-value, the argument of a function call is evaluated prior to substitution, whereas in call-by-name the argument is substituted first. This is implied by the different set of evaluation contexts (E) and the fact that the operational rule uses a more restricted notion of value (V) for substitutable arguments in call-by-value. Note that, there is an interplay between evaluation and typing. In a more general setting where effects are allowed, the typing rule for introducing polymorphism (*i.e.* the rule with $S : \forall a.\tau$ in the conclusion) is only safe for substitutable terms, which imposes the well-known the *value restriction* for call-by-value (limiting S to values), but requires no such restriction in call-by-name where every term is a substitutable value (letting S be any term).

[2] The judgement $\Gamma \vdash \rho$ should be read as: all free type variables in ρ occur in Γ. As usual Γ, a means that a does not occur free in Γ.

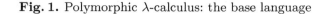

Syntax:

$$
\begin{array}{lrl}
\text{Declaration} \ni & d ::= & \mathbf{data}\ \mathsf{T}\ \overline{a}\ \mathbf{where}\ \mathsf{K} : \overline{\tau} \to \mathsf{T}\ \overline{a}\ \ldots \\
\text{Type} \ni & \tau, \rho ::= & a \mid \tau \to \rho \mid \forall a.\, \tau \mid \mathsf{T}\ \overline{\rho} \\
\text{Term} \ni & t, u, e ::= & x \mid t\ u \mid \lambda x.\, e \mid \mathsf{K}\ \overline{t} \mid \mathbf{case}\ t\ \{\overline{\mathsf{K}\ \overline{x} \to t}\}
\end{array}
$$

Operational Semantics:

Call-by-name

$$V ::= \cdots \mid \mathsf{K}\ \overline{t}$$
$$E ::= \cdots \mid \mathbf{case}\ E\ \{\overline{\mathsf{K}\ \overline{x} \to e}\}$$
$$\mathbf{case}\ (\mathsf{K}\ \overline{t})\ \{\mathsf{K}\ \overline{x} \to e,\ \ldots\} \mapsto e\overline{[t/x]}$$

Call-by-value

$$V ::= \cdots \mid \mathsf{K}\ \overline{V}$$
$$E ::= \cdots \mid \mathbf{case}\ E\ \{\overline{\mathsf{K}\ \overline{x} \to e}\} \mid \mathsf{K}\ \overline{V}\ E\ \overline{t}$$
$$\mathbf{case}\ (\mathsf{K}\ \overline{V})\ \{\mathsf{K}\ \overline{x} \to e,\ \ldots\} \mapsto e\overline{[V/x]}$$

Type System:

$$\frac{\mathsf{K} : \forall \overline{a}.\, \tau_1 \to \cdots \to \mathsf{T}\ \overline{a} \in \Gamma \quad \Gamma \vdash t_1 : \tau_1[\overline{\rho}/\overline{a}] \quad \ldots}{\Gamma \vdash \mathsf{K}\ t_1 \cdots : \mathsf{T}\ \overline{\rho}}$$

$$\frac{\Gamma \vdash t : \mathsf{T}\ \overline{\rho} \quad \mathsf{K}_1 : \forall \overline{a}.\, \overline{\tau_1} \to \mathsf{T}\ \overline{a} \in \Gamma \quad \Gamma, \overline{x_1 : \tau_1[\overline{\rho}/\overline{a}]} \vdash e_1 : \tau' \quad \ldots}{\Gamma \vdash \mathbf{case}\ t\ \{\mathsf{K}_1\ \overline{x_1} \to e_1,\ \ldots\} : \tau'}$$

Fig. 2. λ^{data}: Extending polymorphic λ-calculus with data types

A Language with Data. The first extension of the λ-calculus is with user-defined data types, as shown in Fig. 2; it corresponds to a standard core language for statically typed functional languages. Data declarations introduce a new type constructor (T) as well as some number of associated constructors (K) that build values of that data type. For simplicity, the list of branches in a case expression are considered unordered and non-overlapping (*i.e.* no two branches for the same constructor within a single case expression). The types of constructors are given alongside free variables in Γ, and the typing rule for constructors requires they be fully applied. We also assume an additional side condition to the typing rule for case expressions that the branches are exhaustive (*i.e.* every constructor of the data type in question is covered as a premise).

Figure 2 presents the extension to the operational semantics from Fig. 1, which is also standard. The new evaluation rule for data types reduces a case expression matched with an applied constructor. Note that since the branches are unordered, the one matching the constructor is chosen out of the possibilities and the parameters of the constructor are substituted in the branch's pattern. There is also an additional form of constructed values: in call-by-name any constructor application is a value, whereas in call-by-value only constructors parameterized by other values is a value. As such, call-by-value goes on to evaluate constructor parameters in advance, as shown by the extra evaluation context. In both evaluation strategies, there is a new form of evaluation context that points out the discriminant of a case expression, since it is mandatory to determine which constructor was used before deciding the appropriate branch to take.

Syntax:

$$\begin{array}{lrl} \text{Declaration} \ni & d ::= & \textbf{codata}\ \mathsf{U}\ \overline{a}\ \textbf{where}\ \overline{\mathsf{H} : \mathsf{U}\ \overline{a} \to \tau} \ldots \\ \text{Type} \ni & \tau, \rho ::= & a \mid \tau \to \rho \mid \forall a.\, \tau \mid \mathsf{U}\ \overline{\rho} \\ \text{Term} \ni & t, u, e ::= & x \mid t\ u \mid \lambda x.\, e \mid t.\mathsf{H} \mid \{\overline{\mathsf{H} \to e}\} \end{array}$$

Operational Semantics:

Call-by-name	Call-by-value
$V ::= \cdots \mid \{\overline{\mathsf{H} \to e}\} \quad E ::= \cdots \mid E.\mathsf{H}$	$V ::= \cdots \mid \{\overline{\mathsf{H} \to e}\} \quad E ::= \cdots \mid E.\mathsf{H}$
$\{\mathsf{H} \to e, \ldots\}.\mathsf{H} \mapsto e$	$\{\mathsf{H} \to e, \ldots\}.\mathsf{H} \mapsto e$

Type System:

$$\frac{\mathsf{H} : \forall \overline{a}.\, \mathsf{U}\ \overline{a} \to \tau \in \Gamma \quad \Gamma \vdash t : \mathsf{U}\ \overline{\rho}}{\Gamma \vdash t.\mathsf{H} : \tau[\overline{\rho}/\overline{a}]} \qquad \frac{\Gamma \vdash \mathsf{H}_1 : \mathsf{U}\ \overline{\rho} \to \tau_1 \quad \Gamma \vdash e_1 : \tau_1 \quad \ldots}{\Gamma \vdash \{\mathsf{H}_1 \to e_1, \ldots\} : \mathsf{U}\ \overline{\rho}}$$

Fig. 3. λ^{codata}: Extending polymorphic λ-calculus with codata types

A Language with Codata. The second extension of the λ-calculus is with user-defined codata types, as shown in Fig. 3. Codata declarations in λ^{codata} define a new type constructor (U) along with some number of associated destructors (H) for projecting responses out of values of a codata type. The type level of λ^{codata} corresponds directly to λ^{data}. However, at the term level, we have codata observations of the form $t.\mathsf{H}$ using "dot notation", which can be thought of as sending the message H to the object t or as a method invocation from object-oriented languages. Values of codata types are introduced in the form $\{\mathsf{H}_1 \to e_1, \ldots, \mathsf{H}_n \to e_n\}$, which lists each response this value gives to all the possible destructors of the type. As with case expressions, we take the branches to be unordered and non-overlapping for simplicity.

Interestingly, the extension of the operational semantics with codata—the values, evaluation contexts, and reduction rules—are identical for both call-by-name and call-by-value evaluation. In either evaluation strategy, a codata object $\{\mathsf{H} \to e, \ldots\}$ is considered a value and the codata observation $t.\mathsf{H}$ *must* evaluate t no matter what to continue, leading to the same form of evaluation context $E.\mathsf{H}$. The additional evaluation rule selects and invokes the matching branch of a codata object and is the same regardless of the evaluation strategy.

Note that the reason that values of codata types are the same in any evaluation strategy is due to the fact that the branches of the object are only ever evaluated on-demand, *i.e.* when they are observed by a destructor, similar to the fact that the body of a function is only ever evaluated when the function is called. This is the semantic difference that separates codata types from records found in many programming languages. Records typically map a collection of labels to a collection of values, which are evaluated in advance in a call-by-value language similar to the constructed values of data types. Whereas with codata objects, labels map to *behavior* which is only invoked when observed.

$$\mathfrak{V}\left[\!\!\left[\begin{array}{l}\textbf{data}\ \mathsf{T}\ \overline{a}\ \textbf{where}\\ \quad \mathsf{K}_1 : \overline{\tau_1} \to \mathsf{T}\ \overline{a}\\ \quad \vdots\\ \quad \mathsf{K}_n : \overline{\tau_n} \to \mathsf{T}\ \overline{a}\end{array}\right]\!\!\right] = \begin{array}{l}\textbf{codata}\ \mathsf{T}_{visit}\ \overline{a}\ b\ \textbf{where}\\ \quad \mathsf{K}_1 : \mathsf{T}_{visit}\ \overline{a}\ b \to \overline{\tau_1} \to b\\ \quad \vdots\\ \quad \mathsf{K}_n : \mathsf{T}_{visit}\ \overline{a}\ b \to \overline{\tau_n} \to b\\ \textbf{codata}\ \mathsf{T}\ \overline{a}\ \textbf{where}\\ \quad \mathsf{Case}_{\mathsf{T}} : \mathsf{T}\ \overline{a} \to \forall b.\, \mathsf{T}_{visit}\ \overline{a}\ b \to b\end{array}$$

$$\mathfrak{V}[\![\mathsf{K}_i\ \overline{t}]\!] = \{\mathsf{Case}_{\mathsf{T}} \to \lambda v.\,(v.\mathsf{K}_i)\ \overline{\mathfrak{V}[\![t]\!]}\}$$

$$\mathfrak{V}[\![\textbf{case}\ t\ \{\mathsf{K}_1\ \overline{x_1} \to e_1, \ldots\}]\!] = (\mathfrak{V}[\![t]\!].\mathsf{Case}_{\mathsf{T}})\ \{\mathsf{K}_1 \to \lambda\overline{x_1}.\,\mathfrak{V}[\![e_1]\!], \ldots\}$$

Fig. 4. $\mathfrak{V} : \lambda^{data} \to \lambda^{codata}$ mapping data to codata via the visitor pattern

The additional typing rules for λ^{codata} are also given in Fig. 3. The rule for typing $t.\mathsf{H}$ is analogous to a combination of type instantiation and application, when viewing H as a function of the given type. The rule for typing a codata object, in contrast, is similar to the rule for typing a case expression of a data type. However, in this comparison, the rule for objects is partially "upside down" in the sense that the primary type in question ($\mathsf{U}\ \overline{\rho}$) appears in the conclusion rather than as a premise. This is the reason why there is one less premise for typing codata objects than there is for typing data case expressions. As with that rule, we assume that the branches are exhaustive, so that every destructor of the codata type appears in the premise.

3.2 Compiling Data to Codata: The Visitor Pattern

In Sect. 2.1, we illustrated how to convert a data type representing trees into a codata type. This encoding corresponds to a rephrasing of the object-oriented visitor pattern to avoid unnecessary side-effects. Now lets look more generally at the pattern, to see how any algebraic data type in λ^{data} can be encoded in terms of codata in λ^{codata}.

The visitor pattern has the net effect of inverting the orientation of a data declaration (wherein construction comes first) into codata declarations (wherein destruction comes first). This reorientation can be used for compiling user-defined data types in λ^{data} to codata types in λ^{codata} as shown in Fig. 4. As with all of the translations we will consider, this is a macro expansion since the syntactic forms from the base λ-calculus are treated homomorphically (*i.e.* $\mathfrak{V}[\![\lambda x.\, e]\!] = \lambda x.\,\mathfrak{V}[\![e]\!]$, $\mathfrak{V}[\![t\ u]\!] = \mathfrak{V}[\![t]\!]\ \mathfrak{V}[\![u]\!]$, and $\mathfrak{V}[\![x]\!] = x$). Furthermore, this translation also perfectly preserves types, since the types of terms are exactly the same after translation (*i.e.* $\mathfrak{V}[\![\tau]\!] = \tau$).

Notice how each data type ($\mathsf{T}\ \overline{a}$) gets represented by *two* codata types: the "visitor" ($\mathsf{T}_{visit}\ \overline{a}\ b$) which says what to do with values made with each constructor, and the type itself ($\mathsf{T}\ \overline{a}$) which has one method which accepts a visitor and returns a value of type b. An object of the codata type, then, must be capable of accepting *any* visitor, no matter what type of result it returns. Also notice that we include no other methods in the codata type representation of $\mathsf{T}\ \overline{a}$.

At the level of terms, first consider how the case expression of the data type is encoded. The branches of the case (contained within the curly braces) are represented as a first-class object of the visitor type: each constructor is mapped to the corresponding destructor of the same name and the variables bound in the pattern are mapped to parameters of the function returned by the object in each case. The whole case expression itself is then implemented by calling the sole method (Case_T) of the codata object and passing the branches of the case as the corresponding visitor object. Shifting focus to the constructors, we can now see that they are compiled as objects that invoke the corresponding destructor on any given visitor, and the terms which were parameters to the constructor are now parameters to a given visitor's destructor. Of course, other uses of the visitor pattern might involve a codata type (T) with more methods implementing additional functionality besides case analysis. However, we only need the one method to represent data types in λ^{data} because case expressions are *the* primitive destructor for values of data types in the language.

For example, consider applying the above visitor pattern to a binary tree data type as follows:

$$\mathfrak{V}\left[\!\!\left[\begin{array}{l}\textbf{data}\ \mathsf{Tree}\ \textbf{where}\\ \quad \mathsf{Leaf}\ \ \ \ \ :\mathsf{Int}\to\mathsf{Tree}\\ \quad \mathsf{Branch}:\mathsf{Tree}\to\mathsf{Tree}\to\mathsf{Tree}\end{array}\right]\!\!\right] = \begin{array}{l}\textbf{codata}\ \mathsf{Tree}_{visit}\ b\ \textbf{where}\\ \quad \mathsf{Leaf}\ \ \ \ \ :\mathsf{Int}\to b\\ \quad \mathsf{Branch}:\mathsf{Tree}\to\mathsf{Tree}\to b\\ \textbf{codata}\ \mathsf{Tree}\ \textbf{where}\\ \quad \mathsf{Case}_\mathsf{Tree}:\mathsf{Tree}\to\forall b.\,\mathsf{Tree}_{visit}\ b\to b\end{array}$$

$$\mathfrak{V}[\![\mathsf{Leaf}\ n]\!] = \{\mathsf{Case}_\mathsf{Tree}\to\lambda v.\,v.\mathsf{Leaf}\ n\}$$

$$\mathfrak{V}[\![\mathsf{Branch}\ l\ r]\!] = \{\mathsf{Case}_\mathsf{Tree}\to\lambda v.\,v.\mathsf{Branch}\ l\ r\}$$

$$\mathfrak{V}\left[\!\!\left[\textbf{case}\ t\left\{\begin{array}{l}\mathsf{Leaf}\ n\ \ \ \ \to e_l\\ \mathsf{Branch}\ l\ r\to e_b\end{array}\right\}\right]\!\!\right] = \mathfrak{V}[\![t]\!].\mathsf{Case}_\mathsf{Tree}\left\{\begin{array}{lcl}\mathsf{Leaf} & \to & \lambda n.\,\mathfrak{V}[\![e_l]\!]\\ \mathsf{Branch} & \to & \lambda l.\,\lambda r.\,\mathfrak{V}[\![e_b]\!]\end{array}\right\}$$

Note how this encoding differs from the one that was given in Sect. 2.1 since the $\mathsf{Case}_\mathsf{Tree}$ method is non-recursive whereas the $\mathsf{Walk}_\mathsf{Tree}$ method was recursive, in order to model a depth-first search traversal of the tree.

Of course, other operations, like the `walk` function, could be written in terms of case expressions and recursion as usual by an encoding with above method calls. However, it is possible to go one step further and include other primitive destructors—like recursors or iterators in the style of Gödel's system T—by embedding them as other methods of the encoded codata type. For example, we can represent `walk` as a primitive destructor as it was in Sect. 2.1 *in addition* to non-recursive case analysis by adding an alternative visitor Tree_{walk} and one more destructor to the generated Tree codata type like so:

$$\begin{array}{l}\textbf{codata}\ \mathsf{Tree}_{walk}\ b\ \textbf{where}\\ \quad \mathsf{Leaf}\ \ \ \ \ :\mathsf{Int}\to b\\ \quad \mathsf{Branch}:b\to b\to b\end{array} \qquad \begin{array}{l}\textbf{codata}\ \mathsf{Tree}\ \textbf{where}\\ \quad \mathsf{Case}_\mathsf{Tree}\ :\mathsf{Tree}\to\forall b.\,\mathsf{Tree}_{visit}\ b\to b\\ \quad \mathsf{Walk}_\mathsf{Tree}:\mathsf{Tree}\to\forall b.\,\mathsf{Tree}_{walk}\ b\to b\end{array}$$

$$\mathfrak{V}[\![\mathsf{Leaf}\ n]\!] = \left\{\begin{array}{lcl}\mathsf{Case}_\mathsf{Tree} & \to & \lambda v.\,v.\mathsf{Leaf}\ n\\ \mathsf{Walk}_\mathsf{Tree} & \to & \lambda w.\,w.\mathsf{Leaf}\ n\end{array}\right\}$$

For codata types with n destructors, where $n \geq 1$:

$$\mathfrak{T}\left[\!\!\left[\begin{array}{c}\textbf{codata}\ \mathsf{U}\ \overline{a}\ \textbf{where}\\ \mathsf{H}_1 : \mathsf{U}\ \overline{a} \to \tau_1\\ \vdots\\ \mathsf{H}_n : \mathsf{U}\ \overline{a} \to \tau_n\end{array}\right]\!\!\right] = \begin{array}{l}\textbf{data}\ \mathsf{U}\ \overline{a}\ \textbf{where}\\ \quad \mathsf{Table}_{\mathsf{U}} : \tau_1 \to \cdots \to \tau_n \to \mathsf{U}\ \overline{a}\end{array}$$

$$\mathfrak{T}[\![t.\mathsf{H}_i]\!] = \textbf{case}\ \mathfrak{T}[\![t]\!]\ \{\mathsf{Table}_{\mathsf{U}}\ y_1 \ldots y_n \to y_i\}$$

$$\mathfrak{T}[\![\{\mathsf{H}_1 \to e_1, \ldots, \mathsf{H}_n \to e_n\}]\!] = \mathsf{Table}_{\mathsf{U}}\ \mathfrak{T}[\![e_1]\!] \ldots \mathfrak{T}[\![e_n]\!]$$

For codata types with 0 destructors (where Unit is the same for every such U):

$$\mathfrak{T}\left[\!\!\left[\begin{array}{c}\textbf{codata}\ \mathsf{U}\ \overline{a}\ \textbf{where}\\ \textit{--no destructors}\end{array}\right]\!\!\right] = \begin{array}{l}\textbf{data}\ \mathsf{Unit}\ \textbf{where}\\ \quad \mathsf{unit} : \mathsf{Unit}\end{array}$$

$$\mathfrak{T}[\![\{\}]\!] = \mathsf{unit}$$

Fig. 5. $\mathfrak{T} : \lambda^{codata} \to \lambda^{data}$ tabulating codata responses with data tuples

$$\mathfrak{V}[\![\mathsf{Branch}\ l\ r]\!] = \left\{\begin{array}{ll}\mathsf{Case}_{\mathsf{Tree}} & \to \lambda v.\, v.\mathsf{Branch}\ l\ r\\ \mathsf{Walk}_{\mathsf{Tree}} & \to \lambda w.\, w.\mathsf{Branch}\ (l.\mathsf{Walk}_{\mathsf{Tree}})\ (r.\mathsf{Walk}_{\mathsf{Tree}})\end{array}\right\}$$

where the definition of Tree_{visit} and the encoding of case expressions is the same. In other words, this compilation technique can generalize to as many primitive observations and recursion schemes as desired.

3.3 Compiling Codata to Data: Tabulation

Having seen how to compile data to codata, how can we go the other way? The reverse compilation would be useful for extending functional languages with user-defined codata types, since many functional languages are compiled to a core representation based on the λ-calculus with data types.

Intuitively, the declared data types in λ^{data} can be thought of as "sums of products." In contrast, the declared codata types in λ^{codata} can be thought of as "products of functions." Since both core languages are based on the λ-calculus, which has higher-order functions, the main challenge is to relate the two notions of "products." The codata sense of products are based on projections out of abstract objects, where the different parts are viewed individually and only when demanded. The data sense of products, instead, are based on tuples, in which all components are laid out in advance in a single concrete structure.

One way to convert codata to data is to *tabulate* an object's potential answers ahead of time into a data structure. This is analogous to the fact that a function of type `Bool` $\to$ `String` can be alternatively represented by a tuple of type `String * String`, where the first and second components are the responses of the original function to `true` and `false`, respectively. This idea can be applied to λ^{codata} in general as shown in the compilation in Fig. 5.

A codata declaration of U becomes a data declaration with a single constructor ($\mathsf{Table}_\mathsf{U}$) representing a tuple containing the response for each of the original destructors of U. At the term level, a codata abstraction is compiled by concretely tabulating each of its responses into a tuple using the $\mathsf{Table}_\mathsf{U}$ constructor. A destructor application returns the specific component of the constructed tuple which corresponds to that projection. Note that, since we assume that each object is exhaustive, the tabulation transformation is relatively straightforward; filling in "missing" method definitions with some error value that can be stored in the tuple at the appropriate index would be done in advance as a separate pre-processing step.

Also notice that there is a special case for non-observable "empty" codata types, which are all collapsed into a single pre-designated Unit data type. The reason for this collapse is to ensure that this compilation preserves typability: if applied to a well-typed term, the result is also well-typed. The complication arises from the fact that when faced with an empty object $\{\}$, we have no idea which constructor to use without being given further typing information. So rather than force type checking or annotation in advance for this one degenerate case, we instead collapse them all into a single data type so that there is no need to differentiate based on the type. In contrast, the translation of non-empty objects is straightforward, since we can use the name of any one of the destructors to determine the codata type it is associated with, which then informs us of the correct constructor to use.

3.4 Correctness

For the inter-compilations between λ^{codata} into λ^{data} to be useful in practice, they should preserve the semantics of programs. For now, we focus only on the call-by-name semantics for each of the languages. With the static aspect of the semantics, this means they should preserve the typing of terms.

Proposition 1 (Type Preservation). *For each of the $\mathfrak{V}$ and $\mathfrak{T}$ translations: if $\Gamma \vdash t : \tau$ then $[\![\Gamma]\!] \vdash [\![t]\!] : [\![\tau]\!]$ (in the call-by-name type system).*

Proof (Sketch). By induction on the typing derivation of $\Gamma \vdash t : \tau$.

With the dynamic aspect of the semantics, the translations should preserve the outcome of evaluation (either converging to some value, diverging into an infinite loop, or getting stuck) for both typed and untyped terms. This works because each translation preserves the reduction steps, values, and evaluation contexts of the source calculus' call-by-name operational semantics.

Proposition 2 (Evaluation Preservation). *For each of the $\mathfrak{V}$ and $\mathfrak{T}$ translations: $t \mapsto\!\!\!\rightarrow V$ if and only if $[\![t]\!] \mapsto\!\!\!\rightarrow [\![V]\!]$ (in the call-by-name semantics).*

Proof (Sketch). The forward ("only if") implication is a result of the following facts that hold for each translation in the call-by-name semantics:

- For any redex t in the source, if $t \mapsto t'$ then $[\![t]\!] \mapsto t'' \mapsto\!\!\!\!\rightarrow [\![t']\!]$.
- For any value V in the source, $[\![V]\!]$ is a value.
- For any evaluation context E in the source, there is an evaluation context E' in the target such that $[\![E[t]]\!] = E'[[\![t]\!]]$ for all t.

The reverse ("if") implication then follows from the fact that the call-by-name operational semantics of both source and target languages is deterministic.

3.5 Call-by-Value: Correcting the Evaluation Order

The presented inter-compilation techniques are correct for the call-by-name semantics of the calculi. But what about the call-by-value semantics? It turns out that the simple translations seen so far do not correctly preserve the call-by-value semantics of programs, but they can be easily fixed by being more careful about how they treat the values of the source and target calculi. In other words, we need to make sure that values are translated to values, and evaluation contexts to evaluation contexts. For instance, the following translation (up to renaming) does not preserve the call-by-value semantics of the source program:

$$\mathfrak{T}[\![\{\mathsf{Fst} \to \mathit{error}, \mathsf{Snd} \to \mathsf{True}\}]\!] = \mathsf{Pair}\ \mathit{error}\ \mathsf{True}$$

The object $\{\mathsf{Fst} \to \mathit{error}, \mathsf{Snd} \to \mathsf{True}\}$ is a value in call-by-value, and the erroneous response to the Fst will only be evaluated when observed. However, the structure $\mathsf{Pair}\ \mathit{error}\ \mathsf{True}$ is not a value in call-by-value, because the field error must be evaluated in advance which causes an error immediately. In the other direction, we could also have

$$\mathfrak{V}[\![\mathsf{Pair}\ \mathit{error}\ \mathsf{True}]\!] = \{\mathsf{Case} \to \lambda v.\, v.\mathsf{Pair}\ \mathit{error}\ \mathsf{True}\}$$

Here, the immediate error in $\mathsf{Pair}\ \mathit{error}\ \mathsf{True}$ has become incorrectly delayed inside the value $\{\mathsf{Case} \to \lambda v.\, v.\mathsf{Pair}\ \mathit{error}\ \mathsf{True}\}$.

The solution to this problem is straightforward: we must manually delay computations that are lifted out of (object or λ) abstractions, and manually force computations before their results are hidden underneath abstractions. For the visitor pattern, the correction is to only introduce the codata object on constructed values. We can handle other constructed terms by naming their non-value components in the style of administrative-normalization like so:

$$\begin{aligned}\mathfrak{V}[\![\mathsf{K}_i\ \overline{V}]\!] &= \{\mathsf{Case}_{\mathsf{T}} \to \lambda v.\, v.\mathsf{K}_i\ \overline{V}\}\\ \mathfrak{V}[\![\mathsf{K}_i\ \overline{V}\ u\ \overline{t}]\!] &= \mathbf{let}\ x = u\ \mathbf{in}\ \mathfrak{V}[\![\mathsf{K}_i\ \overline{V}\ x\ \overline{t}]\!] \qquad \text{if } u \text{ is not a value}\end{aligned}$$

Conversely, the tabulating translation $\mathfrak{T}$ will cause the on-demand observations of the object to be converted to preemptive components of a tuple structure. To counter this change in evaluation order, a thunking technique can be employed as follows:

$$\begin{aligned}\mathfrak{T}[\![t.\mathsf{H}_i]\!] &= \mathbf{case}\ \mathfrak{T}[\![t]\!]\ \{\mathsf{Table}_{\mathsf{U}}\ y_1 \ldots y_n \to \mathbf{force}\, y_i\}\\ \mathfrak{T}[\![\{\mathsf{H}_1 \to e_1, \ldots, \mathsf{H}_n \to e_n\}]\!] &= \mathsf{Table}_{\mathsf{U}}\ (\mathbf{delay}\, \mathfrak{T}[\![e_1]\!]) \ldots (\mathbf{delay}\, \mathfrak{T}[\![e_n]\!])\end{aligned}$$

The two operations can be implemented as **delay** $t = \lambda z. t$ and **force** $t = t$ unit as usual, but can also be implemented as more efficient memoizing operations. With all these corrections, Propositions 1 and 2 also hold for the call-by-value type system and operational semantics.

3.6 Indexed Data and Codata Types: Type Equalities

In the world of types, we have so far only formally addressed inter-compilation between languages with simple and polymorphic types. What about the compilation of indexed data and codata types? It turns out some of the compilation techniques we have discussed so far extend to type indexes without further effort, whereas others need some extra help. In particular, the visitor-pattern-based translation $\mathfrak{V}$ can just be applied straightforwardly to indexed data types:

$$\mathfrak{V}\left[\!\!\left[\begin{array}{l}\textbf{data}\ \mathsf{T}\ \overline{a}\ \textbf{where}\\ \quad \mathsf{K}_1 : \overline{\tau_1} \to \mathsf{T}\ \overline{\rho_1}\\ \quad \vdots\\ \quad \mathsf{K}_n : \overline{\tau_n} \to \mathsf{T}\ \overline{\rho_n}\end{array}\right]\!\!\right] = \begin{array}{l}\textbf{codata}\ \mathsf{T}_{visit}\ \overline{a}\ b\ \textbf{where}\\ \quad \mathsf{K}_1 : \mathsf{T}_{visit}\ \overline{\rho_1}\ b \to \overline{\tau_1} \to b\\ \quad \vdots\\ \quad \mathsf{K}_n : \mathsf{T}_{visit}\ \overline{\rho_n}\ b \to \overline{\tau_n} \to b\\ \textbf{codata}\ \mathsf{T}\ \overline{a}\ \textbf{where}\\ \quad \mathsf{Case}_{\mathsf{T}} : \mathsf{T}\ \overline{a} \to \forall b. \mathsf{T}_{visit}\ \overline{a}\ b \to b\end{array}$$

In this case, the notion of an indexed visitor codata type exactly corresponds to the mechanics of case expressions for GADTs. In contrast, the tabulation translation $\mathfrak{T}$ does not correctly capture the semantics of indexed codata types, if applied naïvely.

Thankfully, there is a straightforward way of "simplifying" indexed data types to more conventional data types using some built-in support for *type equalities*. The idea is that a constructor with a more specific return type can be replaced with a conventional constructor that is parameterized by type equalities that *prove* that the normal return type must be the more specific one. The same idea can be applied to indexed codata types as well. A destructor that can only act on a more specific instance of the codata type can instead be replaced by one which works on any instance, but then immediately asks for *proof* that the object's type is the more specific one before completing the observation. These two translations, of replacing type indexes with type equalities, are defined as:

$$\mathfrak{Eq}\left[\!\!\left[\begin{array}{l}\textbf{data}\ \mathsf{T}\ \overline{a}\ \textbf{where}\\ \quad \mathsf{K}_1 : \overline{\tau_1} \to \mathsf{T}\ \overline{\rho_1}\\ \quad \vdots\\ \quad \mathsf{K}_n : \overline{\tau_n} \to \mathsf{T}\ \overline{\rho_n}\end{array}\right]\!\!\right] = \begin{array}{l}\textbf{data}\ \mathsf{T}\ \overline{a}\ \textbf{where}\\ \quad \mathsf{K}_1 : \overline{a \equiv \rho_1} \to \overline{\tau_1} \to \mathsf{T}\ \overline{a}\\ \quad \vdots\\ \quad \mathsf{K}_n : \overline{a \equiv \rho_n} \to \overline{\tau_n} \to \mathsf{T}\ \overline{a}\end{array}$$

$$\mathfrak{Eq}\left[\!\!\left[\begin{array}{l}\textbf{codata}\ \mathsf{U}\ \overline{a}\ \textbf{where}\\ \quad \mathsf{H}_1 : \mathsf{U}\ \overline{\rho_1} \to \overline{\tau_1}\\ \quad \vdots\\ \quad \mathsf{H}_n : \mathsf{U}\ \overline{\rho_n} \to \overline{\tau_n}\end{array}\right]\!\!\right] = \begin{array}{l}\textbf{codata}\ \mathsf{U}\ \overline{a}\ \textbf{where}\\ \quad \mathsf{H}_1 : \mathsf{U}\ \overline{a} \to \overline{a \equiv \rho_1} \to \overline{\tau_1}\\ \quad \vdots\\ \quad \mathsf{H}_n : \mathsf{U}\ \overline{a} \to \overline{a \equiv \rho_n} \to \overline{\tau_n}\end{array}$$

This formalizes the intuition that indexed data types can be thought of as *enriching* constructors to carry around additional constraints that were available at their time of construction, whereas indexed codata types can be thought of as *guarding* methods with additional constraints that must be satisfied before an observation can be made. Two of the most basic examples of this simplification are for the type declarations which capture the notion of type equality as an indexed data or indexed codata type, which are defined and simplified like so:

$$\mathfrak{Eq}\left[\!\!\left[\begin{array}{l}\textbf{data}\ \mathsf{Eq}\ a\ b\ \textbf{where}\\ \quad \mathsf{Refl} : \mathsf{Eq}\ a\ a\end{array}\right]\!\!\right] = \begin{array}{l}\textbf{data}\ \mathsf{Eq}\ a\ b\ \textbf{where}\\ \quad \mathsf{Refl} : a \equiv b \to \mathsf{Eq}\ a\ b\end{array}$$

$$\mathfrak{Eq}\left[\!\!\left[\begin{array}{l}\textbf{codata}\ \mathsf{IfEq}\ a\ b\ c\ \textbf{where}\\ \quad \mathsf{AssumeEq} : \mathsf{IfEq}\ a\ a\ c \to c\end{array}\right]\!\!\right] = \begin{array}{l}\textbf{codata}\ \mathsf{IfEq}\ a\ b\ c\ \textbf{where}\\ \quad \mathsf{AssumeEq} : \mathsf{IfEq}\ a\ b\ c \to a \equiv b \to c\end{array}$$

With the above ability to simplify away type indexes, *all* of the presented compilation techniques are easily generalized to indexed data and codata types by composing them with $\mathfrak{Eq}$. For practical programming example, consider the following safe stack codata type indexed by its number of elements.

$$\begin{array}{l}\textbf{codata}\ \mathsf{Stack}\ a\ \textbf{where}\\ \quad \mathsf{Pop}\ \ : \mathsf{Stack}\ (\mathsf{Succ}\ a) \to (\mathbb{Z}, \mathsf{Stack}\ a)\\ \quad \mathsf{Push} : \mathsf{Stack}\ a \to \mathbb{Z} \to \mathsf{Stack}\ (\mathsf{Succ}\ a)\end{array}$$

This stack type is safe in the sense that the Pop operation can only be applied to non-empty Stacks. We cannot compile this to a data type via $\mathfrak{T}$ directly, because that translation does not apply to indexed codata types. However, if we first simplify the Stack type via $\mathfrak{Eq}$, we learn that we can replace the type of the Pop destructor with $\mathsf{Pop} : \mathsf{Stack}\ a \to \forall b.a \equiv \mathsf{Succ}\ b \to (\mathbb{Z}, \mathsf{Stack}\ b)$, whereas the Push destructor is already simple, so it can be left alone. That way, for any object $s : \mathsf{Stack\ Zero}$, even though a client can initiate the observation $s.\mathsf{Pop}$, it will never be completed since there is no way to choose a b and prove that Zero equals Succ b. Therefore, the net result of the combined $\mathfrak{T} \circ \mathfrak{Eq}$ translation turns Stack into the following data type, after some further simplification:

$$\begin{array}{l}\textbf{data}\ \mathsf{Stack}\ a\ \textbf{where}\\ \quad \mathsf{MkS} : (\forall b.a \equiv \mathsf{Succ}\ b \to (\mathbb{Z}, \mathsf{Stack}\ b)) \to (\mathbb{Z} \to \mathsf{Stack}\ (\mathsf{Succ}\ a)) \to \mathsf{Stack}\ a\end{array}$$

Notice how the constructor of this type has two fields; one for Pop and one for Push, respectively. However, the Pop operation is guarded by a proof obligation: the client can only receive the top integer and remaining stack if he/she proves that the original stack contains a non-zero number of elements.

4 Compilation in Practice

We have shown how data and codata are related through the use of two different core calculi. To explore how these ideas manifest in practice, we have implemented codata in a couple of settings. First, we extended Haskell with codata

n	Time(s) codata	Time(s) data	Allocs(bytes) codata	Allocs(bytes) data
10000	0.02	0.01	10,143,608	6,877,048
100000	0.39	0.27	495,593,464	463,025,832
1000000	19.64	18.54	44,430,524,144	44,104,487,488

Table 1. Fibonacci scaling tests for the GHC implementation

in order to compare the lazy and codata approaches to demand-driven programming described in Sect. 2.2.[3] Second, we have created a prototype language with indexed (co)data types to further explore the interaction between the compilation and target languages. The prototype language does not commit to a particular evaluation strategy, typing discipline, or paradigm; instead this decision is made when compiling a program to one of several backends. The supported backends include functional ones—Haskell (call-by-need, static types), OCaml (call-by-value, static types), and Racket (call-by-value, dynamic types)—as well as the object-oriented JavaScript.[4] The following issues of complex copattern matching and sharing applies to both implementations; the performance results on efficiency of memoized codata objects are tested with the Haskell extension for the comparison with conventional Haskell code.

Complex Copattern Matching. Our implementations support nested copatterns so that objects can respond to chains of multiple observations, even though λ^{codata} only provides flat copatterns. This extension does not enhance the language expressivity but allows more succinct programs [2]. A flattening step is needed to compile nested copatterns down to a core calculus, which has been explored in previous work by Setzer *et al.* [37] and Thibodeau [39] and implemented in OCaml by Regis-Gianas and Laforgue [33]. Their flattening algorithm requires copatterns to completely cover the object's possible observations because the coverage information is used to drive flattening. This approach was refined and incorporated in a dependently typed setting by Cockx and Abel [11]. With our goal of supporting codata independently of typing discipline and coverage analysis, we have implemented the purely syntax driven approach to flattening found in [38]. For example, the `prune` function from Sect. 2.2 expands to:

```
prune = λx → λt →
  { Node     → t.Node,
    Children → case x of
                 0 → []
                 _ → map (prune(x-1)) t.Children }
```

Sharing. If codata is to be used instead of laziness for demand-driven programming, then it must have the same performance characteristics, which relies on sharing the results of computations [6]. To test this, we compare the performance of calculating streams of Fibonacci numbers—the poster child for sharing—implemented with both lazy list data types and a stream codata type in Haskell

[3] The GHC fork is at https://github.com/zachsully/ghc/tree/codata-macro.
[4] The prototype compiler is at https://github.com/zachsully/dl/tree/esop2019.

Syntax

$$\text{Values} \ni \quad V ::= \cdots \mid \{\overline{\mathsf{H} \to V}\}$$
$$\text{Terms} \ni t, u, e ::= \cdots \mid t.\mathsf{H} \mid \{\overline{\mathsf{H} \to V}\} \mid \mathbf{let}_{\text{need}}\ \overline{x = t}\ \mathbf{in}\ e$$

Transformation

$$\mathcal{A}[\![t.\mathsf{H}]\!] = \mathcal{A}[\![t]\!].\mathsf{H}$$
$$\mathcal{A}[\![\{\overline{\mathsf{H} \to t}\}]\!] = \mathbf{let}_{\text{need}}\ \overline{x = \mathcal{A}[\![t]\!]}\ \mathbf{in}\ \{\overline{\mathsf{H} \to x}\}$$

Fig. 6. Memoization of λ^{codata}

extended with codata. These tests, presented in Table 1, show the speed of the codata version is always slower in terms of run time and allocations than the lazy list version, but the difference is small and the two versions scale at the same rate. These performance tests are evidence that codata shares the same information when compiled to a call-by-need language; this we get for free because call-by-need data constructors—which codata is compiled into via $\mathfrak{T}$—memoize their fields. In an eager setting, it is enough to use memoized versions of **delay** and **force**, which are introduced by the call-by-value compilation described in Sect. 3.5. This sharing is confirmed by the OCaml and Racket backends of the prototype language which find the 100th Fibonacci in less than a second (a task that takes hours without sharing).

As the object-oriented representative, the JavaScript backend is a compilation from data to codata using the visitor pattern presented in Sect. 3.2. Because codata remains codata (*i.e.* JavaScript objects), an optimization must be performed to ensure the same amount of sharing of codata as the other backends. The solution is to lift out the branches of a codata object, as shown in Fig. 6, where the call-by-need let-bindings can be implemented by **delay** and **force** in strict languages as usual. It turns out that this transformation is also needed in an alternative compilation technique presented by Regis-Gianas and Laforgue [33] where codata is compiled to functions, *i.e.* another form of codata.

5 Related Work

Our work follows in spirit of Amin *et al.*'s [3] desire to provide a minimal theory that can model type parameterization, modules, objects and classes. Another approach to combine type parameterization and modules is also offered by 1ML [36], which is mapped to System F. Amin *et al.*'s work goes one step further by translating System F to a calculus that directly supports objects and classes. Our approach differs in methodology: instead of searching for a logical foundation of a pre-determined notion of objects, we let the logic guide us while exploring what objects are. Even though there is no unanimous consensus that functional and object-oriented paradigms should be combined, there have been several hybrid languages for combining both styles of programming, including Scala, the Common Lisp Object System [8], Objective ML [34], and a proposed but unimplemented object system for Haskell [30].

Arising out of the correspondence between programming languages, category theory, and universal algebras, Hagino [20] first proposed codata as an extension to ML to remedy the asymmetry created by data types. In the same way that data types represent initial F-algebras, codata types represent final F-coalgebras. These structures were implemented in the categorical programming language Charity [10]. On the logical side of the correspondence, codata arises naturally in the sequent calculus [15, 28, 44] since it provides the right setting to talk about construction of either the provider (*i.e.* the term) or the client (*i.e.* the context) side of a computation, and has roots in classical [13, 41] and linear logic [18, 19].

In session-typed languages, which also have a foundation in linear logic, external choice can be seen as a codata (product) type dual to the way internal choice corresponds to a data (sum) type. It is interesting that similar problems arise in both settings. Balzer and Pfenning [7] discuss an issue that shows up in choosing between internal and external choice; this corresponds to choosing between data and codata, known as the *expression problem.* They [7] also suggest using the visitor pattern to remedy having external choice (codata) without internal choice (data) as we do in Sect. 3.2. Of course, session types go beyond codata by adding a notion of temporality (via linearity) and multiple processes that communicate over channels.

To explore programming with coinductive types, Ancona and Zucca [4] and Jeannin *et al.* [26] extended Java and OCaml with regular cyclic structures; these have a finite representation that can be eagerly evaluated and fully stored in memory. A less restricted method of programming these structures was introduced by Abel *et al.* [1, 2] who popularized the idea of programming by observations, *i.e.* using copatterns. This line of work further developed the functionality of codata types in dependently typed languages by adding indexed codata types [40] and dependent copattern matching [11], which enabled the specification of bisimulation proofs and encodings of productive infinite objects in Agda. We build on these foundations by developing codata in practical languages.

Focusing on implementation, Regis-Gianas and Laforgue [33] added codata with a macro transformation in OCaml. As it turns out, this macro definition corresponds to one of the popular encodings of objects in the λ-calculus [27], where codata/objects are compiled to functions from tagged messages to method bodies. This compilation scheme requires the use of GADTs for static type checking, and is therefore only applicable to dynamically typed languages or the few statically typed languages with expressive enough type systems like Haskell, OCaml, and dependently typed languages. Another popular technique for encoding codata/objects is presented in [31], corresponding to a class-based organization of dynamic dispatch [21], and is presented in this paper. This technique compiles codata/objects to products of methods, which has the advantage of being applicable in a simply-typed setting.

6 Conclusion

We have shown here how codata can be put to use to capture several practical programming idioms and applications, besides just modeling infinite structures.

In order to help incorporate codata in today's programming languages, we have shown how to compile between two core languages: one based on the familiar notion of data types from functional languages such as Haskell and OCaml, and the other one, based on the notion of a structure defined by reactions to observations [1]. This paper works toward the goal of providing common ground between the functional and object-oriented paradigms; as future work, we would like to extend the core with other features of full-fledged functional and object-oriented languages. A better understanding of codata clarifies both the theory and practice of programming languages. Indeed, this work is guiding us in the use of fully-extensional functions for the compilation of Haskell programs. The design is motivated by the desire to improve optimizations, in particular the ones relying on the "arity" of functions, to be more compositional and work between higher-order abstractions. It is interesting that the deepening of our understanding of objects is helping us in better compiling functional languages!

References

1. Abel, A., Pientka, B., Thibodeau, D., Setzer, A.: Copatterns: programming infinite structures by observations. In: Proceedings of the 40th Annual ACM SIGPLAN-SIGACT Symposium on Principles of Programming Languages, POPL 2013, pp. 27–38 (2013)
2. Abel, A.M., Pientka, B.: Wellfounded recursion with copatterns: a unified approach to termination and productivity. In: Proceedings of the 18th ACM SIGPLAN International Conference on Functional Programming, ICFP 2013, pp. 185–196 (2013)
3. Amin, N., Rompf, T., Odersky, M.: Foundations of path-dependent types. In: Proceedings of the 2014 ACM International Conference on Object Oriented Programming Systems Languages & Applications, pp. 233–249 (2014)
4. Ancona, D., Zucca, E.: Corecursive featherweight Java. In: Proceedings of the 14th Workshop on Formal Techniques for Java-Like Programs, FTfJP 2012, Beijing, China, 12 June 2012, pp. 3–10 (2012)
5. Andreoli, J.M.: Logic programming with focusing proofs in linear logic. J. Logic Comput. **2**, 297–347 (1992)
6. Ariola, Z.M., Felleisen, M.: The call-by-need lambda calculus. J. Funct. Program. **7**(3), 265–301 (1997)
7. Balzer, S., Pfenning, F.: Objects as session-typed processes. In: Proceedings of the 5th International Workshop on Programming Based on Actors, Agents, and Decentralized Control, AGERE! 2015, pp. 13–24. ACM, New York (2015)
8. Bobrow, D.G., Kahn, K.M., Kiczales, G., Masinter, L., Stefik, M., Zdybel, F.: Commonloops: merging Lisp and object-oriented programming. In: Conference on Object-Oriented Programming Systems, Languages, and Applications (OOPSLA 1986), Portland, Oregon, USA, Proceedings, pp. 17–29 (1986)
9. Böhm, C., Berarducci, A.: Automatic synthesis of typed lambda-programs on term algebras. Theor. Comput. Sci. **39**, 135–154 (1985)
10. Cockett, R., Fukushima, T.: About charity. Technical report, University of Calgary (1992)
11. Cockx, J., Abel, A.: Elaborating dependent (co)pattern matching. In: Proceedings of the 23rd ACM SIGPLAN International Conference on Functional Programming, ICFP 2018, pp. 75:1–75:30 (2018)

12. Cook, W.R.: On understanding data abstraction, revisited. In: Proceedings of the 24th ACM SIGPLAN Conference on Object Oriented Programming Systems Languages and Applications, pp. 557–572 (2009)
13. Curien, P.L., Herbelin, H.: The duality of computation. In: Proceedings of the Fifth ACM SIGPLAN International Conference on Functional Programming, ICFP 2000, pp. 233–243. ACM, New York (2000)
14. DeLine, R., Fähndrich, M.: Typestates for objects. In: Odersky, M. (ed.) ECOOP 2004. LNCS, vol. 3086, pp. 465–490. Springer, Heidelberg (2004). https://doi.org/10.1007/978-3-540-24851-4_21
15. Downen, P., Ariola, Z.M.: The duality of construction. In: Shao, Z. (ed.) ESOP 2014. LNCS, vol. 8410, pp. 249–269. Springer, Heidelberg (2014). https://doi.org/10.1007/978-3-642-54833-8_14
16. Dummett, M.: The Logical Basis of Methaphysics: The William James Lectures, 1976. Harvard University Press, Cambridge (1991)
17. Gallier, J.: Constructive logics. Part I: a tutorial on proof systems and typed lambda-calculi. Theor. Comput. Sci. **110**(2), 249–339 (1993)
18. Girard, J.Y.: Linear logic. Theor. Comput. Sci. **50**(1), 1–101 (1987)
19. Girard, J.Y.: On the unity of logic. Ann. Pure Appl. Logic **59**(3), 201–217 (1993)
20. Hagino, T.: Codatatypes in ML. J. Symbolic Comput. **8**, 629–650 (1989)
21. Harper, R.: Practical Foundations for Programming Languages, 2nd edn. Cambridge University Press, New York (2016)
22. Howard, W.A.: The formulae-as-types notion of construction. In: Curry, H.B., Hindley, J.R., Seldin, J.P. (eds.) To H.B. Curry Essays on Combinatory Logic, Lambda Calculus and Formalism, pp. 479–490. Academic Press, London (1980). unpublished manuscript of 1969
23. Hughes, J.: Why functional programming matters. Comput. J. **32**(2), 98–107 (1989)
24. Hughes, R.J.M.: Super-combinators: a new implementation method for applicative languages. In: Proceedings of the ACM Symposium on Lisp and Functional Programming, pp. 1–10 (1982)
25. Jacobs, B., Rutten, J.: A tutorial on (co)algebras and (co)induction. EATCS Bull. **62**, 222–259 (1997)
26. Jeannin, J., Kozen, D., Silva, A.: CoCaml: functional programming with regular coinductive types. Fundam. Inform. **150**(3–4), 347–377 (2017)
27. Krishnamurthi, S.: Programming Languages: Application and Interpretation (2007)
28. Munch-Maccagnoni, G.: Focalisation and classical realisability. In: Grädel, E., Kahle, R. (eds.) CSL 2009. LNCS, vol. 5771, pp. 409–423. Springer, Heidelberg (2009). https://doi.org/10.1007/978-3-642-04027-6_30
29. Munch-Maccagnoni, G.: Syntax and models of a non-associative composition of programs and proofs. Ph.D. thesis, Université Paris Diderot (2013)
30. Nordlander, J.: Polymorphic subtyping in O'Haskell. Sci. Comput. Program. **43**(2–3), 93–127 (2002)
31. Pierce, B.C.: Types and Programming Languages. The MIT Press, Cambridge (2002)
32. Plotkin, G.: LCF considered as a programming language. Theor. Comput. Sci. **5**(3), 223–255 (1977)
33. Regis-Gianas, Y., Laforgue, P.: Copattern-matchings and first-class observations in OCaml, with a macro. In: Proceedings of the 19th International Symposium on Principles and Practice of Declarative Programming, PPDP 2017 (2017)

34. Rémy, D., Vouillon, J.: Objective ML: a simple object-oriented extension of ML. In: Proceedings of the 24th ACM SIGPLAN-SIGACT Symposium on Principles of Programming Languages, POPL 1997, pp. 40–53. ACM, New York (1997)
35. Reynolds, J.C.: User-defined types and procedural data structures as complementary approaches to data abstraction. In: Gries, D. (ed.) Programming Methodology. MCS, pp. 309–317. Springer, New York (1978). https://doi.org/10.1007/978-1-4612-6315-9_22
36. Rossberg, A.: 1ML - core and modules united (F-ing first-class modules). In: Proceedings of the 20th ACM SIGPLAN International Conference on Functional Programming, ICFP 2015, pp. 35–47. ACM, New York (2015)
37. Setzer, A., Abel, A., Pientka, B., Thibodeau, D.: Unnesting of copatterns. In: Dowek, G. (ed.) RTA 2014. LNCS, vol. 8560, pp. 31–45. Springer, Cham (2014). https://doi.org/10.1007/978-3-319-08918-8_3
38. Sullivan, Z.: The essence of codata and its implementation. Master's thesis, University of Oregon (2018)
39. Thibodeau, D.: Programming infinite structures using copatterns. Master's thesis, McGill University (2015)
40. Thibodeau, D., Cave, A., Pientka, B.: Indexed codata types. In: Proceedings of the 21st ACM SIGPLAN International Conference on Functional Programming, pp. 351–363 (2016)
41. Wadler, P.: Call-by-value is dual to call-by-name. In: Proceedings of the Eighth ACM SIGPLAN International Conference on Functional Programming, pp. 189–201 (2003)
42. Wadler, P.: Propositions as types. Commun. ACM **58**(12), 75–84 (2015)
43. Weirich, S.: Depending on types. In: Proceedings of the 19th ACM SIGPLAN International Conference on Functional Programming, ICFP 2014 (2014)
44. Zeilberger, N.: On the unity of duality. Ann. Pure Appl. Logic **153**, 66–96 (2008)
45. Zeilberger, N.: The logical basis of evaluation order and pattern-matching. Ph.D. thesis, Carnegie Mellon University (2009)

Permissions

All chapters in this book were first published by Springer; hereby published with permission under the Creative Commons Attribution License or equivalent. Every chapter published in this book has been scrutinized by our experts. Their significance has been extensively debated. The topics covered herein carry significant findings which will fuel the growth of the discipline. They may even be implemented as practical applications or may be referred to as a beginning point for another development.

The contributors of this book come from diverse backgrounds, making this book a truly international effort. This book will bring forth new frontiers with its revolutionizing research information and detailed analysis of the nascent developments around the world.

We would like to thank all the contributing authors for lending their expertise to make the book truly unique. They have played a crucial role in the development of this book. Without their invaluable contributions this book wouldn't have been possible. They have made vital efforts to compile up to date information on the varied aspects of this subject to make this book a valuable addition to the collection of many professionals and students.

This book was conceptualized with the vision of imparting up-to-date information and advanced data in this field. To ensure the same, a matchless editorial board was set up. Every individual on the board went through rigorous rounds of assessment to prove their worth. After which they invested a large part of their time researching and compiling the most relevant data for our readers.

The editorial board has been involved in producing this book since its inception. They have spent rigorous hours researching and exploring the diverse topics which have resulted in the successful publishing of this book. They have passed on their knowledge of decades through this book. To expedite this challenging task, the publisher supported the team at every step. A small team of assistant editors was also appointed to further simplify the editing procedure and attain best results for the readers.

Apart from the editorial board, the designing team has also invested a significant amount of their time in understanding the subject and creating the most relevant covers. They scrutinized every image to scout for the most suitable representation of the subject and create an appropriate cover for the book.

The publishing team has been an ardent support to the editorial, designing and production team. Their endless efforts to recruit the best for this project, has resulted in the accomplishment of this book. They are a veteran in the field of academics and their pool of knowledge is as vast as their experience in printing. Their expertise and guidance has proved useful at every step. Their uncompromising quality standards have made this book an exceptional effort. Their encouragement from time to time has been an inspiration for everyone.

The publisher and the editorial board hope that this book will prove to be a valuable piece of knowledge for researchers, students, practitioners and scholars across the globe.

List of Contributors

Ferdinand Vesely
Tufts University, Medford, USA
Swansea University, Swansea, UK

Kathleen Fisher
Tufts University, Medford, USA

Beniamino Accattoli and Maico Leberle
Inria & LIX, École Polytechnique, UMR 7161, Palaiseau, France

Giulio Guerrieri
Department of Computer Science, University di Bath, Bath, UK

Samuele Buro and Isabella Mastroeni
Department of Computer Science, University of Verona, Strada le Grazie 15, 37134 Verona, Italy

Simon Castellan
Imperial College London, London, UK

Hugo Paquet
University of Cambridge, Cambridge, UK

Ugo Dal Lago and Francesco Gavazzo
University of Bologna, Bologna, Italy
Inria Sophia Antipolis, Sophia Antipolis Cedex, France

Dylan McDermott and Alan Mycroft
Computer Laboratory, University of Cambridge, Cambridge, UK

Paul Downen, Zachary Sullivan and Zena M. Ariola
University of Oregon, Eugene, USA

Simon Peyton Jones
Microsoft Research, Cambridge, UK

Index

Printed in the USA
CPSIA information can be obtained
at www.ICGtesting.com
JSHW051509111223
53612JS00005B/62

9 781647 284398